Deborah Perez

D1452517

A Place in History

A Place in History

Albany in the Age of Revolution, 1775–1825

— Warren Roberts —

excelsior editions

State University of New York Press
Albany, New York

Cover image, *The Van Rensselaer Manor* by Thomas Cole, courtesy of the Albany Institute of History and Art.

Published by
State University of New York Press, Albany

For information, contact State University of New York Press, Albany, NY
www.sunypress.edu

Excelsior Editions is an imprint of State University of New York Press

Production by Ryan Morris
Marketing by Anne M. Valentine

Library of Congress Cataloging-in-Publication Data

Roberts, Warren, 1933–
  A place in history : Albany in the age of revolution, 1775–1825 / Warren Roberts.
    p. cm.
  ISBN 978-1-4384-3329-5 (hardcover ; alk. paper)
  1. Albany (N.Y.)—History—18th century. 2. Albany (N.Y.)—History—19th century. 3. Albany (N.Y.)—Biography. I. Title.

F129.A357R63 2010
974.7-3—dc22   2009054122

10 9 8 7 6 5 4 3 2 1

*To Anne, Tony, and Sam, my travelling companions,
and Daniel, an inspiration to all of us*

Contents

Preface

The inclusion of the French Revolution in a book about this history of Albany requires some explanation. The American Revolution and the Erie Canal, yes, but why the *French* Revolution? There are solid historical reasons for doing so, but I will not rehearse the argument here; it appears, fully orchestrated, in the chapters that follow. There is another reason for including the French Revolution in my early Albany stories: I am an historian of the French Revolution. When I directed my attention to Albany, a city I have lived in since 1963, I saw it through the prism of my previous work on the French Revolution. It wasn't my conscious intention to do this, but in time it is what I did. I can trace my newly found interest in Albany back to June 1998, when I had just finished a book on the French Revolution. More precisely, the book was about two artists who lived through the French Revolution, and whose lives were deeply marked by it. One of them, an illustrator who compiled a remarkable pictorial record of the Revolution, went to the guillotine because of his political involvement. I took a trip to France just before completing my book and walked through the streets of Paris, seeing in my mind's eye the events that this artist illustrated. I had come to know Paris of the French Revolution well by the time of this visit; walking through the city that I knew through this artist's illustrations made the experience one that I shall never forget. It was right after I returned to Albany from this trip to Paris that something happened to trigger an interest in Albany that resulted in this book. Looking back now, it all seems interconnected.

Writing *Jacques-Louis David and Jean-Louis Prieur, Revolutionary Artists* was demanding; it took a lot out of me (I was chair of two departments when I wrote the book, first my own department and then another one). At some emotional level, I suspect, I needed to relieve the accumulated pressure that had built up while writing the book. I needed to try something new. At any rate, I took a bicycle ride the summer I returned to Albany after the trip to France that my wife and I had taken. It was a Sunday morning in late June (as best as I can recall) when I headed out on my bicycle to do some laps around

Figure 1. Anne Roberts took this photograph when we were in Paris in June 1998. I am standing in what was once the Place de Grève, adjacent to the Hôtel de Ville, the center of municipal government in Paris; it was here that two officials were killed and decapitated by a furious crowd on July 14, 1789, in the aftermath of the Storming of the Bastille.

the Averill Harriman State Campus, a usual routine when I want to get in some exercise. I live on Norwood Street, just off Western Avenue and below the University at Albany, where I am a member of the History department. I rode around the University perimeter road until I came to Washington Avenue, when I decided, on the spur of the moment, not to do laps on the Harriman State Campus, but to go down Washington Avenue, into the center of Albany. When I came to the bottom of Washington, which ends at City Hall, I made another spur-of-the-moment decision; I went around Academy Park, heading up Elk Street with its fine row houses on one side and Philip Hooker's 1814 Albany Academy on the other side. I had a palpable sense of Old Albany as I went around Academy Park and decided to continue my exploration, for this is what my bicycle outing had become. I knew there was a bicycle path along

the Hudson River, and I thought I knew how to pick it up, so I rode down
to Broadway and followed it to an exit just past Madison Avenue that feeds
into I-787. This is where the Corning Preserve bicycle path begins. Pleased to
find it, I rode up the bicycle path to its end, across from Troy, passing along
the Hudson for long stretches. As I rode back down the bicycle path I asked
myself where I would go after reaching the beginning of the path. In yet another
spur-of-the-moment decision I decided to see if I could find Schuyler Mansion
and headed up the hill as I continued my Sunday adventure. There it was at
the top of Schuyler Street, one of the finest colonial houses in America, dating
from 1761. Little did I know that the Albany aristocrat who built Schuyler
Mansion, Philip Schuyler, would occupy such an important place in my work
in coming years. Schuyler's residence was one of two Colonial-period mansions
that would occupy much of my time and thought for the next ten years. The
other colonial mansion, Van Rensselaer Hall, constructed in 1765 and located
on the manorial grounds of the Van Rensselaer family, no longer stands; it was
demolished in 1893. At the time of my 1998 bicycle excursion I knew nothing about Van Rensselaer Hall, and little about the Van Rensselaer family. I
had no idea that the manorial grounds of this prominent family were not very

Figure 2. H. H. Richardson's 1880 Albany City Hall at the end of Washington Boulevard, built after a fire destroyed Philip Hooker's 1829 City Hall.

Figure 3. This is where I turned left to go around Academy Park. In early June 1998, I stood in the center of the Place de Grève in Paris; several weeks later I rode around its Albany equivalent, Academy Park.

Figure 4. Elk Street row houses from the 1820s and 1830s are on the right, and Philip Hooker's superb 1814 Albany Academy, the oldest civic building in the city, is on the left.

Figure 5. The beginning of the Corning Preserve bicycle path.

far from today's downtown Albany, and that this was where one of the finest eighteenth-century homes in the mid-Hudson River Valley had been situated. The path that I traversed on my 1998 bicycle adventure went alongside what had been Van Rensselaer Manor.

Having seen Albany on this bicycle excursion as I hadn't seen it before, and with heightened interest in Albany's historic architecture, I made regular trips into the city on my bicycle with a camera in my backpack, taking roll after of roll of slides, compiling a visual record of today's Albany, and most particularly of the city's historic buildings. I did this in the summer of 1998 and in succeeding summers, exploring all of Albany, one end to the other, street by street, with Diana Waite's superb book, *Albany Architecture*[1] as a guide. I wanted to know as much as I could about the city of Albany, its architecture, and its history. I read William Kennedy's Albany novels and his unique book, *O Albany!*[2]; I read everything about Albany I could put my hands on. And I pored over maps of old Albany, trying to trace the growth of the city over time. Of the maps I examined, one in particular stood out: Simeon De Witt's map of 1794 Albany. Here was a map that told me about Albany in a year that was of particular interest to me. It was in 1794 that the Reign of Terror ended in France. Studying this map, and using it as a way to reconstruct Albany, I was doing the same thing here that I had done with maps of Revolutionary Paris. I am unable to say if I made the connection between Albany and Paris immediately, but in time I most certainly did. And there were other connections: Some of the Albanians whose lives I looked into were connected with the French Revolution. One of those persons was Philip Schuyler, who appears in all four of my early Albany stories.

Schuyler is one of the leading figures in my Battle of Saratoga chapter, the first of my narratives. Fought twenty-five miles above Albany, the Battle of Saratoga is a connecting link between the American Revolution and French Revolution, as we shall see. Philip Schuyler appears again in my second chapter, a discussion of seven prominent visitors who came up the Hudson River to see him as the American Revolution ran its course. Two of Schuyler's visitors were in France in 1789 at the beginning of the French Revolution, into whose vortex they would be swept—to follow their paths is to pass through both the American and French Revolutions. Schuyler appears yet again in my story of a French émigré of aristocratic birth, Mme de La Tour du Pin, who came to Albany in 1794 to escape the Reign of Terror in revolutionary France. When Mme de La Tour du Pin fled France she ended up in Albany, having been encouraged to come here by Philip Schuyler. Upon reaching Albany she looked

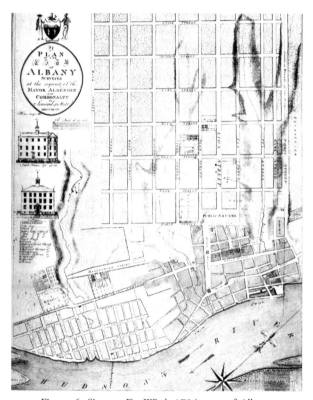

Figure 6. Simeon De Witt's 1794 map of Albany.

up Schuyler, and with him she visited the manorial grounds of his son-in-law, Stephen Van Rensselaer III, which she saw on the day after her arrival. Schuyler even makes an appearance in my last narrative, a chapter on Albany and the Erie Canal, as does Stephen Van Rensselaer III. These Albany aristocrats, both of Dutch ancestry, figure prominently in my early Albany stories—so too do their mansions, both situated just outside Albany at the time of their construction in 1761 and 1765.

It dawned on me only gradually, by steps and stages, often to my considerable surprise, how my understanding of Albany history in these stories drew from my earlier publications. This book encompasses the period 1775 to 1825. Jane Austen, the subject of one of my previous books, was born in 1775. Jacques-Louis David, the subject of my next book, died in 1825. These connections are incidental, but I must say they gave me a feeling that I was meant to write the four stories that are the subject of this book. Over and over, I returned to my earlier books as I thought about the history that was unfolding along the Hudson River, my new area of study. After writing several versions of the Battle of Saratoga, I found myself looking at a military encounter that took place 25 miles above Albany through the prism of a literary scheme that came out of my first book, a study of eighteenth-century French literature. I dare say that previous studies of the Battle of Saratoga have not asked the questions I asked in this chapter. I did not do this to be novel, but because the literary scheme furthered my own understanding of the Battle of Saratoga and the social dynamics that fed into it. Moreover, this scheme helped me to place the historic battle within a framework, that of an Age of Democratic Revolution, which I have been thinking about for the last 45 years, in all of my work.

Of the connecting links between my previous work and the four narratives brought together here, none is more striking than an image that appears on the cover of my last book. It shows two crowds coming together in a Paris street at the beginning of the French Revolution. One crowd brandishes a head on a pike with straw stuffed in the mouth; the other crowd escorts someone in a carriage who turns away in horror from the severed head. I was riveted by this image when I first saw it some 20 years ago, and wanted to understand what it was about. I went to the New York State Library in Albany to see if I could uncover information about the artist, Jean-Louis Prieur, who rendered the image. What I found was a superb facsimile edition of Prieur's entire extant original illustrations done for the finest and most comprehensive set of prints that depicted the main events of the French Revolution, the *Tableaux Historiques de la Révolution Française*. That image triggered my interest in the artist who rendered it; it is at the visual and conceptual core of my last book. I was astonished to discover that Gouveurneur Morris, a downstate New Yorker and one of the most interesting and intriguing characters in my early Albany stories, was in Paris in the summer of 1789, awaiting a carriage, when he received news of the same episode that Prieur depicted in his superb image.

Just as remarkably, a friend of Gouverneur Morris, the Marquis de Lafayette, another character in my early Albany stories, tried unsuccessfully to prevent the lynching and mutilation of the two men that Prieur depicted in his compelling image. Prieur's image is one link among many between my previous work and my early Albany stories, as readers will see as they go through the narratives brought together in this book.

No subject has been more important in my writing and teaching since the 1960s than manners. I devoted a chapter to that subject in my first book, with particular attention given to the prevailing system of manners among the elite in eighteenth-century Paris and at the court at Versailles. To understand eighteenth-century manners I went back to courtier's books, etiquette books, and manuals on civility that first appeared in the sixteenth century, and were instrumental in creating a division that ran through European society, separating a well-mannered, refined elite from ordinary people, those who worked with their hands. This scheme, which I have thought about often, and deeply, is of central importance to the narratives that I have constructed in my early Albany stories. Having seen how manners helped form a barrier between the elite and the people in European society I was fascinated to see how a similar social dynamic was at work in America. Manners, and the mindsets that went with them, help explain some of the prominent figures, American, British, and French, who make appearances in my early Albany stories, and the roles they played on the historical stage that they bestrode in the half century from 1775 to 1825.

The *Memoirs* of Mme de La Tour du Pin are one of the best accounts we have of a French aristocrat who witnessed the gaiety, levity, and freedom that prevailed in elite circles, and at Versailles, in the years before the French Revolution. Looking back many years later, while writing her *Memoirs*, Mme de La Tour du Pin condemned what she regarded as the loose manners and the corrupt morals within her world before the deluge of 1789. She also described her personal response to what happened to her as the Revolution ran its bloody course during the Reign of Terror. She fled to America, and it was there, while living on a farm outside Albany, that she realized what a profound change had taken place within her; she found refuge in religion from a world that had treated her harshly. So too did Jane Austen, who was born five years after Mme de La Tour du Pin, and also experienced the tremors of the French Revolution, as I explain in *Jane Austen and the French Revolution*. Like Mme de La Tour du Pin, Jane Austen lived through the Revolutionary Age, and was profoundly marked by it; she too underwent a deep personal change, with religion assuming a new and more important place within her experience. Society emerged from the upheavals of the Revolutionary Age—in France, England, and America—more serious, and more religious. Some of the leading characters in my early Albany stories are fully intelligible only if they are seen within the context of a vast movement of religious revival that began to pass through America in the period covered by this study.

From the beginning, I intended *A Place in History* to be different from my previous books. I did not see it as a work of specialized scholarship intended for an academic audience; I intended to address a broader audience than an academic one. I wanted to address readers with an interest in Albany, the city, and its history. My writing strategies have been informed by this goal. Some of the figures who will wander into my narratives are remarkably interesting, at least for me. I hope they will be no less so for my readers. The interest in these characters is not merely in their lives and personalities. Some strange and colorful figures will appear on my stage, to be certain; getting to know them was of captivating interest to me, as I hope they will be to my readers. Most important, however, is the history they helped make.

Acknowledgments

I must thank the four people to whom I have dedicated the book. Anne Roberts, Tony Anadio, and Sam Huntington have been traveling companions, and more, as I uncovered history along the Hudson. Anne led the way delving into the Albany experience; it was her sustained efforts to open its history to local audiences that set the stage for my later efforts, following in her path. Her two NEH-funded programs from the 1980s remain landmark events in raising public awareness of Albany's deep and rich history. Tony's assistance goes far beyond the outings that we have together; he has helped me technically and been a constant sounding board as we have talked about Albany and its history. His work on Thomas Cole will constitute his contribution to our appreciation of the cultural riches of the Hudson River Valley. Sam and his parents took Anne, Tony, and me into history that unfolded along the Hudson as no others possibly could have. I sent chapters of my Albany project to Daniel Koch when he was doing doctoral work at Oxford; his comments gave me a lift when I needed it, and his suggestions were as helpful as I would expect from this fine historian. But Daniel did more than read chapters; he has shown me how much the relationship between teacher and student is one of reciprocal benefit, with the teacher ending up as the principal beneficiary. I should also like to thank the audiences that listened to me as I gave talks on my Albany adventures. These audiences were brought together by the Albany chapter of OASIS, the Humanities Institute of Lifelong Learning, a fine organization founded by Helen and Fred Adler, and a University at Albany audience that Miriam Trementozzi organized with her usual efficiency. All of these audiences have been an ongoing source of support. So too have undergraduate students who have taken my course on Albany at the University at Albany. We hit the pavement many times, sharing Albany and its history together. It is audiences such as these that I had in mind when I wrote the narratives in this book. Most pointedly, I must give the fullest possible measure of thanks to James Peltz and Ryan Morris of the SUNY Press. James Peltz's forbearance has taken him far beyond the call of duty as I have inflicted more copies of my chapters on him than I can recall. Or, I have no doubt, than he would like to recall. Ryan Morris' editorial skills are commendable and greatly appreciated; I alone am responsible for the flaws, technical and otherwise, that remain in the text. I might also thank the people who make Trek bicycles for providing me with the transportation without which these stories would not be quite the same. Seeing Albany at street-level is an experience unlike any other.

Introduction

At 315 miles in length the Hudson River is not among America's largest rivers. From its headwaters in the Adirondacks it flows in a southerly direction until, just below Lake George, it turns sharply to the east for several miles, and then proceeds almost due south until it passes into the Atlantic. Just after turning to the south in the final stage of its passage to the Atlantic, the Hudson passes alongside Fort Edward. Fort Edward is some 30 miles below Whitehall, which lies on a watershed that separates bodies of water that flow in opposite directions; it is from this watershed that water passes into Lake Champlain, which empties into the Richelieu River. That river flows into the Saint Lawrence, which, in turn, passes into the Atlantic. These two waterways, the Hudson and Champlain, were discovered in the same year, 1609; it was in that year that Henry Hudson sailed up the river that was named after him, and Samuel de Champlain sailed along a lake that was named after him. Were it not for the 30 miles of forest that separate the two waterways the Hudson-Champlain corridor would be continuous; the stretch of wilderness that separates the Hudson River from the headwaters of Lake Champlain is of no small historical significance. A battle was fought a few miles below Fort Edward that changed the course of world history. The Battle of Saratoga was the turning point of the American Revolution, and it set in motion a chain of events that led to the French Revolution. The geography of New York contributed to the outcome of that historic battle.

England and France waged four wars between 1689 and 1783, a period of just under one hundred years. These wars were fought most importantly in Europe, but they were also fought overseas, nowhere more importantly than in North America. Within the North American theater of war throughout this period no geographical area was of greater military significance than New York. This was owing to New York's location between England's and France's colonial holdings in North America. Beginning with raids and skirmishes back and forth between New York and Canada in 1690, carried out by parties of several hundred or so, the struggle increased in scale and intensity until Britain achieved an overwhelming victory over France in 1763. Britain's victory over France in

Figure 7. Whitehall in the summer of 2006. Originally Skenesboro, it is here that waters flow in different directions, north into Lake Champlain and south into the Hudson. Knowing that the wooded area between Skenesboro and Fort Frederick presented serious problems for Burgoyne's army on the march to Albany, I wanted to see it for myself. Seen here are Sam Huntington, a former student of mine who lives just above Whitehall, another student, Tony Anadio, and my wife Anne. Tony, Anne, and I spent a weekend with Sam and his parents; Sam drove with us from Whitehall to Fort Edward, observing what was once a stretch of wilderness that contributed to the outcome of a battle that changed the course of world history.

Figure 8. South Bay, between Lake Champlain and Whitehall. I took this photograph from Mount Defiance (originally Sugar Loaf Hill).

Figure 9. Fort Edward, next to the Hudson River. Visiting the physical ground on which history unfolded in 1777 was an exercise in historical recovery. This is what I have done throughout my Early Albany Stories on similar trips.

the French and Indian War was complete; she forged the most far-flung global empire up to that time, vaster even than the Roman Empire at its height. The cost of these wars was staggering for both Britain and France; both were fiscally exhausted and forced to search for additional sources of revenue. For Britain, the problem was exacerbated by a large-scale Indian uprising, Pontiac's Rebellion, which broke out in the aftermath of the French and Indian War. Britain had to build forts and maintain garrisons along the western frontier, at no small cost, adding to the heavy burden of the war debt. Under these circumstances, Britain imposed taxes on the American colonies, direct beneficiaries of the victory over France and of her continuing military presence along a troublesome western frontier. The problem was that the colonies did not want to pay taxes; within a mere 12 years colonial opposition to taxes and other imperial measures culminated in armed conflict at Lexington and Concord, the beginning of the American Revolution. Fiscally exhausted as France was, she threw her support behind the American war for independence after the American victory at Saratoga. Without France's intervention the American cause looked bleak; with it, victory was possible. Revenge against Britain was sweet for France, but the cost was more than the French treasury could bear; within three years of the 1783 Treaty of Paris, France was faced with a fiscal crisis that led to the French Revolution. And within another four years France and Britain were at war again, the beginning of a struggle between two imperial powers that ended with Napoleon's defeat at Waterloo in 1815.

Two rivers that come together just above Albany, the Hudson and Mohawk, had major strategic and military importance in wars fought between 1690 and 1815. The same was true of two lakes north of Albany, Lake George and Lake Champlain. It became evident during the French and Indian War that control of the Mohawk River valley was one of the keys to victory; another was control of Lake George and Lake Champlain. Forts were built along these waterways; rival armies passed back and forth, fighting for control of the forts and the waterways along which they lay. As the military historian John Keegan has said, these river corridors were among the most bitterly contested places on earth in the second half of the eighteenth century. This was true of the French and Indian War, and it was true again during the American Revolution. In 1777, the third year of the revolution, one British strategy was to gain control of the Hudson-Champlain corridor by sending armies down Lake Champlain, up the Hudson, and across the Mohawk. All armies were to meet at Albany. Had the strategy succeeded Britain would have sealed off New England from the rest of the Revolution, thereby assuring victory. Of course, this is not how it turned out; the American victory at Saratoga, fought 25 miles above Albany, was a major defeat for Britain. An entire British army surrendered, along with arms and gunpowder; this was the turning point of the American Revolution.

The story of New York's waterways in time of war did not end with the American Revolution. Once again, during the War of 1812, British armies would pass across New York's waterways, along the Saint Lawrence to Lake Ontario and down Lake Champlain toward Albany; battles of great significance were fought along these historic waterways, most importantly in the Battle of Plattsburgh in 1814. Again, an American force prevailed, as an earlier one had at Saratoga during the Revolution. As wars were fought along New York's river corridors during the Revolution, and again in the War of 1812, Americans became aware of the potential of these waterways as avenues of commerce. For this potential to be realized, canals could be built that would facilitate trade between New York and the vast area beyond its western frontier, and with Canada to the north. Commercial traffic passing along canals from the west and the north would arrive at their natural terminus, Albany; it would then proceed down the Hudson to New York Harbor, making it the leading port in America, and one of the most important in the world. This is precisely what happened with completion of the Erie and Champlain canals.

The historian Norman Cantor has said that throughout most of history

> only the aristocracy had any real consciousness of its identity, its rights, or its destiny. The aristocrats held a monopoly of power, learning, and culture, and they alone had a sense of their special

and privileged place in the world . . . As late as 1700, the prevailing European social system was still one in which vast power, the greater part of landed wealth, and the prime control of political life belonged to the hereditary landed aristocracy.[1]

It was during the eighteenth century that domination of the aristocracy was first challenged. This happened on both sides of the Atlantic, in Europe and America, and particularly after 1760, when democratic stirrings were felt throughout Western society. How this happened is anything but straightforward. The aristocracy had always held power and been socially and culturally dominant in Europe, but in America it was only in the course of the eighteenth century that an aristocracy coalesced. America became more aristocratic during the eighteenth century; paradoxically, it also became more democratic. The democratic impulse did not come exclusively from above or below; it came from both the elite and from the people. How this complex dynamic played out during the half century between 1775 and 1825 is one of the central themes of this book.[2] Two Albany aristocrats and their Hudson River mansions will be focal points and provide physical settings for the narratives in which this theme will be traced.

After 1720, the members of leading families in America began consciously to emulate the way of life of the English elite, whose refinement they admired.[3] In acquiring refinement, prominent Americans formed themselves into a civilized elite, thereby separating themselves from the coarse people, who lacked social polish. A courtesy book whose precepts George Washington copied at age 17, *Youth's Behaviour, or Decency in Conversation among Men*, sheds light on the historical process by which Americans from prominent families acquired refinement. The book from which Washington hand-copied 110 precepts of proper behavior was a seventeenth-century English manual that was derived from a 1595 book written by French Jesuits that, in turn, borrowed from one of the most important of all etiquette books, Giovanni della Casa's *Il Galateo*, first published in 1558. Renaissance Italy was a seedbed of good manners, where forms of proper conduct were first set down in courtier's books, and then in etiquette books and manuals of civility.[4] By the time the system of manners contained in this literature was assimilated—over a period of several centuries—Western society was transformed; a divide ran through society, with a well-mannered and refined elite on one side of the division, and the uncultivated people on the other side.[5] The book from which Washington copied precepts of behavior was part of a sizeable body of etiquette books that told readers how to dress, converse, maintain proper comportment, and conduct themselves at the dinner table; these manuals told readers how to acquire the social skills that constituted good manners. Members of the well-mannered American elite acquired the trappings of gentility: articles of clothing, furniture, interior décor, material objects that marked one as refined. Many of the fine things that marked a person as refined came from Europe; imported from abroad, these items were costly, beyond the means of ordinary people, accessible only to the well-to-do. But refinement was not only about observing the outer forms of proper behavior and surrounding oneself with tasteful objects; refinement involved a state of mind—it contributed to the formation of personal and social identities. To be refined was not only to be polished and genteel, it was to occupy a different mental sphere, separate from the less elevated world of the people.

George Washington's contemporary, Philip Schuyler, is an object lesson in the process by which an elite American acquired refinement. From a Dutch family originally of middling background, Schuyler's ancestors married well and climbed the ladder of success over several generations. He inherited family properties, was economically astute, and amassed a considerable fortune, offering him the means to achieve the social ambitions of a man of refinement. As with other elite Americans, construction of a mansion marked him as a person of distinction; if ever there was a bastion of American refinement and elitism it was Philip Schuyler's Albany mansion. When Schuyler purchased a 24-acre plot of land for his mansion, it was a mile south of a stockade that still encircled Albany. Only after American victories in the French and Indian War in 1759 and 1760 was it deemed safe to build on a site such as the one chosen by Schuyler for his mansion. Schuyler had served under Major General John Bradstreet in the French and Indian War, and with keen mathematical skills he brought order to Bradstreet's account books. He went to England in 1761 to present Bradstreet's account books to the authorities, just as construction began on his mansion, with Bradstreet overseeing it during his absence. While in London, Schuyler acquired fine objects for himself and for his mansion, all in the latest fashion, all marking him as a person of taste, discernment, and refinement. Before returning to America he compiled a list of objects he had purchased in England, valued at £645 13s, that included "window glass, fabrics, silver and brass items, glassware, hardware, a theodolite, Hadley's quadrant, a reflecting telescope, a magic lantern, and a crane-necked chariot."[6] Also among the articles Schuyler acquired in England was wallpaper for his mansion, a fashionable commodity that had only recently appeared on the market. The wallpaper that Schuyler selected depicted scenes of the "Ruins of Rome," a subject that evoked the Grand Tour and reflected elite taste of the time.

Lord Adam Gordon, son of the second Duke of Gordon, traveled along the Atlantic seaboard in 1765, the year in which construction of Schuyler Mansion was completed. Having gone from Charleston to New York and then made his way up the Hudson, Lord Gordon had seen houses of the great as he proceeded. Upon arriving in Albany, he made note of the "dull and ill-built" town, but he added, "One Mr. P. Schuyler has a good house near it, lately built in a better Stile, than I have generally seen in America."[7] It is difficult for us today to imagine the impact Schuyler's mansion would have had on contemporaries. It is in a style that, broadly speaking, may be called Georgian,

Figure 10. Schuyler Mansion.

with rows of windows running along the front and sides of the brick building, a grand total of 26, each with 24 panes of glass that Schuyler had purchased in England, having paid £68 15s for "1500 feet [of] the best London crown glass."[8] Brick mansions stood apart from wooden houses that were the norm in mid-eighteenth-century America; to build in brick was to be fashionable, and to build a house in a Georgian style just outside Albany between 1761 and 1765 was to place oneself in the stylistic vanguard. The first house in the town of Albany done in this style was the Stevenson House on State Street, built between 1770 and 1780. Earlier Albany houses were typically in a Dutch vernacular style, with gables facing the street. It was Schuyler who introduced the new style, and he did so in grand manner in a building whose size and fineness could only have had dramatic effect on contemporaries.

To carry off a statement such as this it was necessary to bring in a master carpenter from Boston, along with other skilled craftsmen. The staircase, one of the stylistic centerpieces has hand-turned balusters of varied and complicated design, in imitation of the finest houses in America, such as the Hancock House in Boston. One entered Schuyler's refined residence in a main hall, a rectangular room that was an appropriate space to receive guests. On both sides of the great hall there were parlors, intended for the use of the family and for guests. The very word parlor is indicative of the thinking that attended the design of eighteenth-century mansions. Derived from the French word *parler* ("to speak"), the parlor was a room intended for the use of refined people who came together in proper sociable interaction, people who had learned to converse easily and correctly, who dressed well, and in the fullest sense of the word were refined. The parlor was a civilized space, and as such it was part of what one might call a "parlorization" of elite society. Behind one of the parlors was Philip Schuyler's study, a place to which a man of parts, and learning, could retire. The staircase was in the room behind the main hall, and on the other side was the dining room. Upstairs, running the entire length of the building, was the saloon, the largest room in the house, and in many respects the most important. This is where formal entertainments took place; this is where the important guests who came to meet with and receive the hospitality of Philip Schuyler assembled.

Driving all of this was the reality of power, of utmost importance to someone of Philip Schuyler's station and ambitions. A list of the guests who received Schuyler's hospitality in The Pastures and assembled in its most important room, the saloon, is impressive. We will be meeting some of these dignitaries in the early Albany stories that follow. When we come to them it will be useful to keep the saloon in mind; this is where they will gather. Like the parlor, the saloon says much about the refining process. Derived from the French word *salon*, it denotes a coming together of civilized people in convivial and informed gatherings. The other four upstairs rooms are bedrooms, intended for members of the Schuyler family and for guests. What is missing from both floors is a kitchen, or any workspace whatever. The kitchen was in a separate building attached to the rear of the house, as were quarters for servants. All of this is congruent with a pattern of architectural thinking that relegated workspaces and those who occupied them to the rear of houses, or to buildings outside houses. The thinking that resulted in arrangements of this type is integral to the civilizing process that ran its course from the time of the Renaissance to the eighteenth century, and resulted in the separation of a refined elite from an unrefined people.

Construction began on another mansion overlooking the Hudson in 1765. This mansion was in Watervliet, north of Albany, on the manorial grounds of the largest estate in New York, Rensselaerwijck, comprised of some 700,000 acres. The origins of the Van Rensselaer land holdiing went back to Kilian Van Rensselaer, a Dutch diamond merchant who called for investment groups to establish large estates, patroonships, along the Hudson River valley. The Van Rensselaer patroonship, initially 24 miles wide and 24 miles in length, was enlarged later and ran along both sides of the Hudson. Kilian Van Rensselaer never set foot on the patroonship that he founded; but his son, Jan Baptiste, came to America in 1651, and from this time on the Van Rensselaers lived on and continued to develop their extensive land holding, making them one of the wealthiest of all American families. Jeremias Van Rensselaer, the third patroon, built a new house on the manorial grounds north of Albany after floods destroyed the previous farm house in 1666. This house was near the grist mill and a new brewery, close to Patroon's Creek that passed through the Van Rensselaer manorial grounds before emptying into the Hudson. That house served as the manor house until Stephen Van Rensselaer II began construction of a grander mansion in 1765, Van Rensselaer Hall. Stephen Van Rensselaer II died in 1769, before construction of his riverside mansion was completed. It was his brother-in-law, Abraham Ten Broeck, who oversaw the completion of Van Rensselaer Hall in the years after Stephen Van Rensselaer II's death. Ten Broeck was also the ward of his nephew, the next patroon, Stephen Van Rensselaer III, a child of five at the time of his father's death. Befitting someone of his station, Stephen Van Rensselaer III attended Harvard, from which he graduated in 1782. He married a daughter of Philip Schuyler, Margarita, in 1783, and two years later they moved into Van Rensselaer Hall. Margarita climbed out of her second-floor room in her father's mansion to elope with her 19-year-old husband. She was 25 and six years older than her husband. From this time on there was close contact between Albany's two most important families, the Schuyler and Van Rensselaer families, whose mansions, one south of Albany and one north of the city, were among the finest in the Hudson River Valley.

The front entrance of Van Rensselaer Hall opened into a central great hall that was 47 feet in length, had a 12-foot ceiling, and was 24 feet in depth. By the standards of the landowning elite of the mid-Hudson River Valley this was a most impressive house, as one would have expected given the status and

Figure 11. Van Rensselaer Hall, demolished in 1893.

wealth of the patroon who built it. If there was a nodding acknowledgment of the Dutch heritage in the gambrel roof of Van Rensselaer Hall, the design was basically Georgian, placing it in the same stylistic category as Philip Schuyler's mansion. The great hall was decorated with hand-painted wallpaper purchased by Philip Livingston, Stephen Van Rensselaer II's father-in-law, when he was in London in 1768. Made by the firm of Neate and Pigou, the wallpaper designs included scenes of the "Ruins of Rome" and pastoral landscape scenes loosely paraphrased from the rococo paintings of Nicolas Lancret, a student of Antoine Watteau. The hand-painted wallpaper scenes, smart and fashionable, were placed within borders of flowing arabesques, decorative motifs such as one might have seen in the estates of French and English aristocrats. Visitors to Van Rensselaer Hall would have seen the same "Ruins of Rome" wallpaper design in Philip Schuyler's mansion if they had visited the riverside mansion of Albany's other leading aristocrat. The important personages who visited these two mansions and enjoyed the hospitality of Philip Schuyler and Stephen Van Rensselaer III will play a central role in the four stories brought together in this book.

1

The Battle of Saratoga

Epic, Tragedy, or Comedy of Manners?

The Battle of Saratoga, comprised of two pitched battles fought 25 miles north of Albany on September 19 and October 7, 1777, has been called the most important battle in the last thousand years.[1] It was not among the largest eighteenth-century battles in terms of the size of the two armies, or in terms of casualties. The British army, which included German mercenaries, loyalists, and Indians, totaled some 8,000 men, and the American army, made up of Continental regulars and militiamen, totaled some 8,000 to 12,000. These numbers are approximate, and they changed between the Battle of Freeman's Farm, fought on September 19, and the Battle of Bemis Heights, fought on October 7. The British army was considerably smaller than the American army at the time of the second engagement; after news of the first battle passed through New York and New England men poured into Saratoga for what they hoped would be—and was—a final and decisive battle. Altogether, there were some 1,200 British casualties (dead and wounded) in the two pitched battles at Saratoga, and some 450 American casualties. In the Battle of Bemis Heights, 184 British and Germans were killed and about 30 Americans. These numbers are miniscule when compared to the size of armies and the number of casualties in the Seven Years War, waged between 1756 and 1763, when the combined combatant armies could be as large as 60,000 men (Battle of Lobositz), and total casualties could number over 22,000 (Battle of Prague). On the losing side alone some 5,000 men are thought to have been killed or wounded on the battlefield at the 1757 Battle of Rossbach; by contrast, at the Battle of Bemis Heights 20 years later, barely over 200 men were killed in total. It is the later, much smaller battle that is vastly more important in terms of its historical fallout; Rossbach was one of many bloody encounters in a war that was waged over a seven-year period; the Battle of Saratoga changed the course of history. How was this so? What is the importance of the Battle of Saratoga?

A straightforward answer to the above question is as follows: The Battle of Saratoga was the pivotal battle of the American Revolution. Before it was fought the American cause looked bleak, with little chance of ultimate success; the American victory at Saratoga changed everything. Upon receiving news of the American victory at Saratoga the American envoy in Paris, Benjamin Franklin, met with Charles Gravier, Comte de Vergennes, France's foreign minister, who had previously given covert support to the rebellious colonies and now considered it feasible to join the American cause openly. Louis XVI agreed, and in February 1778 France joined the war against Britain. She did so not only in America; France escalated the conflict by sending fleets to the West Indies and to the Mediterranean, where Britain had interests that she had to defend. Up to this point Britain had waged war just against the American colonies; now she had to divert her resources to a struggle that had different, more extensive parameters, fought not just along the Atlantic seaboard but on the high seas. The burdens of the expanded war made it ever more difficult for Britain to supply her armies and fleets engaged in the American theater of war. To add to her burdens, Spain joined the war against Britain, and then Holland. But it was France whose intervention in the war that was decisive; it was she that played the leading role in the climacteric battle of the American Revolution: The American victory at Yorktown in 1781 was the result of a strategy devised by the French commander in America, General Jean-Baptiste Donatien, Comte de Rochambeau, and made possible by a French fleet under the command of Admiral François, Comte de Grasse, who sailed to Chesapeake Bay from the West Indies and blockaded its mouth, isolating the British army under General Charles, Second Earl Cornwallis and bringing about his surrender after a combined French and American army lay siege to a fortress that had become a trap. With no way to escape Cornwallis had to capitulate, setting the stage for Britain's acceptance of America's independence. The role of France in the Battle of Yorktown was but the most dramatic example of her contribution to the American victory over Britain: Ragtag American soldiers used gunpowder supplied by France at Saratoga; by the end of the Revolution; American soldiers wore proper uniforms, thanks to French aid; they fought alongside French soldiers; and they used armaments that France had provided. There is no way to determine how the American Revolution would have ended had France not intervened, but there can be no doubt that her support was important, and probably decisive.

Why France, a monarchical state, supported a colonial revolt in North America, and a republican one at that, seems strange, misdirected, and in light of the ultimate outcome disastrous from the point of view of those who made the decision to intervene on the side of the Americans. In 1787, four years after the Treaty of Paris ended the American War for Independence, France undertook measures to address a fiscal crisis that her support of the American cause had helped bring about. Ninety-one percent of the monies that France spent in support of the American Revolution came from loans, most of them raised through the sale of government securities.[2] Altogether, the amount came to 1.3 billion livres. Along with the cost of France's earlier eighteenth-century wars, the public debt was crushing, as became evident when the king's finance minister, Charles-Alexandre Calonne, drew up the 1786 budget, the first ever under the Bourbon monarchy. Unable to win support for new taxes necessary to make France solvent, the King summoned the Estates General, the only apparent way out of the fiscal impasse. Within two months of the arrival of assembled deputies of the Estates General at Versailles in May 1789 forces were unleashed that plunged France into revolution. What this means, in effect, is that the two revolutions, the American and the French, were joined at the hip, and it was the Battle of Saratoga that was the connecting link. Thus, the Battle of Saratoga was not only the turning point of the American Revolution, it also helped set in motion events that culminated in the French Revolution. The Revolution plunged France into civil war and the Reign of Terror and it plunged all of Europe into protracted warfare fought on a scale vastly larger than all previous European wars. By the time the dust settled on the Revolutionary and Napoleonic wars some 2,500,000 soldiers and some 1,000,000 civilians were dead, wounded, or missing. All of this can be traced back to the Battle of Saratoga, instrumental in bringing France into the American Revolution and in the creation of a fiscal crisis that played into the French Revolution. And the long-term fallout went beyond Europe and America: Ideas spawned by the French Revolution ignited protest movements in the West Indies in the 1790s, slave revolts whose long-term impact it is all but impossible to measure. Moreover, independence movements that erupted in an already tottering Spanish Empire can be understood only within the larger context of movements set in motion by the French Revolution.[3] If the British Empire crumbled amidst the struggles of the Revolutionary Age, another empire was rebuilt on new foundations in the aftermath of her defeat in the war against the American colonies. Britain took steps almost immediately to rebuild her Empire, tightening her hold on India and colonizing Australia. Having lost an entire army at Yorktown, Cornwallis went to India five years later, in 1786, where he fought battles that helped establish British dominance in Southern India, the base of a reconstituted Empire. The world was profoundly different as a result of revolutions in America and in France; all of this can be traced back, at least plausibly, to the Battle of Saratoga.

Much has been written about the Battle of Saratoga, fittingly, considering its importance. Nothing that I might say about it factually is new; I have no information to add to that used by other historians. As a piece in a collection of early Albany stories I can emphasize the importance of Philip Schuyler, an Albanian who played an important role in the Battle of Saratoga, even though he was not there. And I will pay attention to Schuyler, a central figure in this Albany story and in the narratives that follow this one. In earlier versions of this piece the central theme was Schuyler's role in the Battle of Saratoga, but as I continued to read and think about the historic battle I came to see it from a different perspective, that of an historian with an interest in relationships between literature and society in eighteenth-century France and eighteenth-century England.[4] Strange as it might seem, I came to see the Battle of Saratoga within the context of a literary scheme that includes three genres of literature: epic, tragedy, and comedy of manners. One of my underlying assumptions is that works of literature do not appear in a vacuum, but draw from and in some measure reflect the societies from which they emerge; a work of literature, as I think about it, is part of history. Similarly, genres of literature, such as epic, tragedy, and comedy of manners, are conditioned by social change. The more I read and thought about the Battle of Saratoga, the more inclined I was to consider it within a scheme that included these genres of literature. By seeing the Battle of Saratoga through this prism I found myself understanding it differently than before I followed this approach. I hope in my conclusions to convey the understanding I achieved after having asked if the Battle of Saratoga fits best with epic, tragedy, or comedy of manners. But first, some old-fashioned narrative history.

When long-simmering discontents turned into armed protest at Lexington and Concord on April 19, 1775 Americans were quick to recognize the importance of the Hudson-Champlain corridor in the struggle that lay ahead. Key fortresses at Ticonderoga and Crown Point on Lake Champlain had been important in the French and Indian War, and both the Americans and British expected them to be important again in the Revolution. As soon as news of Lexington and Concord spread through New England, American patriots marched on and took the two Lake Champlain fortresses, setting the stage for an invasion of Canada that was launched at the end of August 1775. The American assault of Quebec that began on December 31, 1775 failed, and in spring 1776 a British army pushed the battered American army out of Canada and down Lake Champlain in a campaign that had joining forces with another British army in New York as its ultimate goal. By the time the British army reached Ticonderoga in October 1776 it was too late in the year to continue the passage to New York and the army returned to Quebec. When the 1777 campaign began, a British army followed the same path as that of the 1776 force that invaded America from Canada, again moving down Lake Champlain as it headed toward the Hudson River. The objective was to seize the Hudson-Champlain corridor, whose control would enable the British to sever New England from the rest of the colonies, thereby assuring victory. The British army that invaded America from Canada in June 1777 passed down Lake Champlain as it made its way toward the Hudson River, as the British army had in the previous year. This

time the army took Fort Ticonderoga and continued south as it headed toward
Albany, its immediate destination. This British army never reached Albany; it
was stopped at Saratoga.

As I turn to leading figures in the Battle of Saratoga I begin with the rival
generals, John Burgoyne (1722–1792), commander of the British army, and
Horatio Gates (1727–1806), commander of the American army. The commanding generals of the combatant armies were both British, one of several paradoxes
of this many-sided and problematic battle. Not only were Burgoyne and Gates
both British, they were once fellow officers in the same British regiment.[5] In
fact, their names appeared next to one another on the same regimental roster
in 1745 when both were junior officers hoping to achieve high rank within the
British military system. This Burgoyne was able to do, thanks to his aristocratic
birth, a strategic marriage, and political influence that came from sitting in
Parliament. Yet, all did not go easily for Burgoyne. Very possibly the illegitimate
son of powerful Lord Bingley, gossip swirled about him throughout his life.
Given to extravagant living, gambling, and free-spending, he lived beyond his
means, considerably beyond his means, and was in difficult financial straits even
after marrying the daughter of powerful and wealthy Lord Derby in 1743. So
unhappy were his wife's parents over the marriage that they allowed her but a
small dowry and refused to see her or her husband in their country estate. Living
under straitened circumstances in London, Burgoyne gambled and frequented
smart clubs. With money from his wife's dowry he purchased a lieutenancy in
1745, and a captaincy later in the year, but he was so far in debt by 1747 that
he sold his commission and he and his wife retired to the Continent. Living
in France, he met influential aristocrats with whom he went to Rome, where
he posed for the prominent portraitist, Allan Ramsay. His wife had a daughter
in 1754 and in 1755 they returned to England, where a reconciliation was
effected with her parents. Lord Derby gave his daughter a £400 annuity and
the expectation of an estate of £25,000.

Burgoyne was reinstated in the army and climbed the ladder of promotion rapidly; by May 1758 he was lieutenant colonel. Britain was now in the
thick of the Seven Years War, and it was at this time that he made his mark
both in Parliament and on the battlefield. He was in a campaign in Portugal
in 1761 when he ran for Parliament, without opposition thanks to powerful
support; he took his seat in 1762, the same year in which he distinguished
himself on the battlefield in Spain. As MP, Burgoyne supported the Stamp Act
and indeed all British imperial initiatives in North America, which gave him
influence within British leadership in Parliament, and with the King. A man
of parts, Burgoyne belonged to fashionable clubs and wrote plays that were
well received; he was known for his wit and clever repartées, and moved easily

in the most elevated stratum of elite British society. As a political storm was brewing in North America in 1774, Burgoyne gave a party that celebrated the marriage of the daughter of the Duke of Hamilton to Lord Stanley, grandson of the Earl of Derby; even by aristocratic standards of the day the event was something special. The party was staged as a fête champêtre, reported to have been the first in England. Robert Adam, the sought-after architect, a friend of Burgoyne, designed a pavilion for dancing and theatricals, which Garrick staged. Burgoyne himself wrote a two-act play, *The Maid of Orleans*, which Garrick later expanded into a five-act play that he gave successfully at Drury Lane. Three hundred guests attended the evening, many of them MPs. Salvos of French horns greeted the guests when they arrived in their carriages; shepherds and shepherdesses appeared on the lawns and then performed a masque. Two cupids gave each guest a bouquet and singers serenaded Lord Stanley. Dinner began at 11:30 and dancing lasted until 3:00. The estimated cost of the entertainment was £5,000, a huge sum. Horace Walpole wondered if Burgoyne had "bought all the orange trees around London" for the festivities, and if the haycocks were "made of straw coloured satin."[6] So many MPs attended the party that Lord North was without a quorum when Parliament met the following Monday.

As Britain found herself on a collision course with the colonies, Burgoyne saw the Hudson-Champlain corridor as the key to British efforts to bring the contentious Americans into line. Advocate of a forceful policy toward the colonies, he argued the importance of the Hudson-Champlain corridor in conversations with Lord North and the King in February 1775, before protest in the colonies erupted in revolution. Burgoyne maintained that by seizing the strategic waterway that extended from Canada to New York, the British could stifle resistance in Boston, the center of the rebellion. He was unable to sell his plan; the government decided instead to send a force to Boston to aid General Thomas Gage in an effort to maintain order in that city. Burgoyne set sail for Boston with Generals William Howe and Henry Clinton on April 20, 1775, the day after Lexington and Concord. When he returned to London in December 1775, having fought in the bloody Battle of Bunker Hill, everything in America had changed. The rebellion had turned into revolution, the British army under Howe and Clinton occupied Boston but it was under siege, Canada had been invaded by two American forces, and General Guy Carleton at Quebec needed reinforcements. Burgoyne was put in command of a fleet of 34 ships that sailed to Canada in April 1776 with an army of 13,000 men to join forces with Carleton and drive out the Americans. By the time of Burgoyne's arrival in Canada in May 1776 the American force outside Quebec was greatly weakened, and one of its leaders, Benedict Arnold, had departed for Montreal with men under his command. Burgoyne was at the head of a British force that pursued Arnold; by the time he caught the Americans they were at Saint Johns, which they were leaving at the very time of Burgoyne's arrival. Bizarrely, in light of what would transpire at Saratoga, Arnold was the last of the Americans to depart; he was the last American to jump aboard the last ship as Burgoyne reached Saint Johns. Two of the principal adversaries at Saratoga missed one another by minutes. Even more bizarrely, when Burgoyne and Arnold fought at Saratoga, Arnold was under the command of Horatio Gates, commanding general of the American army, once a fellow officer of Burgoyne and a member of the same regiment.

Horatio Gates' path to Saratoga could hardly have been more different from that of Burgoyne. The son of a Thames River boatman and a servant, Gates had none of the advantages of Burgoyne. His ambitious and intensely status-conscious mother married her considerably younger second husband under circumstances that raise questions about Gates' paternity. It is possible that he was fathered by an aristocrat, which could explain why a boatman would have married an older woman who already had children. According to this line of thinking, Gates' legal father was paid to marry his mother. This could also explain the military commission that someone purchased for Gates when he was 18, at which time his name appeared on the same regimental roster as Burgoyne. As a boy, Gates received a decent education, which gave him a smattering of Latin and Greek and fluency in French. His schooling also left him with clear, precise use of English. As a fledgling officer he developed skills that would serve him well in the military; he became expert at bureaucratic and organizational minutiae, his chosen channel of advancement. When his regiment was disbanded in 1749, at the end of the War of Austrian Succession, he went to Halifax as Cornwallis' aide at half-pay. Back in London in 1753, he wanted a proper, full-time military position, and when he received news that troops were needed in America at the beginning of the French and Indian War he put money down on a captaincy and joined Braddock's army in Maryland and marched with him to Fort Duquesne. He was with Braddock at the Battle of Monongahela, at which Braddock was killed and Gates himself seriously wounded. It was at this time that Gates met George Washington. He went to Fort Oswego to recover and then to Forts Herkimer and Edward. As if to anticipate his future role, he went to Saratoga and Stillwater and became involved in New York politics through his supporters, Cornwallis and Monckton, generals with clout and influence. In effect, Gates enjoyed the patronage of these important men. When Monckton led an expedition to Martinique in 1762 Gates joined him as an aide, and it was Gates who bore the news of victory to London, with Monckton's recommendation that he be rewarded for outstanding service. Gates was appointed major and given £1,000 to purchase a colonelcy, but his pay was cut, the colonelcy he sought was filled, and he again entered the orbits of Cornwallis and Monckton, his patrons. He made the fatal mistake of quarrelling with Cornwallis' wife, apparently over one of her officer friends. She attacked him angrily and he responded in kind; his apology to Cornwallis was not accepted. In despair he commented, "I am Soliciting from the Hard Hand of Power." His family life took a turn for the worse, he turned to drink and gambling, tried Methodism, and became obstinate and demanding. At this point he sold his commission and left the army. Monckton was now his patron, and he tried to find a place for him in India, but Monckton himself lost out in India, owing to a ruling in Parliament by a committee that included John Burgoyne. Doors were closed to Gates and, having been thwarted repeatedly, latent republicanism, acquired in part in New York taverns, surfaced. His New York friend, William Smith, who was in London and with whom Gates spent evenings, wrote "with the Aid of Bacchus and in the Pride of Philosophy, we laughed at the shining Anxieties of the Great."[7]

The period after the Seven Years War saw the emergence of radical movements in Britain, most strikingly in London, with John Wilkes a polemicist who stirred contemporaries dissatisfied with a political system that turned on personal influence and within which corruption was pervasive.[8] Horace Walpole, son of Robert Walpole, the prime minister who was instrumental is constructing a political system that depended on influence and patronage, and himself an MP, said that when "Parliament opens, everyone is bribed." Among Gates' friends at this time were Henry Cruger, a New York merchant who argued against the Stamp Act and was a Wilkite radical, Isaac Barré, another radical, and Jack Hale, a Whig outsider who declared war on the corrupt political establishment. Charles Lee, who like Gates had fought in the French and Indian War and was part of Hale's radical circle; he too was placed on half-pay after serving in America under Braddock. Braddock had nicknamed Lee "the Vagabond"; he was an eccentric and an intellectual who read Rousseau and looked to the Anglo-Saxon past as a time of liberty before the Norman Conquest brought tyranny to Britain. Benjamin Franklin invited Gates and Lee to dinner in 1768; in 1770 a friend called Gates a "red hot Republican"; in 1772 Gates used the money he had received from Parliament after the Martinique expedition to buy a plantation in Virginia. He had written Washington before going to Virginia; with the purchase of a plantation he became a fellow planter in the same colony as Washington. Gates rushed to Mount Vernon when he received news of Lexington and Concord, and both he and Washington proceeded to Philadelphia. When Congress appointed Washington head of the Continental Army, Gates was given the rank of brigadier general and made Washington's aide, but Gates wanted a field command and worked assiduously to get one. Long familiar with political networking, he courted favor with politicians in Congress, particularly those from New England, whose champion he became. Finally the day Gates had long awaited arrived in April 1776, when he was placed in command of a broken American army that had laid siege to Quebec and desperately needed relief. The army that he was to take command of is the one that fought at Saratoga. As it turned out, Gates was not given undisputed command of the American army that fought at Saratoga until August 1777. Before exploring how Gates ended up as commander of this army, it is time to introduce the two heroes of the 1777 battle, Benedict Arnold and Daniel

Morgan, and to trace their paths to Saratoga. Then we will turn to another American who played an important role in the American victory but was not at the Battle of Saratoga—the Albany aristocrat, Philip Schuyler. These men, and the paths they took, say much about the Battle of Saratoga, about the American Revolution, and about the social dynamic that fed into it.

Benedict Arnold (1741–1801) was from a prominent Rhode Island family that first came to Providence in 1636 and included a governor of the colony and a member of the assembly. His father moved to Connecticut, held local offices in Norwich, and as ship owner and merchant carried on trade while Britain was at war with France. With cessation of hostilities in 1749 trade declined, Arnold's father experienced economic difficulties, and he began a long slide into alcoholism. Benedict received a proper education and was a good student, but there were problems. The school headmaster wrote Arnold's mother about a terrifying incident in 1754 when her son, age 13, walked across the ridgepole of a barn that was on fire, passing over flames below him. The headmaster said of the boy who had brazenly courted danger that he was bright, but "so full of pranks and plays."[9] His father lost his business in the same year as this incident and was kept out of jail by relatives who protected him from creditors. To escape misery, Arnold's father frequented local taverns, became drunk, and had to endure taunts as he made his way home, sometimes attended by Benedict, who suffered the catcalls and jeers along with his father. It was from episodes such as these that Arnold acquired a lifelong hatred of alcohol. Unable to return to school in the fall of 1754, Arnold spent time with the remnants of Indians who lived in the area surrounding Norwich, from whom he learned to paddle a canoe, stalk deer, and adopt their ways. With them he swam and leaped from high cliffs into water below, hunted, trapped, and rode horseback. He also fell in with town boys who imitated Indian raids they had heard about from their parents, and they staged mock battles. To prove his daring he jumped onto a rotating waterwheel and riding it downward plunged into the water below, thoroughly doused after completing the stunt. Arnold said years later to Benjamin Rush that he had been "a coward until [he] was fifteen."[10] His actions in years before he reached that age belie this assertion, but the comment reveals something essential about Benedict Arnold: For some internal reasons he had to prove himself, and his courage. Young Arnold carried off his most brazen caper on Thanksgiving Day 1754 at an outdoor town dinner when he and friends stole barrels of tar and set them afire, a fierce blaze that the constable and assistants rushed to put out. To protect his boon companions who were escaping, Arnold tore off his shirt and confronted the forces of law and order until he was subdued. Clearly, something was wrong; clearly, Arnold's mother decided, something had to be done. Among her relatives was a Dr. Daniel Lathrop, a Yale graduate, trained as a physician but an apothecary by trade, the only one between Boston and New York City. Arnold was apprenticed to Dr. Lathrop towards the end of 1754 and moved into his New Haven mansion, one of the finest homes in

Connecticut. There he learned all that was needed to become an apothecary, and there, under the gentle influence of Dr. Lathrop's wife, Jerusha, he acquired the manners of polite society and the appreciation of fine things, gardens with flowers, vegetables, and herbs, all lifelong interests of Arnold.

Within Benedict Arnold there were two interior persons, the daredevil driven to perform deeds of audacious courage, willing and even eager to court danger, and the gentleman who had come to appreciate fine things, the amenities of civilized life. In early 1758 it was the first of these persons that surfaced when Arnold, age 17, left the Lathrop mansion and walked all the way to Westchester to join a militia that was on its way to attack Fort Ticonderoga. When Arnold's mother heard that he had run away to join the army, she persuaded a friend to have him brought back by force; he ran away again and on this occasion it was Dr. Lathrop who got him back. In 1759 he persuaded his mother to let him enlist in a New York militia unit. He marched to Albany as his unit made ready to move toward Forts Ticonderoga and Crown Point before laying siege to Montreal and Quebec. Arnold reveled in demonstrating prowess and bravery to fellow militiamen, but he found the drilling and preparations for the campaign tedious. Before having a chance to prove himself in battle he received news of his mother's serious illness and deserted in order that he could see her. A notice of his desertion was published; he was home when his mother died. He did not return to military service, but he had come to appreciate the strategic importance of the Lake Champlain forts at Ticonderoga and Crown Point in the war against France in the French and Indian War.

We move forward in time; it is now 1775, and Arnold is an apothecary in New Haven; ambitious and enterprising, he has also built up a commercial firm whose ships plied the waters of the Hudson and Lake Champlain, passing by the forts that had been so important in the French and Indian War. When news of Lexington and Concord reached New Haven on April 20, Arnold assembled 63 men in the governor's guard on the college green with the intention of taking them to Boston, but Brigadier General David Wooster thought he should wait until he received proper orders; moreover, local officials refused to give him guns and ammunition. When Arnold threatened to break into the magazine, officials opened it and Arnold and his men appropriated arms and marched straightaway to Cambridge, where they met with the local Committee of Safety. Arnold announced his intention of marching to Forts Ticonderoga and Crown Point, known for their strategic importance and known to have cannon that if taken could help the American cause. Arnold and a force of New England militiamen, with the approval of and orders from the Massachusetts provincial congress, set out for the New York forts on May 3, but along the way they met another group of militiamen, the Green Mountain Boys under Ethan Allen, that was heading the same way and bent upon carrying out the same mission.

Arnold's first encounter with Green Mountain Boys took place in a tavern in Bennington, a contentious scene that anticipated much that was to follow. When Arnold entered the tavern he wore a red uniform and had a saber at his side, the attire of a British officer, which made an immediate impression on men in fringed buckskin hunting shirts and high boots who raised their muskets and pointed them at the very correct person who unexpectedly entered their midst. The dynamics of this encounter say much about Arnold and men who were instantly and instinctively on their mettle when they first saw him. The gulf between him and them was personal, and it was cultural; they were moving toward the same destination and for the same political and military purpose, the capture of Fort Ticonderoga and its cannon, but they brought different habits of mind, feelings, attitudes, values, and prejudices to the undertaking. They adhered to different systems of manners; one was elite and refined, the other popular and coarse. Arnold showed the men in the tavern his papers and they lowered their guns; they then mocked him by mimicking his correct behavior and sense of rectitude, conveyed by body language, movement, and gesture; they jumped on tables and danced about, ridiculing a strange intruder who resembled nothing as much as a British officer, and was accompanied by an orderly. The encounter between Arnold and Ethan Allen was no less confrontational when they met the next day and Arnold showed Allen papers that he maintained placed him in command of the forces that were now approaching Ticonderoga. Allen was inclined to accept orders that put Arnold in command of the expedition, but his men were not; some stacked their muskets and others shouldered them, as if they were about to leave rather than serve under someone such as Arnold, a clear case of insubordination insofar as Arnold was concerned. Under the circumstances an arrangement was worked out under which Arnold would lead his contingent, and Allen would lead the Green Mountain Boys; it was now a joint expedition, with two leaders.

The Americans caught the British at Ticonderoga completely by surprise and took the fort with virtually no opposition. Then things turned ugly, at least as far as Arnold was concerned. The Green Mountain Boys discovered 90 barrels of rum in a cellar, and availing themselves fully of their contents went on a three-day drunken spree, replete with looting and pillaging, a scene that horrified the very correct Benedict Arnold. Allen did nothing to put an end to the rampage, worsening relations between him and Arnold. Problems between the two leaders continued after their combined force took Crown Point, again with virtually no resistance; now both Arnold and Allen, eager to continue a campaign that had been so successful, mounted separate efforts to push into Canada with boats they appropriated, competing with one another for pride of achievement. In this contest Arnold bettered Allen, a source of further and deepening hostility, from which there would be ongoing fallout. Having taken Ticonderoga and Crown Point, Arnold seized several ships, outfitted them with guns, and sallied forth on Lake Champlain, in search of British warships. Laying anchor below Saint Johns, Arnold and his men rowed all night, and early the next morning they surprised the British garrison in an attack that Arnold led, sword in hand. He and his men seized the British outpost without firing a shot; leaving a few guards behind he boarded the British warship *George*, which he took, again without firing a shot. Arnold's successes on Lake Champlain were a prelude to an American invasion of Canada. Two armies invaded Canada in 1775, one passing down Lake Champlain in late August and the other marching through Maine in September.

Placed in command of the army of 1,050 men that marched through Maine, Arnold sailed from Cambridge to the Kennebec River on September 11 and then moved across rugged wilderness to Quebec. On the last night before their departure Arnold and his officers had dinner at the mansion of a friend who served fine wines and fine dishes on white linen while his men were confined to their ships to prevent looting, which had become a problem in previous days. The march to Quebec was fearsomely difficult, and along the way one contingent of Americans returned to Massachusetts, in effect deserting. By the time Arnold reached Quebec, wearing his gold-braided uniform when he approached his destination, his force was considerably smaller and weakened by illness. The other force in the 1775 invasion of Canada, under the command of Richard Montgomery, was late in arriving. They finally reached Quebec in December, and in a blizzard on December 31 the combined forces launched an assault on Quebec that was under the command of Sir Guy Carleton. The assault failed, Arnold was shot in the leg, and Montgomery was killed. Still hoping to take the fortress, Arnold held on grimly until early April 1776, at which time he left Quebec and moved to Montreal. From this point on Arnold's story, marked by sudden twists and turns and ongoing controversy, becomes one of high melodrama, petty disagreements, political intrigue, and heroic deeds. There is no stranger path to Saratoga than that taken by Benedict Arnold. Having led a battered force of 786 men (out of an original force of 2,250) to Montreal, Arnold ran afoul of junior officers, who filed charges against him of plundering, charges that were never proven and would seem unlikely given Arnold's strong feelings about plundering. These charges would be used against Arnold in the future by enemies in Congress who opposed both Washington and Arnold. The ongoing story of Arnold before Saratoga is one of heroic deeds and conflict with enemies in his own ranks and most importantly with enemies in Congress; repeatedly Arnold would achieve spectacular military successes; repeatedly Congress would work against him, most vexingly from his point of view by promoting officers over him whose achievements did not match his. A man of intense pride and vanity, Arnold reached a point at which he could no longer take the abuse heaped upon him: the endless calumnies, refusal to recognize his heroics, the promotion of others over him. On July 10, 1777 he resigned his commission. This was exactly when Burgoyne broke through at

Ticonderoga; hearing of the disaster in upstate New York, Washington wrote Congress, saying that Arnold was urgently needed in New York. Congress refused to accept Arnold's resignation and he rode north to participate in the struggle against two seemingly irresistible British forces that were moving toward Albany, one proceeding down the Hudson-Champlain corridor, the other down the Mohawk corridor. Arnold would play a critical role in the obstruction of one of those forces and in the defeat of the other.

Fighting alongside Arnold at Saratoga was Daniel Morgan (c. 1735–1802), whose path to Saratoga could hardly have been more different from that of all the other major figures in the historic battle. Virtually nothing is known about Daniel Morgan until he was 17, at which time he left his family in New Jersey and moved to Virginia, apparently after having had a serious disagreement with his father. When he arrived in Virginia in 1753 he had to fend for himself; he had little but physical brawn and raw energy to further whatever schemes he might concoct, or ambitions he might harbor. He had no connections, could barely read or write, his manners were coarse, he was given to gambling and hard drinking, and he fought at the least provocation. At a solid six feet and strong as an ox he seldom lost altercations when they took place, which was not infrequently. The backwoods of Virginia he settled in were peopled by men such as he —tough, blunt, direct—and free of the softer ways and habits of city people in more settled zones along the eastern seaboard. Daniel Morgan was the prototypical American frontiersman. If he was to achieve anything it would be by dint of his own effort, and from the beginning Morgan had plans to better his position. A tireless worker and trustworthy, he hired himself out as a farmhand and within a year he was put in charge of a sawmill. He saved whatever money he could, bought a wagon and team, and set himself up as a wagoner bringing supplies to farmers in his part of the country. He also hauled supplies for the British at the beginning of the French and Indian War, which broke out at the very time he became a wagoner. He hauled supplies for Braddock, and was with his army when it was attacked by an enemy force in 1755; he now hauled dead bodies for the British. He had an altercation with a British officer and hit him in the face, for which he received 500 lashes; he continued to work with the British and ran messages for them. While doing this on one occasion he was chased by Indians who shot at him along the way. A bullet passed through his neck, took out several teeth, and left a deep mark on his left cheek. The Indians caught one of Morgan's men and scalped him. Morgan settled near Winchester, Virginia in 1758, resumed wagoning, trading items such as rum and cards; this was a rough world and it was one that he fit into; he was an excellent horseman, a fast runner, and a wrestler who seldom lost when he took on opponents, whom he joked with after beating them. He hated to lose and had a fierce temper. Intensely proud, he was not to be crossed. His gang, the Morgan gang, had brawls with other gangs, most notably the Davis gang, in which no holds were barred, with kicking, biting, and gouging accepted by both sides. Charged with assault and battery, Morgan defied the sheriff who was sent to bring him in. He was in court 22 times for indebtedness between 1767 and 1774. Morgan's ways began to change in 1761 when he bought a "gentleman's" hat, a watch, several combs, and sleeve buttons. He also bought a handkerchief, ribbon, and silk, presents for Abigail Curry, daughter of a prosperous nearby farmer in her late teens. She moved in with him and they had two children before they were married. Abigail had some civilizing effect on Morgan, and she helped him improve his reading and writing. By the time Morgan and Abigail were married in 1773 or 1774, he was a prosperous farmer and captain of the local militia. When the Continental Congress gave instructions for the formation of two companies of riflemen from Virginia in 1775 Morgan was the unanimous choice to raise and lead the unit from his county.

The Kentucky Rifle was integral to life on the American frontier, an instrument of the time and the place; it had deadly accuracy and with a range of 250 yards it was a potent weapon. It was much slower to load than the smooth-bore musket, however, and was unable to accommodate the bayonet, making it useless for soldiers who marched into battle in formal lines, discharging rounds as they proceeded until engaging the enemy with bayonets when they clashed in hand-to-hand combat. But with its remarkable range and accuracy the rifle had the potential of inflicting serious damage on the battlefield. Having raised a company of riflemen, Morgan followed Washington to Boston after Lexington and Concord, marching the entire distance. He reached Cambridge on August 6, where he and his men made an immediate impression on New Englanders. More importantly, Morgan's riflemen made an impression on the British by accurate sniping at unheard of and terrifying distances. The impact of the rifle went beyond its ability to kill at long distance; every bit as important was its emotional impact, tearing away a barrier of safety dictated by the range of the smooth-bore musket, the established weapon of the time. If having Morgan's riflemen in Boston had an upside, there was also a downside; the frontiersmen did not accept discipline easily, and not infrequently they fell into fighting amongst themselves, and with others.

Morgan's riflemen took aim, often deadly aim, at officers, whom they sought deliberately to kill, in violation of an established eighteenth-century military code. Washington recognized the value of the rifle in military terms, but did not want Morgan's men to snipe at British officers. Morgan's men brought something new to warfare, but they were disorderly, unkempt, and quarrelsome, a particular problem to someone who valued order and discipline as Washington did. So when Washington sent Morgan and his riflemen into Canada with Arnold, his motives were most likely mixed. He would have recognized the fighting prowess of Morgan's men, and the military value of their weapon, the rifle; at the same time he would seem to have been relieved to be rid of these rough, contentious men of the frontier. As for Arnold, he was quick to recognize the toughness of Morgan's men, who made their way through the Maine upcountry with a facility and dexterity that was in contrast to the difficulties felt by New Englanders on the expedition. Arnold made Morgan commander of his first division; he and Morgan respected one another and worked well together, as different as they were in appearance and manner. Arnold brought his gold-braided uniform with him and wore it on proper occasions, whereas Morgan wore the same buckskin shirt and leather leggings as his men. The high rhetoric of Arnold's letters suggests a use of language that placed him on a different linguistic planet than that of Morgan, whose letters—at least those of his early years—are without proper spelling, grammar, or syntax. The one altercation between Arnold and Morgan took place when Morgan's men were caught stealing and plundering, for which Arnold held Morgan responsible. Yet Arnold would seem to have recognized that Morgan's men were essential to the success of his operation; when it was time for the attack on Quebec to begin, a vote was taken and plundering was to be allowed.

As the American force shelled Quebec with artillery while preparing to storm the city, Morgan's men sniped at anyone who came into their sights. When a rifleman shot a sentry in the head at long range, a loyalist, Captain Ainslie, complained of the "skulking riflemen . . . These fellows who call themselves soldiers . . . are worse than savages. They lie in wait to shoot a sentry! A deed worthy of Yankee men of war!" When the attack on Quebec took place in a snowstorm on December 31, Arnold led the charge with a sword. Inside the town he entered a narrow street, Morgan right behind him; faced with two cannon at the far end of the street Arnold ordered some of his men to move to the left and come up behind the two cannon, but before this happened he was fired upon, hit in the leg, and seriously wounded. Other officers insisted that Morgan take the lead, but Arnold had given no instructions for anyone to take command of his forces in the event he were hit, a failure that would seem to have contributed to the ultimate American defeat. Morgan threw all caution to the winds as he took initiative after initiative to secure victory, but the various American contingents failed to work together and soon isolated groups had no choice but to surrender. When a British soldier told Morgan to surrender, Morgan shot him in the head. Morgan was in the last group that lowered their arms, which his men did against his orders. His back to a wall, he stood alone and told his assailants to try and take his sword. The British threatened to shoot him; his men pleaded with him to give up; he saw a priest in the crowd, and gave his sword to him, proclaiming, "Not a scoundrel of those cowards shall take it out of my hands."[11] Morgan was placed in decent confinement by the British and in August he and the other Americans went by ship to New York, the idea being to exchange them for British prisoners held by Americans. Morgan was allowed to return to his family in Virginia with the understanding that he would remain there until agreement was reached for the exchange of prisoners. This happened in January 1777, a year after his capture.

Aware of Morgan's achievements, Washington placed him in command of another unit of riflemen; it was those men, with Morgan at their head, who would ride north to play an important role at the Battle of Saratoga later in the year.

We come now to Philip Schuyler (1733–1804), the Albany aristocrat who had been head of the Northern Army that fought the Battle of Saratoga until he was relieved of his command a month before the battle took place. Schuyler's great grandfather, Philip Pieterse Schuyler (1628–83), a carpenter who came to America from Holland in the middle of the seventeenth-century, was active in the fur trade, acquired land north of Albany, built a house in Albany on what is now State and Pearl Street, and fathered 12 children. The eldest son, Pieter Schuyler (1657–1724), married Maria Van Rensselaer, connecting his family to the largest landowning family in New York. He joined his father in trade with Indians, learned Iroquois, was a leader in resistance to the Leisler Rebellion in 1690, and was the first mayor of Albany. Pieter's sister, Alida, married another member of the Van Rensselaer family, and after his death she married Robert Livingston, a powerful Hudson River landowner. The youngest son of Pieter Schuyler, Johannes Schuyler (1668–1747), married a woman ten years older than he, to his considerable material advantage; he continued his father's business enterprises, was active in Indian affairs, and was mayor of Albany for four terms. His son, Johannes Schuyler, Jr. (1697–1741), the father of Philip Schuyler, married Cornelia Van Cortlandt, who brought a large dowry and substantial inheritance to the marriage. Continuing the well-travelled path of his father and grandfather, Philip Schuyler married advantageously in 1755; his wife was from the Claverack branch of the Van Rensselaer family. He inherited an estate in Saratoga (present-day Schuylerville) of 10,000 to 20,000 acres from an uncle in 1763, which he turned into a thriving and highly prosperous enterprise with a sawmill, grain mill, and facilities for the making of flax. He built ships that conveyed commodities grown and produced on his estate to markets in New York, as well as fish that he brought from the waters of the Hudson. Wealthy and allied to powerful aristocratic families with estates along the Hudson, Schuyler became a member of the New York Assembly in 1768. He was a close personal friend of General John Bradstreet, under whom he served in the French and Indian War, and after whom he named one of his sons. Well-disposed to Britain and to English civilization, Schuyler had to make hard choices as political storms gathered over the colonies in years before the Revolution. Like others of his class he supported protests against British taxes, but without wanting to sever ties with Britain.

In all of these respects Schuyler took a line similar to that of George Washington, a Virginia aristocrat with whom he had much in common. They were almost exact contemporaries; Washington was born in 1732 and Schuyler in 1733. Both were landed aristocrats; both emulated their English counterparts, the country gentry; both strove to and did expand their landed holdings—Washington through acquisition of patents in the unsettled area that lay to the west of Mount Vernon, Schuyler by speculating in land in western New York. Both inherited land from relatives and added to their prestige and wealth by marrying into powerful families; both fought in the French and Indian War but returned to their estates before the conflict ended; both became active in local and colonial politics; both saw themselves as natural leaders, innately better than those of lower station; both thought that the wealthy should rule; both saw themselves as men of virtue and dedicated to the public good, prepared to make all necessary sacrifices to the cause they served; both placed value on honor and pride, transmitted by the classical tradition that shaped the ethical thought of the elite ruling class, to which both belonged.

Among the precepts that Washington hand-copied at age 16 from *The Rules of Civility and Decent Behaviour in Company and Conversation* was one that said "Every action done in company ought to be done with some sign of respect to those that are present."[12] This was the very first precept of *The Rules of Civility*; others spelled out the endless distinctions that one should make when showing respect to others. One was to respond differently to someone "of Greater Quality than oneself" than to "Artificers & Persons of Low Degree. . . . In writing or Speaking, [one should] give to every Person his due Title According to his Degree & the Custom of the Place. . . . Associate yourself with men of good Quality if you esteem your own Reputation. . . ." The rules of etiquette that Washington learned as a youth involved many aspects of proper behavior, including eating and speaking correctly, when and how to laugh, how to walk, how to be graceful, how to dress, and how to set a good example. Being polite when in the company of others is a common theme. The respect of others, which Washington was told was essential to proper behavior, expresses something central to a system of manners that originated within the ruling elite and served its ends, a system that at once validated those who observed the proper forms of behavior within the system and separated them from those outside it.[13] The child who learned to show respect for others would, as an adult, gain respect; out of engrained habits came discipline, limits on individual behavior that resulted in self-mastery; out of self-mastery came a sense of mastery, the stuff of which leaders were made. Washington assimilated all of this, along with acute sense of pride, honor, and dedication to the public good, transmitted by the classical heritage, a Ciceronian tradition that spoke directly and eloquently to men of Washington's class. So too did English literature of the Augustan Age that conveyed Senecan ideas of fortitude and resignation. Among the plays that Washington read as a young man was Addison's *Cato* (1713), in which the protagonist utters the words "A day, an hour, of virtuous liberty is worth a whole eternity in bondage."[14] Washington internalized the ideas of fortitude and dedication to liberty that were at the core of this play, which officers' wives performed at Valley Forge in the harsh winter of 1777–78.

The Dutch tradition from which Schuyler sprang was different in some respects from the English tradition that framed Washington's formative

Figure 12. Schuyler house on the corner of State and Pearl before its demolition in 1887

experience. Children in Albany, which was still predominantly Dutch, grew up not on plantations but in town, where they were brought together according to fixed arrangements. Boys and girls were formed into separate groups, where they were allowed to play together, but always under supervision. Raised in a house on the corner of the two main streets passing through Albany (present-day State and Pearl Streets), Schuyler participated in the same pastimes as other children of his station. The habits of discipline elders imparted to Schuyler when he was a boy are suggested by an incident when he was about ten and his mother had a servant place a dish before him at dinner, which he said he did not want to eat, asking for something else instead. His mother told the servant to take the dish away and nothing else was brought to him. At supper

Figure 13. The IBM Building at the corner of State and Pearl today, where the 1667 Schuyler house once stood.

the servant brought in the same dish that Schuyler had refused to eat, and still refused to eat; again he left the table having eaten nothing, this time going to bed more than a little hungry. In the midst of these episodes Schuyler's mother (his father died when he was eight) said nothing, uttered no rebukes, and was nothing but civil. But she made the point, and Schuyler knew that she had. He apologized the next day for his bad behavior, and ate the meal that he had rejected on two previous occasions.[15] This is a small incident, to be certain, but it evokes life in a household within which a well-established system of manners determined forms of conduct. If there is a Dutch flavor to this episode, it suggests common affinities between Schuyler's boyhood experience and that of Washington, within which expectations of proper behavior were well known. Like Washington, much of Schuyler's education was at the hands of tutors; his education included study of the classics, works that helped impart a code that, in broad, general terms, both he and Washington absorbed. That code helped determine how they thought about themselves, about those of their own class, and about those below them in the social order. So between Schuyler and Washington there were shared affinities, mental and emotional qualities held in common. Moreover, both built or improved mansions, symbols of power and statements of family importance. Mount Vernon overlooked the Potomac and Schuyler's mansion overlooked the Hudson. Both men were formal, well-read, and placed emphasis on proper manners, a system of etiquette within which one showed respect to others through a carefully calibrated set of observances known by all who subscribed to this system, as Washington and Schuyler most certainly did.

Schuyler met Washington in Philadelphia at the second Continental Congress in 1775. Introduced to one another, they would have recognized shared manners in an instant. This they seem to have done; they got on well from the beginning. When Washington was appointed commander in chief of the Continental Army he recommended to Congress that Schuyler be placed in command of one of four regional armies, the Army of the Northern Department, which included New York and Canada. The recommendation was approved. It was Schuyler's army that was to carry out the invasion of Canada that Congress decided to undertake on June 17. When Washington left Philadelphia for Boston on June 23, he rode with a group that included Schuyler. After stopping at New York City for a few days, Washington continued to Boston to organize the army that was to confront the British army that occupied that city; whereas Schuyler went to Ticonderoga to prepare for the invasion of Canada, stopping off at his mansion in Albany along the way. From the time Washington and Schuyler parted company in New York City in late June 1775 until the departure of Schuyler's army from Ticonderoga for the invasion of Canada at the end of August the two leaders maintained a regular correspondence; altogether, Washington and Schuyler exchanged seven letters each between June 25 and September 8, 1775, in which they kept one another informed of their plans and the formidable problems they faced. This correspondence reveals much about the two leaders, one a Virginia planter and the other a New York landowner.

The Washington-Schuyler correspondence during this two-month period shows both men as highly organized leaders, as one would expect of landed aristocrats with much experience running their own estates, and accustomed to giving orders. This is evident in Washington's first letter to Schuyler, written on June 25. "You are to take upon you the Command of all the Forces destined for the New York Department," the letter begins, "and see that the Orders of the Continental Congress are carried into the Execution with as much Precision and Exactness as possible . . . You will be pleased also to make regular Returns once a Month to me and to the Continental Congress (and oftener as Occurences may require) of the Forces under your Command—Of your provisions, Stores &c. and give me the earliest Advises of every piece of Intelligence, which you shall judge of Importance to be speedily known." The voice is authoritative, but at the same time there is recognition on Washington's part that he is dealing with a person of worth, someone who like himself is accustomed to exercising authority. "Your own good Sense must govern in all Matters not particularly pointed out, as I do not wish to circumscribe you within too narrow Limits."[16] Schuyler was still in New York City when he wrote his first letter to Washington on July 1, 1775, by which time Washington had departed for Boston. He explained that he would carry out Washington's directions with all possible dispatch; he gave specific information on what he was doing and what he had to do; he told Washington that he hoped to leave for "Albany in my way to Ticonderoga on Monday next"; and he wrapped the project in which he and Washington were involved in a banner of high purpose: "That Success and Happiness equal to the Merit & Virtue of my General may crown all his Operations is the Wish of every honest American by none more sincerely than me."[17] The sense of high purpose in Schuyler's letters also came through in Washington's letters: In his July 28 letter to Schuyler, Washington wrote that "I am much easier with Respect to the public Interests since your arrival at Ticonderoga, as I am persuaded those Abilities and that Zeal for the common Welfare which has led your Country to repose such Confidence in you will be fully exerted."[18] Both men were dedicated to the public weal; both adhered to Ciceronian notions of virtue, as did other Americans of their class and time. Mingled with Classical Ideas of serving the public weal was a sense of Stoic resignation and rectitude, also part of the code of the aristocratic landowning class. Writing Schuyler on August 20, Washington said, "Animated with the Goodness of our Cause, and the best Wishes of your Countrymen, I am sure you will not let Difficulties not insuperable damp your ardour. Perseverance and Spirit have done Wonders in all ages."[19] Schuyler was fully aware of the obstacles he faced as he was about to undertake the invasion of Canada; just before his departure from Crown Point on August 31 he wrote, "so Critical is my Situation that I sacrifice every thing to the Grand Object." He had expected more cannon than he had gotten, "but I have promised not to Complain." Schuyler closed this letter with a token of friendship: "Adieu, my Dear General."[20] In the course of their correspondence, Washington and Schuyler addressed one another in terms or mutual respect and admiration, befitting aristocrats who pursued the same high-minded cause: service of their country.

It is hardly surprising that both Washington and Schuyler, fellow aristocrats, sought to impose discipline, and considered subordination of inferiors to superiors essential to the maintaining of proper order. Washington was reluctant initially to tell Schuyler how bad conditions were in Boston. Writing from Cambridge on July 27, he commented, "Our army is in good Health & Spirits well supplied with Provisions of all Kinds—The Situation of the Enemy is directly the reverse in every Respect and we have Reason to think [their] Desertions will be very great."[21] Washington's letter to his half brother, John Augustine Washington, written on the same day, gives a different picture: "I found a mixed multitude of People here, under very little discipline, order, or Government—I found the Enemy in possession of a place called Bunkers Hill . . . I found part of our army . . . in a very insecure state."[22] Clearly, Washington experienced disorder in units that he wanted to form into a disciplined army, but initially he was reluctant to discuss these problems with Schuyler. This changed as Schuyler brought up the problems of discipline that he encountered in his army. In a July 15 letter to Washington, he said, "Be assured my General that I shall use my best Endeavours to establish Order and Discipline in the Troops under my Command . . . It is extremely difficult to introduce a proper Subordination amongst a People where so little Distinction is kept up . . . I shall have an Augean Stable to clean here."[23] Having received news of Schuyler's problems with discipline, Washington explained that he understood them full well: "From my own Experience I can easily judge of your Difficulties to introduce Order & Discipline into Troops who have from their Infancy imbibed ideas of the most contrary Kind: It would be far beyond the Compass of a Letter for me to describe the Situation of Things here on my arrival, perhaps you will only be able to judge of it, from my assuring you that mine must be a portrait at full Length of what you have had in Miniature."[24] Schuyler wrote in a letter of August 6 that having to put up with such matters as Washington did was far from pleasant. "I foresaw, my Dear Sir, that You would have an Herculean Labour, in Order to introduce that proper Spirit of Discipline & Subordination, which is the very Soul of an Army, and I felt for You with the utmost Sensibility, as I well knew the Variety of Difficulties, You would have to encounter, and which must necessarily be extremely painfull & disgusting to You, accustomed to Order & Regularity, I can easily conceive, that my Difficulties are only a faint Semblance of Yours."[25]

Schuyler suffered from rheumatic gout, a congenital illness that flared up when he was heavily stressed, as he certainly was when he undertook the invasion of Canada at the end of August 1775. He did not feel well before departing from Crown Point for Canada on August 31, three days after his second in command, Richard Montgomery, had set out with an advance force. Already "much indisposed" before setting forth on Lake Champlain, Schuyler's condition grew worse, and on September 17, barely able to hold his pen when he drew up reports, he returned to Ticonderoga, still officially in command of the Northern Army but separated from it, as he would be throughout the disastrous Canada campaign. In the two-year interval between Schuyler's return to Ticonderoga in 1775 and the Battle of Saratoga in 1777, he and Washington continued their correspondence; Schuyler wrote Washington a total of 108 letters, and Washington wrote Schuyler 79 letters. They never saw one another during this period; their only contact was through the letters they exchanged. In the course of their correspondence they maintained a relationship of sorts; while the purpose of the epistolary exchanges was always official they also took stands on issues that said much about themselves politically, militarily, and ideologically. It turned out that they were in fundamental agreement on a host of important issues, some of them controversial, making them allies in ongoing struggles with adversaries within the Revolution's political and military leadership. Throughout the correspondence both men described in clear and precise terms the logistical and organizational minutiae that occupied much of their time and energy: supplies they needed and were often unable to obtain; the disposition and movement of troops, theirs and those of the enemy; desertions; difficulties attracting recruits; disciplinary problems; the endless complications they had to deal with, day in and day out, week after week, month after month. How they responded to the myriad problems they faced and the overwhelming pressures they were under says much about the two men. What comes through in the Washington-Schuyler correspondence is constant adversity and pressure. Amidst all of this what also comes through are feelings of mutual respect, very much the stuff of aristocratic friendship—and friendship does not seem too strong a word to characterize the relationship that developed between Washington and Schuyler. As it turned out, Washington had no choice but to acquiesce to Congress' decision to remove Philip Schuyler from command of the Northern Army in August 1777, a month before the Battle of Saratoga. It was Washington's own former aide, Horatio Gates, who won Congress' support and was given command of Schuyler's army, a blow of devastating severity to the proud Albany aristocrat. But this is to get ahead of ourselves; what we must now do is follow the course of events as the principal players in the drama work their way toward the historic Battle of Saratoga.

Schuyler remained in New York throughout the agonizing campaign in Canada, first at Ticonderoga, then with onset of winter in Albany; he was still head of the Army of the Northern Department, but separated from it and from the campaign that was carried out in his absence. On June 17, 1776 Congress, knowing that the army in Canada was in desperate straits, ordered Horatio Gates to take over its command. Gates rode to Albany to consult with Schuyler on his way to Canada. When he arrived on June 26, Schuyler showered him with his usual hospitality, but relations soured as soon as Gates showed Schuyler his orders. Gates' understanding was that he was now in charge of Schuyler's army, but paying close attention to the wording of the orders Schuyler pointed out to Gates that his command applied only to the army that was in Canada; he explained that the army was no longer in Canada, having returned to New York, which meant that he, Schuyler, was still the commanding general of the Army of the Northern Department. Schuyler and Gates both appealed to Congress for clarification; Congress decided that since the army was back in America Schuyler remained in command. Gates was given the choice of serving under Schuyler or rejoining Washington. He decided to remain with Schuyler, and together they rode to Crown Point, where they met with Benedict Arnold, who had fled Saint Johns just before Burgoyne almost caught up with him on June 13.

It was Arnold who spoke first when he, Schuyler, and Gates met at Crown Point on July 5. Arnold explained that a British force of formidable size would soon appear on Lake Champlain in a mass invasion of New York, for which preparations needed urgently to be made. The three men agreed on a division of responsibility: Arnold moved to Skenesboro (now Whitehall) at the headwaters of Lake Champlain to build a fleet that would obstruct the passage of the British flotilla as best as possible; Schuyler returned to Albany to raise militia, to tend to organizational matters, and to sort out problems with Indians in western New York, a problem of some urgency; and Gates took charge of building up defenses at and around Fort Ticonderoga. Of the three initiatives, Arnold's was of the greatest immediate importance. He was a fireball of energy at Skenesboro, building ships that were to take on the larger British fleet certain to appear on the waters of Lake Champlain. When he began the formidable task confusion reigned at Skenesboro, but carpenters arrived from Albany on July 24 and by July 31 six row galleys were on stocks. By August 15 Arnold was ready to sail for Crown Point with the ships he had built in five weeks, half the number he had hoped for. Attired in his new navy-blue uniform, buff sash, and gold-braided tricorn hat, Arnold led his fleet onto the waters of Lake Champlain on August 24. The first skirmish took place at Isle LaMotte on September 21. Arnold then moved to Valcour Island five miles below Plattsburgh and lay in wait for the British fleet as it made its way along the western side of Lake Champlain. Arnold's fleet of 16 ships was half the size of Carleton's fleet of some 30 ships; to gain tactical advantage he positioned his ships in a narrow strait between the shore and Valcour Island, and camouflaged them so they would be unseen by the British fleet. When Carleton's flotilla arrived on October 11 and sailed past Valcour Island, Arnold sent three ships after it, decoys that drew British ships back for the naval engagement that continued into the night and resulted in heavy losses for both the British and American fleets. All of Arnold's ships took hits, several were destroyed, and all were leaking, but Arnold had devised an escape strategy, which he put into effect under cover of darkness. By putting shirts around oars his men rowed silently through British ships in a single file, coming so close they could hear the voices of British men on board their ships. When Carleton discovered that the Americans had escaped he gave pursuit; he encountered difficulties owing to weather, but caught up with Arnold the following day, October 13. Arnold sent slower ships ahead and he entered a cove awaiting the British fleet. A five-hour battle ensued, at the end of which Arnold and his men, some of them wounded, scuttled their ship, waded ashore, and walked ten miles to Crown Point, which Arnold burned, and then made his way to Ticonderoga. Carleton reached Crown Point on October 20, by which time snow was already falling. He then sailed to Ticonderoga, whose defenses had been shored up by Gates, forcing Carleton to make a hard decision: Should he take Ticonderoga and continue down the Champlain-Hudson corridor and join Howe in New York, or should he abandon the campaign and return to Quebec? Burgoyne, who had sailed down the eastern side of Lake Champlain and joined Carleton at Ticonderoga, wanted to push on to New York, but Carleton decided to return to Quebec. Returning with Carleton to Quebec, Burgoyne claimed illness, went to London that winter, and gave his version of what had happened and what had gone wrong.

Back in London in December 1776, Burgoyne again pushed his plan for a British army to move down the Champlain-Hudson corridor, only this time not with the overly cautious Carleton in command; he would bring the needed decisiveness to the 1777 campaign and exuded confidence with everyone with whom he discussed his plan. He placed a bet that he would be back in London in time for Christmas after securing victory over the Americans; as a man of the theater and aristocratic clubs, Burgoyne certainly did not want to spend the holiday season in America, whose harsh winters he did not care for. Both Germain and George III approved Burgoyne's plan, according to which he was to sail at the head of a fleet to Quebec with orders that put him in command of the army that was to pass down Lake Champlain on its way to Albany. In his original thinking about the Champlain-Hudson strategy Burgoyne had envisaged two British armies joining forces somewhere along the Hudson, one coming from the north and the other from the south. When he was in London in the winter of 1775–76 he had drawn up a proposal for the British War Department, *Reflections upon the War in America*, in which he wrote that "two armies should advance, one from the North in Canada, and one from the South, join at some given point, and cut the colonies in half."[26] Since that time Burgoyne had modified the original plan and made it a three-pronged attack, with one British force coming from the north, one from the south, and one from the west, all converging at Albany. In the final plan that Germain and the King accepted, definite arrangements were made only for two parts of the plan: the invasion from the north passing down Lake Champlain, and one from the west that proceeded down the Mohawk. What the plan did not do was specify what role the British army at the southern end of the Champlain-

Hudson corridor under the command of General William Howe would play in the 1777 campaign. The assumption was that Howe would lead his army up the Hudson and join Burgoyne's army at Albany, but this part of the British war plan was not nailed down. That Germain did not spell out this part of the invasion plan in clear, unambiguous directives says much about how he fit into the complicated British social, political, and military structure as the 1777 campaign was about to get under way. The seeds of failure were deeply embedded within that complex system.

Lord George Germain (1716–85), a younger son of the Duke of Dorset, was appointed to the office of Secretary of State for the American Department by George III, who viewed him with personal favor. This was in November 1775, after the Battle of Bunker Hill. The king wanted someone who would bring decisive leadership to the struggle with the incorrigible colonies; it was to Germain that he turned at this point. The man who was to direct the British war effort from late 1775 to 1782 was born into the powerful Sackville family. His father, Lionel Sackville, the Duke of Dorset, was Lord High Steward of England and Lord Lieutenant of Ireland. As the third son, George Stainville—his name at the time of his birth—grew up on the family estate in Kent, Knowle House, noted for its 52 staircases and 365 rooms, one for each day of the year. It was only in 1769 that George Stainville became Lord George Germain, when his aunt, Lady Betty Germain, bequeathed her estate in Northamptonshire to him, under the proviso that he take her surname.

In British political life under the Hanoverians a constant theme was enmity between the King and the Prince of Wales, heir to the throne. Constellations of placemen and favorites gathered around the King and prime minister at Whitehall; whereas discontented outsiders surrounded the Prince of Wales, awaiting opportunities that might come their way with the next succession to the throne. These relations extended outward into political life across Britain, into the military establishment, and they fed into power struggles within the high command. As a younger son of the Duke of Dorset, Germain purchased a commission and in 1745 he fought bravely at the Battle of Fontenoy in the War of the Austrian Succession, in which he was wounded and cited for bravery. Promoted to major general, he fought at the Battle of Minden in 1759 in the Seven Years War, in which he failed to lead a cavalry charge in a British defeat. His commanding officer, Prince Ferdinand of Brunswick, related by blood to George II, reprimanded Germain severely and when Germain returned to Britain he was stripped of his command. Germain demanded a court martial, at which he was declared unfit to serve under George II. The king added to Germain's disgrace by stripping him of his rank and ordering that the court-martial verdict be read to every regiment in the army. From this time on Germain was known as the "Coward of Minden" in circles that were hostile to him.

It was in the year after Minden that George III came to the throne, and with his accession much changed. The new king despised George II's ministers, and in 1765 he made Germain one of his secretaries of state, the first step in his rehabilitation. Yet Germain never lived down the disgrace of Minden; scarred by it emotionally, he would do nothing that might suggest weakness on his part. More importantly, insofar as carrying out Burgoyne's 1777 strategy was concerned, Germain was uneasy about the commander of British forces in North America, General William Howe, who was not only a relative of the King but was also known for his bravery. Howe had his own ideas for the 1777 campaign, which Germain considered in London, agreeing with him when possible but when necessary refusing requests for reinforcements in numbers too great to meet; what Germain never did was to insist that Howe and Burgoyne work together in a unified strategy for the 1777 campaign. Basically, Germain left Howe to his own devices; he was reluctant to tell Howe what to do, but he did act decisively in one quarter: He placed Burgoyne in command of the army that was to move down the Hudson-Champlain corridor, removing Carleton from that command. In this connection it should be noted that Carleton had been at Minden, and he was on the court-martial committee that briefly consigned Germain to political oblivion. Placing Burgoyne in command of the invasion army, rather than Carleton, could not have been displeasing for Germain.

Both Germain and Burgoyne steered shy of Howe; Germain made no reference to him in his final plan for the 1777 campaign that logically should have taken Howe into account. Howe had crushed Washington's army at the Battle of Long Island in the 1776 campaign, and his army was at the southernmost end of the Hudson when Burgoyne's 1777 campaign began. Militarily, the British strategy should have coordinated efforts between Burgoyne's army that moved down the Hudson-Champlain corridor and Howe's army that was at its southernmost end, but this did not happen. Wanting to avenge Washington's successes at Trenton and Princeton, Howe decided to take Philadelphia; personal honor became a factor as he played out his role in the fateful British campaign of 1777. The two British armies, Howe's and Burgoyne's, acted separately; at no point did Germain, in London, issue directives saying that they should work together in a coordinated strategy. Howe was bent upon pursuing an independent course of action, not wanting to share glory with Burgoyne, and Germain was reluctant to tell Howe what to do. And, of course, the delay in back-and-forth communications between London and America, something like three months, complicated Germain's efforts to give effective direction to the 1777 campaign. With a free hand, Howe decided to strike a decisive blow at the Revolution by taking the American capital, Philadelphia, which he occupied on September 25, 14 days after defeating Washington's army at Brandywine. As it turned out, Howe's victory was hollow; Congress left Philadelphia as the British army advanced; no political or military advantage was gained by Howe's occupation of Philadelphia, which the British had to abandon in 1778. For his part, Burgoyne also acted independently, although he assumed, or hoped, that Howe would join forces with him in Albany. Pursuing different strategies, both Howe and Burgoyne tried to crush the Revolution in the 1777 campaign;

Howe's occupation of Philadelphia on September 25 took place between the two battles of Saratoga, fought on September 19 and October 7. Had Howe sent a strong force up the Hudson in support of Burgoyne, he would have applied pressure on the Americans who opposed Burgoyne; in the absence of this pressure the Americans were able to concentrate on stopping Burgoyne. This they did at Saratoga.

Divisions within the political and military establishments in America were no less complicated than in Britain. Of the rifts, tensions, and conflicts in Congress none were deeper, arguably, than those between delegates from New England and New York, the supporters, respectively, of Horatio Gates and Philip Schuyler. It was when Gates went to Boston in July 1775 as Washington's aide that he began to build a base of support that enabled him to replace Schuyler as head of the Army of the Northern Department two years later. To understand how Gates built a base of support in New England one can do no better than consider how differently he and Washington responded to conditions in Boston at the time of their arrival in the summer of 1775. The soldiers who assembled in Boston were described by New Englander loyalist Benjamin Thompson as "the most wretchedly clothed, and as dirty a set of mortals as ever disgraced the name of soldier . . . They would rather let their clothes rot upon their backs than be at the trouble of cleaning 'em themselves." Washington had been forewarned by the Massachusetts Provincial Congress that he should not expect "regularity and discipline"[27] among his soldiers; this was a remark that tallied all too well with Washington's own perception of the men he saw in Boston, men who had left their farms, their homes, and their daily callings to join in an armed struggle against Britain, whose army of well-drilled professional soldiers Washington's army would meet in battle.

As commander in chief of the American army Washington had the mindset of a Virginia planter; a member of the Virginia elite, he was accustomed to fine things, and to special treatment. Upon arriving in Boston he was offered the home of the President of Harvard for his residence, but he found it inadequate, and chose instead the larger home of a loyalist who had left Cambridge for Boston. Staying there he lived, to the extent possible, in a manner to which he had long been accustomed, which included maintaining a fine table and showing hospitality on a proper scale. He had two cooks and a staff of ten, not including several slaves, one of whom was his personal attendant who rode with him on his daily rounds, inspecting troops and defenses. Washington did not like what he saw on these inspections. He wrote to his cousin Lund Washington, who managed Mount Vernon during his absence, that Yankees were an "exceeding dirty and nasty" lot. He wrote Richard Lee, a fellow Virginian and member of Congress, that there was an "unaccountable kind of stupidity in the lower class of these people, which believe me prevails but too generally among the officers . . . who are near[ly] of the same kidney with the privates." Particularly distressing to Washington was familiarity between officers and men; to make matters worse, officers strove to "curry favor with the men" so they could be re-elected. To someone of Washington's mindset and sense of proper relations it was decidedly irregular that men elected officers; in his view there should be distance between officers and men, as there should be between gentlemen and ordinary folk. He advised his officers to "Be easy . . . but not familiar" with your men, "lest you subject yourself to a want of that respect, which is necessary to support a proper command." To his chagrin, the men he hoped to turn into an effective fighting force capable of doing battle with an army of professional British soldiers were undisciplined and seriously in need of correction. Punishments were harsh for those who broke the rules. Floggings were customary; the incorrigible were told to leave camp. Washington disciplined not only the men under his command but officers as well. Writing Richard Lee in August 1775 he said, "I have made a pretty good Slam among such kind of officers as the Massachusetts Government abound in since I came to this Camp, having Broke one Colo. and two Captains for Cowardly behaviour in the action on Bunker's Hill—Two captains for drawing more provisions and pay than they had men in their Company—and one for being absent from his Post when the enemy appeared there, and burnt a House just by it. Besides these, I have at this time one Colo., one Major, one Captn, & two Subalterns under arrest for trial."[28]

Washington was unhappy with the officers Massachusetts had given him, with the New England practice of enlisted men electing officers, with militias made up of New Englanders, and with the very idea of fighting a war with militia units rather than a permanent army of trained soldiers, the Continental Army. Philip Schuyler was in full agreement with Washington on all of these issues, as his correspondence with Washington makes crystal clear. Writing Washington from Ticonderoga on November 22, 1775 Schuyler said, "Our Army requires to be put on quite a different Footing. . . . I cannot without the most extreme Pain, see that disregard of Discipline, Confusion, & Inattention which reign in this Quarter . . . Nothing can surpass the Impatience of the Troops from the New England Colonies, to get to their Fire Sides—Near three hundred of them arrived a few Days ago, unable to do any Duty, But as soon as I administered that Grand Specific, *a Discharge*, they instantly acquired Health. . . ."[29] Schuyler was so weary of the conditions he faced, he explained to Washington, that he was "determined to retire." Of course, Schuyler did not retire, although there can be little doubt that men serving under him, and particularly New Englanders, wished that he had. The hostility New Englanders felt toward Schuyler, instrumental in his eventual downfall, can be traced back to the beginning of his military career.

If Schuyler was in basic agreement with Washington on a need for strict discipline, particularly among New Englanders, Horatio Gates, Washington's aide, thought differently. Gates did not demand mindless obedience of soldiers, and he said he "never desired to see better soldiers than the New-England made men."

It was to politicians that Gates made this pronouncement; long accustomed to making such adjustments as were necessary with those in power, Gates carefully courted favor with New England politicians. He met and became friendly with John Adams in December 1775; soon they were exchanging letters, in which Gates professed republican political views that conformed perfectly with those of Adams. Washington still hoped for reconciliation with Britain, as did Schuyler, but not the resolute Gates, who took a firm, unyielding line, insisting that there could be no objective short of full independence. These were words that Adams liked to hear. Moreover, Gates accepted the New England practice of enlisted men electing their officers; he would work with men and officers; he would observe the principle of accommodation rather than subordination; he did not call for rigid separation between officers and men, or on strict discipline. Here was a man for John Adams: "A letter from you," Adams wrote Gates, "cures me of all Anxiety and ill Humour, for two or three Days at least; and, besides that, leaves me better informed in many Things and confirmed in my good Resolutions, for my whole Life."[30] Here was someone, Adams had come to feel, who should have a field command rather than waste his skills, understanding, and military experience as an aide doing the work of a desk-job functionary.

When Adams nominated Washington as commander in chief of the Continental Army in the Second Continental Congress he did so for political reasons, not because he thought Washington was the most qualified person. That Washington wanted to command the American army was indicated by the fact that he wore his military uniform in meetings of Congress, the only delegate to do so; Adams' nomination was not mere acquiescence to Washington's wishes; Adams wanted to tie Virginia, the most heavily populated of the colonies, to the Revolution as firmly as possible; the appointment of Washington as commander in chief served that end. The appointment of Philip Schuyler as major general and head of the Army of the Northern Department was also dictated by political considerations, made in part as a concession among New England delegates to New York delegates. Relations between New England and New York had long been strained, partly owing to contested land between the two colonies. There was no fixed boundary between New York and Massachusetts; rural disturbances broke out in 1751–57 and on a larger scale in 1766 when interlopers from New England encouraged tenant farmers on Hudson River estates in New York to rise up against their landlords, aristocrats mainly of Dutch ancestry, in order that they could occupy land whose ownership they disputed.[31] These agrarian disturbances sent waves of discontent into assemblies in Massachusetts and New York that left a large residue of mutual ill-feeling.

In addition to problems between New York and Massachusetts there was controversy over the New Hampshire Grants, a large expanse of land that later became the state of Vermont, but only after much controversy with New York. Philip Schuyler was involved in all of these issues, and was disliked by New England delegates not only for these reasons but also because they disliked him personally. Schuyler had no personal interest in the New Hampshire Grants, but he represented New York in the contentious meetings. It does not require oversized imagination to sense the hostility Schuyler stirred in these negotiations. New Englanders saw enough of Schuyler to regard him as arrogant, a perception that never went away. John Adams and John Hancock both despised Schuyler, whom they regarded as a haughty aristocrat, aloof and prideful. They were not altogether wrong in the way the way they viewed Schuyler. As similar as Schuyler and Washington were in many respects, there were clear personal differences between them. Aristocrat that Washington was, he was not overbearing or arrogant; in his personal code one should be "amiable," "modest," and easily familiar with others. Yes, he maintained distance between himself and those of lower station, but in a way that others seem typically not to have found objectionable. His code was of the time; contemporaries of different social stations, in some measure, understood and accepted it. Washington did not set the teeth of others on edge; in terms of ordinary human interchange he got on well with others across a broad social spectrum. With Schuyler it was different. Many did not like him, and delegates in Congress from New England most certainly did not like him. They were willing for political reasons to support him as Major General of the Army of the Northern Department in a calculated effort to tie New York as firmly as possible to the Revolution, but when opportunity arose to support someone else they were quick to seize it. That opportunity arose in June 1776 when Schuyler was in his Albany mansion, separated from his army during the disastrous campaign in Canada. The appointment of Horatio Gates as commander of the American army in Canada came out of a deep division in Congress, which it revealed with perfect clarity. Gates' appointment set the stage for a running struggle in Congress between the supporters of Gates and Schuyler, and most dramatically, it set the stage for bitter conflict between Gates and Schuyler themselves.

Initially Gates and Schuyler got on well; they worked in tandem as they—and Arnold—cooperated in a common effort to block the British invasion of America from Lake Champlain in the summer and fall of 1776. The outcome of their efforts proved successful when Carleton and Burgoyne withdrew from a seemingly well defended and fortified Ticonderoga in November, vindicating the decision that all three leaders had agreed on to abandon Crown Point and to concentrate on putting Ticonderoga's defenses in order. Yet, 21 junior officers disagreed with the decision to abandon Crown Point and said so in a July 8 letter to Schuyler, written in respectful language, setting forth seven reasons for their disagreement. Among the signatories were men such as Nathan Hale, John Stark, and Enoch Poor, men of ability and devotion to the Revolutionary cause. The signatories were largely New Englanders who thought for themselves, had definite opinions, and were not reluctant to question the authority of superior officers. They had a looser, freer idea of rank and its prerogatives than the authoritarian Philip Schuyler, who found the questioning of a decision he and other superior officers had made intolerable. Both Gates and Schuyler defended the decision and criticized the officers who had gone over their heads to Congress. Gates said the officers did not know what they were talking about, but Schuyler went farther when he wrote to Washington, threatening to resign unless Congress rebuked the junior officers. Not only had the junior officers been out of line, they had impugned his honor. Writing Congress on August 7, Schuyler said, "That an ignorant multitude, instigated not only by my own enemies, but by those of the country, should have been instigated to traduce my character is not very surprising, and I had already made myself easy on that score, but a late transaction of a council of officers held at New York is so injurious that I have found it necessary to resent it in a letter to General Washington. . . ."[32] Schuyler saw a conspiracy among those who worked against him; they were "not only my own enemies, but . . . those of the country." Washington found the abandonment of Crown Point difficult to understand, and wrote a sharp letter to Gates to that effect. Under criticism from many quarters for abandoning Crown Point, the ensuing flap had the effect of driving Gates and Schuyler together. Writing Gates on August 3, Schuyler said, "It is incumbent on us, my dear sir, to do justice to our injured reputations: as it is our duty to go hand in hand in opposing the enemies of the public, so we ought heartily to join in defeating the insidious foes who basely aim at the destruction of our characters. We shall discover who he or they are, and I trust I will be able to cover them with confusion."[33]

As the two leaders worked together, Schuyler came under a barrage of criticism from Congress, against which he repeatedly defended himself, and which he found intolerable. After constant inquiries into his management of accounts and the monies he had dispersed as head of a much beleaguered army, Schuyler resigned his command on September 14, 1776. How serious he was when he resigned is uncertain; at any rate, Congress declined the resignation. Why Congress pressed Schuyler to explain and justify his expenditures is also not altogether clear. In part, this would seem to have been done out of authentic concern over finances in time of acute fiscal shortage, but also Schuyler's enemies in Congress would seem to have wanted to discredit him. The questions Congress put to him, and the innuendo of corruption sometimes associated with the questions, was more than the prideful Philip Schuyler could bear. Eventually, exhaustive inquiries were conducted and Schuyler was fully exonerated of any wrongdoing, but before that happened Schuyler vented his frustrations to endless questions and charges that as a man of honor he deeply resented. And it is above all as a man of honor that Schuyler revealed himself when he felt that his honor had been impugned. "I have suffered such brutal outrage from Congress," he wrote on October 18, "that every gentleman who has ever honored me with his friendship ought to blush for me if I did not resent it. The treatment I have experienced puts it out of my power to hold any office, the appointment of which must be made by Congress." What added to Schuyler's resentment was that, when a committee traveled into the Northern Department to investigate conditions there, its members consulted not with him but with Horatio Gates. For Schuyler this was "conduct towards me [that] is replete with brutality and folly. . . ."[34] It is important to note that Schuyler did not find fault with Gates, "my inferior officer," on this occasion; in fact, he and Gates continued to work, or seemed to work, on favorable terms. Gates did not take sides in the controversy between Schuyler and Congress, but maintained a discreet distance. When a dispute arose between Schuyler and antagonists in Congress over the appointment of head of the Commissary, Gates responded by saying, "It is a matter of moonshine to me who is Commissary, so [long as] the troops are well supplied." Schuyler made it clear to Gates and to others that upon resigning, which he continued to say he was determined to do, he expected Gates to take over command of the Army of the Northern Department. Yet this did not happen as expected. Congress refused to accept Schuyler's resignation; he remained head of the army that Congress had originally placed under his command. Amidst the controversy that swirled about Schuyler in Congress he knew that some delegates were working against him, as Samuel Chase warned him: "You have many Enemies" in Congress, Chase said; this Schuyler knew anyway.[35]

Both Schuyler and Gates had supporters and opponents in Congress; now the wind blew in one direction, then in a different direction. Congress made a request for Gates to resume his post as adjutant-general of the army, but Gates was indignant over the request: "I had last year the honor to command in the second post in America, and had the good fortune to prevent the enemy from making their so much wished for junction with General Howe. After this, to be expected to dwindle again to the adjutant-general requires more philosophy on my part and something more than words on yours."[36] Gates wanted command of the Northern Army, and his New England supporters wanted him to have that position. What they needed was an occasion to take down Schuyler. It was Schuyler who gave them the occasion they sought when he wrote Congress a letter on February 4, 1777 protesting several matters under his jurisdiction. The letter received little attention initially, but several New England delegates saw a few words in Schuyler's letter that could be deemed offensive to Congress, and argued that this was the case. When New York delegates were absent from Congress, New England delegates passed resolutions reprimanding Schuyler. What Schuyler had written was "highly derogatory to the honor of Congress"; in the future his letters should be "written in a style more suitable to the dignity of the representative body of these free and independent states, and to his own character as their officer"; what he had done was "altogether improper and inconsistent with the dignity of Congress."[37] Upon receiving this reprimand Schuyler finally made the appearance before Congress that he had long wanted to make, but before doing so he went to Kingston, where the New York Assembly elected him as a delegate to Congress. When he appeared before Congress in Philadelphia he was an elected member of that body and other New York delegates were there with him to take up his cause. In a concerted counteroffensive mounted by Schuyler and New York delegates against Gates and his supporters, Schuyler received vindication from Congress in May and remained in command of the Northern Army. The fat was in the fire; he and Gates were in full and open conflict, as were their respective supporters in Congress.

When Congress reprimanded Schuyler in March, it ordered Gates to take up command of Fort Ticonderoga, where he was to be in charge of building up defenses against a possible British offensive along the Hudson-Champlain corridor when the 1777 campaign got under way. The question of who commanded the Northern Army was not made clear, but it seemed that it was Gates. Schuyler was given administrative responsibilities in Pennsylvania, which he carried out dutifully as Congress debated the larger question of who was in command of the Northern Army. So, as winter turned into spring in the year 1777, it was unclear who was in a position of ultimate authority in the Northern Department; the expectation was that a British force would attack America from the north and move down the Hudson-Champlain corridor, but Congress gave itself over to debating who was in charge in New York, Gates or Schuyler. In London, plans were moving ahead for the British invasion; in Philadelphia Congress argued back and forth. Gates was placed in command of the army in Ticonderoga, but he did not go to Ticonderoga; rather, he set up headquarters in Albany and remained in contact with friends in Congress who were working on his behalf in what he and they hoped would be the final stage in their effort to bring about Schuyler's dismissal as head of the Northern Army and Gates' appointment in Schuyler's place. At this stage Gates was more occupied with dislodging Schuyler from his command of the Northern Army than working on the critically important defenses at Ticonderoga. He wrote his friend James Lovell on May 12 that "If General Schuyler is solely to possess all the power, all the intelligence, and that particular favorite, the military chest, and constantly reside at Albany, I cannot, with any peace of mind, serve at Ticonderoga."[38] When Gates received news that Congress had reaffirmed Schuyler's full command of the Northern Army on May 15, that he was removed from his command of the army at Ticonderoga (which he had never undertaken), and that he was given the choice of serving under Schuyler or taking up his former post as Washington's adjutant, he rushed to Philadelphia. Gates went ballistic before Congress on June 18 when he appeared before that body, describing himself as "extremely ill-used," "greatly chagrined," and "enraged."[39] Congress did not appreciate Gates' fulminations and he was ordered from the chamber within which he had unleashed feelings of keen abuse. Deeply frustrated and offended over what had happened, Gates remained in Philadelphia, refusing to serve under Schuyler and awaiting future developments. Hoping that things would turn out to his advantage, Gates continued to cultivate friends in Congress who would support his cause if the right moment were to appear; all was in flux, but if circumstances were propitious, if the stars above were lined up right, if the gods were to smile, Horatio Gates might finally have his day. And he did. Burgoyne's campaign created a set of circumstances that finally put Gates in command of the American army that would fight at Saratoga; it was here that the two generals, Gates and Burgoyne, once officers in the same regiment, would fight one another in two pitched battles that comprised the Battle of Saratoga.

As the Schuyler-Gates opera buffa was playing in Philadelphia, General John Burgoyne, "Gentleman Johnnie," was poised to carry out his part of the 1777 British campaign. He arrived at Quebec on May 6, filled with optimism and bearing orders that placed him in command of the army of 3,700 British regulars, 3,000 German mercenaries, mainly Hessians under the command of the able Baron von Riedesel, 650 Tories and Canadians, and 400 Iroquois, altogether a formidable force of some 8,000 men. Moreover, he had the organizational capacity of the greatest empire on earth behind him, backed up by the greatest navy on earth. All of this Burgoyne felt; all of this fed into the high confidence he brought to the grand enterprise that was soon to unfold. Moving down Lake Champlain with a massive flotilla of gunboats and pinnaces manned by 700 Royal Navy sailors, 260 bateaux carrying rank-and-file soldiers, and canoes paddled by Indians, Burgoyne's passage was uneventful until he came to Fort Ticonderoga, the first obstacle up to that point. It was here that the British campaign of the previous year had floundered when Carleton decided to return to Quebec. Since then, the Americans had had ample time to further shore up defenses at Ticonderoga, and in fact much had been done, but as it turned out, the considerable efforts made to strengthen defenses were of no avail. Burgoyne took Ticonderoga without firing a shot. When he came to within four miles of Ticonderoga on July 5, a loyalist who accompanied him told Burgoyne that by cutting a path around Ticonderoga they could reach the base of Sugar Loaf Hill (now Mount Defiance), which rose 750 feet above Ticonderoga; if cannon were taken up Sugar Loaf Hill they would give the British decisive advantage over the American army that defended Fort Ticonderoga. The loyalist who understood the importance of Sugar Loaf Hill was not the only person to do so, or the first.

When Horatio Gates had been responsible for shoring up Fort Ticonderoga in the summer of 1776, a junior officer serving under him, John Trumbull, son of the Governor of Connecticut and a recent graduate of Harvard, was part of a team that inspected the terrain around Fort Ticonderoga. Trumbull was an aspiring artist, and would go on to become one of America's leading painters, specializing in depictions of great battles of the American Revolution. With the eye of an artist he walked the terrain around Fort Ticonderoga, and recommended fortifications on a hill below and east of Ticonderoga, Rattlesnake Hill. Others agreed with these suggestions, and they were put into effect. Trumbull also climbed a hill to the south and west of Ticonderoga, Sugar Loaf Hill,

Figure 14. This is a picture of me taking a photograph of Fort Ticonderoga from Mount Defiance. It was taken by Tony Anadio, who later told me, "I wanted a picture of you doing something you've done countless times and shown to decades of students." I had no idea that Tony was snapping this picture of me; having taken several of my courses he had seen many slides that I had taken over the years.

which he thought might be of crucial importance should the British lay siege to Fort Ticonderoga. To find out if he was right he conducted a test, which he felt demonstrated that if the British were to climb Sugar Loaf Hill with cannon they could fire down on Fort Ticonderoga with impunity, but no one took Trumbull's warnings seriously, and Sugar Loaf Hill was left unprotected. In spring 1777, Tadeusz Kosciuszko, a Polish military engineer who had joined the American cause and was on the staff of Horatio Gates, pointed out the importance of Sugar Loaf Hill in preparing defenses of Ticonderoga, but again nothing was done. Gates, his superior, was in Albany, doing everything possible to persuade Congress to remove Schuyler and place him in command of the Northern Army; no one at Ticonderoga paid attention to Kosciuszko's warnings. Schuyler, restored to command of the Northern Army, visited Ticonderoga on June 20 to inspect the fortifications. He inquired about Sugar Loaf Hill; all officers maintained that the side of the hill was too rugged to bring cannon up it, a verdict that both Schuyler and General Arthur St. Clair, who was put in command of Ticonderoga on June 12, accepted. St. Clair did what he could to shore up the defenses of Ticonderoga, and to strengthen those on Rattlesnake Hill, but he did nothing with Sugar Loaf Hill. When Burgoyne reached Ticonderoga he had 400 men cut a path around the fortress and build a road up the side of Sugar Loaf Hill, enabling an artillery detachment to take two 16-pound cannon up the hill to a high point, where they were installed and made ready to fire. Seeing the cannon the next morning, and understanding the predicament he was in, St. Clair had to make a decision: Would he defend the fortress as long as possible, slowing down Burgoyne's march to Albany, or would he abandon it to the enemy? While he had substantial provisions and could have held out for some time, he knew he could not hold out indefinitely, and were he to surrender his army of some 2,000 men they would become prisoners of the British and no longer be capable of participating in the struggle against Britain. At that point St. Clair decided, knowing full well that he would come under heavy criticism, that saving as much of his army as possible was the best course of action, so before the British could stop him he marched out of Ticonderoga with his army, leaving behind only the wounded and a few men who were to defend a bridge he had built across the narrowest part of the inlet below Fort Ticonderoga. Burgoyne took the fort and most of its supplies without firing a shot, but St. Clair and his army got away, marching south toward Schuyler's army that he hoped to join at some unknown point.

Up to now everything had gone Burgoyne's way. Before leaving Canada he had discussed the coming campaign with Friedrich Adolph, Baron von Riedesel, commander of the Hessian troops that made up an important part of Burgoyne's force. Both generals scorned their adversaries, lowly Americans. As Riedesel wrote his wife, who was soon to join him on the march to Albany, "There are only a few dozen ambitious people who direct this whole affair and who make the whole land unhappy. As for the others, they do not know why they fight."[40] That Burgoyne and Riedesel viewed their American adversaries with disdain was not unusual; this had been the prevalent British attitude during the French and Indian War, expressed with particular clarity in the remarks of General James Wolfe, the self-anointed hero and martyr of the 1759 Battle of Quebec. He had called Americans "the dirtiest, most contemptible, cowardly dogs you can conceive. There is no depending on them in action. They fall down in their own dirt and desert by battalions, officers and all. Such rascals as these are rather an encumbrance than any real strength to an army." The conqueror of Fort Duquesne, General John Forbes, had described American troops as "an extream [sic] bad Collection of broken Innkeepers, Horse Jockeys, and Indian traders . . . a gathering from the scum of the worst people."[41] Attitudes of British superiority extended from the French and Indian War into the revolutionary war and were widespread; the assumption was that Britain would put the Revolution down summarily. When Lord Sandwich, First Lord of the Admiralty, addressed the House of Lords in 1776 he said, "Suppose the Colonies do abound in men, what does that signify? They are raw, undisciplined, cowardly men. I wish instead of forty or fifty thousand of these *brave* fellows they would produce in the field at least two hundred thousand; the more the better, the easier would be the conquest; if they did not run away they would starve themselves into compliance with our measures. . . ."[42] A British major said a month before Lexington and Concord that "I am satisfied that one active campaign, a smart action, and burning two or three of their towns, will set everything to rights." General James Murray called Americans "the worst soldiers in the universe."[43] Some felt that the Americans did not want to fight. Thomas Anburey, a junior British officer serving under Burgoyne, said on June 30, before Burgoyne's flotilla reached Ticonderoga, "it is an invariable maxim with the Americans, of which there are numberless instances in the last campaign, never to face an enemy but with very superior advantages, and the most evident signs of success. . . ."[44]

As if to confirm the British view that Americans preferred not to fight, St. Clair's army of 2,000 men departed from Ticonderoga in the night, allowing Burgoyne to take what the British thought was the main obstacle on the march to Albany without opposition. From then on, however, the march to Albany became more difficult. Far more difficult. St. Clair sent a few supplies and some of his wounded men by water to Skenesboro at the headwaters of Lake Champlain while he, at the head of his retreating army, marched to Hubbardton, some 24 miles to the south and east of Ticonderoga, where his men clashed with a British contingent led by General Simon Fraser in a sharply contested and bloody battle. The British were surprised at how well the rebels fought, a harbinger of things to come. Thomas Anburey wrote that "Some of [the American] detachments, notwithstanding an inferiority, most resolutely defended themselves, and the fate of the day was undecided till the arrival of the Germans, who, though late, came in for a share of the glory in dispersing the enemy in all quarters. . . ."[45] The British commander of the light infantry, Lord Balcarres, said that the Americans had "behaved" well at Hubbardton and fought "with great gallantry."[46]

Burgoyne proceeded by water to Skenesboro, following Americans that conveyed supplies to that settlement before retreating to the south. Staying with Philip Skene, a loyalist and the leading landowner in the region, Burgoyne settled into a comfortable routine before continuing the march to Albany. Discussing his circumstances with Skene, he considered how his army might best proceed toward the Hudson. He could continue to Albany by taking one of two routes: He could return by water to the narrows below Ticonderoga, which were connected to Lake George, and then sail down that body of water to its far end, which was connected by road to the Hudson River, his destination; or he could continue by land from Skenesboro to the Hudson River, which he would reach at Fort Edward 22 miles to the south. Philip Skene seems to have urged Burgoyne to take the direct route, by land, along a path that he had built, and which Burgoyne's engineers would turn into a proper road capable of conveying Burgoyne's army and supplies as they made their way south. The road, once built, would be of obvious benefit to Skene. There is no way to tell to what extent Skene offered advice that Burgoyne followed; the fact is that this is the route Burgoyne took. Following this path he took the most direct route south, avoiding a portage between the southern end of Lake Champlain and Lake George. Burgoyne proceeded down the path alongside Wood's Creek that led to Fort Edward and to the Hudson River, working on it as he proceeded. The path he took went through heavily wooded terrain, bogs, swamps, rivers, and ravines. The going was brutal for the men who made their way toward the Hudson River; the conditions Burgoyne and his men encountered as they made their way from Skenesboro to Fort Edward took a heavy toll. Geography was one of the factors in the military outcome at Saratoga; had it not been for the 22 miles of untamed land in upstate New York between Skenesboro and the Hudson River, the Battle of Saratoga could have turned out differently.

Philip Schuyler was another factor in the outcome at Saratoga. His estate lay just below Fort Edward. The rugged terrain Burgoyne and his army had to traverse was well known to Schuyler, as were the families in the region. The Battle of Saratoga was fought, so to speak, in Schuyler's own backyard; no one in a position of leadership could have been better suited and more qualified than he to throw up obstacles that obstructed Burgoyne's march to Albany. A superb organizer, Schuyler had a strategy that was perfect for the time and the place. With the assistance of Tadeusz Kosciuczko he tore up the corduroy road that Philip Skene had built, he ordered the bridges that Burgoyne's force had to cross on its way to Fort Edward destroyed, he had trees felled, he had streams dammed; he did everything possible to create obstacles for the British. His policy was the classic one when enemy armies invade a foreign land, that of scorched earth, forcing the invading army to depend on supplies that it provides itself, rather than to forage and live off the land it crosses. To demonstrate the depth of his own commitment, as well as to do his own part in a massive effort to thwart the British offensive, Schuyler ordered his own crops burned. His wife, Catherine Van Rensselaer Schuyler, is said to have set them afire herself. He urged local farmers to hide or drive away cattle in order that the British could not appropriate them. The farther south Burgoyne went, the more difficult provisioning his army became. Nature and the elements came to Schuyler's aid; as chance had it July was unseasonably hot and rainy, making marching difficult and sleeping at night all but impossible, the air being alive with all manner of insects: mosquitoes, chiggers, no see-ums, horseflies, and deerflies. At times Burgoyne's army was able to go no farther than a mile a day, and in the hot, humid, unhealthy atmosphere disease took a heavy toll. What made matters worse were the soldiers' heavy wool uniforms and the 60-pound packs they had to carry. And there was fear of wild animals, seemingly of all types, that inhabited the wilderness through which Burgoyne's men had to pass, not to mention rodents and snakes. In contrast to the hardships of the men who made their way to Albany was the different passage of Burgoyne and high-rank-ing officers. As a man of parts, and exquisite taste, Burgoyne felt it essential to surround himself with the amenities of civilized life, which translated into over 30 wagons laden with his own personal belongings as he and his army made their way through rugged terrain on the way to Albany. Among the belongings were silk beds and cases of champagne and claret; Burgoyne was not to spend his nights with his mistress, the wife of a junior officer, without champagne and fine wine. Burgoyne allowed Baron von Riedesel to have his wife and three daughters join him; he and other officers were accompanied by wives, servants, and their personal baggage, which had not been reduced to essentials, adding to the difficulties of proceeding south from Skenesboro to Fort Edward.

After waiting at Skenesboro for the arrival of needed supplies, Burgoyne pressed south and arrived at Fort Edward on July 30. The Fort Edward that Burgoyne entered was desolate; the fort had been burned and the surrounding countryside laid waste, but at least he had reached the Hudson. His supplies were exhausted and Riedesel's Hessian units said they needed cattle and horses. Believing that horses could be obtained somewhere in the vicinity of Benning-ton, Burgoyne sent a detachment of Hessian soldiers to get them; the Hessians were instructed to muster support from loyalists and to obtain such provisions as were possible from local farmers, who were supposed to be friendly. What Burgoyne did not understand was the fierceness of resentment amongst local farmers whose lands his men crossed. That resentment was made more intense by his use of Indians for military support and in a deliberate attempt, which he announced in a proclamation, to terrorize patriot farmers who sided with the Revolution. Burgoyne ordered Indians not to harm women and children and not to take scalps, but sometimes his orders were not followed. This happened most famously on July 27 near Fort Edward when Indians found an American woman hiding in a cellar. Jane McCrea, a loyalist who was engaged to an English officer, told the Indians she was their friend. Under circumstances that are still not clear, the Indians killed and scalped Jane McCrea; this happened just before Burgoyne entered Fort Edward and less than two weeks before he sent the detachment of Hessians to the south to get horses and provisions. The time between the Jane McCrea incident and the departure of the Hes-sians from Fort Edward to Bennington was sufficient for news of the atrocity to spread like wildfire across the surrounding New York countryside and into nearby New England.

As a detachment of some 600 men under Colonel Friedrich Baum set out for Bennington, a call went out for militias to take on the Hessians. Men arrived in surprising numbers under an independent-minded New Englander who marched to his own beat, Brigadier General John Stark. Stark had fought at Quebec in 1759, at Bunker Hill at the beginning of the Revolution, and at Trenton and Princeton with Washington. Washington followed events in upstate New York closely; he hoped that some part of Burgoyne's force could

Figure 15. Historical marker at Fort Edward indicating the approximate place of Jane McCrea's murder. The exact place of the incident is unknown.

be separated from the rest: "Could we be so happy as to cut one [of Burgoyne's units] off, supposing it should not exceed four, five or six hundred men, it would inspirit the people and do away with much of the present misery."[47] Just what Washington hoped would happen, did happen. As Stark moved toward the encounter with Baum's force he called upon Seth Warner to bring in the Green Mountain Boys, and by the time Baum and the Hessians were within ten miles of Bennington, New England militiamen awaited them. Stark's and Warner's militiamen put Baum's men to rout on August 15; Baum himself was killed in the encounter and his detachment was completely lost to Burgoyne; all men were killed, wounded, taken captive, or fled. When Burgoyne sent another detachment of 500 under Breymann to give support to Baum's contingent they too were routed. Altogether some 1,000 men were lost at Bennington. Washington had wished that somehow Burgoyne would detach and lose a unit, perhaps between 400 and 600 men; as it turned out, something better happened for the Americans—Burgoyne lost something like one-sixth of his army in the Bennington episode.

Philip Schuyler was in Albany when he received news on July 7 that Burgoyne had taken Fort Ticonderoga the previous day. He left Albany at once for Fort Edward, where he set up his headquarters, hoping somehow to join forces with St. Clair, writing letters as he headed north calling for militiamen to join in the resistance to Burgoyne's army. When he heard on July 10 that

St. Clair was some 50 miles to his east, he assumed that he had no more than 1,000 men and that his army would be depleted by further desertions. Hoping at this stage to put together a force of 3,000 Continentals and 1,000 militiamen, Schuyler was keenly aware of the dilemma he and fellow patriots faced. To make matters worse, Schuyler received a report that a British army had left Oswego and was moving down the Mohawk toward Albany. This army, under Barrimore St. Leger, was carrying out Burgoyne's strategy that called for two armies to converge at Albany and, joining forces there, to continue down the Hudson. Schuyler now faced a two-pronged attack. "I am to face a powerful enemy from the north, flushed by success, and pressed at the same time from the west by St. Leger's army." Aware of the urgency of his situation, Schuyler did everything possible to organize resistance to Burgoyne and St. Leger, and he berated those who were not doing all that he felt they should do. He told authorities in Tryon County that he was disgusted by their "pusillanimous spirit," and that he regretted their asking for Continental troops "when the militias of every other county in the State, except yours, is called out. For God's sake, do not forget that you are an over-match for any force the enemy can bring against you, if you act with spirit." He wrote a committee of safety in Cambridge (New York) that they should not be afraid of Indians, as Burgoyne wanted them to be, and that they should ignore his promises of clemency. Responding to a request for clothing and money, Schuyler wrote that he was sending both, and that local patriots should make every effort to round up cattle and wagons so Burgoyne would not get them, to drive out Tories, and above all to stay close to Burgoyne's army. "Be vigilant; a surprise is inexcusable . . . If we act vigorously, we save the country. Why should we despond? Greater misfortunes have happened, and have been retrieved. Cheer up the spirits of the people in your quarter."[48]

The urgency and sharpness of Schuyler's letters as he organized support against Burgoyne is in striking contrast to the complacency and inflated rhetoric of Burgoyne's pronouncements, at least at the beginning of his campaign. In his first manifesto Burgoyne claimed to speak "in consciousness of Christianity and the honor of soldiership," and listed his various titles: "John Burgoyne, Esquire, Lieutenant-General of his Majesty's forces in America, Colonel of the Queen's regiment of Light Dragoons, Governor of Fort William in North Britain, one of the Commoners of Great Britain in Parliament, and commander of an army and fleet employed in an expedition from Canada."[49] Just before reaching Ticonderoga, Burgoyne announced that he was embarked on "a cause in which His Majesty's Troops and those of the Princes his Allies, will feel equal excitement. The services required of this particular expedition are critical and conspicuous . . . This army must not retreat."[50] After taking Ticonderoga Burgoyne announced his success: "The rebels evacuated Ticonderoga on the 6th, having been forced into the measure by the presence of our army. On one side of the lake they ran as far as Skenesborough; on the other side as far as Hubbardton.

They left behind all their artillery, provisions, and baggage."[51] As the summer wore on, and Burgoyne's arduous and debilitating march to Albany brought him closer to Saratoga, the tone of his letters changed, and increasingly they were tinged with despondency and a sense of fatalism. He wrote Germain that "The great bulk of the country" supported the American cause, and wherever his men went they were confronted by well-provisioned militias that could withdraw as suited their purposes, only to appear again, sometimes three or four thousand at a time. To make matters worse, he wrote, Vermont, recently unpopulated, now "abounds in the most active and most rebellious race of the continent and hangs like a gathering storm on my left." Vermont had declared itself a state on July 8; a storm was indeed gathering on Burgoyne's left. The farther south Burgoyne went, the more aware he was that the Americans were gaining and that he was losing the advantage. Where, he asked on August 20, was Howe? There would be no relief from that quarter; the fundamental flaws in the 1777 campaign were becoming painfully evident. Burgoyne now said that if he were not committed to joining forces with Howe he would stay where he was or retire to Fort Edward, where he would be in a better position to get needed provisions and reinforcements. By August 20 Burgoyne was clearly discouraged. "Whatever may be my fate . . . whatever decision may be passed upon my conduct, my good intent will not be questioned."[52]

By the time Burgoyne wrote the August 20 letter to Germain, Philip Schuyler had been relieved of his command of the Northern Army. The main charge leveled against Schuyler was that he was responsible for the fall of Ticonderoga, which Burgoyne had taken without firing a shot. For his part, Schuyler was incredulous over what had happened. "What could induce General St. Clair and the general officers with him to evacuate Ticonderoga, God only knows."[53] Wild rumors circulated over a seemingly inexplicable turn of events, in which Schuyler was seen as a traitor who had sold the fortress to the British. The surgeon James Thacher, who tended to wounded Americans in Albany, wrote in his journal that "It has been industriously reported that Generals Schuyler and St. Clair acted the parts of traitor to their country and that they were paid for their treason by the enemy in *silver balls* shot from Burgoyne's guns into our camp and that they were collected by order of General St. Clair and divided between him and General Schuyler."[54] Schuyler was well aware of the rumors of his treachery. He wrote Washington on July 26 that "The People, especially in the Eastern States, are industriously propagating that the General Officers who were at Ticonderoga, and myself are all a Pack of Traitors; this doctrine has been preached in the Army to many of the People that have come up from New England, and by some from this State, which greatly prejudices the Service, as it tends to destroy that confidence which troops ought to have in their Officers."[55] Rumors of Schuyler's treachery were not new; he had written Washington over a year earlier, on May 31, 1776, that "I am informed by persons of good Credit that about one hundred persons, living on what are commonly called the New Hampshire Grants, have had a Design to sieze me as a Tory, and perhaps still have—There never was a Man so infamously scandalized and ill-treated as I am. . . ."[56] Amidst the panic that followed the fall of Ticonderoga, New Englanders were inclined to believe crazy rumors about Philip Schuyler, long their bête noir. A New England minister, William Gordon, repeated the story of Schuyler's treachery in a letter to Washington; he had been told that "the *silver* bullets flew plentifully at Ticonderoga;" a person of "rank and character" had "declared upon his honor that there was bribery and treachery."[57]

Schuyler himself, for all of his protestations of innocence in the loss of Ticonderoga, helped bring about his own downfall; the person who had been instrumental in throwing up obstacles before Burgoyne that contributed to his defeat was the victim of his own desperate pleas to Washington and to Congress to provide needed assistance in the Northern Department. To those who received Schuyler's letters detailing the crisis he faced, it must have seemed as if things were falling apart along the Hudson-Champlain corridor, and that a change of leadership was urgently needed. Also, Horatio Gates had—again—been lobbying his supporters in Congress; he was now blaming Schuyler for the fall of Ticonderoga. In fact, he had been in charge of building up defenses at Ticonderoga a year earlier; he had paid no heed to the warnings of his own underling, John Trumbull, who told him that if the British were to take cannon up Sugar Loaf Hill they would be in a position to take Fort Ticonderoga, the very thing that Burgoyne had done when he captured the American fortress. But Gates was not interested in fair assessment of blame; he wanted command of Schuyler's army. And Schuyler himself gave Gates just what he needed to achieve his goal, arguments that Gates' supporters in Congress could use against him. When Schuyler wrote Washington on July 28, he explained that he was unable to get urgently needed support from New England. "So far from the Militia that are with me encreasing, they are daily diminishing, and I am very confident that in ten Days, if the Enemy should not disturb us, we shall not have five hundred left, and altho' I have entreated this and the Eastern States to send up a Reinforcement of them, yet I doubt much if any will come up, especially from the Eastern States, where the Spirit of Malevolence knows no Bounds, and I am considered as a Traitor."[58]

Washington was well aware of Schuyler's inability to persuade New England militias to answer his call for support. He wrote to Schuyler on June 20: "I cannot concieve what occasions the Delay of the Massachusetts and New Hampshire Troops. I have repeatedly wrote to them in the most pressing Manner to send them on, but in vain."[59] Washington wrote Schuyler on July 24, again expressing regret over the refusal of New England to send militias that would help Schuyler block Burgoyne's march to Albany: "I lament that you have not yet been joined by a larger Number of Militia . . . I cannot but think the Eastern States, who are so deeply concerned in the Matter will exert themselves to enable you by effectual Succours to check the progress of the Enemy, and repel a Danger with which they are so immediately threatened."[60] Schuyler's August 8 letter to Washington conveyed a similar message: "It is much to be lamented that Massachusetts and Connecticut appear so loath to afford us any assistance . . . I know that from their unjust and ill founded prejudices against me arose that universal Clamor which I sustained."[61] An August 11 letter from Samuel Adams to his friend Roger Sherman confirmed Schuyler's and Washington's worst fears about New England hostility to Schuyler. "Schuyler has written a series of weak and contemptible *things* in a style of despondency which alone, I think, is sufficient for removal of him . . . for if his pen expresses the true feelings of his heart, it cannot be expected that the bravest veterans would fight under such a general." Even worse, from Adams' point of view, was Schuyler's well-known contempt for men that he expected to bear arms against the British. "[Schuyler] seems to have no confidence in his troops, nor the states whence reinforcements are to be drawn. A third of the Continental troops, he tells us, consists 'of boys, Negroes, and aged men not fit in the field or any other service . . . A very great part of the army naked, without blankets, ill armed, and very deficient in accoutrements, without a prospect of relief . . . Many, too many of the officers would be a disgrace to the most contemptible troops that ever was collected.' "[62] Schuyler unwittingly gave Congress good and sufficient reasons to remove him from command of the Northern Army; if the stated reason for his dismissal was the fall of Ticonderoga, for which he was not primarily responsible, his own words revealed a problem that could be solved only by his removal; New England militias, essential if Burgoyne's march to Albany was to be blocked, would not fight under Schuyler. This both Schuyler and Washington understood; both made repeated appeals to New Englanders to join in the struggle against Burgoyne's army; the pleas were not answered; the men who achieved victory at Saratoga would not have fought under Schuyler's command. Gates was the darling of the New Englanders; with him in command they answered the call to battle. As soon as Gates took charge of the Army of the Northern Department troops began to move toward New York and toward a site just below Philip Schuyler's estate where a battle would be fought that would change the course of history.

Schuyler was about to ride from Albany to join his army at Stillwater on August 10 when a courier from Philadelphia arrived notifying him that Congress had passed two resolutions: There was to be an enquiry into the abandonment of Fort Ticonderoga, and he and St. Clair were to appear at Washington's headquarters in New Jersey, which Schuyler believed almost certainly meant that he was to face a court martial. Relieved of his command of the Northern Army, Schuyler insisted on a court martial, and did receive one in the following year, in the course of which he was acquitted of all charges. He resigned his commission at that time, thereby ending his military role in the American Revolution. Upon receiving news from Congress that he was no longer in command of the Northern Army, Schuyler went into several days of depression so dark that he was virtually unable to speak to anyone; his considerable pride had been cut to the quick. As for Gates, he took two weeks to make a leisurely trip from Philadelphia to Albany. Until the time of Gates' arrival, Schuyler continued the work of organizing forces that were no longer under his command. When Gates assumed command of the Northern Army on Van Schaik's Island on August 19, he summoned a war council to discuss plans for the imminent battle with Burgoyne's army, from which he excluded Schuyler. In some measure his exclusion of Schuyler is understandable; Schuyler's plan had been to withdraw farther to the south with his army rather than to advance toward the enemy and engage him in battle, the course of action that Gates had decided upon. Yet, it is difficult not to think that there was something personal in Gates' decision not to include Schuyler in discussions concerning the showdown with Burgoyne and his army, soon to take place. Gates and Schuyler had worked together a year earlier, but that was then and this was now; Gates left Schuyler out of all discussions and did not consult him in any way, even though Schuyler had unique understanding of local geography and knew as no one else what had been done up to that point to build up a force that would confront the British army. By the time of Gates' arrival to take command of the Northern Army, Burgoyne's supply lines, thanks in no small measure to the efforts of Philip Schuyler, were stretched almost to the breaking point; Schuyler's work helped make possible the American victory that was soon to take place.

Schuyler had received news on July 26 that a British army under Barrimore St. Leger was proceeding from Oswego to Fort Stanwix (which had recently been renamed Fort Schuyler, in his honor); this fortress on the Mohawk River was the major obstacle in St. Leger's way as he moved toward Albany, carrying out his part of the strategy that Burgoyne had formulated for the 1777 campaign. When Schuyler held council with his advisers to consider what action to take in response to St. Leger's march down the Mohawk, some of them felt that Burgoyne's army was such a threat that all forces should be concentrated to deal with it, rather than send men elsewhere to address a problem that they regarded as one of lesser gravity. Schuyler felt otherwise, and asked for a brigadier general to lead a detachment up the Mohawk to bring relief to the men who were defending Fort Stanwix. At this point a major general who had just arrived in Schuyler's camp volunteered for the assignment; that person was Benedict Arnold, sent to New York by George Washington. At the time of his arrival at Schuyler's camp Arnold was eager to throw himself into the struggle and, once again, to prove himself in battle. Schuyler gave orders to Arnold to make his way up the Mohawk toward Fort Stanwix, to persuade "such of the militia as you can prevail upon to join your troops," and to do whatever possible to stop St. Leger's march to Albany. The obstacles were formidable: St. Leger had a force of some 2,000 men comprised of British troops, loyalists, and Indians; the garrison at Fort Stanwix was made up of 750 men who lacked sufficient provisions, had little gunpowder, and whose ammunition did not always match their guns. A bloody battle between local militia and a force comprised of Indians and loyalists had been fought at Oriskany, some seven miles east of Fort Stanwix, on August 6 in which there had been heavy losses by both sides, including General Nicholas Herkimer. The veteran American general calmly gave orders to his men during the fierce six-hour encounter, smoking a pipe after receiving a shot in the leg that resulted in his death after the battle.

By the time Arnold neared Stanwix, St. Leger's men were within 150 yards of the fort, having dug trenches up to that distance; the position of the Americans was desperate. Arnold came up with a wild scheme to disrupt the British and their Indian allies. Among the loyalists taken captive by the Americans was a somewhat daft distant cousin of Philip Schuyler, Hon Yost Schuyler, who in moments of excitement spoke in tongues, as if he were in touch with higher spirits, and whom Indians considered a sort of holy man. The idea was for him to meet with Indians who were part of St. Leger's war party, and to put on his wildest and most extravagant performance for their benefit. With his brother held hostage by the Americans, Hon Yost Schuyler took readily to the plan. Shots were fired through his coat, as if he had been attacked by patriot soldiers; with an Oneida Indian to back up his story he made his way to St. Leger's camp, where he found some Mohawk who were part of the British war party, and he told them about an immense American army that was advancing toward Fort Stanwix. When a British officer asked

Figure 16. Reconstructed Fort Stanwix, situated in the middle of Rome, New York. I took this photograph in June 2008, while taking a trip along the Mohawk River Valley, following the same path that Benedict Arnold took in the summer of 1777. The Visitor Center here contains much valuable information on Fort Stanwix and its historical significance

Hon Yost Schuyler for more particular information, meaning how large the force was, he rolled his eyes and looked upward at trees above, as if to say there were more men than there were leaves in the trees. He then repeated the same story when he met with St. Leger, giving more specific information: He said that Arnold was 24 hours from Stanwix, at the head of an army of over 3,000 men (his actual force was barely over 1,000); the ruse worked, and the already disaffected Mohawk took flight, taking with them the British officers' liquor and clothing. Without the needed support of Indian allies St. Leger's army returned to Oswego, with Indians in pursuit, attacking stragglers who lagged behind and taking scalps along the way. From Oswego St. Leger's army left the southern shore of Lake Ontario by boat, unable to pass down the Mohawk and join Burgoyne's army in the decisive battle with the Americans, soon to take place. It was Arnold and his 1,200 men who passed down the Mohawk corridor, not St. Leger and his army, and it was he who played an important role in the Battle of Saratoga. Schuyler had gambled when he sent Arnold at the head of a contingent up the Mohawk to obstruct the British force under St. Leger; he had gone against advisers who opposed the plan; the outcome could not have been more successful. Yet, by the time of Arnold's return to Schuyler's camp, Schuyler was not there. He had been relieved of his command and it was Horatio Gates who had taken his place.

Gates moved with his army northward from its camp just above the Mohawk on September 7 and reached Stillwater, a few miles below Saratoga, on September 9. Militiamen were arriving from the east, eager to serve under a general they had long viewed with favor; clearly, Gates was a much-needed tonic, just the person to replace the despised Schuyler. Spirits rose among American forces who made ready for battle, and it was they who would determine its location. When Gates was told the best place to do battle was at Bemis Heights, a hilly area alongside the Hudson that Burgoyne's army had to pass through, he inspected the site and gave orders to throw up earthwork fortifications, designed by the Polish engineering officer Tadeusz Kosciuszko, with Arnold also playing a role. Some 7,000 men worked for a week building up layers of earth, forming abates by placing trees with sharpened limbs along the long line of the earthwork fortifications, and positioning cannon so they could rake the river road, forcing the advancing British to march into the fortified position along the crest of Bemis Heights. It was only when Americans fired on some of Burgoyne's men on September 18 that the British general realized where the American army was situated. Following a strategy that he had devised, Burgoyne attacked the Americans the next day, sending three columns across a four-mile front, with himself astride his white horse in the center, so he could give orders, according to how the fighting progressed. Horatio Gates was at his headquarters at Bemis Heights, where he received news of the fighting, which he never saw. A former British officer, Gates was deeply impressed by the discipline and battlefield capabilities of British redcoats, among the best-trained soldiers of the time, as were the German mercenaries under Riedesel. Gates understandably had less confidence in his own American soldiers, made up of Continentals who had received but perfunctory training and had limited combat experience, and militiamen who had had little military training and were not even dressed as soldiers. With men like this Gates was not eager to join the enemy in open battlefield combat. His idea was to wait for the enemy to reach his lines; his strategy was basically defensive.

As it turned out, the first battle of Saratoga, the September 19 Battle of Freeman's Farm, did not follow the defensive plan that Gates had decided upon. The battle was a compromise between Gates' defensive strategy and one urged on Gates by Benedict Arnold, who pleaded with Gates to send men forward in order that they could engage the enemy rather than wait for them to attack. Reluctantly, several hours after the British column under Simon Fraser was spotted moving along the right-hand side of the British advance, Gates agreed to send in several units to do battle with the British. The first of the American units was led by Daniel Morgan, whom Washington had directed on August 17 to proceed up the Hudson in order that he and his men could join the Northern Army. As the Battle of Freeman's Farm unfolded, two key figures on the American side were Morgan and Benedict Arnold, who had fought together at Quebec when Arnold had been wounded and Morgan had been the last

Figure 17. Bemis Heights, above the Hudson River, where fortifications were built as Burgoyne headed toward Albany.

Figure 18. Historical marker on the Saratoga battlefield showing the site of the September 19 Battle of Freeman's Farm. Words are insufficient to convey how superbly the National Park Service has laid out the Saratoga battlefield, with markers that visitors can see as they drive through the historic site.

American to surrender. They had taken different paths to Saratoga, but once again they were together, fighting against the British. When Horatio Gates finally yielded to Arnold's request to send men forward to engage the advancing British units under Simon Fraser, it was Morgan's riflemen who took up positions in a wooded area by Freeman's farm where they could inflict serious punishment on an exposed enemy in a 350-yard opening. As British troops came into sight Morgan and his men communicated by turkey calls, and they took particular aim at the "kingbirds," officers who could be identified by their uniforms. It was here that the most concentrated fighting took place. As fighting between Morgan's and Fraser's men went back and forth, Arnold was in the rear; observing the fighting he joined the action, spurring his men on, shouting encouragement, personally leading charges, and exposing himself to fire. When a British force advanced Arnold rallied his men, shouting, "Come on boys. Hurry up, my brave boys!" He led a charge at the head of five regiments, trying to drive a wedge between the British lines, always responding to the dynamics of the battle. One witness described Arnold "riding in front of the lines, his eyes flashing, pointing his sword to the advancing foe, with a voice that rang clear as a trumpet and electrified the line."[63]

The intense fighting in which Arnold was directly involved lasted some-where between 30 and 45 minutes; neither side was able to gain decisive advantage; Arnold rode back to headquarters and asked Gates to send in additional men so the Americans could deliver a decisive blow to the British and achieve victory. At this point Gates and Arnold had a sharp disagreement and Gates refused to allow Arnold to return to the battle. Relegated to inactivity, Arnold reached a point where could take it no longer; shouting, "By God, I will soon put an end to it," he mounted his horse and rushed toward the fighting. Gates sent one of his officers after Arnold and told him to return to headquarters, a direct order that Arnold had no choice but to obey. By this time it was getting dark and the Battle of Freeman's Farm was winding down; soon it would end as the Americans retreated into the woods. The British held the field, allowing Burgoyne to claim victory, but it was his army that sustained the greatest losses. The American casualties included 63 dead, 212 wounded, and 38 missing; British casualties came to 160 dead, 364 wounded, and 42 missing. Of surviving accounts of the Battle of Freeman's Farm, that of Lieutenant Thomas Anburey is of particular interest. Reflecting on all that happened, he was "astonished" that the Americans fought so well; indeed, they were "not the contemptible enemy we had hitherto thought them to be." Anburey was assigned the grim duty of burying the British who had died on the battlefield, which he did according to established custom; officers and men were buried separately. "I . . . observed a little more decency than some parties had done, who left heads, legs, and arms above ground. No other distinction is paid to officer or soldier than that the officers are put in a hole by themselves. Our army abounded with young officers, in the subaltern line, and in the course of this unpleasant duty, three of the Twentieth Regiment were interred together, the age of the eldest not exceeding seventeen."[64] Separation of officers from men was so embedded in the mindset of Thomas Anburey that when burying the dead he was bothered that he could make no other distinction than burying officers and men separately. This British officer was not the only combatant who made a distinction between officers and men at the Battle of Freeman's Farm; so too had Daniel Morgan.

In the weeks after the Battle of Freeman's Farm, Burgoyne's army was weakened by nightly attacks. To make matters worse, his supply lines to Canada were all but severed, and he was badly outnumbered. Under these circumstances Burgoyne's senior officers advised him to retreat, but on October 6 he decided on the attack that took place on the next day, the Battle of Bemis Heights. His hope had been that his glorious victory in America would culminate in a knighthood; unable, or unwilling, to accept failure he decided on one last throw of the dice, his biggest gamble yet. He lost, and Britain lost North America. As for the Americans, confusion and ill-feeling reigned within their camp, owing to a bitter quarrel between Horatio Gates and Benedict Arnold. The immediate cause of the quarrel was Gates' report to Congress on the Battle of Freeman's

Farm, which omitted mention of Benedict Arnold, the battle's hero. To further anger Arnold, Gates removed Morgan's riflemen from Arnold's command and placed them under his own command.

Relations between Gates and Arnold had been complicated from the beginning. Arnold's first encounter with Gates was at Washington's camp at Dorchester Heights during the siege of Bunker Hill in 1775, when Arnold gave papers from Congress to Gates, that Gates put on his desk rather than giving them directly to Washington. It was a small thing, but for someone as thin-skinned as Arnold it could have been conceived as an insult, and as such festered over time. Arnold and Gates came together more directly in July 1776 when they met at Ticonderoga, along with Philip Schuyler, to make preparations to obstruct Carleton's invasion of America by way of Lake Champlain. Arnold, always in difficulties, was under attack by men hostile to him who made serious charges, to which Congress paid serious attention; under these circumstances Gates defended Arnold, recognizing his importance in efforts to stop the British advance along Lake Champlain. Gates also worked with Schuyler at this time. Since then relations between Gates and Schuyler had become venomous, a change to which Arnold seemingly paid no attention. Upon arriving at Gates' camp on August 30, he befriended Schuyler's former aides, and placed Brockhorst Livingston, a friend and relative of Schuyler, on his staff, insensitive to the poisoned atmosphere that he entered. But that was Arnold. If he were to choose friends, he would choose them as he wished. He may well have had a sense of loyalty to Schuyler, and to those who had moved within his orbit. Moreover, when Arnold went on a military mission up the Mohawk, where he was at his most imaginative and brilliant, achieving results far beyond any reasonable expectations, he was under Schuyler's orders. Gates welcomed Arnold at the time of his arrival, seemed well-disposed to him, and put him in charge of one of his units; but seeds of mutual dislike would seem to have been planted within both men before the Battle of Freeman's Farm. It was at that battle that underlying suspicions and resentments burst into the open, laying bare dislike and hostility.

When Arnold learned that Gates had omitted any mention of him in his report to Congress on the Battle of Freeman's Farm, he stormed into Gates' headquarters and unleashed pent-up anger in a furious outburst. In return, Gates belittled Arnold, making comments that were like daggers inserted into Arnold's most vulnerable points, where his pride made him susceptible to the criticisms of an officer of superior rank; Gates knew that in the military chain of command he had the last word. Having returned to his quarters in a white heat, Arnold drew up a list of grievances and sent them to Gates with a request to be transferred to Washington's command. Rather than reply to Arnold's letter directly Gates gave him a copy of a letter he had sent to John Hancock saying that Arnold had permission to leave his army. A ten-day quarrel followed these acrimonious exchanges, during which Arnold announced his intention to leave

Saratoga; responding to that announcement all but two officers signed a petition requesting that Arnold remain with the army. This Arnold did; he was still
with the army and under Gates' command when the Battle of Bemis Heights
began on October 7. When firing started Arnold asked Gates for permission
to reconnoiter, to see what was happening. Gates replied, "I am afraid to trust
you, Arnold." Arnold assured Gates that he would be cautious; he received the
permission he sought, and when he returned 30 minutes later he informed
Gates of the enemy's troop movements. The orders that Gates gave to counter
the British offensive struck Arnold as absurd: "That is nothing; you must send
a strong force." Gates had had enough of Arnold: "General Arnold, I have
nothing for you to do. You have no business here."[65]

And so the Battle of Bemis Heights began without Arnold. As the battle
raged away Arnold was at the rear of the action, hearing the sound of guns
and cannon, seething with frustration and anger. Finally, he could take it no
longer and, throwing down a tankard of rum and mounting a horse, Arnold
rode into the thick of the action, a reprise of the Battle of Freeman's Farm,
and again Gates sent someone after him, a major who was to order him back
to camp. Seeing Gates' messenger pursuing him, Arnold spurred his horse and

Figure 19. The Neilson farmhouse on Bemis Heights. Gates' headquarters were just
below the Neilson farmhouse. This photograph shows a reconstruction of that one-
room building.

Figure 20. Posts run alongside the Neilson farmhouse, as seen in this photograph, indicating the disposition of the American lines that awaited the British attack, which never reached this point.

outran him, looking "more like a madman than a cool and discreet officer," as his pursuer said later.[66] Having reached the fighting, Arnold shouted at men who were not under his command to follow him, in clear breach of battlefield protocol; the men followed Arnold, cheering as they went. It was Arnold who took charge of the American army; it was he who led the way. The fighting went back and forth; toward the end of the day the outcome was not yet clear. Arnold wanted to avoid a stalemate; itching for a decisive victory he abandoned all caution as he rode through American and British lines, exposed to fire by both, and paid the price for his foolhardiness. He was shot in the leg, the same leg that had been injured before at the Battle of Quebec; this time he was pinned under his dead horse. Writhing in pain, Arnold saw that one of his men had captured the soldier who had shot him, and was about to dispatch him with a bayonet. Arnold shouted for the American to save the soldier; he had only done his duty. Throughout the fighting Gates never moved from his headquarters. Arnold was the energizer, the catalyst of victory over Burgoyne's army that had seemed invincible four months earlier, after taking Ticonderoga without firing a shot.

After the Battle of Bemis Heights Burgoyne regrouped his army, still at something over 5,000 men and still a force to be reckoned with, and marched

Figure 21. Historical marker that shows the location of Burgoyne's camp at the northern end of the National Historical Park at Saratoga. Burgoyne's marquee stands above the tents used by foot soldiers, one indication among many of the separation of gentleman officers from the men who served under them. This same separation comes through

north, hoping to return to Ticonderoga. Starks' militiamen had taken Fort Edward, cutting Burgoyne off from supplies; in a grueling 24 hour march Burgoyne advanced to his former camp on Philip Schuyler's estate, staying in and burning Schuyler's home, the finest in the region, along the way. Militia-men blocked the passage to Ticonderoga and the British camp was subjected to bombardment from American artillery. Further to obstruct the British and to clarify their vulnerability, Morgan's riflemen sniped at their camp from batteries to the rear and from across the Hudson. Burgoyne had no choice but to enter into negotiations with Gates. He sent a messenger, Major Robert Kingston, to confer with Gates. Kingston was told he had to wear a blindfold when he was escorted to the meeting with Gates; he objected to the "indignity" but he agreed to wear it. The blindfold was removed when he arrived at Gates' tent and he addressed Gates politely. "General Gates, your servant." Gates' reply was polite, even familiar: "Ah! Kingston, how do you do?"[67] Burgoyne had decided, after conferring with officers, that he was prepared to surrender under honorable terms, which he spelled out in a document that Kingston handed to Gates. To Kingston's considerable surprise, Gates' handed him a set of conditions that in effect were an ultimatum calling for unconditional surrender. After further negotiating, an agreement was reached and the two generals, once fellow officers, met, Burgoyne dressed in full uniform, wearing a hat with flowing plumes. A German officer who was there said Burgoyne had "bestowed so much care on his whole toilet that he looked more like a man of fashion than a warrior."[68] A painting of Burgoyne's surrender to Gates, done later by John Trumbull, the aide who had urged Gates to defend Sugar Loaf Hill when defenses were made at Ticonderoga, shows Burgoyne and Gates as sartorial equals, but this was not the case; Gates wore a plain blue frock. According to one version of the surrender, Burgoyne raised his hat and bowed before Gates, saying, "The fortune of war, General Gates, has made me your prisoner." To this salutation Gates responded, "You will always find me ready to testify that it was not brought about through any fault of your excellency."[69] In another version it was Gates who spoke first: "I am glad to see you," he said, as Burgoyne pulled up on his horse. "I am not glad to see you. It is my fortune, sir, and not my fault that I am here."[70] In both versions the exchanges are those of officers who adhere to the same code, men who deem themselves gentlemen and address one another as such. Burgoyne offered his sword to Gates in surrender, but Gates declined to take it. There is no sense in these exchanges between two gentlemen, once fellow officers, of the gravity of what had just happened. In fact, negotiations had been hard; initially Gates had imposed demands that were not only difficult for Burgoyne to accept but humiliating, a point that could have hardly been lost on Burgoyne. What had just happened changed the tide of the war irreversibly; Burgoyne had to surrender to the Americans his entire army, the very force that London had expected to deliver a final and crushing blow to the Americans. This was a devastating defeat to Burgoyne and to Britain, and yet in the polite civilities that both observed at the time of surrender there was no sense of this; outwardly all was personal; both Burgoyne and Gates behaved as gentlemen.

At the time of Burgoyne's surrender to Gates his entire army of 5,752 men fell into American hands, along with 42 brass cannon, 7,000 muskets, and large stores of materiél. After the British surrendered they found the Americans who lined up to see them a strange and curious sight. A British officer was mortified by the playing of "Yankee Doodle" at the time of their surrender. A Hessian who was there saw the Americans who lined the hills as something altogether new, soldiers such as he had never seen: "Each man had on the clothes he was accustomed to wear in the field, tavern, the church, and in everyday life. Yet no fault could be found in their military appearance, for they stood in an erect and soldierly attitude, and remained so perfectly quiet that we were utterly astonished. Not one of them made any attempt to speak to the man at his side; and all the men who stood in array before us were so slender, fine-looking, and sinewy, that they were a pleasure to behold."[71] A British officer said, as he looked at the American farmer-soldiers, that they appeared

Figure 22. Victory Monument, Schuylerville (formerly Saratoga). This 1876 monument marks the place of Burgoyne's surrender to Gates on October 17.

to be a new race. According to the terms of surrender a clear distinction was made between officers and men; officers were to be separated from the men; they were to be placed on parole, allowed to keep sidearms, and their baggage was not to be searched. Burgoyne was invited by his one-time fellow officer Horatio Gates to join him for dinner, an invitation that he accepted. The meal was a bountiful repast that included ham, goose, beef, boiled mutton, and New England cider and rum. In the course of the dinner Burgoyne offered a toast to George Washington; Gates responded, politely, by offering a toast to George III. By the time dinner was served Philip Schuyler had arrived, having received news in Albany of Burgoyne's surrender. Gates did not invite Schuyler to dinner, so Schuyler ate separately, but he did not eat alone. Baroness von Riedesel had observed British and American officers milling about before dinner on an "extremely friendly footing." Schuyler saw her and invited her to join him for dinner: "It may be embarrassing to you to dine with all these gentlemen; come now with your children into my tent, where I will give you, it is true, a frugal meal." The baroness replied, "You are certainly a husband and father, since you show me such kindness." The meal was, in fact, not exactly frugal, consisting of "excellent smoked tongue, beefsteaks, potatoes, good butter, and bread."[72]

The Baroness von Riedesel was not altogether pleased with Burgoyne, who "liked a jolly time and spending half the night drinking and amusing himself in the company of the wife of a commissary, who was his mistress and, like him, loved champagne."[73] The baroness thought it strange for officers, British and American, to be consorting amiably with one another after the British surrender. Her perspective was that of a wife whose husband, and the men under his command, had fought against an army in two pitched battles, in which there had been pain, suffering, and death, which she witnessed directly and described in her memoirs:

> Soon after our arrival [at the Battle of Bemis Heights], a terrible cannonade began, and the fire was principally directed against the house, where we had hoped to find a refuge, probably because the enemy inferred, from the great number of people who went toward it, that this was the headquarters of the generals, while, in reality, none were there except women and crippled soldiers. We were at last obliged to descend into the cellar, where I laid myself in a corner near the door. My children put their heads upon my knees. An abominable smell, the cries of the children, and my own anguish of mind, did not permit me to close my eyes, during the whole night . . . Eleven cannon-balls passed through the house, and made a tremendous noise. A poor soldier, who was about to have a leg amputated, lost the other by one of these balls. All his comrades ran away at that moment, and when they returned, they found him in the corner of the room, in the agonies of death.[74]

After all that she had seen and heard, the baroness found it disconcerting when officers from opposing armies who had inflicted pain, suffering, and death upon one another came together so easily. Were these not enemy armies?

Throughout the long campaign that ended in defeat of the British Army at Saratoga, Burgoyne and fellow officers lived apart from ordinary soldiers: the British redcoats and German mercenaries who slept in the field, carried their packs, endured extreme hardships, and were a universe apart from the officers above them. A few years earlier, Dr. Samuel Johnson visited an army camp while traveling to the north of England; he commented that the English class system was never as evident as on this occasion. Conditions similar to those that Dr. Johnson observed pertained to Burgoyne's army as it moved toward Albany in upstate New York. Rank-and-file soldiers slept on the ground, trying to ward off insects, rodents, and animals; Burgoyne, their commanding general, slept on the silk bed he had brought with him. This is not to say that Burgoyne's men resented Burgoyne, were hostile toward him, or that there was bad feeling between him and them. On the contrary; Burgoyne's men seem to have viewed him favorably; "Gentleman Johnnie" was not a strict disciplinarian; he was a leader who retained the loyalty of his troops by treating them fairly, and by sharing danger with them in battle. Burgoyne's critics came not from men who served under him, ordinary soldiers, but from his own world, that of the elite, men of prominence and political importance who opposed his role in the war and were critics of the war itself. Burgoyne's pronouncements, couched in high-flying phrases and as flamboyant as the man who uttered them, struck opposition members of Parliament as fatuous and absurd. When Burgoyne announced that he would use Indians to terrorize American patriots but that the Indians were not to do harm to women or children, or to take scalps, Edmund Burke set forth gales of laughter in Parliament when he said (according to Horace Walpole) that what Burgoyne proposed "was just as if, at a riot on Tower Hill, the keeper of the wild beasts had turned them loose, but adding, 'my gentle lions, my sentimental wolves, my tender-hearted hyenas, go forth, but care not to hurt women, or children.' "[75] To Horace Walpole, Burgoyne was "vaporing Burgoyne," "Hurlothrumbo," and, perhaps most wickedly, "Pomposo."[76] Burgoyne and his British critics belonged to the same or similar clubs; they moved in the same elite circles, they shared the same tastes. Horace Walpole, Burgoyne's clever critic, was an arbiter of taste, and was, in fact, a key figure in the appearance of a new style, Gothic Revival, both as a writer and in additions he made to Strawberry Hill, his estate outside London, fanciful and daring in its Gothic ornament. When Burgoyne was in Montreal in 1776 biding his time, he threw up a building in the Gothic style, with pointed arches and ornament, almost certainly the first structure in North America done in a style that drew from an impulse that originated within elite arbiters of fashion in England, men of his class.

The Albany aristocrat, Philip Schuyler, treated General John Burgoyne, the English aristocrat, with utmost respect. When Burgoyne apologized to Schuyler for burning his mansion at Saratoga, as well as other houses on his property, Schuyler (according to Burgoyne) told Burgoyne he should "think no more of it . . . that the occasion justified it according to the principles of war, and he should have done the same upon the occasion. . . ."[77] Schuyler invited the Baroness von Riedesel to accept hospitality at his mansion in Albany when he had her to dinner after Burgoyne's surrender. The baroness accepted the invitation after speaking to her husband and he also accepted Schuyler's invitation, as did a retinue of English and German officers whom Schuyler invited to stay at The Pastures under polite captivity. At the head of the party that traveled to Albany to enjoy Schuyler's hospitality was the guest who would seem to have been most honored, General John Burgoyne. According to the Marquis de Chastellux, Burgoyne "was lodged in the best apartment in the house. An excellent supper was served him in the evening, the honors of which were done with so much grace, that he was affected even to tears. . . ."[78] Schuyler remained in Saratoga, staying in a tent on his property so he could begin construction of a new house; once again he was the man in charge. Schuyler sent his aide, Colonel Varick, ahead to Albany so he could help Mrs. Schuyler make necessary preparations for the guests. The English and German officers were not the only ones who went to Albany; so too did foot soldiers, riflemen, and light infantry who camped on the hill behind Schuyler's mansion, where they were a nuisance to Mrs. Schuyler and her guests. She had to delay sending servants to Saratoga to help her husband because someone had to guard her potatoes from men who could not be trusted. To make matters worse, soldiers built makeshift shelters from boards taken from Schuyler's fencing. John Lansing said entertaining Burgoyne and his entourage "entirely discomposed the Oconomy [sic] of the Family and have given no small Degree of Trouble to Mrs. Schuyler."[79] Aristocratic hospitality was not without its burdens. Such hospitality did not end with that of Schuyler in Albany; upon leaving Albany as he began to make his way to Boston, Burgoyne stayed with another family of Dutch patricians, the Pruyns, in Kinderhook, on the other side of the Hudson.

Burgoyne finally reached Boston at the beginning of November. Hannah Winthrop of Cambridge was at Prospect Hill when Burgoyne rode into town at the head of his army. The procession was headed by "a noble looking advanced guard," followed by Burgoyne and other generals, British and Hessian, on horseback. After them came the soldiers, "poor, dirty, emaciated men [and] great numbers of women, who seemed to be beasts of burden [with] bare feet, clothed in dirty rags; such effluvia filled the air while they were passing, had not they been smoking all the time, I should have been apprehensive of being contaminated by them." The generals went to a tavern, "Bradishs," while the "privates trudged through thick and thin to the hills. . . ." Soon there were complications, Hannah Winthrop explained, about quartering the defeated British army. Some Bostonians, "polite ones," felt that "we ought not to look on [officers] as prisoners. They are persons of distinguished rank." Her ironic response to this point of view was that "Perhaps, too, we must not view them in the light of enemies. I fear this distinction will soon be lost."[80] Everywhere Burgoyne went crowds gathered; nowhere were there signs of disrespect or hostility. "Sir, I am astonished at the civility of your people," Burgoyne said to his escort, General William Heath, "for were you walking the streets of London, in my situation, you would not escape insult." Upon reaching Cambridge things did not go so well. Burgoyne wrote Gates on November 14:

> The officers are crowded into the barracks, six and seven in a room of about ten feet, & *without distinction of rank* (my italics). The General officers are not better provided for. I & Genl. Phillips after being amused with promises of quarters together, are still in a dirty miserable tavern lodging in a bed room & all the gentlemen of our suite lodge upon the floor in a chamber adjacent a good

deal worse than their servants had been used to . . . the publick faith is broke.[81]

That Burgoyne complained to Gates about the accommodations that he and fellow officers had to endure suggests that he would have expected a sympathetic response from a fellow general. The list of complaints that Burgoyne laid before Gates came out of an elite mindset within which there were endless distinctions of rank. What is paradoxical in all this is that the mindset was not limited to Britain, America's adversary; a British elite mindset had taken hold in America in some quarters, as we have seen in the hierarchical mind of Philip Schuyler, with its emanations of pride and personal honor, qualities and values that brought him and Burgoyne together after the Battle of Saratoga.

What happened to Burgoyne, his officers, and his enlisted men after the Battle of Saratoga says much about the social code of the time. Eighteenth-century British society was stratified, with a dividing line separating a privileged few from common folk. That code, attenuated to be certain, applied to America as well. This can be seen in the treatment Schuyler extended to John Burgoyne and to his officers, all gentlemen, as he fancied himself to be. Judging from his actions after the Battle of Saratoga, Schuyler would seem to have felt closer ties to British and German officers than to his own farmer soldiers; the letters he sent to Congress when mobilizing defenses against Burgoyne's advancing army suggest that he viewed the men who served under him with contempt. Horatio Gates was more politically astute than Schuyler; he courted favor with New Englanders, particularly delegates in Congress, and told them what they wanted to hear. Some of what Gates said about New England militiamen and their right to elect officers he could well have meant; he could have been sincere taking this position; he had absorbed elements of republicanism before coming to America, when he moved in radical Wilkeite circles, along with Charles Lee, another disaffected British officer who became a general serving under George Washington. However deep the republicanism of these American generals went, it was not deep enough for them to transcend an elite identity and mindset that was integral to their experiences. In fact, both generals had large ambitions, with personal pride to match, that put them on a collision course with Washington. Both harbored ambitions of replacing Washington as commander in chief of the Continental Army; both paid the price for their ambitions; both ran afoul of Washington, at their cost. A relaxed attitude toward his men placed Gates closer to Burgoyne than to American rivals for power, Philip Schuyler, Benedict Arnold, and George Washington, all strict disciplinarians. What bound all of these men together, American and British, Gates, Lee, Schuyler, Arnold, Washington and Burgoyne, was a keen sense of pride and honor.

One American officer stood apart from all others at the Battle of Saratoga— Colonel Daniel Morgan. A product of the frontier, Morgan was stamped from a different mold than Gates, Arnold, or other American leaders who fought at Saratoga. Morgan was not a theoretical republican in the manner of Gates; he emerged from the democratic impulses of a rough-and-ready borderland region where men made their own way, and within which the refined and genteel values of the more civilized coastal region had not yet taken hold. Morgan brought a different identity to the struggle with Britain than other American officers; he brought memories that did not make him inclined to view the British, and particularly British officers, with favor. He had not forgotten the 500 lashes meted out after he hit a British officer in the face at the beginning of the French and Indian War; he said that he had counted the lashes, that he had received only 499, and that he had one to return. Morgan did not view British officers as fellow gentlemen; this placed him in a different mental realm from that of elite officers he fought with. He went into the Battle of Saratoga with a different mindset from that of Benedict Arnold, he fought with a different weapon, and he fought with a different purpose. Morgan fought with a rifle, a weapon of the frontier, used with deadly accuracy by him and his men to kill British soldiers, particularly officers; Arnold fought astride a horse and with a saber, the weapon of a gentleman, an aristocrat not of the blood, as with European aristocrats, but of the mind, in the manner of Americans who internalized a code that came out of aristocratic British life. Both Morgan and Arnold brought something decisive to the Battle of Saratoga, essential to victory. Morgan and his riflemen changed the dynamics of the battle, shooting from trees or wherever they could best position themselves, a violation of the informal but established ground rules of eighteenth-century warfare.[82] This was partisan warfare, from which rules that applied to professional armies had been waived; for Morgan and his riflemen this was warfare as it had taken form on the frontier, fighting Indians, and it was fought with no holds barred. No holds had been barred in fights between Morgan's gang and the Davis gang, and so it was now, on a hilly place overlooking the Hudson, Bemis Heights. Arnold rode into battle, saber in hand, as a knight of old, keen to prove himself, risking anything and everything, exhorting his men to brave deeds, and setting an example of bravery that they could follow. In this he was, if anything, more British than the British; in this he had something to prove, which he did. Benedict Arnold descended from a prominent New England family of distinguished pedigree that provided the crucible within which his identity was formed. It was a fundamentally different identity than that of Daniel Morgan; each identity represented something basic about an America that was striving to break free from Britain, and to chart its own destiny. As the turning point of the Revolution, the Battle of Saratoga was of pivotal importance; by bringing France into the war against Britain, Saratoga set the stage for Yorktown. Important in the American victory at Saratoga was the combination of two very different types of warfare, one of the frontier, that of Daniel Morgan, and one of the elite, that of Benedict Arnold.

Horatio Gates saw both pitched battles at Saratoga only from a distance, from his headquarters well behind the fighting; Benedict Arnold, by contrast, threw himself into the fighting and fought with consummate heroism, rallying his men and exhorting them to give their utmost by his own personal example. Arnold and ordinary soldiers fought together, giving no quarter. The men responded to Arnold as to no other officer. Yet there is a discernible difference between Arnold and the men who fought alongside him; he fought out of personal courage, to prove himself, to become a hero, as he was. Within three years Arnold went over to the British, becoming the most notorious American traitor ever. The seeds of his disaffection can be seen in events leading up to the Battle of Saratoga, and in the battle itself. Brilliant as Arnold was, and fearless in battle, he was driven by something within himself, a need to prove himself and to garner honors. At Saratoga this consuming passion led to collisions with his commanding officer, General Horatio Gates, in both pitched battles and in a bitter confrontation with Gates between the two battles, owing to Arnold's feeling (entirely justified) that he had been slighted. Arnold was so caught up in conflicts with Gates that the fighting became an occasion for him to vindicate himself as much as to defeat adversaries on the battlefield. An excavation of Arnold's mindset, to the extent such an investigation is possible, suggests that Arnold was driven as much by a thrusting need to prove himself as to submerge himself in a concerted patriotic effort to defeat the British and to achieve independence for America. Arnold was surely a patriot, but his patriotism hung in a precarious balance with a sense of honor, deeply rooted in personal pride, that was part of a most complicated mindset. The farmer-soldiers who fought alongside Arnold were less complicated; they fought against British and German soldiers, all mercenaries, to preserve their way of life; they fought for their farms and their families; republican—and incipiently democratic—they fought the paid agents of an imperial power across the sea that would hold them in its thrall. It cannot be said too often, these soldiers, ordinary Americans, were the real victors of the Battle of Saratoga.

The Battle of Saratoga was a most important battle in its own right, judged by some the most important battle of the last millennium. It is a problematic battle, even paradoxical; the two opposing generals, Burgoyne and Gates, were once officers in the same British regiment; an undisputed hero of Saratoga, Benedict Arnold, went over to the British and fought against fellow Americans; the American general, Philip Schuyler, who played an important role in the Battle of Saratoga by throwing up obstacles that put Burgoyne's army in a precarious position by the time they reached Saratoga was not at that battle, fought just below his own estate; and it was Schuyler, whose house at Saratoga Burgoyne burned, who extended his finest hospitality to Burgoyne and to high-ranking British and German officers at his Albany mansion. The Battle of Saratoga offers the historian occasion to consider its various paradoxes, and to consider the meaning of the battle—to place it within a scheme that will reveal something of its importance, and its place in the larger struggle of which it was a part. The way that struggle is conceptualized is one of the keys to how the historian might understand the Battle of Saratoga. It was, by common agreement, the turning point of the American Revolution; also, it occupied a crucial place in what the American historian, R. R. Palmer has called the Age of Democratic Revolution, a struggle that took place within a North Atlantic community of nations.[83] Liberal concepts that came out of the Enlightenment created a seedbed within which ideas of liberty and equality struck root, and within which established, monarchical systems of government came under ever sharper criticism. Ideas of the natural man and of natural rights took hold within this body of thought, and in the liberal culture within which it flourished. Among those who responded to news from America were British and French observers; both contributed to the American cause, in word and in deed. Among those who did so was an immigrant to America, Thomas Paine, who told the Americans at a critical time that there could be no solution to the crisis facing them short of gaining full independence. Drawing from his disaffection with Britain and its political institutions, Paine urged the Americans to dedicate themselves to the struggle for independence. Nobles from France also came to America, some seeking adventure and glory, some out of idealism born of the liberal spirit that passed through France and the enlightened circles within which they moved. The Battle of Saratoga took place at a most important moment in this democratic struggle, in which Europeans were directly involved. It is no accident that a Polish engineer, Tadeusz Kosciuszko, was a participant at the Battle of Saratoga; his being there underscores the larger importance of this epochal event.

When George Washington and Philip Schuyler exchanged letters in the early months of the American Revolution they often expressed need for gunpowder, essential to fighting a war with Britain, as well as need for countless other supplies and materiél. America did not have the material resources to carry on a demanding and debilitating struggle with Britain; in terms of resources America was at a huge disadvantage to Britain. France's intervention in the struggle changed this significantly. While the Battle of Saratoga was decisive in bringing France into the war on America's side openly, France had already intervened in the war, unofficially, and herein lies a most intriguing story. It is a story that says much about the social and cultural dynamics of the Age of Democratic Revolution, an aspect that R. R. Palmer did not treat in his magisterial study undertaken some 50 years ago. If Palmer looked at the Age of Democratic Revolution in essentially political and institutional terms, today's historians are more inclined to bring out its social and cultural aspect. This brings us to the problem of gunpowder and other supplies that Washington and Schuyler discussed continually in their correspondence in the opening months of the Revolution. As it happens, a French adventurer and writer, Pierre-Augustin

Caron de Beaumarchais (1732–99; note that his are the same as Washington's) played an important role making needed supplies, and particularly gunpowder, available to the Americans. Beaumarchais had been sent to London in 1774 to obtain or destroy all copies of a scurrilous publication that revealed the scandalous relationship between Louis XV and his official mistress, Mme du Barry, a former prostitute. Beaumarchais was successful in this mission, and was sent to London again in the following year, 1775, this time to sort out complications with a cross-dressing French adventurer-intriguer-diplomat, the Chevalier d'Eon. While Beaumarchais was in London he was caught up in the sound and fury of Britain's struggle with the American colonies, now at the boiling point. He wrote the King (it was Louis XVI, who came to the throne in 1774) in September 1775 about what he had seen and heard in London:

> Sire, the Americans, resolved to go to any lengths rather than yield, and filled with the same enthusiasm for liberty which has so often made the little Corsican nation formidable to Genoa, have 38,000 men under the walls of Boston . . . all who were engaged in the fisheries which the English have destroyed have become soldiers . . . all who were concerned with maritime trade which the English have forbidden have joined forces with them . . . the workers in the ports and harbours have swelled this angry array . . . and I say, Sire, that such a nation must be invincible.

Filled with enthusiasm for the American cause, Beaumarchais took it upon himself to give it urgently needed support, most importantly arms and gunpowder. Beaumarchais floated a loan of a million livres in 1776 and formed a company, Roderigue Hortalez et Cie, with secret funds provided by the French and Spanish governments in the amount of one million livres each, in order that he could aid the cause of "My friends, the free men of America."[84] Working with Silas Deane, an American representative in France, Beaumarchais helped put together a fleet that delivered military equipment for 25,000 men in the spring of 1777, including guns and gunpowder that are thought to have been essential to the American victory at Saratoga. Of particular importance was the supply of gunpowder, without which, it has been maintained, the American victory at Saratoga would not have been possible.[85]

It was while Beaumarchais gave himself over to the American cause that he began *The Marriage of Figaro*, essentially completed in 1778. The principal characters in this play were carried over from Beaumarchais' earlier play, *The Barber of Seville*, completed in 1772. Changes in the relationship between the central protagonists, Count Almaviva and the commoner Figaro, in the two comedies say much about Beaumarchais, about his own experience in the courtly world of the Ancien Regime, and in the Age of Democratic Revolution. The son of a watchmaker and himself a highly successful one with access to the court, Beaumarchais climbed the social ladder through marriage to aristocratic ladies (there were two such marriages), by acquiring a landed estate, and by purchasing offices that held out hope of becoming a noble. Nobles resented the upstart Beaumarchais and worked against him, throwing up barriers in his way. Amidst many conflicts with men in high position, Beaumarchais proved his mettle in published exchanges with antagonists that brought him to the attention of all Paris, and to readers everywhere who followed his trials and tribulations. Skilled polemicist that he was, Beaumarchais also wrote plays, *The Barber of Seville* being his first important work. In it a barber-factotum, Figaro, assists Count Almaviva in his pursuit of Rosine, whom the Count marries after overcoming obstacles in his way, with Figaro's help. Completed some six years later, *The Marriage of Figaro* presents the same two protagonists, although now in a different light; now they are hostile competitors in pursuit of the same prize, Suzanne, a servant like Figaro, whom Figaro is engaged to marry, but whom the Count wants to possess before the marriage takes place, which is to be on the evening in which the action begins. The central theme of the comic play is conflict between a noble and his servant; the noble would exercise the *droit de seigneur*—first grabs on a female servant before she marries; Figaro would thwart him in that effort. Central to the unfolding action are heated exchanges between the servant and his master in which the servant proclaims his superiority; his merit is based not on birth but on superior energy and resourcefulness. These are democratic pronouncements, sounded with striking clarity, that reflect Beaumarchais' own experience and his personal involvement in the democratic forces that the American Revolution unleashed, a political struggle carried out by a republican people who would throw off the shackles of despotism and tyranny.

   The Marriage of Figaro had the most sensational opening at the Odéon on April 27, 1784 of any play in eighteenth-century France; it was a landmark event, one of the most noteworthy in the entire annals of French theater. Those who wanted to see the play started forming a line to get into the theater by ten in the morning for the eight o'clock performance, altogether some four to five thousand in number. People were crushed to death in efforts to get into the theater. Having banned the play for several years, Louis XVI finally succumbed to pressure mounted, among others, by the Queen, the king's younger brother, the Comte d'Artois, and members of the court nobility, to give a performance of a play that the King correctly considered inflammatory. Beaumarchais was at his most ingenious concocting strategies to break down royal resistance to a play that was, by intention, subversive. *The Marriage of Figaro* came out of an Age of Democratic Revolution and was written by an author who sounded the call of liberty and equality; egalitarian in conception, this play was of the Revolutionary Age. When Beaumarchais wrote *The Marriage of Figaro* France was still a stratified society, and the established order remained intact, in some respects more rigidly than ever. At the same time, subterranean change had taken place within France, and indeed throughout Western society, European and American. Aristocracies there were, and they were separated from the people, but an egalitarian spirit was weakening the division between the two. As a work of literature, Beaumarchais' *The Marriage of Figaro* throws light on the social dynamics of the time in which it was written.

A long-term perspective might be useful at this point. One of the central features of the literature of Classical Antiquity was the separation of styles, a literary scheme that reflected the dominance of the ruling elite in this world.[86] Epic and tragedy were the highest literary forms; both were vehicles for celebrating the great achievements, or tragic fates, of heroes and heroines that dwelled on a higher sphere than ordinary people, who were outside the central action of epic and tragedy. While this system broke down with the collapse of antique civilization, it was restored with the Renaissance, and again it became a way of shedding luster on the great, meaning those who belonged to the privileged order, the aristocracy, and separating them from the people. The separation of styles in the domain of literature ran parallel to class separation in the hierarchical society that took shape as Europe passed from the Middle Ages to the Early Modern period. In the course of the eighteenth century, and particularly after the 1750s, this system began to weaken. Increasingly, leading thinkers and writers called for literature that was less exclusive socially, more inclusive; literature in which heroes and heroines were no longer limited to aristocracy. Beaumarchais was among the advocates of a more inclusive literature, along with Jean-Jacques Rousseau, Denis Diderot, Louis-Sébastien Mercier, and others. *The Marriage of Figaro* is the best-known work to come out of this effort.[87]

We turn now to the question posed earlier in this chapter, and indicated in its title: If we are to find a literary counterpart to the Battle of Saratoga where is the best fit, epic, tragedy, or comedy of manners? The Battle of Saratoga does not fit well with epic as a literary type; it does not have a "principal hero," nor is it "mythical in its content," but it is certainly epic in its "scale" and "mold, as *epic* actions." The historic battle fought 25 miles above Albany in 1777 was epic in this sense of the word. It changed the world forever, but it does not fit well with epic as a literary category. Nor does the Battle of Saratoga fit well with tragedy, "a dramatic composition [that] excites pity and terror by a succession of unhappy events" and in which the leading figure is "brought to a catastrophe." Yet, it is tragic in its consequences; it is "characterized by, or [involves] death or calamity or the suffering implied in tragedy." The tragic dimension of Saratoga comes through in the graphic accounts of Thomas Anburey and the Baroness von Riedesel, to mention but two observers whose descriptions bring out the pain, the suffering, even the smell of death, the burying of men without covering dead limbs with earth, and the house within which wounded are placed for shelter, only to be wounded anew from enemy fire from which there is no escape. The slow death that follows is without relief. Suffering and death there were, the stuff of the tragic, although not tragedy in the literary sense of the word. What we are left with in our search for a literary counterpart to the Battle of Saratoga is comedy of manners, and here the fit works, if we use Beaumarchais as our guide.

As a comedy of manners, *The Marriage of Figaro* was a projection of Beaumarchais' own experience—his conflicts with others in the hierarchical, stratified monarchical world of France on the eve of the French Revolution. That he wrote a comedy of manners at the very time he was sending arms to America, through a company that he organized, arms that contributed to the American victory at Saratoga, suggests another way of viewing this historic battle—seeing it through the lens of manners and what they reveal about the leading players in the Battle of Saratoga. Indeed, we can see the battle as a comedy of manners. The rival generals, two of the leading protagonists, heroes as it were, are old comrades-in-arms, once fellow officers in the same regiment. In a perfect comic script one hero is an aristocrat, a gambler, a man-about-town, a courtier type of sorts who has won favor with the King, to whom he has sold his idea for a campaign that will gratify the King's fondest wish, total victory over the upstart Americans. He moves at the head of his army through the American wilderness, sleeping with a junior officer's wife on a silk bed he has brought with him. Filled with confidence and certain of the superiority of his army, he is eager to use it to gain a knighthood. His counterpart, the other leading figure, the other general, is a commoner who was thwarted in his efforts to climb the ladder of success in Britain. He had quarreled with the wife of his patron, who was having an affair with an officer; he had not played the game by the right rules. Confused and angry, he had tried Methodism, but that hadn't worked out. He became a republican and went to America to achieve success. This he did, big time; he was the victor at Saratoga, defeating his aristocratic rival and one-time fellow officer, a nice theatrical ending. The two protagonists encounter one another after a battle brings them together after many years of separation; one holds out his sword to the other in surrender; both are gentleman; the victor declines the sword. Missing from the comic scene is any sense, any awareness, that something momentous has happened; all is polite civilities; all is personal. As these actors in the play make ready for supper, with officers of their respective armies coming together in a convivial gathering, another actor appears from the wings, an aristocrat who has lost command of his army, a proud and haughty Dutch type who has fallen from grace; unkind gods have given his army to an English adventurer who has reaped laurels of victory that were rightly his. In a nice theatrical touch he comes upon the wife of a German officer and invites her to a frugal meal that turns out to be a fine repast; he then invites her and her husband to stay in his mansion in Albany, the very Hudson River town where two triumphant British armies were to have joined forces. Our Dutch aristocrat also invites the fallen British general to his mansion so he too can enjoy his hospitality. The scene shifts to the Albany mansion. Inside are officers of a defeated army, all gentlemen, who exchange polite civilities with their American hostess, a grand aristocratic lady; outside are ordinary soldiers, men who have won a battle. They have set up a camp, but they are a nuisance; there is serious fear that they will steal potatoes, a problem of such gravity that the very aristocratic lady of the house has to keep servants on hand to watch over the potatoes, rather than send the servants to her husband, who is building a new mansion to replace the one that his dignified guest had burned that was just above the battlefield where he was conspicuous by his absence. A comic scene indeed.

So much for the two commanding generals at the Battle of Saratoga, once fellow British officers. The most intriguing, and problematic actor is a New Haven apothecary and merchant who played a role of singular importance at Saratoga. He is the hero, the catalyst of victory. In scenes that would seem to have come out of a play this actor clashed with his superior, the general who reaped the laurels of victory in battles that he saw only from a distance, in which he was not a direct participant. In both pitched battles at Saratoga, in both acts of the play, our apothecary-merchant-hero is ordered to remain in the rear lines, not to ride forth and join the fighting; both times our hero sputters and fumes until he can no longer take it; both times, in defiance of his superior's commands, he rides into battle; both times the superior sends someone after the hero. In act one the pursuer catches up with the hero and orders him back to the rear lines, a scene of frustration and despair; in act two the same scenario is repeated, only this time the hero outruns his pursuer and throws himself into the thick of the battle, sword in hand, calling upon the fighting men, farmer-soldiers, to achieve final victory over their red-coated adversaries, men from a foreign land. This they do, but the hero pays the price of his heroism; he is shot in the leg, injured in a previous battle; he falls under his horse and is almost crushed by the dead animal. We turn now to the scene between the two battles, between the two acts; it is an interlude, a scene out of a comedy of manners, in which the setting is the quarters of the superior, the general, who has written a report of a battle; absent from the report is any mention of the hero of the battle. This hero, a man of great pride and no small amount of vanity, storms into the quarters of his superior and unburdens himself of frustration and anger. The superior, no less prideful and vain, understands that he has the upper hand; there are rules by which exchanges between those of different rank take place, in the military as in society, and he understands the rules; in fact, both men understand the rules; the hero rages and fumes, but there are limits beyond which he cannot go; the superior needles the hero; the hero does not receive satisfaction; a comic scene, this episode is played out amidst fierce passions that will feed into the second and final act, with vindication of the hero but at a price that goes beyond his injury, sustained in battle. It has been said that tragedy is sometimes found buried within the folds of comedy; if we see the Battle of Saratoga through the lens of comedy of manners this is surely true here: The apothecary-merchant-hero who plays his finest role at Saratoga will betray his country; he will go over to the British, he will join them in the struggle against fellow Americans, against the very cause he served with valor and courage in a battle that made American victory possible. In a character as complicated as our apothecary-merchant-hero there are no easy explanations, there is no certain way to explain his treachery, but one source of the hero's acute feeling of abuse can be traced to a battle fought along the Hudson River 25 miles above Albany, the Battle of Saratoga, in which the hero's superior had not given him just due.

Of the main participants in the Battle of Saratoga one stands out from the rest, an officer who headed a unit of riflemen. A man of the frontier, he does not belong to the elite leadership; he does not move within the same world as the other leaders; he does not observe the polite forms that officers of both armies observe. This means that placing him within comedy of manners is not so easy; in fact, if we are to do so we will have to set the stage. In comedies of manners written when the established social and political order was stable, or seemed stable, that is to say during the reign of Louis XIV (we turn to France as we observe change within comedies of manners for reasons that will become evident as we proceed), the principal characters were members of the elite, bourgeois and aristocrats who were separated by birth but shared a common culture, one of refined people who observed a system of manners that determined polite forms of behavior. People who worked with their hands had no role in these comedies; servants there were, but they were present only to serve the needs of the elite, and to help carry the comic action forward. As the established social and political order in France began to weaken in the course of the eighteenth century, as forces of change were felt across many fronts, as new ideas were in the air, ideas that came out of the Enlightenment, ideas that in some variants were egalitarian and espoused principles of liberty and equality, change took place within an established literary genre, the comedy of manners. We have already identified the key figure in this change, Pierre Augustin Caron de Beaumarchais, a writer who was caught up in enthusiasm for the American Revolution and was instrumental in sending arms and gunpowder to America when they were urgently needed. Beaumarchais wrote his comic masterpiece as a saga was unfolding in upstate New York that would change the course of history, a saga in which he played a role; this play is at the center of an historical episode whose importance is by no means limited to America; it includes France as well. This play comes not just out of the author's experience within the hierarchical society of France in a time of flux and change; it comes out of his enthusiasm for the American Revolution and all that it represented. A protagonist of Beaumarchais' play is a servant-factotum who stands up to and asserts his superiority over his aristocratic master; he is not a conventional figure in a comedy of manners; he is not a subordinate figure who defers to his master; he breaks down the barrier within which someone of his station should remain; he is a new type of character, one for whom the old ground rules no longer apply. All of this happens in a play that has thrown aside the established conventions of French theater, according to which there is strict separation between classes; also jettisoned are proprieties, the *bienséances*, rules that determine forms of address, tone, diction, the subtle and varied precepts that were embedded within the established system of manners and determined behavior in official French theater. Beaumarchais' protagonist, Figaro, belongs to the Age of Democratic Revolution.

So too does his real-life counterpart and contemporary, Daniel Morgan. Like Figaro, Morgan belongs to the people, not the elite; like Figaro, Morgan breaks the rules. If Figaro does not observe rules that apply to a servant, Morgan does not observe those that apply on the field of battle, within which there are established conventions; with him the invisible wall that protected officers disappears; with him officers are fair game, the "kingbirds" that he and his men pick off, not only to gain military advantage, but in Morgan's case, it would seem, to settle old accounts. He had defied rules that applied to someone of his station when he hit a British officer in the face in the French and Indian War, an offense that resulted in severe punishment, 500 lashes that left permanent scars on his body, but one short of the prescribed number, according to his count; now he would return the missing lash, a nice and deft comic touch. Comic sounds are heard in both pitched battles at Saratoga: the turkey calls that men send to one another, a battle cry that comes from the American wilderness, whence these men came, men trained in warfare with Indians, their former adversaries, whom they now drive from the battlefield with the mere sound of their rifles. Morgan is a new type of character, a man who has become an officer, but does not dress or behave like one, on the battlefield or off it; he is a particularly American type in the Age of Democratic Revolution, similar to Figaro in his violation of an established code but utterly American in the way he does so.[88]

Within the democratic forces in the Age of Democratic Revolution there was a most important division, in America and in Europe, one that separated the elite from the people. In eighteenth-century society the most important division was between people who worked with their hands and those who did not. This division was more pronounced in Europe than in America, but it was present on both sides of the Atlantic. In revolutions that surfaced in the course of the Age of Democratic Revolution, elites and the people fought for a common cause, but with different agendas. The dynamic interplay between elite leaders and ordinary people in democratic revolutions is one of the most important problems facing the historian. To what extent did elite leaders dictate the course of events; what was the role of ordinary people in the revolutions? This question is of utmost importance to historians who seek to understand both the American and French revolutions, which were, as we have seen, joined at the hip. One way to think about the Battle of Saratoga is to place it within the context of a scheme within which there is dynamic interplay but also polarity between elite officers and farmer soldiers; it is within this context that the importance of ordinary soldiers becomes evident; it is they who were the real victors of this epochal battle. Most interesting within this scheme is the division that revealed itself in the aftermath of the battle, when generals and officers of the two armies came together in camaraderie, in which the victors extended hospitality to enemy officers, to whom they would seem to have felt closer ties than to their own men, without whom victory could not have been achieved. Placed in the context of the Age of Democratic Revolution, the Battle of Saratoga reveals class divisions in America that are deeper than one might have expected to find. And yet those divisions are nothing when compared to class divisions that would open up on the other side of the Atlantic in France, when that nation moved inexorably toward her revolution.

The surrender of Burgoyne's entire army at Saratoga came as a bolt from the blue when news of the disaster reached London. The British press had reported success after success as Burgoyne moved south on his triumphant march to Albany; Burgoyne himself fed hopes for a decisive victory in the 1777 campaign in letters sent to London that exuded confidence. When George III heard that Burgoyne had taken Ticonderoga he exclaimed, "I have beat them! I have beat them!" What was to have been a glorious victory was a calamity; indignation against Burgoyne was great when he returned to Britain in early 1778. He requested a court martial in order that he could clear his name; the request was denied. When Burgoyne defended himself in Commons on May 26, 1778 the house was packed, and nerves were on edge. He cast blame for the fiasco on Germain; for his part, Germain blamed Howe. Still under the shadow of Minden, Germain was sensitive to attacks, and when one was made that he felt was personal he reached for his dress sword as pandemonium erupted on the floor of Commons. After testifying before Commons, Burgoyne retired to Bath and its civilized pastimes. Unwinding at the gambling tables, he received a note from another man-about-town and gambler, Charles James Fox, an opposition MP who was a severe critic of the war in America, and of those in office who continued to support it. "At whist, as you very well know, it is often right in a desperate case to play upon a supposition of your partner's having a good hand, though there might be the strongest symptoms of the contrary; because if he has not, the game is lost."[89] Fox was feeling Burgoyne out; might he join him and his political allies who opposed the American war? Bizarrely, Burgoyne did join the opposition; he turned against a war in which he had been one of the principal players; it is as if he were an actor on the stage in a play that combined tragedy, farce, and comedy, with many strange and unexpected scenes. When Burgoyne's political friends came to power briefly in 1782 he was restored to his rank and held office in Ireland, but the ministry to which he had attached himself fell from office in 1783 and he withdrew to private life. Fittingly, he gave himself over to literary pursuits before his death in 1792. All four of his illegitimate children were born from 1782 to 1788. Burgoyne's mistress was an opera singer, Sarah Caulfield; one of the sons, John Fox Burgoyne, received a commission at age 16 and pursued a military career, as his father had; he fought in the Napoleonic Wars, the War of 1812, and the Crimean War. He received a baronetcy in 1856 and retired in 1868 as a Field Marshal. He was as serious and dutiful as his father was wayward and flamboyant; one was an earnest Victorian type, the other an actor in an eighteenth-century comedy of manners.

Britain was divided over the policies that led to the American War of Independence from the beginning; opposition continued throughout the war, with the volume turned up as it ran its agonizing and costly course. The government had poured the massive resources of the most powerful nation on earth into the 1776 campaign, and Howe won a crushing victory over Washington at the Battle of Long Island, but at the end of the year, unable to finish Washington off, he retired to his hospitable lodgings in New York, and to the consoling arms of his mistress. 1777 was to be the year of victory; two British armies were to end the Revolution by joining forces in Albany; the plan failed and an entire army was lost. Howe requested his recall when he heard news of the outcome at Saratoga, and his resignation was accepted in February 1778. His successor, Sir Henry Clinton, asked for more troops, more supplies, more everything, but Britain's resources were stretched to the limit. When Clinton received news that French troops had landed in Newport, he had to abandon Philadelphia, whose capture by Howe had sabotaged the 1777 British campaign. As ongoing reports of failure in America reached London the political climate in Britain heated up; critics of the war became more vocal in Commons and in the press. Britain was flooded with satirical anti-war pamphlets; political, cartoonists had at it, lampooning those deemed responsible for a misdirected and inconclusive war effort. A petition to end the war was sent to Parliament from Norfolk. Edmund Burke ridiculed the King in Commons; he called for Crown lands to be put up for sale and for the elimination of useless offices and sinecures. Charles James Fox, a political ally of Burke, proposed a toast to George Washington. William Pitt, now Lord Chatham, appeared in Lords three times in 1778 and proclaimed that if he were an American he would never lay down his arms, "Never, never, never!" Richard Sheridan's play, *The Camp*, satirized the military. Horace Walpole commented wryly, "We are in the oddest situation that can be; at war in fact, but managed like a controversy in divinity."[90]

A war in distant America exacerbated underlying social tensions in Britain. Politicians lashed away at one another as dislocations from the war led to lower wages and increased unemployment. Out of these conditions came the most explosive and destructive London riots ever. The 1780 Gordon Riots drew from instabilities stirred by the war in America, from ancient hatreds embedded within the English class system, and most immediately from the Papist

Act of 1778, which removed some civil disabilities to which Catholics were subject. Anti-Catholic feeling in Britain was pervasive and rooted in centuries of struggle with Catholic Spain and Catholic France. Protestantism was the very badge of English identity; to be British was to fear and hate the nation's Catholic enemies. In 1780 Britain was at war with both France and Spain, and the war was taking a heavy domestic toll, politically and socially. Under these circumstances legislation giving greater toleration to Catholics was seen as a threat to all that true Britons held dear. Some 40,000 to 60,000 Londoners appeared before Parliament on June 2 with banners proclaiming "No Popery," and a petition calling for repeal of the Papists Act. The people were kept from forcing their way into Commons, but Lord George Gordon, an eccentric MP, presented their petition to the members of that body. Outside Parliament matters changed suddenly, and explosively, as throngs of angry Londoners began a series of attacks that lasted five days, until the army was called in on June 7 with orders to fire on groups of four or more that refused to disperse. Some 285 people were shot dead; by the time order was restored, parts of London lay in smoking ruins.

Among those that rampaging mobs targeted were members of the government who led Britain's war against America, such as John Montagu, Fourth Earl of Sandwich (1718–92), First Lord of the Admiralty from 1771 to 1783. It was he who headed Britain's navy as the war in America ran its course; in the opinion of some he was both incompetent and corrupt. Lord Sandwich (yes, the sandwich was named after him) was a longtime opponent of John Wilkes, a champion of the people and an active supporter of the American Revolution. At the beginning of the Gordon Riots a mob stopped Lord Sandwich's carriage and proceeded to strip and destroy it. Another mob forced its way into the London mansion in Bloomsbury Square of William Murray, First Earl of Mansfield (1705–93), forcing him and his wife to flee. Lord Mansfeld had submitted Benjamin Franklin to a degrading dressing-down in Whitehall in 1774, an incident that was instrumental in turning Franklin, a loyal supporter of the British Empire, into an American patriot. Lord Mansfeld also handed down a judicial ruling that was favorable to Catholics; he was among those targeted by angry Londoners on the first day of the Gordon Riots. As the Gordon Riot ran their five-day course, mobs went after their enemies, and they forced their way into buildings that they associated with an oppressive social order. One crowd torched debtor's prison; another marched to Newgate and set fire to the prison roof. The Gordon Riots were a protest not only against measures favorable to Catholics; the protest agenda included assaults on many perceived injustices, large and small, including pawnshops and Thames tollhouses As a contemporary commented, "This is a deep laid Re[v]olt . . . The ringleaders at least act with a deliberate rage and upon a deliberate plan."[91]

The Battle of Saratoga was the turning point of the American Revolution, setting the stage for independence; that same battle brought France into the war, making victory possible but with unexpected and momentous results, nothing less than the French Revolution. The American Revolution had other unexpected results; it changed the political landscape of Britain. In the final stages of the war in America coalition ministries fell apart amidst embittered fighting between hostile groups of politicians as former enemies came together in fragile coalitions that collapsed, one after the other. In the last two years of the war five ministries rose and fell; parliamentary government had all but broken down at the end of the war. It was at that critical moment, at the end of 1783, that William Pitt the Younger, son of William Pitt, the Great Commoner, the architect of victory in the Seven Years War, accepted an offer by George III to head a new ministry. He was 24 years old. Upon assuming office, Pitt's enemies, led by Charles James Fox, were certain that they would bring him down in no time at all, but they were mistaken; William Pitt the Younger was to have the longest term in office of any British Prime Minister, ever. It was he who would lead Britain through the forthcoming struggle with Revolutionary France, and with Napoleonic France, until the time of his death in 1806. What gave Pitt support when he needed it at the end of 1783 was an outpouring of popular support. Weary Britons sent over 200 messages to the King, giving him their support; they carried the banner, "The King! The Constitution! The People! And Pitt Forever!"[92] There had been a shifting of tectonic plates in Britain; the foundations of government stood on a more solid footing after the desolation spread by a war in America that resulted in defeat and breakdown of Empire. In that struggle the Battle of Saratoga was the turning point; its impact on America, France, and Britain was of profound historic importance. Some historians consider it the most important battle of the last thousand years.

Philip Schuyler's Hudson River Visitors, 1776–83

As soon as news of the April 19, 1775 battles of Lexington and Concord spread through New England, militiamen moved to Forts Ticonderoga and Crown Point to seize cannon and to gain control of Lake Champlain, essential to an American invasion of Canada that followed later in the year. The disastrous American invasion of Canada set in motion a struggle for the Hudson-Champlain corridor that culminated in the Battle of Saratoga, the turning point of the American Revolution. That battle did not end conflict along the Hudson-Champlain corridor, which continued to the end of the Revolution, even though the main theater of war shifted to the South in the course of the 1779 and 1780 campaigns. This chapter is about men who appeared in Albany between 1776 and 1783 as the historic struggle between America and Britain over control of the Hudson-Champlain corridor ran its course. Altogether, we will observe seven visitors who came up the Hudson River, all of them to see Philip Schuyler. He is a fixed point in all of the narratives in this chapter. Of the visitors whose paths we will follow, five were American and two were French; two of them were in Paris at the beginning of the French Revolution; five of them lived through both the American and French revolutions. To follow the paths of these men is to pass through two revolutions, and it is to follow private and public lives of bewildering complexity and no small amount of historical interest.

A sloop with five passengers docked at Albany at seven thirty in the morning on April 7, 1776, where a tall, very correct Albanian awaited them. Several members of the party recognized the person who stood on the dock, having sat with him in the Second Continental Congress in Philadelphia in the previous year. The Albanian who stood on the dock, Phillip Schuyler, had commanded the army that had invaded Canada in 1775. Unable to remain with the invading army because of illness, Schuyler had been at his Albany mansion, his estate at Saratoga, or northern forts along the Hudson-Champlain corridor as he received news of reversal after reversal from the American forces that had experienced extraordinary hardship in the failed campaign. Unwilling to accept the hard fact of failure, Congress still hoped to secure Canada's support in the war against Britain in 1776.

The idea of bringing Canada into the Revolution was fundamentally flawed from the beginning, owing to the wise and prudent efforts of the leading British official in Canada, Sir Guy Carleton, who understood that if British rule in Canada were to be effective it was necessary to win the loyalty of a predominantly French population, recently placed under British rule. To that end, Carleton persuaded the political leadership in London to pass the pro-French and pro-Catholic Quebec Act in 1774, which succeeded admirably in its express goal, not only because it extended freedoms to French-speaking, Catholic subjects of the British crown but also because Americans in Congress denounced the measure. One member of Congress, the New Yorker John Jay, warned that the greater freedoms and rights of Catholics in Canada would spread "impiety, bigotry, murder, and rebellion throughout every part of the world."[1] At the time of the 1775 invasion of Canada the thinking had been that Canadians would probably want to join the American cause, and that if they did not side with the Americans, a little force would be sufficient to make them change their minds. Few Canadians answered the American call, the American siege of Quebec failed miserably, and in its aftermath the elements and disease took a terrible toll on the remnants of the invading American forces. Congress understood that if American efforts were to succeed in Canada in 1776 it was necessary to secure the support of Canadians, and it was for that reason that it sent a commission of three to Canada; it was those men, along with two others who traveled with them, who stopped at Albany to meet with Phillip Schuyler on April 7, 1776.

Prominent among the three Canada Commissioners was the most famous American of the time, Benjamin Franklin (1706–1790), who had been in Albany before, in June 1754, to attend an intercolonial conference summoned as storm clouds were gathering in North America. France was making plans in 1754 to retake Nova Scotia, lost to Britain 40 years earlier, and to extend her influence into the Ohio Country, an undefined frontier territory west of Britain's American colonies. An incident had taken place near the Forks of the Ohio River a month before the delegates arrived in Albany to discuss measures that might be taken against the French threat. The torch of war had already been lit by a 21-year-old lieutenant colonel from Virginia who led a force of militiamen and Indians through the Pennsylvania wilderness in May 1754. Some 40 miles before reaching the Forks of the Ohio this lieutenant colonel received news that French soldiers had been seen. Not knowing that they were on a peaceful mission, he found them with the help of Indian guides, gave orders to his men to fire, and after a brief skirmish the French surrendered. Following their own rules of war, the Indians massacred several of the French, including their commander, Ensign Joseph Coulon de Villiers de Jumonville. After Jumonville had been killed the leader of the Indians pulled his brain from the cleaved skull and brandished it triumphantly as a sign of victory. Among those who witnessed the grotesque spectacle was the lieutenant colonel who headed the expedition into the Ohio country. His name was George Washington; it was he, in this incident, who triggered the French and Indian War.

By the time Benjamin Franklin and other delegates drew up the 1754 Albany Plan of Union and presented it to the colonies and to London it had been overtaken by events and received no support on either side of the Atlantic. Looking back at the Albany Plan years later, Franklin wrote, "I am still of the opinion it would have been happy if it had been adopted. The colonies, so united, could have been sufficiently strong to have defended themselves; there would have been no need for troops."[2] Britain waged war against France, first in America and then in a global conflict that ended with an overwhelming British victory in 1763. When Franklin arrived in Albany again, in 1776, it was America and Britain that were at war; the idea at this point was to persuade French Canadians to join the American War for Independence.

Now in his seventieth year, Franklin was renowned as a scientist, inventor, and writer; he held honorary BA degrees from Harvard, Yale, and William and Mary and honorary doctorates from the universities of Edinburgh and Oxford; and he was a member of the Royal Academy of Science in London. Successful and wealthy, he had retired from profitable business concerns in Philadelphia at age 42 and spent 16 years in England, where he moved in cultured and aristocratic circles until he sided with the rebellious colonies and returned to America. Franklin had given serious thought to Canada long before becoming a member of the Canada Commission in 1776. He had written a piece on Canada in 1760, "The Interest of Great Britain Considered," now referred to as "The Canada Pamphlet," when he was in London representing several interests in the Pennsylvania colony. A strong advocate of the British Empire, Franklin wrote this piece in the aftermath of the 1759 Battle of Quebec, the pivotal battle in the French and Indian War. By this time it was clear that Britain had gained the upper hand in the war with France, and that she would have to decide which French colonial possessions she might gain as fruits of victory. Franklin felt it imperative that Britain give first priority to Canada, and advanced arguments for doing so. He maintained that as long as France ruled Canada she could keep the "extended [American] frontier in continual alarm," but "with Canada in our possession our people in America will increase amazingly." Franklin's position was that as long as France possessed Canada it would be a check on the growth of the British colonies in America; conquest of Canada would bring the American colonies and Canada together; doing so would define "the frontier of the British empire on that side." Were Britain to gain possession of Canada, the French-speaking inhabitants would quickly assimilate British culture; they would "be blended and incorporated with our people both in language and manners."[3] When Congress appointed Franklin to the Canada Commission in 1776 he had been transformed from an outspoken champion of the British Empire to an outspoken patriot, convinced that the breach with Britain was irreparable and that America should do everything possible to bring Canada into the war against Britain on the side of America.

If Franklin was appointed to the commission because of his fame and diplomatic experience, another member, Charles Carroll from Maryland, was chosen, at least in part, because he was Catholic. Charles Carroll was not only Catholic but an important member of the Continental Congress and one of the two or three wealthiest men in America, giving him prestige that Congress felt would be useful in negotiations that were to take place in Canada. Moreover, Carroll had studied in France at the Collège Louis-le-Grand in Paris, where Voltaire had studied earlier and a boarding student from Arras, Maximilien Robespierre, would be a student some years later. Fluent in French, Charles Carroll was well suited to carry out negotiations with French Canadians whose support Congress felt was of major importance in the revolutionary struggle. The third member of the commission was another Marylander, Samuel Chase, a lawyer who in later years would be appointed to the Supreme Court by George Washington. Also traveling with the commissioners was John Carroll, a Jesuit priest and a cousin of Charles Carroll, who had also studied in France and was also fluent in French. Having a Jesuit priest who had spent years in France would be advantageous in conversations with Canadians aware of well-known anti-Catholic feeling in America. The fifth member of the group was Frederick William, Baron von Woedtke, a former Prussian officer who was not part of the Canada Commission but was sent by Congress to serve as a military advisor to Schuyler and was to join the American forces outside Quebec.

Franklin had written Schuyler from Philadelphia on March 11, telling him about the Canada Commission and about the men who were to carry it out, at the behest of Congress.[4] For Schuyler these were important men and this was an important mission, one that called for proper hospitality, for which he was well-known. Charles Carroll, who kept a journal while making the trip to Canada, said that when Schuyler greeted his visitors at the landing where the sloop docked he was accompanied by "2 daughters, lively, agreeable, black-eyed girls." One of the girls, "Betsey," was Elizabeth Schuyler, the other daughter, "Peggy," was Margarita Schuyler. Schuyler had a carriage at the ready for his guests, and in it they made their way to Schuyler's mansion overlooking the Hudson River. As he was passing through Albany, Charles Carroll noted that Fort Frederick was in near ruins, that there was not a single cannon in sight, that the town had a heavily Dutch appearance, that most residents spoke Dutch, but that English "language and manners" were gaining currency. By the time the distinguished guests in Schuyler's carriage arrived at The Pastures they were well south of Albany; they were entering a rural paradise, which the name of Schuyler's mansion consciously evoked. The distinguished Commissioners sent to Albany by Congress spent two days at The Pastures with their aristocratic host, Philip Schuyler, who according to Charles Carroll "behaved with great civility."[5] Writing to his mother of the visit, John Carroll said Schuyler extended many courtesies to his guests, and that he entertained them "with great politeness and very genteely."[6]

Having shown the members of the Canada Commission proper hospitality in Albany for two days, Schuyler accompanied them to his estate at Saratoga in one of his wagons, "in company with Mrs. Schuyler and her 2 daughters," as Charles Carroll noted in his *Journal*. The trip to Saratoga was exhausting but spectacular.

> At 6 miles from Albany I quitted the wagon and got on horseback to accompany the Generals [they were accompanied by General John Thomas, who was on his way to Quebec] and got on horseback to view the falls on the Mohawks' River, called the Cohoes. The perpendicular fall is 74 feet and the breadth of the river in this place, as measured by Gen. Schuyler, is 1,000 feet. The fall is considerably above 100 feet, taken from the first ripple or still water above the perpendicular fall. The river was swollen with the melting of the snows and rain, and rolled over this frightful precipice an impetuous torrent. The foam, the irregularities in the fall broken by projecting rocks, and the deafening noise presented a sublime but terrifying spectacle.

The party arrived at Schuyler's Saratoga estate "a little before sunset, having "spent the whole day in the journey, occasioned by the badness of the roads and the delay the wagons of the roads met with in crossing two ferries." Along the way the travelers passed alongside Bemis Heights, where a battle would be fought in the following year as the capstone of a sequence of events for which this trip helped set the stage. Upon arriving at Saratoga, Schuyler took his guests on a tour of his estate, which Charles Carroll found impressive.

> The lands about Saratoga are very good, particularly the bottom lands. Hudson's River runs within a quarter of a mile of the house, and you have a pleasing view of it for 2 or 3 miles above and below. A stream called Fish Kill, which rises out of Lake Saratoga about 6 miles from the General's house, was close by it and turns several mills, viz., a grist mill, two sawmills, one of them carrying 14 saws, and a hemp and flax mill. The mill is of a new construction and answers equally well in breaking hemp or flax.

Carroll was impressed both by Schuyler and his Saratoga estate.

> General Schuyler is a man of a good understanding and improved
> by reflection and study. He is of a very active turn and fond of
> husbandry, and when the present distractions are composed, if his
> infirm state of health will permit him, will make Saratoga a most
> beautiful and valuable estate.[7]

Schuyler, the Baron de Woedtke, and General John Thomas left for Lake George
the next morning to carry out military preparations for the forthcoming Canada
campaign. Schuyler was to organize a shipment of "military stores and supplies"
to Canada, whereas General Thomas and the Baron de Woedtke left Schuyler
at Lake George as they made their way to Canada, where Thomas was to take
command of the battered American army outside Quebec. The three Commissioners and John Carroll remained at Schuyler's home in Saratoga for four days,
held back by a blast of severe weather that struck on April 12. Having spent
four days at Schuyler's house, Charles Carroll wrote that he "parted with regret
from the amiable family of Gen. Schuyler. The ease and affability with which
we were treated, and the lively behavior of the young ladies made Saratoga a
most pleasing séjour, the remembrance of which will long remain with me."
Continuing his account of the trip to Canada after leaving Schuyler's estate,
Charles Carroll described the battered fortifications he and his companions
observed as they headed north, at Fort Miller, Fort Edward, and Fort George,
and the complete destruction of Fort William Henry, where a massacre had
taken place 19 years earlier. Carroll and the members of the party were passing through a part of upstate New York in which some of the most brutal
fighting had taken place during the French and Indian War, when Americans
and British had fought together against a common enemy, France, and their
Indian allies. As the Commissioners made their way north they were joined
unexpectedly by Schuyler, and together they sailed along Lake George, breaking through pieces and blocks of ice at the northern end, where they entered
narrows that led to Lake Champlain. They crossed the portage between Lake
George and Lake Champlain and made their way to Fort Ticonderoga, which
was in a "ruinous condition." "In the present state of affairs," Charles Carroll
wrote, "this fort is of no other use than as entrepôt or magazine for stores, for
from this place all supplies for our army in Canada are shipped to go down
Lake Champlain." Having stayed at Ticonderoga "about an hour or two" the
party "embarked at 11 o'clock and reached Crown Point a little after 3 with
the help of our oars only." This fort, some 15 miles above Ticonderoga, was "in
ruins; it was once a considerable fortress, and the English must have expended
a large sum in constructing the fort and erecting the barracks, which are also
in ruins."[8] Leaving Crown Point the next day, April 24, the party sailed down
Lake Ticonderoga to St. Johns. Having reached St. Johns on April 27, the

Commissioners made their way to Montreal, which they reached on April 29. They were received at Montreal

> . . . by General [Benedict] Arnold on our landing in the most polite and friendly manner, conducted to headquarters where a genteel company of ladies and gentlemen was assembled to welcome our arrival. As we went from the landing place to the General's house, the cannon of the citadel fired in compliment to us as the Commissioners of Congress. We supped at the General's, and after supper were conducted by the General and other gentlemen to our lodgings, the house of Mr. Thomas Walker, the best built and perhaps the best furnished in this town.[9]

Everywhere the Commissioners went they were welcomed by dignitaries, elite hosts who lavished on them their finest hospitality.

The trip had been arduous, but the Commissioners had reached their destination without major incident, and they were now ready to achieve their goal: arriving at an agreement with Canadians that would bring them into the war against Britain. The goal, never more than a fantasy, soon had a major reality check. The elite Canadians who welcomed the Commissioners were English; they were not French Canadians and were in fact despised by French Canadians. Problems piled up rapidly. The Commissioners wrote Congress on May 8, describing the difficulties they faced; they were in desperate need of money to purchase urgently needed provisions and to repay creditors who had been promised repayment on outstanding loans. "Our Enemies take the advantage of this Distress, to make Us look contemptible in the Eyes of the Canadians. . . ."[10] By the time of the Commissioners arrival in Montreal the American army outside Quebec was on the verge of collapse. General John Thomas had left Schuyler and the Commissioners at Saratoga on April 11 and made his way to Quebec, where he took command of an American army that was depleted by sickness, hunger, and the effects of a long and debilitating winter. To make matters worse, much worse, the first British ships arrived in the Saint Lawrence on May 5, part of a fleet that conveyed some 13,000 men to Quebec under the command of General John Burgoyne. The British army drove out the Americans as if they were the last autumn leaves swept away before a severe winter storm. The Commissioners in Montreal received news of a British attack on May 6 that "so dispersed" the American forces that "not more than two hundred could be collected at Head Quarters. In this situation a retreat was inevitable and made in the utmost precipitation and confusion with the loss of our cannon on the batteries, provisions, five hundred stand of small Arms, and a batteau load of powder. . . ." So hopeless was the situation, the Commissioners explained in their May 10 report to Congress, that reinforcements would "only increase our distress."[11]

The Commissioners were unable to enter into serious negotiations with the Canadians and became apprehensive over their hosts, Mr. and Mrs. Thomas Walker. Under these circumstances the commissioners wrote Philip Schuyler on May 11, asking him to show "every civility in your power and facilitate [Mrs. Walker] on her way to Philadelphia; the fear of cruel treatment from the enemy on account of the strong attachment to, and zeal of her husband in the cause of the united Colonies induces her to depart precipitately from her home; and to undergo the fatigues of a long and hazardous journey."[12] Charles Carroll and Samuel Chase remained almost an additional three weeks in Canada, trying against all odds to hold the scattered American forces together, but realizing that the case was hopeless they left Montreal on May 29, two days after sending Congress a detailed report of utter and complete disarray along the Canadian front.[13] In a postscript to the report the Commissioners wrote that "General Arnold arrived on Sunday evening with the troops at St. Ann's, just in time to see the savages carrying off from an island the last load of our unhappy prisoners; we had no boats to follow them." Conditions could hardly have been bleaker as Charles Carroll and Samuel Chase departed from Montreal and made their way back to New York, meeting with Philip Schuyler along the way at Skenesboro (Whitehall). Charles Carroll noted in his *Journal* on June 6 that he "Parted with Gen. Schuyler this morning. He returned to Fort George on Lake George. We rode to Saratoga, where we got by 7 o'clock but did not find the amiable family at home." He wrote on the next day that "Our servants and baggage being come up, we left Saratoga this morning at 9. Took boat and went down Hudson's River thro' all the rapids to Albany. . . ."[14] He arose early the next day and set sail for New York, which he reached on June 9. He met with Washington that afternoon at his headquarters at Richmond Hill in upper Manhattan, along with Horatio Gates and other members of the American high command. The Commissioners' trip to Canada had been a complete fiasco.

Benjamin Franklin had not remained with his two colleagues throughout the increasingly difficult Canada expedition, as Charles Carroll noted in his Journal on May 11. "Doctor Franklin left Montreal this day to go to St. Johns and from thence to Congress. The doctor's declining state of health and the bad prospect of our affairs in Canada made him take this resolution."[15] At age 70 the trip had been arduous for Franklin from the beginning. He wrote his filend Josiah Quincy, Sr. from Saratoga on April 15, early in the expedition to Canada, that "I have undertaken a Fatigue that at my Time of Life may prove too much for me, so I sit down to write a few friends of Farewell."[16] Franklin suffered from swelling of the legs and from boils while in Montreal, and by the time of his departure the failure of the mission was all too clear. He had done everything possible to further the mission, even advancing £333 from his own purse to assuage creditors in Montreal. When he left Canada on May 11 the roof was falling in militarily, and the day after he departed Father John Carroll also left. Franklin wrote Schuyler from St. Johns on May 12, explaining that without provisions the American "Army must starve, plunder, or surrender."[17] Franklin arrived in New York on May 26 and wrote Philip Schuyler a letter the next day, thanking him for the kind assistance of Mrs. Schuyler and her servant Lewis when he arrived in Albany.

> We arrived here safe [in New York] yesterday Evening, in your Post Chaise driven by Lewis. I was unwilling to give so much Trouble, and would have borrowed your Sulkey, and driven myself: but good Mrs. Schuyler insisted on a full Compliance with your Pleasure, as signify'd in your Letter, and I was oblig'd to submit; which I was afterwards very glad of, part of the Road being very Stoney and much gullied, where I should probably have overset and broke my own Bones, all the Skill and Dexterity of Lewis being no more than sufficient. Thro' the Influence of your kind Recommendation to the Innkeepers on the Road, we found a great Readiness to supply us with Change of Horses. Accept our Thankful Acknowledgements; they are all the Return we can at present make."[18]

Having reached New York, Franklin proceeded to Philadelphia to meet with Congress, which put him on a committee that was to write the Declaration of Independence. In September Admiral Sir Richard Howe requested a meeting with Americans to see if it was possible at this late date to work out a political settlement, hoping no doubt that the crushing British victory over Washington's army on Long Island on August 27 would have weakened the will of the Americans. Congress appointed Franklin to the contingent that met with Howe, whom he had known and been friendly with in England when he represented several American colonies, but the point of no return had been reached and the conversations on Staten Island on September 11 went nowhere. Once a proud champion of a British Empire that emerged victorious over France in the French and Indian War, Franklin was now poised to play an important role in securing France's support of America in the war against Britain. Having been appointed one of three commissioners to France, Franklin left Philadelphia on October 2, 1776 and reached Paris on December 21; his charge was to do everything possible to bring France into the war against Britain. By the time he received news of the American victory at Saratoga on December 4, 1777, he had ingratiated favor with Vergennes, the French foreign minister, who wanted to join the war against Britain but awaited a positive signal from across the Atlantic. As it happened, the American victory that conveyed that signal—the Battle of Saratoga—had been achieved on ground that Franklin had traversed when he had traveled to Canada in 1776. This battle was fought just below the estate of Philip Schuyler, whose hospitality Franklin had enjoyed as he made his way to Canada; the same person, Benjamin Franklin, who had headed the failed Canada Commission in 1776, entered into negotiations with Vergennes after the American victory at Saratoga that brought France into the American war against Britain.

Franklin had been to France twice before he arrived as American Ambassador at the end of 1776; he had been there in 1767 and 1769, when he was feted as the ingenious American who had made such interesting and important scientific discoveries. Soon after arriving in Paris in 1767 he wrote his London landlady's daughter, Polly Stevenson, that he was becoming a Frenchman.

> I had not been here Six Days before my Taylor and Peruquier had transform'd me into a Frenchman. Only think what a Figure I make in a little Bag Wig and naked Ears! They told me I was become 20 Years younger, and look'd very galante; so being in Paris where the Mode is to be sacredly follow'd, I was once very near making Love to my Friend's Wife.[19]

Franklin's nine years in Paris between 1776 and 1785 were among the happiest of his life. Having been elected to the Royal Academy of Science as a foreign associate in 1772, he was known for his scientific discoveries and for the experiments he conducted amidst great public acclaim. Moreover, his social skills were finely attuned to the sophisticated, elite world in which he moved while in France. He had an innate reserve and an impeccable sense of timing, knowing just when to drop the right bon mot when conversing in the select social circles that welcomed him. Having broken from his early Puritan background and embarked on a life of worldly success and worldly pleasure, Franklin was on the same wavelength as members of the French elite whose company he enjoyed. In this, he was the very opposite of fellow American John Adams, who found pliable Parisian manners irregular and offensive.

Elite Parisian manners were far from strict. A novel written by an army officer who had close ties to the court and was part of Marie Antoinette's select circle at Versailles, Pierre Victor, Baron de Besenval's *La Spleen* (1777, published at the very time of Franklin's arrival in France), portrayed married life within the aristocratic elite. The husband and wife in this novel enjoyed one another briefly after they were married but fleeting pleasures were soon followed by indifference. Understanding this, the husband rationalized his thoughts on marriage: "This sentiment [love between husband and wife], source of true love, is no longer supported by our manners; it constrains liberty, the charm of the society of our time."[20] Having come to see marriage as a mere convenience, the husband discovered that his wife had arrived at a similar point of view; when he returned home unexpectedly from military duty his wife had invited friends to spend the evening with her, including her lover. Recognizing how the ground lay, the husband accepted the arrangements his wife had made; no questions were asked; relations remained courteous; both parties were free to select lovers as they saw fit. And so it was amongst elite Parisians in whose circles Franklin moved during his nine years in Paris. Living at Passy, between Paris and Versailles, Franklin spent much time with ladies in nearby châteaux, often exchanging declarations of love with married women to whom he was clearly attracted, as they were to him. He was particularly taken by one of the women he was close to in these years, Anne-Catherine de Ligniville d' Autricourt Helvétius, widow of Claude-Adrien Helvétius, an advanced thinker whose major work, *De l'Esprit* (1758), marked a sharp departure from conventional morality and openly espoused a philosophy of hedonism. A beauty at age 60 when Franklin met Mmc. Helvetius, he proposed marriage to her repeatedly, an offer that was made with proper levity and was not accepted. Franklin had never been happier than he was in France and sometimes thought he would like to remain there. He wrote in 1784 that

> I am here among a People that love and respect me, a most sensible Nation to live with, and perhaps I may conclude to die among them; for my Friends are dying off one after another, and I have been so long abroad that I should now be almost a Stranger in my own Country.[21]

At the same time that Franklin was blending into the world of elite Paris society and becoming increasingly French in feeling and identity, he was, paradoxically, becoming more American. Franklin played a clever and pragmatically effective role as a plain American during his years in Paris, a virtuous primitive who bedecked himself in ordinary, homespun attire. No fancy hats, no embellishments, no sword for this diplomat, just a plain jacket, trousers, and white shirt, topped by a marten-fur hat. As one Parisian observed, "Everything about him announces the simplicity and innocence of primitive morals . . . The people clustered around as he passed and asked: 'Who is this old peasant who has such a noble air?' "[22] If this was a disguise, it nonetheless brought Franklin into contact with an earlier identity, that of the American he had once been: apprentice, worker, printer, someone who began at the bottom of the social ladder. The disguises were not just disguises; at one level the assumed persona *was* Franklin. Having played the role of an American in France, Franklin felt American; perhaps it was time for him to return to America. By the time of his departure in 1785 he had completed his work in France; he had helped win France over to the American cause and he had played the leading role in negotiating terms for the 1783 Treaty of Paris that ended the American Revolution. While carrying out these negotiations Franklin entered into secret negotiations with Britain in order to work out the best possible terms for America, in spite of an understanding with France that he would not do so. His diplomacy had served America well; he had done everything possible for his country; he was tired, and if he were to see America again it would have to be soon. He was

79 when he returned to an America that was plunged into uncertainty and internal conflict. When the Constitutional Convention met in Philadelphia in 1787 Benjamin Franklin was there, a capstone event in his support of the American Revolution.

Horatio Gates arrived in Albany on June 26, 1776 to meet with Philip Schuyler, a month after Franklin returned to New York in the aftermath of the failed Canada expedition. Gates had been placed in command of the battered American army "in Canada" after Samuel Chase guaranteed him that his power would be that of "a Roman dictator." When Gates showed his orders to Schuyler the two men quarreled bitterly over who commanded the Northern Army; both appealed to Congress for clarification; and, as we have seen, Congress ruled in Schuyler's favor. We need not retell the story of conflict between the two generals, or of Gates' victory at Saratoga, but we can follow Gates' path after Saratoga, not in close detail, but briefly. Gates' path to Saratoga had been difficult and presented many obstacles, which he managed to surmount; his path after he achieved a pinnacle of success at Saratoga was less than heroic. Congress rewarded Gates for his victory at Saratoga, naming him head of the Board of War, but he aspired to even greater authority and power. Swollen with pride and more ambitious than ever, Gates tried to undermine Washington's position as Commander of the Continental Army, hoping to assume that position himself. He was drawn into the Conway Cabal, which was not a conspiracy in the strict sense of the word, but a sustained effort by factions in the army and Congress to take advantage of Washington's weakened position after he had been pummeled at Brandywine while Gates garnered victory laurels at Saratoga.[23]

Aware that invidious comparisons were being made between himself and Gates, Washington explained in a letter to Patrick Henry that conditions at Saratoga and Brandywine had been very different, favoring Gates and placing him at a disadvantage. To assume from the outcomes of the two battles that Gates was the superior officer, Washington maintained, was mistaken. That Washington felt obliged to defend himself to fellow Virginian Patrick Henry shows that he was aware of his vulnerability, and of efforts to undercut his position. Among those in Congress who were working against Washington was John Adams, still a supporter of Horatio Gates. Also conniving against Washington was Benjamin Rush, whose backstabbing Washington discovered to his considerable dismay. Thomas Conway, an Irishman who became an army officer in France before coming to America, and after whom the Cabal was named, ended up having a duel with a fellow intriguer in May 1778. By this time efforts to remove Washington from the command of the Continental Army had failed, and Gates, unable to achieve his goal, spent parts of 1779 at his estate in Virginia. His military role had not ended however; in 1780 the British strategy had changed, with the South as the main theater of war. When Congress learned that Henry Clinton had taken Charleston in January 1780, it placed Gates in command of the Army of the Southern Department, against Washington's wishes. Having received news of the appointment on May 7, 1780, Gates moved from Virginia to the Carolinas, where he made ready for a showdown with a British army under Cornwallis' command. The American and British armies blundered into one another at Camden, South Carolina on August 15, after Gates had marched a fatigued and hungry army through swampy country, leaving it weakened by the time of the battle on the following day. Gates placed militiamen who were eager to fight but untrained in formal warfare on his left flank, opposite well-drilled, proven English units under the command of Banastre Tarleton, known for unrelenting cruelty toward Americans, particularly after they were defeated. As British redcoats unleashed deadly volleys and advanced with lowered bayonets they spread panic among the Americans, whose flight soon turned into a general rout. Americans who fled from the chaos of the battlefield were overtaken by their commanding general, Horatio Gates, who rode an impressive 170 miles in three days, leaving his men to fend for themselves. Gates was never placed in field command again. His path after Saratoga was serpentine, covered with pitfalls of his own making, ending in defeat and ignominy at Camden in June 1780. Horatio Gates died in 1806, having returned to Virginia after the Revolution but moving to New York at the urging of John Adams. He lived in the upper part of Manhattan and served a term in the New York legislature. By the time of his death Gates had alienated some of his closest friends, including John Adams, who had championed his cause before the Battle of Saratoga, which brought him fame and glory that was to prove short-lived.

Another battle was fought in South Carolina five months after Camden, with a strikingly different outcome. Frustrated after being passed over for promotion by Congress and not in good health, Daniel Morgan had retired to his farm in Virginia in June 1779, but after the disaster at Camden he decided to participate in the Southern campaign, putting his personal feelings aside. He was placed in command of an army that marched deep into the southern back-country, pursued by Banastre Tarleton, who issued orders to push Morgan "to the utmost," "anywhere he is within your reach." Tarleton finally caught up with Morgan on January 17, 1781 at Cowpens, a field where cattle were brought for sale. It was here that Morgan won a stunning victory over a British army that appeared to have every advantage. Morgan met with his men the night before the battle, joking with them and showing them the lash marks on his back, inflicted years earlier by the British. The "Old Waggoner" would use his whip on "Benny" the next day; he and his men, fellow backwoodsmen, would teach these Brits a lesson or two: "Just hold up your heads, boys, give them three fires, and you will be free. . . . Then when you return to your homes, how the old folks will bless you and the girls will kiss you."[24] Morgan's strategy was to set a trap by lining his men up as Gates had done with his men at Camden, placing militia units along his left flank, directly opposite highly-trained British units. They were to wait for the advancing British units to come close enough to fire at them accurately, but just two rounds; they were then to pull back, leading the British to think that they had panicked and were in flight. The British took the bait and rushed forward up a hill, behind which Morgan had stationed units that suddenly appeared with loaded rifles that poured volleys of deadly fire into the British, including officers on horseback. This time it was the British who were in disarray; this time it was they who left the battlefield, resulting in an American victory, one of the most unexpected and stunning of the entire American Revolution. As at Saratoga, Daniel Morgan's rapport with his men, fellow backwoodsmen, ordinary Americans, was one of the keys to victory at the Battle of Cowpens.

Gouverneur Morris (1752–1816), a downstate New Yorker of important family, formidable intelligence, and imposing size—at six feet, three inches he was the same size as George Washington—arrived in Albany on July 14, 1777, having been sent up the Hudson by the Committee of Safety of the New York Provincial Congress, of which he was a member. Morris's family had been torn asunder by the Revolution. His mother, a staunch loyalist, turned the family estate in Westchester over to the British for military use after the British victory at the Battle of Long Island in August 1776, but he sided with the Patriot cause from the beginning, in spite of his aristocratic outlook and mindset. His position was not unlike that of George Washington and Philip Schuyler, both aristocrats who had to make difficult decisions when push came to shove over issues that were beyond resolution between Mother Country and the colonies. Morris's half-brother served as an officer in the British army during the Revolution; he represented the family estate in an extralegal body, the New York Provincial Congress, organized by Patriots in 1775. He attended King's College (later Columbia University) from age 12 to the time of his graduation at age 16, and subsequently became a lawyer. Morris had the ability to conceptualize problems and understand complex issues; clever with words, not hesitant to speak out and sometimes outspoken, his long and distinguished political career is now seen, at least by some historians, as one that rightly places him among America's Founding Fathers, a measure of respect that he has not generally received. He was one of the principal authors of the 1777 New York State Constitution, and he held the pen that wrote the American Constitution in Philadelphia in 1787. He arrived in Paris at the beginning of the French Revolution, and was American Ambassador in France from 1792–1794. No other American experienced the two great revolutions of the Age of Democratic Revolution, the American and French Revolutions, as directly as he did. Moreover, as we shall see, his personal life was as varied and complicated as his public life, with unexpected twists and turns at various bends of the road

When news of Burgoyne's capture of Fort Ticonderoga reached Kingston, where the New York Provincial Congress met, it threw its members into high panic. Desperate to stop Burgoyne's march to Albany, the Committee of Safety of the New York Congress sent Morris to meet with Philip Schuyler, commander of the Army of the Northern Department, to gather such information as he could, and to relay it back to Kingston. Upon arriving in Albany on July 14 as he made his way toward Schuyler's headquarters at Fort Edward, Morris stopped to write a letter to the president of the Committee of Safety, in which he discussed rumors he had heard of "disasters" in the north and "depredations" in the west. His next letter was from Fort Edward. Having talked with Schuyler, Morris reported that "the state of our affairs . . . are far from being such as could be wished." There were but 2,600 continental troops and 1,000 militia, no match for Burgoyne's army, reported as 10,000 in number. "If the enemy would follow, I know not when we should stop, as matters now stand. We have only two old iron field pieces . . . [and] can get no more . . . Fort Anne is abandoned, and Fort George will be so by tomorrow. . . ." Morris wrote the Committee of Safety from Saratoga the next day, reporting the destruction of Fort George by the Americans and the removal of all supplies. Things were so desperate that the Americans would have to "break up all the settlements upon our northern frontier . . . drive off the cattle, secure or destroy the forage, and . . . destroy all sawmills. These measures, harsh as they may seem, are . . . absolutely necessary."[25] Morris' next letter, written the following day, said that an American unit had just been attacked by "savages and British troops" and suffered heavy losses, with 12 killed and one man scalped.[26] When Morris returned to Kingston he requested—and received—permission to travel to Washington's headquarters, in order that he could explain that Schuyler needed reinforcements if he were to stop Burgoyne's march to Albany. Washington explained to Morris that he was unable to send men to Schuyler; he had to maintain contact with a British army under William Howe that was considerably larger than Burgoyne's army—with which, as it turned out, he would soon do battle. Morris rushed to Philadelphia, hoping to secure help from Congress for the Northern army, but he arrived after Congress had replaced Schuyler with Gates. When he returned to Kingston Morris wrote Schuyler, explaining that he was "exceedingly distressed" over Gates' appointment, and that while he regarded Gates as a friend he regretted that he was "acquiring honor . . . at your expense."[27] He also explained to Schuyler that Congress' decision was understandable, for "eastern folks" would not "march while [he] had the command." Schuyler wrote back to Morris, thanking him "for sympathizing with me . . . My crime consists in not being a New England man in principle . . . General Gates is their man."

Morris was elected to Congress and traveled to Valley Forge in January 1778 to gather information on Washington's army, which was at low ebb after the reversals of the previous campaign. He was shocked by what he saw, and convinced that serious measures were needed to strengthen Washington's army. He felt that as long as the army was dependent on funding by the separate states it would not have adequate support; only if Congress provided funding would the army rest on a sound fiscal base. This conclusion made Morris the advocate of strong national government, a position that he would retain through the vicissitudes of coming years, to the end of the Revolution and beyond. Articulate and by no means reluctant to speak out on issues under debate, Morris spoke frequently in Congress, often irritating others. He was not re-elected to Congress in 1779, to his relief; he had grown weary of debates that seemed to him to go nowhere. Leaving Congress, Morris gave himself over to the company of women, which he enjoyed unabashedly. He also established a legal practice and pursued his own private interests with no small measure of success, thanks to astute speculations in real estate and whatever other opportunities for profit presented themselves. Morris's acumen brought him to the attention of Robert Morris, the leading financier in America (they were not related to one another), whose assistant he became. The two Morrises met with the French Minister La Luzerne and General Rochambeau in August 1781, a most propitious moment militarily; news had arrived that a French fleet was on its way to Chesapeake Bay, setting the stage for the Battle of Yorktown. For this operation to succeed American and French armies had to move south; the problem was that one of Washington's armies under Benjamin Lincoln threatened to abandon the march to Yorktown unless they received a month's back pay. The French had 20,000 dollars in hard currency that they were prepared to turn over to the Americans, but for that to happen it was necessary to find a French official and to secure his approval to release the funds. To do this Robert and Gouverneur Morris rode off posthaste to seek out the French officer whose signature was needed. The two men must have made for a strange spectacle; Robert Morris was middle-aged and fat, and Gouverneur Morris, who had suffered an accident in Philadelphia in the previous year, had but one leg. According to one version of the accident, a carriage ran over and injured Morris's leg; in a different version, Morris injured his leg jumping from a window to escape a husband with whose wife he was having a tryst. When the doctor who attended to Morris told him he would have to amputate the leg below the knee a friend told him that loss of his leg would help him to build character; making light of the incident, Morris replied that he was "almost tempted to part with the other."[28]

Gouverneur Morris resigned as Robert Morris's assistant in 1784, and in the next several years he tended to his own affairs, with considerable success. To his surprise he was elected by the Pennsylvania Assembly to sit in the Constitutional Convention in 1787 as one of its three delegates (he received barely enough votes, the least of the three delegates). As a delegate to the Constitutional Convention Morris spoke 173 times, more than any other member. He sat on a committee of five that that prepared a draft of the proposed Constitution;

it was he who held the pen that wrote the Constitution and provided some of its finished language. His considerable social and verbal skills helped resolve differences between delegates who were often deeply divided; having helped write the New York Constitution in 1776, he advanced some of the same core ideas in Philadelphia 11 years later: religious liberty, respect for the rule of law, opposition to slavery, and the consent of the governed as the basis of political authority. After the Constitutional Convention ended, Morris went to Virginia to sort out Robert Morris' accounts with tobacco planters. Robert Morris had a tobacco monopoly in France, and owing to the vagaries of the market he was overextended. Under these circumstances he turned to Gouverneur Morris, not only to sort out matters in Virginia but to do so in France. Morris sailed from Philadelphia for France in December 1788 and arrived in Paris in February 1789. While in France he carried out negotiations pertaining to Robert Morris's tobacco monopoly and in the servicing of America's war debt, in which Robert Morris had an interest. Gouverneur Morris would be in Paris for the next five years, a period that coincided almost exactly with the French Revolution. His *Diary*, which he began soon after he arrived in Paris, is a remarkable record of his experiences in Paris during the French Revolution.

Among those Morris saw after he arrived in Paris was Thomas Jefferson, the American Minister since 1784. He wrote in his *Diary* on May 5 that Jefferson was "very civil but the English of it seems to be that he had already more Trouble than he desires with Strangers. We shall see."[29] Morris found Jefferson reserved but he continued to see him regularly in coming weeks and months, up to the time of Jefferson's return to America in October 1789. Gregarious, sociable, inquisitive, and fluent in French, Morris sought out people in high position, including the Marquis de Lafayette, whom he had known in America, and others who were to play various roles in the French Revolution: Necker, Castries, Condorcet, Talleyrand, Clermont-Ferrand, Besenval, Lavoisier, La Rochefoucauld, Malesherbes, and a Spanish beauty, Mme Cabarrus, not a major actor on the Revolutionary stage but a woman who moved easily in liberal elite circles that supported reform and were caught up in the revolutionary dynamic. To follow Morris's visits on a given day is to be constantly on the move, going from one place to another, sometimes just in Paris, sometimes at Versailles. He must have been a strange spectacle, an American with a wooden leg and six feet three in height, particularly when seen with fellow American Thomas Jefferson, almost as tall as he. Sometimes Morris visited Jefferson at his fine residence, the Hôtel de Langeac, on the fashionable Champs Elysées, west of his lodgings on the rue de Richelieu; sometimes he met Jefferson at elite gatherings that they both frequented. Moving in politically alert circles, Morris and his friends and acquaintances exchanged views constantly on the dramatic events that were unfolding in Paris in the weeks and months before the summoning of the Estates General on May 5. He observed the life of Paris, the social interaction, the social contrasts, the brutality, and the injustice, as on March 4 when he saw a noble riding through a dimly-lit Paris street in a coach run into a horse and then berate the owner of the animal he had killed. Morris wrote a sardonic poem about the episode that ended with the noble saying: "Had I supposed a Horse lay there I would have taken better Care, But by St. Jacques [I thought] t'was nothing but a Man."[30]

Morris was keenly aware of the emerging crisis in Paris. He wrote on April 18 that

> A Man in Paris lives in a Sort of Whirlwind which turns him round so fast he can see nothing . . . The Ministers have disgusted this City by the Manner of convoking them to elect their Representatives for the States General, and at the same Time Bread is getting dearer . . . with Hunger and Discontent the least Spark would set every Thing in a Flame.[31]

He wrote in his *Diary* two days later that

> The Court is so extremely feeble and the Manners are so extremely corrupt that they cannot succeed if there be any consistent Opposition, unless the whole Nation be equally depraved. The Probability I think is that an Attempt to retreat at this late Period of the Business will bring the Court into absolute Contempt.[32]

Morris met with Jefferson at the Hôtel de Langeac on April 22, where Lafayette joined them. Concerned over the mounting pressures in Paris, Morris offered advice to Lafayette, recommending that the Estates General, soon to assemble at Versailles, remove Swiss Guards "from about the King's Person," and that they make "a Compliment . . . to the National Troops. Mr. Jefferson does not seem to think this important, but I urge it to the Conviction of Lafayette."[33] Morris had dinner two days later with the Baron de Besenval, the worldly commander of troops responsible for maintaining order in an increasingly volatile Paris. This was the same Besenval who wrote a novel in 1777, *La Spleen*, in which he depicted the civilized arrangements among aristocratic husbands and wives, a fictional depiction of his own way of life. Morris described the dinner conversation at Besenval's: "We hear a great Deal about the Disturbances for want of Bread. These give Pleasure to the Company here, who are all averse to the present Administration." The people at Besenval's evening hoped for bread riots that they reckoned would drive Necker, a liberal minister, from office, and bring in a more conservative ministry. Morris did "not believe in a Change just now."[34] He hoped the pending crisis could be averted. When a riot erupted three days later, on April 27, it was Besenval who quelled it. The Réveillon riot broke out in the faubourg Saint-Antoine when workers at a wallpaper factory protested a cut in wages. Besenval moved two cannon into place, persuading the crowd to disperse, leading him to feel that he was able to subdue a riotous people. Order was restored only after the furious crowd went on a rampage, burning Réveillon's house and factory, a portent of things to come.

The fashionable, urbane Besenval, who moved easily at court and had been close to Marie Antoinette, was hardly the best person to maintain order in Paris as pressures were mounting that culminated in the insurrection of July 12–14, triggered by the King's dismissal of Jacques Necker, a favorite of the people. When a crowd clashed with Swiss Guards in the finest public square in Paris, the Place Louis XV (now the Place de la Concorde), Besenval sent in additional units, but they encountered unexpectedly strong resistance, forcing Besenval to make a difficult decision. Rather than order his men to fire on the people he had them withdraw to Saint-Cloud, west of Paris, leaving the city in the hands of the people. Gouverneur Morris's residence on the rue de Richelieu

Figure 23. Jean-Louis Prieur, *The Busts of the duc d'Orléans and Necker are carried in Triumph and broken in the Place Louis XV*, July 12, 1789. Both Gouverneur Morris and Thomas Jefferson witnessed this episode, which triggered the Paris Insurrection of 12–14 July 1789. What happened during this three-day period transformed the French Revolution. Up to this point the Revolution had been centered at Versailles and was carried out by elite deputies; the people carried out a very different revolution in Paris, which culminated in the Storming of the Bastille on July 14.

was a short distance from the Place Louis XV. When told of Necker's dismissal he was "much affected," fearing that the danger was "infinitely greater than [the King] imagines." He visited several friends, whom he found apprehensive, and then made his way toward the Hôtel de Langeac, to discuss the crisis with Jefferson. As he moved along the rue St. Honoré he encountered utter confusion, with carriages and people on foot heading in all directions. Passing alongside the Place Louis XV he heard people shouting and observed Swiss Guards arriving to confront a furious crowd; he witnessed a scene of pandemonium and violence, the first of the Paris Insurrection.

> When we come to the Place Louis Quinze [we] observe the People . . . picking up Stones . . . the Cavalry cannot act . . . One of the Soldiers is either knocked from his Horse or the Horse falls under him. He is taken Prisoner and at first ill treated. They had fired several Pistols . . . A Part of the Swiss Guards are posted at the Champs Elisées with Cannon. Proceed to Mr. Jefferson's.[35]

Having arrived at the Hôtel de Langeac, situated beyond the Place Louis XV, he and Jefferson discussed what both witnessed on this tumultuous day; Jefferson had also seen the people clashing with armed cavalry in the Place Louis XV. The clash between the people of Paris and Swiss Guards that Gouverneur Morris and Thomas Jefferson observed triggered a three-day uprising that culminated in the Storming of the Bastille. The Paris insurrection of July 12–14 transformed the French Revolution. Elected deputies at Versailles had carried out the first, constitutional stage of the Revolution at the Palace of Versailles; the people carried out the second stage, saving the Revolution but also casting it in a new mold. As news of the Paris Insurrection spread through France uprisings broke out in towns and cities across the nation, along with a massive peasant revolt, the Great Fear, which brought down an agrarian order that went back to feudal times. By the time the dust settled in early October France was no longer the same; the people had taken matters into their own hands. The key event in the popular revolution, politically and symbolically, was the Fall of the Bastille, achieved by workers from faubourgs in the eastern part of the capital, whose seizure of a hated fortress on the afternoon of July 14 brought the Paris Insurrection to a bloody but triumphant end.

Recognizing the importance of the Fall of the Bastille, Gouverneur Morris wanted to see the historic site, but to go through the battered fortress, whose demolition was soon to begin, he needed to receive a pass. He sought out his friend Lafayette, now commander of the National Guard, from whom he received the pass, and on July 21 Morris went through the Bastille, which he saw only with difficulty, owing to disarray everywhere. "The storming of the Castle was a bold enterprise," he concluded, but the ancient fortress "stinks horribly."[36] The hatreds that fed into the Paris Insurrection had not ended, as Morris was soon to discover. On July 22, the day after he visited the Bastille, he had dinner at the Palais Royal, and was awaiting his carriage afterward, taking a "walk under the Arcade," when a strange spectacle unfolded before him.

> The Head and Body of Mr. de Foulon are introduced in Triumph. The Head on a Pike, the Body dragged naked on the Earth. Afterwards this horrible Exhibition is carried thro the different Streets. His crime is to have accepted a Place in the Ministry. This mutilated Form of an old Man of seventy five is shown to Bertier, his Son in Law, the Intdt. of Paris, and afterwards he also is put to Death, and cut to Pieces, the Populace carrying about the mangled Fragments with a Savage Joy. Gracious God what a People.[37]

Francois Foulon de Doué was a wealthy grain merchant who had been appointed to a conservative ministry on July 11 when Louis XVI dismissed Necker, a decision that precipitated the Paris Insurrection that broke out the next day. Louis-Jean Bertier de Sauvigny was the Intendant of Paris, and as Morris indicated, the son-in-law of Foulon. Both men had good reason to feel uneasy when the Paris Insurrection erupted on July 12. Foulon was thought to have said during a famine years earlier, in 1775, that if the people were hungry they could eat hay, as his animals did; long-simmering hatred of Foulon reached a new level when he was appointed to a reactionary ministry by the king on July 11. Hatred of Foulon's son-in-law, Bertier, was tied to his efforts as a reforming official to address the problems of chronic unemployment, vagrancy, and crime in Paris. By removing people from the street and teaching them practical skills in workhouses that he organized they could become productive members of society, but to do this coercion was necessary, which stirred resentment amongst the people. Aware of popular hostility, Foulon and Bertier de Sauvigny fled Paris on July 12 and went into hiding. Both were recognized on July 22 and taken forcibly to Paris, first Foulon and then Bertier; both were taken to the Hôtel de Ville, where angry crowds that received news of their capture awaited their arrival.

Foulon was the first to feel the wrath of the people, and to receive the justice they dispensed on that fateful day. Officials took him inside the Hotel de Ville, hoping to protect him from an angry crowd, but the people seized Foulon and dragged him outside and hung him from a lamppost in the adjacent Place de Grève. The crowd severed Foulon's head from the dead body, stuffed hay in the mouth—a sardonic reminder of his supposed earlier comment that the people could eat hay if they were hungry—and stuck it on a pike. A triumphant crowd then proceeded up the Rue St. Martin, brandishing the head of Foulon on a pike and dragging the body through the street. Bizarrely, as the crowd moved up the Rue St. Martin it encountered another crowd heading in the opposite direction, taking Foulon's son-in-law, Bertier de Sauvigny, to the Hôtel de Ville. As the two processions encountered one another, and Bertier

Figure 24. Jean-Louis Prieur, *The Intendant Bertier de Sauvigny, led to the Hôtel de Ville, recognizes the Head of Foulon*, July 22, 1789. This image is on the cover of my last book, published by SUNY Press. More than any other image, it helped me to understand the pent-up hatreds that fed into the French Revolution. Class anger, rooted in French history, drove the French Revolution in a very different direction than that taken by the American Revolution. I was thunderstruck when I learned that Gouverneur Morris heard of this event as he was awaiting his carriage at the Palais Royal.

Figure 25. The church of St. Merry on the rue St. Martin. This is the church that Prieur depicts in his tableau, *The Intendant Bertier de Sauvigny*, seen in the previous illustration. I took this photograph in June 1998 when Anne Roberts and I walked up the rue St. Martin after visiting the Place de Grève, where both Foulon and Bertier were lynched and decapitated. Anne can be seen in the right-hand side of this photograph.

saw the head of his father-in-law stuck on a pike with straw stuffed in the mouth, a crowd chanted the refrain, "Kiss Papa!," "Kiss Papa!," a vivid example of the gallows humor of the people. The crowd took Bertier to the Hôtel de Ville, hung him from a lamppost, decapitated him, ripped his heart from the eviscerated body, and stuck both the head and heart on pikes. Again a crowd passed through the streets of Paris brandishing its trophies, the head and heart of Bertier de Sauvigny, singing the refrain, "A party isn't a party/When the heart isn't in it."[38] Gouverneur Morris's response to this grisly episode—"Gracious God, what a People!"—was that of an American who had experienced revolution in his own country, but that revolution was utterly different than the one that exploded with such anger and fury in Paris in July 1789.

Riots were commonplace in the eighteenth century, in France, Britain, and America. Common rituals unfolded in all three countries when riots broke out; there were similar dynamics whenever anger turned into protest. This was the case in Paris, London, and Boston, to mention three cities in which riots took place, but it was only in Paris that angry mobs lynched and mutilated their enemies.[39] A close observer of the Paris scene, Louis-Sebastien Mercier, commenting on the 1780 Gordon Riots in London, wrote in 1783 that "The sedition led by Lord Gordon in London is unimaginable to Parisians." Mercier felt that that in Paris the forces of order held the people in check: "If the Parisian, in a moment of excitement, were to riot, he would soon find himself inside an immense cage in which he lives, refused bread, and when he no longer had anything to eat he would immediately plead misery and beg to be pardoned." Mercier added, "A riot that would turn into an uprising [in Paris] is morally impossible. The surveillance of the police, regiments of Swiss and French guards, billeted and everywhere ready to march . . . [along with] the King's body-guard [and] fortresses that surround Paris . . . make the chances of a serious revolt most unlikely." Yet, Mercier reflected, if "the people of Paris" were to be "freed of restraint" and "no longer held back by the police . . . they would recognize no measure in their disorder. The populace, released from its accustomed control, would be all the more cruel because they would not know when to stop."[40] Mercier was wrong when he said that a riot that would turn into an uprising was inconceivable in Paris, but he was deadly accurate when he added that if the populace were free to act on their own they would "be all the more cruel because they would not know when to stop." As it happened, an American in Paris, Gouverneur Morris, had a front-row seat as an angry populace settled accounts with their enemies, not only killing them but dismembering them as well.

Keen observer of political life in Paris that he was, Morris did not neglect his private life; from the beginning he made frequent social calls, which he discussed in his *Diary*. In his first *Diary* entry, made on March 1, 1789, he described an afternoon at the theater, after which he attended a supper where he met Mme de La Suze, the mistress of the baron de Besenval. Morris first met the 66-year-old

Besenval a few days later. "I observe all pay a very kind Attention to the Baron de Bezenval, whose grey Hairs designate the Father than the Lover. But it seems he has been remarkably successful in seducing the Sex." Age, it seemed, was no bar to having lovers; it soon became clear to Morris that there were few bars of any type to sexual affairs, at least in the circles in which he moved. From his residence on the rue de Richelieu he was close to the Palais Royal, a protected space in the center of Paris given over to pursuit of pleasure, in whatever form it might take. Built by Cardinal de Richelieu in the first half of the seventeenth century, the Palais Royal was taken over by the Ducs d'Orléans, a branch of the house of Bourbon whose line went back to Louis XIV's younger brother. The current Duc d'Orléans, Philippe, opened up the Palais Royal to the public in 1780, providing entertainments of all type. Prostitutes had free rein; liberty gave way to license; sexual trysts were arranged with ease. Morris frequented the Palais Royal regularly and met a prostitute early on, which did not make him feel particularly pleased with himself. "I walk in the Palais Royal, am picked up and return Home at twelve, the Object of my own Contempt and Aversion."[41] He also met people of stature at the Palais Royal, or who had close ties to it, including the Duchesse d'Orléans, whom he met when visiting Mme. de Chastellux, the widow of a French officer who fought in the American Revolution and whom Morris had known in America. The Marquis de Chastellux, Rochambeau's chief of staff, died in October 1788, four months before Morris' arrival in Paris. Morris thoughtfully looked up his widow, who was lady-in-waiting and confidant of the Duchesse d'Orléans. Mme de Chastellux presided over a circle of friends that were quick to befriend Morris, and to introduce him around. A womanizer of no small proportion, Morris had to feel his way as he made the rounds of circles to which he gained access almost as soon as he arrived in Paris. His reputation for "gallantry" had preceded him; the question was what might his French acquaintances think of him? In America he was considered a rake; how might his civilized friends in Paris regard him? It turned out that Gouverneur Morris fit into the social scene of elite Paris easily; his quick wit, urbane manner, and worldliness made him attractive to his aristocratic acquaintances. He visited people constantly; he was completely in his element. At six feet three in height and with a wooden leg he was an American exotic, as much as Franklin had been in his different way. To be American was fashionable, and Morris, sensing this, took full advantage of his appeal. When he met the widow of the previous Duc d'Orléans, a prince of the blood, on March 21 he felt he made a favorable impression. As she left she said she was "glad to have met me, and I believe her. The Reason is that I dropped some Expressions and Sentiments a little rough and which were agreeable because they contrast with the palling Polish she constantly meets with everywhere."[42]

Like Franklin, Morris was a perfect fit in the salons to which he had access. Typically, females presided over these circles, and typically conversation turned upon politics.[43] Thomas Jefferson found it intrusive for women to concern themselves with politics, an exclusively male domain, but Morris liked to discuss politics with women. He would seem to have found women more interesting, more appealing, *because* they had minds and liked to use them. The discussion of politics had become a central feature of salon life in the last several decades of the eighteenth century and now, as the Estates General were about to be summoned and as Paris was flooded by political pamphlets, salon conversation often turned on politics. The circles in which Morris moved rejected the constraints of the past and espoused the principle of liberty. The call for liberty in enlightened circles in Paris sometimes had double meaning; it applied not only to the public realm, that of politics, but to the private sphere, and to personal relations. The principle of liberty in elite Parisian circles extended to sexual relations, and to marriage; sex and politics were inextricably intertwined in France in the decades before the French Revolution. Beaumarchais' runaway hit, *The Marriage of Figaro*, combined sex and politics in a heady brew that implicitly undercut the established social order. It was in the eighteenth century that feudalism came to mean the antiquated, the tyrannical, the despotic; privileges derived from the feudal past had become so many abuses, anomalous and intolerable. So in *The Marriage of Figaro* the count, who wants to sleep with his wife's servant before she marries, will exercise the *droit de seigneur*, giving him first grabs on the bride. Behind the levity of Beaumarchais' comic masterpiece there was a clear social message. Not that Beaumarchais was a moral censor, a puritanical reformer; far from it. The mocking, satirical, tone of his writing in this play and throughout his *oeuvre* placed him in a cultural milieu that combined the serious with the urbane, ironic, satirical, and playful. Sex and politics were also combined in the scandalously successful novel, *Les Liaisons Dangereuses*, published in 1782 and written by an artillery officer, Choderlos de Laclos, who entered the service of the Duc d'Orléans before the Revolution and was one of his strategists devising schemes to undermine the position of the King and to advance the Orléanist cause. As a protected space, the Palais Royal was a distribution point for subversive literature, some of it pornographic, that undermined monarchy and the court, depicted as a scene of license and depravity. If sex and politics came together anywhere it was at the Palais Royal, right next to where Morris took up residence, and which he frequented regularly in the months before the beginning of the French Revolution.

When Morris looked up the Marquise de Chastellux as soon as he arrived in Paris he found the grieving widow, who was heavily pregnant, "not the less lovely for the Tears she shed."[44] Among those in her circle was Mme Rully, whom Morris met on April 2:

> Visit Madame de Chattelux. Madame Rully, another of the Duchess of Orleans' Women of Honor, comes in and with very fine Eyes which she knows very well how to make Use of seems to say that she has no Antipathy to the gentle Passion. Nous verrons.[45]

The women Morris met were interesting, and they were flirtatious. This included the Duchesse d'Orléans, whose husband's philandering was notorious. Morris wrote on March 25 that "The Duchesse [d'Orléans] is affable, and handsome enough to punish the Duke for his irregularities."[46] "She has perhaps the handsomest arm in France, and from habit takes off her glove and has always occasion to touch some part of her face as to show the hand and arm to advantage."[47] He met her again on March 21 while visiting Mme de Chastellux:

> After being there some Time the Duchess of Orleans enters. We have a Trio for Half an Hour. She has something or other which weighs very heavy at her Heart. Perhaps the Besoin d'etre aimée, that 'painful Void left aching in the Breast.' I make an Apology for her Husband's Wildness . . . She repeats that she is very glad to see me there. This is very kind but I do not really know what it means.[48]

Morris met the Duchesse d'Orléans again ten days later, while visiting Mme de Chastellux:

> A Look from her royal Highness opens the idea that Monsr. Morris est un peu amoreux de Madame la Marquise [Mme de Chastellux], but Madame la Duchesse is mistaken.[49]

Much was suggested by a glance, a furtive look, in a setting such as this. Innuendo was sometimes the key, sometimes badinage; all was fleeting and elusive, difficult to detect, requiring seismic sensitivity to subtle vibrations. But sometimes comments were direct and straight to the point. Philippe, the Comte de Ségur, thought he detected knowing glances between Morris and Mme de Chastellux; his recommendation was that he should "have an Affair with the Widow," as he intended to do himself. When Morris was leaving Mme de Chastellux on April 9 after the other guests had already departed she told him, speaking plainly, that "Mme de Rully is a slut."[50] Behind the innuendo of conversation and the flirtatious glances there were real people with real appetites, which they did not hesitate to indulge.

Morris was at the Palais Royal on March 28 having dinner at one of its several restaurants, that of "Monsr. de la Bretêches . . . [when] presently," as he explained in his *Diary*,

> . . . enters Monsr. de Ségur. Madame de Durfort makes place for him. After Dinner he applies to me on the Subject of Gallantry and I assure him there is nothing of the Kind in America. He seems incredulous but is positive that it could easily be introduced. Next enquiries of my Amours here. I tell him with great Truth I

have none and I am not likely to have any, besides that I dare not hazard offending a virtuous Woman. This as I expected he laughs at and says no Woman is offended at a Thing of the Kind. That it will frequently succeed and can do no Harm if it fails—Rare Morality this; but I believe there are many Instances in this Country to justify it. After a good Deal of this Kind of Talk a striking Instance of the Facility of Manners is presented for my Meditation and Edification.[51]

Ségur told his wife, who on that occasion was with him, that he wanted to show her something and took her to a nearby room and closed the door. Inside, Mme Ségur called after Morris several times, but after a few minutes Ségur emerged, having, "as Sterne says, gratified the Sentiment [and] in a few Minutes takes Leave and steps into his Cabriolet." It would seem that the Vicomte de Ségur, having offered advice to Morris on satisfying one's desire took it upon himself to give him a practical demonstration, showing him how easy it was to carry out.

Ségur was not the only French aristocrat who took an interest in Morris' sex life. His reputation for "gallantry" having preceded him, there was curiosity over how matters might work out for him in Paris. Among those whose interest had been piqued was Adelaide Filleul, Comtesse de Flahaut, a married woman nine years younger than Morris, known to her friends as Adèle. Mme de Flahaut was the daughter of Marie Irene Catherine de Buisson, who is thought to have been one of Louis XV's kept girls at his private brothel, the Parc aux Cerfs. Adèle's mother married Charles-François Filleull after she received a pension for services rendered the king, but her biological father is thought to have been Michael Bouret, a farmer-general who committed suicide; Adèle's mother died when she was six, at which time she was sent to a convent, where she learned English. When she was 18 arrangements were made for her to marry Alexandre-Sébastien, Comte de Flahaut, 35 years older than she. Adèle lived in the Louvre, where her husband, Keeper of the King's Gardens, had an apartment. He lived on one floor and she on another; they went separate ways. The priest who married M. and Mme de Flahaut was from an aristocratic family of ancient pedigree in the south of France. This priest had suffered a nasty accident as an infant when his governess placed him on the drawer of a dresser from which he fell, breaking his foot and leaving him a cripple with an iron rod in his leg and requiring him to wear a special shoe. Unable to enter the military, he was given an office in the Church, but with no priestly calling whatever he lived the life of an aristocrat, and betook of the pleasures owing someone of his social station. He was known for his many affairs, his sophistication, his clearheaded pragmatism, his intelligence, and his cynicism. His name was Charles-Maurice de Talleyrand-Périgord. Today he is simply referred to as Talleyrand; he is one of the more interesting figures thrown up by the French Revolution. When

Talleyrand married M. and Mme de Flahaut he would seem to have felt that the vivacious and clever 18-year-old bride could hardly be expected to find satisfaction from her much older husband, and decided himself to provide what was beyond the presumed capacities of the husband. He, not the Comte, was the father of Adèle's six-year-old son. Having begun a liaison with the bride after he presided over the wedding ceremony, Talleyrand continued to be her lover, and still was when Morris met her.

Morris saw Adèle at Versailles, as he noted in his *Diary* on March 21: "Madame Flahaut enters shortly . . . She speaks English and is a pleasing Woman. If I might judge from Appearances [she is] not a sworn Enemy to Intrigue."[52] Morris found Adèle interesting, and having heard about his reputation she wanted to know more about him. She made it known through friends that she would welcome a visit, and Morris sought her out in her apartment at the Louvre. Morris and Adèle went to Versailles together on May 4, the day before the opening of the Estates General, to observe the preliminary ceremonies. This is a most striking scene. Gouverneur Morris, an American, was sitting next to a woman, soon to be his lover, whose mother had been the kept girl of Louis XV, whose scandalous reign contributed to meltdown of the monarchy in 1787–88 that set the stage for the summoning of the Estates General at Versailles, where the first stage of the Revolution was to unfold. Morris visited Adèle on June 21, the day after he heard news of the Tennis Court Oath, an event of greatest political significance.

> From one Thing to another fell into Conversation on her domestic Affairs. She seems inclined to make me her Confidant: but for what? She talks to me of certain Affairs of Gallantry which she has been told I was once engaged in. I assure her that these are idle Tales, unworthy of Credit. She nevertheless persists in her Belief. I tell her that I have a perfect Respect for the Lady supposed to be the principal Object. She questions me as to the Term Respect and I take the Occasion to assure her of a Truth that (without Reference to any particular Person) I have never lost my Respect for those who consented to make me happy on the Principles of Affection. This Idea will I know dwell on her Mind, because the Combination of Tenderness and Respect with Ardency and Vigor go far towards the female Idea of Perfection in a Lover.[53]

It was in the ensuing five-week period that Morris and Mme de Flahaut went from the exploratory stages of sniffing about to a full-blown, torrid affair. The amorous progress of Morris and Mme de Flahaut unfolded amidst the explosive events that culminated in the French Revolution, an instance of sex and politics coming together in real life. On July 20, six days after the fall of the Bastille, Morris went to the Hôtel de Ville to see Lafayette, commander of the

National Guard, which had been formed to prevent descent into anarchy after the unleashed violence of the Paris insurrection of 12–14 July. Morris wanted to see the Bastille, but to do that he needed to obtain a pass, which Lafayette gave him. Having secured the pass to see the Bastille, Morris paid a visit to Mme de Flahaut. It was on this occasion that he spelled out the proposed terms of an affair that he was ready to begin, as he explained in his *Diary*:

> I cannot consent to be only a Friend . . . I know myself too well . . . [A]t present I am perfectly my own Master with Respect to her, but . . . it would not long be the Case . . . [H]aving no Idea of inspiring her with a Passion I have no Idea either of subjecting myself to one.

He added that he knew the proposed arrangement was "wrong," but he could not suggest anything else. Their affair would be strictly for pleasure; they would be lovers in the physical sense, underscored by intellectual compatibility, but without emotional attachment. "She thinks it a very strange Conversation, and indeed so it is, but I am much mistaken if it does not make an Impression much greater on Reflection than at the first Moment. Nous verrons."[54] The next day, July 21, Morris and Mme de Flahaut visited the Bastille, which they saw together. It was on the following day, July 22, that Morris received news of the lynching and mutilation of Foulon and Bertier de Sauvigny while awaiting his carriage at the Palais Royal. Adèle sent Morris a note the next day, July 23, inviting him to come and see her, as he did. She had reflected on the affair that he had proposed a few days earlier and agreed to it, but only after attaching one of her own conditions. She admitted to having a "Marriage of the heart," meaning that she was having an affair with someone else, and was not prepared to end it. She would maintain the other affair while entering into one with him. The lover she referred to but did not identify was Talleyrand, as Morris understood. The question at that point was "whether our Conversation is to break off or go farther. I think one as likely as the other."[55] The answer to that question came five days later when Morris went to Adèle's apartment in the Louvre at 5 pm. "She is at her Toilet. Monsr. [her husband] comes in. She dresses before us with perfect Decency even to the Shift. Monsieur leaves us to make a long Visit and we are to occupy ourselves with making a Translation. We sit down with the best Disposition imaginable but instead of a Translation . . ."[56] The unfinished sentence alludes to the beginning of an affair that they agreed was to be a matter of convenience and pleasure but became more than that as their lives were caught up in the turbulence of the French Revolution.

In early August business matters summoned Morris to London, on what turned out to be a six-week trip. When he returned to Paris in September Adèle was away, but he received a note from her when she returned to Paris a few days later and they saw one another briefly. "We talk a little Politics and a little of family." He paid her a visit at the Louvre the next day, but she was expecting someone else and sent him packing. He saw her again after dinner. She was "fatigued," having slept badly the previous night, but they "performed" the "Rites" anyway, after which she went to her convent school to see a nun. When he saw her the next morning, September 24, she was "At her toilette"; they discussed political and financial matters, in which both had keen interest. From the beginning of their affair they had been drawn together not only sexually but intellectually as well. Morris woke up "listless and feeble" on September 29, but he felt better after seeing Adèle: "We converse a good Deal about [political] Measures to be pursued and this amiable Woman shews a Precision and Justness of Thought very uncommon indeed in either Sex."[57] Yet relations became strained at this very time. When Morris visited Adèle on October 1 he found her uneasy, beset by feelings of insecurity. She feared that she had become pregnant while her husband was in Spain. The future seemed uncertain to her. She had two lovers; one was the father of her child, the other was her lover in the physical and intellectual sense of the word. Morris and Adèle had agreed at the beginning of their affair that it was for their mutual satisfaction; Adèle now wanted more; she wanted some stability. Alluding to Adèle's possible pregnancy, Morris wrote in his *Diary* on October 1 that "if nothing happens [if she is not pregnant] we are to take Care for the future until the Husband returns, and then exert ourselves to add one to the Number of human Experiences. This is a happy Mode of conciliating *Prudence and Duty*."[58] Referring to the possibility that they might have a baby together in this way suggests how casual Morris was about their life together. This was distressing to Adèle. Her state of mind at the time of Morris' next visit four days later, on October 5, was troubled, as was the city of Paris.

It was on that day that 10,000 women marched on Versailles, followed by Lafayette and the National Guard, who hoped to maintain order and, if necessary, to protect the King and Queen from an angry mob. People were hungry, rumors of intrigue and treachery were rife, a sense of imminent violence charged the atmosphere. Morris wrote in his *Diary* on October 5 that "The Town is in Alarm. Visit Madame de Flahaut. Stay with her till near one o'clock. She wishes me to make some more Sacrifices but this is I know a Business to which there is no End and therefore I refuse." Adèle's position was that if Talleyrand were to abandon her she would be lost; what would she do? What *could* she do? Yes, she and Morris had agreed to be lovers without any obligations to one another, but everything seemed precarious. Morris was unwilling to alter the conditions of their relationship and said they should keep things as they were; they became "good Friends again by Means of my Sang-froid," and made love on his terms. His conclusion was that "This Liberty is the Devil when we know not what to do with it."[59] Having had sex with Adèle, Morris left her apartment at the Louvre. Sex and politics went together on this day, October 5, as they had before; now it was in a new configuration. Inside the Louvre,

Morris and Adèle made love uneasily, fitfully, amidst conflicted feelings; outside a political storm was brewing as the women of Paris, *Poissardes*, were making ready to march to Versailles.

> Go into the Tuileries. A Host of Women are gone towards Versailles with some Cannon. A strange Manoeuvre . . . This Tumult is the Continuation of last Night, a wild, mad Enterprize . . . Lafayette has marched by Compulsion, guarded by his own Troops who suspect and threaten him. Dreadful Situation, obliged to do what he abhors or suffer an ignominious Death, with the Certainty that the Sacrifice of his Life will not prevent the Mischief.

When Morris awoke the next day, October 6,

> Paris [was] all in Tumult. Two Heads of the Gardes du Corps are brought to Town; and the royal Family . . . are to come this Afternoon. At half past two I will go to dine with Madame de F[lahaut]. She is very much hurt that I will not promise to marry her; that it is because she appears despicable in my Eyes from having had a Lover. I assure her that this is not the Reason. Laugh. Jest. She joins in all this but returns to her Point, 'with all the Arts of wily Woman working to her Purpose.' I see the Game but yet appear the Dupe . . . Tears. A countenance of Anguish . . . She feels guilty.

Morris made concessions to Adèle, agreeing that perhaps they would marry, and they made love. She vowed to be his. They left the Louvre together to visit friends, and then returned to Adèle's apartment. She wanted news of what had happened at Versailles, which they received. The Queen had fled in "her Shift and Petticoat with her Stockings in Hand to the King's Chamber for Protection, being pursued by the *Poissardes*."[60] This day, October 6, when the King and Queen moved from Versailles to Paris, was a turning point in the French Revolution. Forced to take up residence in the Tuileries, Louis XVI and Marie Antoinette were no longer personally free. They tried to escape from Paris in 1791 but were apprehended before they crossed the French border. They returned ignominiously to Paris, which they never left again. The women of Paris who forced the King and Queen to move from Versailles to Paris unwittingly set the stage for their execution.

Morris' affair with Mme de Flahaut lasted three years, from the summer of 1789 to the summer of 1792. It began right after the Paris insurrection of 12–14 July, its exploratory stages coinciding exactly with political shock waves that culminated in an uprising that cast the Revolution in a new mold; it ended when Paris was again shaken by political upheaval, the Storming of the Tuileries on August 10, 1792, the most violent Paris uprising of the French Revolution.

Their affair began against a background of upheaval and violence, and it ended against a background of upheaval and violence. Morris and Adèle were separated several times during this three-year period when he traveled to London on business. There were tensions when he returned to Paris in September 1789, and there were tensions again in November 1790 when he returned from another and longer trip to London. On this occasion he was away for a period of eight months. When Morris saw Adèle on November 7, 1790 they quarreled, as they did again the next day. By the time he saw Adèle two days later, on November 10, he had received a note from her, indicating, he thought, that she was ready to receive him as a lover. Yet, when he was again with her and was "proceeding immediately to the Object" Adèle let it be known that she had a plan: She was henceforth "to be merely her friend. I tell her that this cannot be but if she wishes to get Rid of me Nothing is so easy, and immediately wish her a Good Morning." At that point her husband returned. "He stays some Time and when he is gone we have a strange mingled Scene of Sentiments, Caresses and some Tears . . . She says I may if I please possess her. I agree to do so pour la dernière fois . . . She says I am a Cheat in telling her it is for the last Time."[61] And Adèle was right; the affair lasted almost another two years. As lovers they were reckless, taking crazy chances, flouting rules of propriety or correctness, as when Morris and Adèle made love in the same room as her niece, who was playing a harpsichord, or when they made love in a coach.

Morris was appointed American Minister to France on April 6, 1792, as war was about to erupt between France and Austria. By June, Paris was in turmoil. Morris wrote Jefferson on June 10 that "The best Picture I can give of the French Nation is that of Cattle before a Thunder Storm,"[62] and on June 17 he wrote that "we stand on a vast Volcano, we feel it tremble and we hear it roar but how and when and where it will burst and who may be destroy'd by its Eruptions it is beyond the Ken of mortal Foresight to discover."[63] In another letter to Jefferson, written on August 1, Morris commented on "the instability of human Affairs, especially of those which depend on the Opinion of an ignorant Populace." Morris felt that if revolutions were to succeed stability was essential, and for him this meant keeping the people, potentially turbulent, in check. Morris' apprehensions toward the people of Paris were evident at the beginning of the Revolution when he described a mob carrying the remains of hated officials through the streets of Paris. His comment on this occasion was "Gracious God what a People!" Now, on August 1, 1792, Morris feared the worst from the people of Paris. "I verily believe that if Mr de La Fayette were to appear just now in Paris unattended by his Army he would be torn to Pieces. Thank God we have no Populace in America and I hope the Education and Manners will long prevent that Evil."[64] Having lived in Paris during the first three years of the French Revolution, Morris' comment that America was fortunate not to have a "Populace" expressed a linguistic distinction that he had come to feel articulated an important difference between American and

French societies: In America there were "the people," whereas in France there was a "Populace." Historians today sometimes make the same distinction. It was a politicized "populace," the sansculottes of the eastern Sections of Paris, who stormed the Tuileries on August 10, 1792, the bloodiest day of the entire French Revolution. Parisians took vengeance on the Swiss Guards who fired on them, stuffing body parts into their mouths, and killing those who were fallen but not yet dead.

Morris carried on extensive correspondence with politically important Americans in the months following the Storming of the Tuileries and the subsequent September Massacres: Thomas Jefferson, George Washington, Alexander Hamilton, Thomas Pinckney, and Rufus King, and with French officials and friends—Le Brun, Lafayette, and the Duchesse d'Orléans. The correspondence contains a wealth of information and analysis about the August 10 insurrection, and about the September Massacres carried about by vengeful and angry Parisians. He wrote in his *Diary* on September 3 that "The murdering continues all Day. I am told that there are about eight hundred Men concerned in it." On the following day, September 4, he wrote that "The Murders continue. The Prisoners in the Bicêtre defend themselves and the Assailants try to stifle and drown them." In his September 6 *Diary* entry, Morris wrote, "There is

Figure 26. Jean-Louis Prieur, *Siege and Capture of the Tuileries*, August 10. 1792. This was the most violent uprising of the entire French Revolution; it created a fissure in France that resulted in civil war and the Reign of Terror.

nothing new this Day. The Murders continue and the Magistrates swear to protect Persons and Property. The weather is pleast. . . ."[65] The remaining *Diary* entries for September are terse and virtually without comment. His entries for October are limited to brief, descriptive sentences. Most of his entries comment on the weather. The November *Diary* entries are even briefer, and except for a few remarks on his health, one reference to Robespierre, and mention of papers found in the Tuileries they too comment on the weather. The December and January *Diary* entries are much like those in November; to read them one would think that little of consequence was taking place in Revolutionary France. Morris made his last *Diary* entry on January 5, 1793: "I go out this Morning but am glad to get Home. The Streets are a Glare of Ice. Horses tumbling down and some killed. Mine come off tolerably. . . ."[66] And at this point the *Diary* of Gouverneur Morris comes to an end. He was in France throughout the Terror, but his *Diary* is silent about events for which he had a front-row seat. To keep a diary in times such as these would have been imprudent in the extreme, as Morris understood full well. It comes as no surprise that Morris did not discuss his role in an unsuccessful effort to save the King by spiriting him from Paris after the Storming of the Tuileries on August 10.

Morris was able to assist Adèle, who rushed to see him after the Storming of the Tuileries, requesting his protection, which he provided, as he did to others. He managed to get Adèle a passport so she could go to London, and gave her money for the trip. This ended their affair. An affair that began during the Paris insurrection of July 1789 ended after another insurrection, that of August 10, 1792. Adèle was soon joined in London by Talleyrand, who fled France in September, but they went separate ways, as he had already entered into an affair with Germaine de Staël, Necker's daughter. Talleyrand moved in elite circles in London, and struck up a friendship with the John Barker Churches, the daughter and son-in-law of Philip Schuyler, who would help him travel to America in 1794. Adèle met Morris one more time, at Hamburg in November 1794. James Monroe had replaced Morris as American Minister in Paris on July 29, 1794, but before returning to America Morris traveled to Switzerland, then to Germany, and it was there that Adèle and her son met with him. She needed money, which he gave her. Adèle finally found the security she wanted by marrying a Portugese diplomat in 1802, and as Madame Souza-Botelho she lived on to 1836. The life of this woman, whose mother was mistress of Louis XV, had been most extraordinary, as if it had come out of a novel. Adèle was, in fact, a novelist, well-known during her time, but her fiction has long since fallen from fashion; its interest now limited to specialists who traffic in obscure literary texts. Adèle's own life reads like fiction with romantic entanglements, some of them set against the background of the first three years of the French Revolution. Upon returning to America, Morris settled into the family estate, Morrisania, in what was then Westchester and is now the Bronx, which he had purchased from a half-brother who inherited the property. Living alone and trying to maintain his estate proved a problem. Servants were not to be relied upon, so he invited Anne Cary Randolph, a 35-year-old woman who lived in New York in a boarding house, to oversee his household. She was from the powerful Randolph family of Virginia, but there had been family scandal, with rumors of incest and murder. She had been turned out of her sister's home and moved to New York, where she was penniless. As the daughter of an old friend, Morris decided to knock off two birds with one stone; he would come to the aid of the indigent daughter of a deceased aristocratic friend, and he would install someone at his estate who would impose needed order. Anne Cary Randolph performed admirably in her new role, and with proven acumen and common sense she soon accompanied Morris on business trips. They married, and at age 61 Morris became a father. This was three years before his death in 1816.

A 22-year-old aide-de-camp of George Washington arrived in Albany on November 5, 1777 after riding 300 miles in five days. Washington sent his aide to Albany because he needed help after suffering a punishing defeat at Brandywine Creek, fought on September 11. Washington had not blocked the British advance to Philadelphia, and desperate, he sent two of his most trusted officers and eight cavalrymen up the Schuylkill River to burn flour mills before they fell into the hands of the advancing British army. While the American contingent was torching one of the flour mills a sentinel signaled that the British were arriving, so one of the officers and three of his men jumped into a boat to escape as the other officer and his men fled by horse. The officer who fled on horse looked back at his comrades who were in the boat, "struggling against a violent current, increased by the recent rains," and pursued by English soldiers who raked the boat with gunfire and, he thought, killed the Americans. He sent a note to Washington describing the fate of his comrades, but it proved inaccurate when the officer he believed to be dead walked through the door of headquarters, accompanied by cheers and laughter. One of the men in the boat had been killed, but not the others. The officer who wrote the note to Washington was Captain Charles Lee, the father of Robert E. Lee; the officer who walked into headquarters, waterlogged but very alive, was the aide-de-camp that Washington sent to Albany two months later. His name was Alexander Hamilton.[67]

Of all the men who sprang from obscurity to prominence because of their role in the American Revolution, no one rose—and fell—as spectacularly as Alexander Hamilton (with the obvious exception of Benedict Arnold); of all the Founding Fathers his story might be the most extraordinary. Born on the West Indies island of Nevis in 1755, the illegitimate son of a Scottish adventurer who abandoned him at age ten, Hamilton was an orphan at age 12. He became a clerk for Nicholas Cruger, a merchant on the nearby island of Saint Croix, who did a sizable business in New York, where he had his own wharf. As Cruger's clerk the young Hamilton learned the ins and outs of trading, shipping, and fluctuating markets; he had to monitor inventories, chart the courses of ships, keep track of freight, and compute prices. He had an enormous capacity for work, and showed remarkable acumen and capacity for organizing affairs when Cruger left him in charge of his operations at age 14, when Cruger traveled to New York on business. Successful as Hamilton was, he hated working as a clerk; his father had been from a family of Scottish lairds, and his mother's family, French Huguenot in background, had belonged to the plantation class before falling on hard times. Raised amidst real hardship but hearing about his family's importance in better times, he aspired to something higher than the position to which fate had cast him as a lowly clerk. He received practically no formal schooling but he did receive some tutoring, and his mother, hoping to maintain a patina of respectability, had 34 books on her shelf. Among the authors he read were Alexander Pope, Plutarch, and Machiavelli, and he read devotional tracts and sermons as well. It seems that he took Pope as a stylistic model; words were to be his vehicle of upward mobility; it was through flourishes of elevated prose that he first made his mark. His opportunity came when a Presbyterian minister on Saint Croix, Hugh Knox, read a fine essay on hurricanes that Hamilton had written. Knox got the essay published, it made a stir, and he arranged for Hamilton to get a scholarship so he could study in America. And it was to America that he went in 1771, at age 15. The timing could not have been more propitious.

Feeling stranded on a remote West Indies island in 1769, Hamilton wished a war would break out; were that to happen opportunities would surely open up to someone of talent and ambition such as himself. When he went to New York in 1771, the colonies were on a collision course with Britain that resulted in the American Revolution; the war that he had fantasized about actually happened. He was in New York when Washington marched into the city after the Battle of Bunker Hill; he enlisted in a military unit in February 1776 and was appointed captain a month later; he was 21. He was with Washington at the disastrous Battle of Long Island in August 1776, and first brought himself to Washington's attention when the battered Continental Army fled a more powerful British force up Manhattan to Harlem Heights. It was there that Washington saw Hamilton's superb organizational skills at work as he oversaw men who were building earthwork fortifications. Washington sought Hamilton out and spoke to him in his tent a few days later. Hamilton was with Washington during the retreat across New Jersey to the Delaware, and he participated in the daring raid at Trenton on Christmas night, forcing himself from a farmhouse sickbed before crossing the partly frozen Delaware and marching eight miles in the surprise attack on unaware Hessians. He also participated in the raid on Princeton on January 3, 1777. An eyewitness described the diminutive Hamilton (he was 5'7" tall) as he marched into the village that Washington's men had taken. "I noticed a youth, a mere stripling, small, slender, almost delicate in frame, marching beside a piece of artillery, with a cocked hat down over his eyes, apparently lost in thought, with his hand resting on a cannon, and every now and then patting it, as if it were a favorite horse or pet plaything."[68] Much impressed by Hamilton's role in these successes, Washington wrote a personal note to him on January 20, 1777, asking him to become one of his aides-de-camp. It was in that capacity that Hamilton became indispensable to Washington. With remarkable facility he was able to intuit what Washington thought and felt, as if he entered into his mental processes, and he was able to put into words just what Washington wanted to say, in language that conveyed his wishes and instructions directly and concisely. Knowing the objectives Washington wanted to achieve, Hamilton learned to take into account the reasons behind them. Hamilton was someone Washington came to feel he could entrust with matters of utmost importance.

The mission Washington entrusted to Hamilton at the beginning of November 1777 when he sent him on horseback 300 miles to Albany was important, and it was fraught with difficulty. The summer campaign had gone badly for Washington after his defeat at Brandywine. Soon winter would set in and Washington's Continental Army would set up camp at Valley Forge, a time of unrelieved hardship and misery. At this juncture he needed help, and after consulting with other generals he decided to turn to Horatio Gates, who had just won the Battle of Saratoga. No British initiative would be mounted in the Northern Department in the waning months of 1777, and under these circumstances Washington decided that his overall strategy could be served best by having some of Gates' troops join him and his forces in New Jersey. When he sent Hamilton to Albany he gave him a letter that he was to present to Gates. This letter introduced Hamilton and described the nature of his mission: He was "to lay before you a full state of our situation and that of the enemy in this quarter. He is well-informed . . . and will deliver my sentiments upon the plan of operations . . . now necessary."[69] Washington did not make a specific request for Gates to send him a certain number of troops; rather, he left it to Hamilton to feel his way in the conversation, knowing what the real objective was, and giving him discretion to work out the particulars according to his exchanges with Gates. Knowing Washington's goals, Hamilton was to act as his surrogate; he was to advance arguments in his exchanges with Gates that would achieve Washington's objectives as best as possible. Predictably, the exchanges did not go easily. Gates' position was that his men were still needed in the Northern Department; Hamilton explained Washington's overall strategy and how important Gates' troops were to its accomplishment; Gates continued to advance counter-arguments. Under pressure from Hamilton, Gates agreed to send one brigade to Washington, not the three that Washington wanted. When Hamilton asked others about the brigade Gates had decided upon he was told that it was "by far the weakest of the three here," and with this information he confronted Gates in an acrimonious exchange. Gates finally relented and sent two brigades to Washington, but he complained about having to enter into important discussions with an aide who had been sent "300 miles distant" and vested with "dictatorial powers." As for Hamilton, he commented on Gates' "impudence, his folly, and his rascality."[70]

There is a four-day gap in Hamilton's expense report to Washington, suggesting that he stayed with Philip Schuyler. One thing is certain: Hamilton did visit with Schuyler while in Albany, and while seeing Schuyler in his Albany mansion he met his daughter, Elizabeth. They met again in 1780 when Elizabeth, "Betsey" as she was called in the family, visited an aunt in Morristown, and carried letters from her father to the Baron von Steuben and Washington, whose camp was close by. Schuyler had resigned his commission in 1778 after being exonerated of all charges in the court martial that he insisted on after he was blamed for the fall of Ticonderoga, but he continued to play an active role in the Revolution, working hand-in-glove with Washington, who asked him to serve on a committee that he asked Congress to form. Washington said of Schuyler, "There is no other man who can be more useful as a member of this Committee than General Schuyler. His perfect knowledge of the resources of the country, the activities of his temper, his fruitfulness of expedients and his sound Military sense make me wish above all things [that] he may be appointed." Schuyler accepted the appointment, and it was while serving in that capacity that he sent messages to von Steuben and Washington, delivered by his daughter Elizabeth.

Alexander Hamilton was drawn to females from families of distinguished rank. A romantic opportunity came his way in Morristown in 1780 when Elizabeth Schuyler, the daughter of Philip Schuyler, head of an important old Dutch family and the friend of George Washington, made an appearance. Elizabeth Schuyler was attractive to Hamilton, and he was attractive to her. Poised, urbane, and sophisticated, Hamilton had the social skills that allowed him to win favor with important people. In 1777 he and two other officers formed a smart trio, ornaments of Washington's Continental Army. One of the young officers was John Laurens, the son of a South Carolina planter, Henry Laurens, who followed John Hancock as president of the Continental Congress. The other officer in this distinguished trio was a French aristocrat, the Marquis de Lafayette, at age 19, three years younger than Hamilton and Laurens. Lafayette had married before coming to America, but both Laurens and Hamilton were single and very eligible bachelors. That they discussed prospective wives is made clear in a letter from Hamilton to Laurens in 1777 when he described, partly in jest and partly seriously, his qualifications for a wife:

> She must be young, handsome (I lay most stress upon a good shape).
> Sensible (a little learning will do), well-bred (but she must have an
> aversion to the word ton), chaste and tender (I am enthusiast in
> my notions of fidelity and fondness), of some good nature, a great

deal of generosity (she must neither love money nor scolding, for I dislike equally a termagant and an economist). In politics, I am indifferent what side she may be of; I think I have arguments that will easily convert her to mine. As to religion, a moderate streak will satisfy me. She must believe in god and hate a saint. But as to fortune, the larger the better. You know my temper and circumstances and will therefore pay special attention to this article in the treaty. Though I run no risk of going to purgatory for my avarice, yet as money is an essential ingredient to happiness in this world—as I have not very much of my own and as I am very little calculated to get more either by my address or industry—it must needs be that my wife, if I get one, bring at least a sufficiency to administer to her own extravagancies.[71]

When Elizabeth Schuyler arrived at Washington's camp in February 1780, she and Hamilton recognized one another; they made polite exchanges that soon turned into a full-blown romance. Within a month Hamilton proposed marriage and Elizabeth accepted; in one step Washington's 25-year-old aide-de-camp, nine years removed from a life of misery and destitution in a remote West Indies sugar island, born out of wedlock and orphaned, was about to ally himself through marriage to one of the most powerful families in New York. Hamilton did not hesitate to ingratiate himself with the members of the Schuyler family. After seeing a picture of Elizabeth's younger sister Margarita, Hamilton wrote a letter to her in which he described the woman he was to marry:

I venture to tell you in confidence that by some odd contrivance your sister has found the secret of interesting me in everything that concerns her . . . She is most unmercifully handsome and so perverse that she has none of those pretty affectations which are the prerogatives of beauty. Her good sense is destitute of that happy mixture of vanity and ostentation which would make it conspicuous to the whole tribe of fools and foplings . . . She has good nature, affability, and vivacity unembellished with that charming frivolousness which is justly deemed one of the principal accomplishments of a belle. In short, she is so strange a creature that she possesses all the beauties, virtues, and graces of her sex without any of those amiable defects which . . . are esteemed by connoisseurs necessary shades in the character of a fine woman.[72]

Hamilton struck a somewhat different chord when he told his friend John Laurens that "I give up my liberty to Miss Schuyler. She is a good-hearted girl who, I am sure, will never play the termagant. Though not a genius, she has good sense enough to be agreeable, and though not a beauty, she has fine black eyes, is rather handsome, and has every other requisite of the exterior to make her happy." Were Laurens to think his attraction to the woman he was about to marry tepid from this description, Hamilton assured him that "I am [a] lover in earnest, though I do not speak of the perfections of my mistress in the enthusiasm of Chivalry."[73]

Philip Schuyler was greatly distressed over the elopement of his eldest daughter, Angelica, as Hamilton understood full well. He would not commit the same wrong, and properly asked Philip Schuyler for the hand of his daughter in marriage. In April Schuyler wrote Hamilton to say that he had discussed the marriage proposal with Mrs. Schuyler and that they had accepted it. Both Philip and Mrs. Schuyler were in Morristown in June, and while staying in the house they had taken Hamilton paid them regular visits. By the time of the wedding in December 1780, Hamilton was on close terms with his wife's parents, and with her siblings as well. Having married into the Schuyler family, Hamilton secured the admiration of his difficult and demanding father-in-law. Schuyler wrote Hamilton on January 25, 1781, a month after the marriage, telling him, "You can not my Dear Sir be more happy at the Connection you have made with my family than I am, until a child has made a judicious choice the heart of a parent is continually in anxiety but this anxiety vanished in the moment that I discovered w[h]ere you and she had placed your affections."[74] When Schuyler wrote Elizabeth about her husband in 1782, he said: "Participate afresh in the satisfaction I experience from the connection you have made with my beloved Hamilton. He affords me happiness too exquisite for expression. I daily experience the pleasure of hearing encomiums on his virtue and abilities from those who are capable of distinguishing between real and pretended merit. He is considered, as he certainly is, the ornament of his country."[75] From this time on Hamilton's life was closely bound up with the Schuyler family. And it was also bound up with Schuyler's Albany mansion, where he and Elizabeth were married. From this time until his tragic death 24 years later this mansion was the one fixed place in Hamilton's life, to which he would return as soldier, lawyer, Treasury Secretary, and prominent member of the Federalist Party; he returned to Schuyler's mansion from military campaigns, from his New York law office, and from Philadelphia. This Albany home was the center of gravity for Hamilton and for his wife Elizabeth; she returned to her family home to bear children, to be with her parents, and to find solace in the life of remarkable success and equally remarkable turmoil and conflict that she shared with her husband Alexander Hamilton.

After spending his honeymoon at his father-in-law's mansion, Hamilton rejoined Washington in early January 1781 at army headquarters, now located in a farmhouse outside New Windsor, where he was joined by his wife. It was from New Windsor that Elizabeth wrote a letter to her sister Margarita on January 21, in which she said, "I am the happiest of Woman; my dear

Hamilton is fonder of me every day; get married, I charge you." Hamilton read Betsey's letter to her sister and added a postscript in which he offered his own views of marriage.

> Because your sister has the talent of growing more amiable every day, or because I am a fanatic in love, or both—or if you prefer another interpretation, because I have address enough to be a good dissembler, she fancies herself the happiest woman in the world, and would persuade all her friends to embark with her in the matrimonial voyage. But I pray you do not let her advice have so much influence as to make you matrimony-mad. 'Tis a very good thing when their stars unite two people who are fit for each other, who have souls capable of relishing the sweets of friendship, and sensibilities. The conclusion of the sentence I trust to your fancy. But it's a dog of life when two dissonant tempers meet, and 'tis ten to one but this is the case.[76]

Beneath the levity of Hamilton's postscript to his sister-in-law there was uneasiness about his marriage, which had presented problems from the beginning. Writing his friend John Laurens after he had become engaged to Elizabeth Schuyler, Hamilton said she "was not a genius," that she had "good sense enough to be agreeable," and that "though not a beauty, she has fine black eyes, is rather handsome, and has every other requisite of the exterior to make *her* [my italics] happy." Hamilton did not say that these attributes were sufficient to make *him* happy. Hamilton's marriage to Elizabeth Schuyler was an important stage in his relentless drive for success, carried out methodically and with characteristic energy. The campaign to advance himself through marriage was driven by hard calculation. From all accounts, Hamilton was strongly drawn to women; Martha Washington named a prowling cat in the camp at Morristown "Hamilton." But he was not strongly drawn to Elizabeth Schuyler, the woman he married. The letters Hamilton wrote to Elizabeth in Morristown when he courted her were couched in the language of rapturous love, but their lofty phrases came from the head more than the heart.

Within weeks of Elizabeth's arrival at New Windsor in January 1781 Alexander Hamilton had a falling out with George Washington. There had been several mutinies of New Jersey and Pennsylvania troops, and Washington and those around him were under heavy stress, with nerves on edge. After working until after midnight February 15, Hamilton was going down a flight of stairs the next day, tired from recent exertions, when someone told him Washington wanted to see him. Hamilton finished the errand he was on and talked briefly to Lafayette before seeing Washington. In his account of the incident written to Philip Schuyler two days later Hamilton said,

> Instead of finding the General as usual in his room, I met him at
> the head of the stairs, where accosting me in a very angry tone,
> "Col[onel] Hamilton," (said he), "you have kept me waiting at the
> head of the stairs ten minutes. I must tell you, sir, you treat me
> with disrespect." I replied without petulancy, but with decision, "I
> am not conscious of it, sir, but since you have thought it necessary
> to tell me so, we part." "Very well, sir." (said he), "if it be your
> choice," or something to this effect and we separated. I sincerely
> believe my absence, which gave so much umbrage, did not last
> two minutes.[77]

Washington tried to make amends, but Hamilton would not reverse his decision; he resigned his position as Washington's aide-de-camp. This episode did not come out of the blue, but was driven by pent-up frustrations; Hamilton had long wanted a field command and had made repeated requests to that effect. Washington turned down Hamilton's requests, explaining to him that he could not promote him over other officers with higher rank than his. A month after resigning his position as Washington's aide-de-camp Hamilton traveled to Albany for a stay at the mansion of his father-in-law. When he returned to military duty he continued to carry out his duties for Washington, but set about trying to find a place for himself in the army as a line officer.

Hamilton's wish finally came true on July 31, 1781, when he was given command of a New York light-infantry battalion. In late August he and his troops were marching toward Yorktown, where the climacteric battle of the American Revolution would be fought. The bombardment of Yorktown began on October 5, so weakening Cornwallis' army that the allied forces could storm the fortifications. The French had dug a trench to within 600 yards of the British lines, setting the stage for the attack that was soon to take place. It was customary to celebrate the completion of the last trench in the siege of a fortress, and as chance had it Hamilton and his men were chosen for this honor. When they reached the end of the trench Hamilton and his men climbed out of it at his orders and performed a parade ground drill, smartly as could be, an act of bizarre bravado, enacted before the incredulous British. Just beyond the range of British shot this strange escapade was carried out without loss to the Americans who performed it; its significance is what it says about Hamilton's quest for glory, and his willingness to throw chance to the winds to achieve it. When the storming of the British fortifications began, Lafayette was entrusted with the responsibility for deciding on the unit that would participate in one of two main lines of attack. He chose a French unit, against the vociferous protest of Hamilton, who sought out Washington and pressed him to designate an American unit instead. Washington overrode Lafayette's instructions and chose an American unit, Hamilton's, for the attack; finally Hamilton was to have his moment of glory. He ordered his men to charge the

British lines with muskets unloaded and bayonets lowered, shouting at the tops of their lungs as they rushed forward to strike at the enemy. When Hamilton reached a parapet he leaped over the shoulders of a crouching soldier into the midst of the British, whom he and his men subdued. He was brave in victory; he was also magnanimous. When he saw an American about to dispatch a British soldier with his bayonet he shouted at him to show mercy; however savage war was, it was to be waged according to rules, the rules of gentlemen. One of Hamilton's finest moments, his role in the Battle of Yorktown capped five years of military service as a patriot whose contributions to the American Revolution were considerable, although they were not the ones he wanted, at least not until the very end, at the Battle of Yorktown.

War with Britain stretched on for another two years, but with the American victory at Yorktown the outcome had, in effect, been decided. In the following March Hamilton resigned his commission, surrendering "all claims to the compensation attached to my military station during the war or afterwards."[78] This grand gesture was that of a gentleman of means who would not diminish himself by receiving material gain for rendering patriotic service to the nation. Grand as the gesture was, it was one that Hamilton was hardly in a position to make, and it was one that his widow would regret in later years, after his death. When he resigned his commission in March 1782 Hamilton was a father; Elizabeth had given birth to a son, Philip, named after her father, in January 1782. Hamilton joined his wife, son, and the Schuyler family in Albany three months later, where he studied to become a lawyer through a nine-month program of self-study. He passed the bar exam and at the end of 1783 moved to New York, where he set up a law practice. From this time on he would be one of the leading lawyers of his generation, but the practice of law never monopolized his time and energy. As Washington's aide-de-camp Hamilton had been faced constantly with problems concerning an army that Congress never provided for adequately. He was not content to grumble or complain about the condition of the army; rather, he thought about how the problem might be solved. He stood back from day-to-day realities of provisioning the army and devised conceptual schemes that pointed toward long-term solutions. He read economic treatises, corresponded with experts on financial matters, including Philip Schuyler, and reached the conclusion that only if the army were funded by Congress and not the states could it have the support it needed, the same conclusion that Gouverneur Morris reached, and at much the same time. These were two of the most brilliant men who rose to positions of eminence during the American Revolution, and in the difficult, unstable, problematic years that followed. Both Hamilton and Morris reached the conclusion that America needed a strong central government if she were to achieve her vast potential; both sat in the Constitutional Convention in Philadelphia; as Federalists both were driving forces behind the forging of the American Nation.

When Washington was inaugurated as President in April 1789 he chose Hamilton as Treasury Secretary. This was just after Gouverneur Morris' arrival in Paris in mid-February. It was at this precise time that they both initiated sexual affairs under unusual circumstances. Morris' affair, as we have seen, was with Mme de Flahaut, whose current lover was the priest who had presided over her wedding ceremony and was the father of her child. Alexander Hamilton's affair was with his sister-in-law, Angelica Schuyler Church, whom he first met when she accompanied her sister Elizabeth to Morristown in 1780. There is no evidence of conversations between Angelica and Hamilton in Morristown, but they met at that time, and they met again when she was present at the marriage of Hamilton and her sister in December 1780. There can be little doubt that there were sparks between Angelica and Hamilton from the beginning. Vivacious, charming, urbane, flirtatious, cosmopolitan, well-traveled, Angelica was the opposite of her serious, dutiful, domestic, reserved, stay-at-home sister. Of the two, it was Angelica to whom Hamilton was magnetically drawn, and for her part Angelica, far from happy with her husband, was attracted to her brother-in-law, Alexander Hamilton. Angelica wrote her sister after her marriage that she should "Embrace poor Hamilton for me . . . I am really so proud of his merit and abilities that even you, Eliza, might envy my feelings." Angelica told her sister that she could "pass with you the remainder of my days, that is if you will be so obliging as to permit my brother to give me his society, for you know how much I love and admire him."[79] Among the more problematic aspects of the affair between Hamilton and Angelica is the position of Elizabeth Hamilton. When Angelica left for Europe in 1782, Elizabeth became ill and took to her bed; Angelica's response was to write Hamilton, asking him please to "soothe my poor Betsey. Comfort her with assurances that I will certainly return to take care of her soon."[80] By the time Angelica came to America again it was not only her sister she wanted to see; also in her sights was her brother-in-law, Alexander Hamilton. In the absence of full or even substantial documentation, reconstructing the evolving affair between Hamilton and Angelica Schuyler Church is fraught with difficulties, the opposite of Gouverneur Morris' affair with Mme de Flahaut, with his *Diary* offering a remarkably full account not only of the affair but also of Morris' innermost thoughts and feelings as it proceeded. Still, there are sufficient documents to lay bare the essentials of Hamilton's affair with his sister-in-law Angelica, and even the impulses that drew them together.

John Barker Church and his wife returned to England in 1782, by which time he had become wealthy supplying the French army in America. In subsequent years he pursued business interests in America, England, and France. Church and his wife were in Paris for much of 1783 to 1785, when Angelica met and charmed Benjamin Franklin; it seemed that charming men of importance was one of her specialties. She wrote Eliza from Paris on January 27, 1784, that "I should like Paris if it was nearer to America . . . Mr. Franklin has the gavel [kidney stones] and desires to return to America. They talk of Papa or Col. Hamilton as his successor. How would you like to cross the Atlantic? Is your lord a Knight of the Cincinnati?" Angelica asked her sister to send her newspapers, "but the papers must be those that contain your husband's writings . . . Adieu, my dear, embrace your master for me, and tell him that I envy you the fame of so clever a husband, one who writes so well. God bless him, and may he long continue to be the friend and brother of your affectionate Angelica." Closing the letter with a postscript, Angelica said: "P.S. Tell Colonel Hamilton, if he does not write to me, I shall be very angry."[81] Church had extensive business dealings in America, and he and Angelica made a trip to New York in the summer of 1785, at which time he discussed his business affairs with his brother-in-law Alexander Hamilton, initially his lawyer and then his agent. Judging from a letter that Hamilton wrote to Angelica on August 3, 1785, after the Churches returned to England he and Angelica had become closer during the brief visit. "You have been much better to me My Dear friend since you left America, than I have deserved, for you have written to me oftener than I have written to you."[82] Hamilton had gone to Philadelphia to see the Churches sail for England, which, as he explained in a letter to Angelica, he observed with "uneasiness, as if foreboding you were not to return . . . I confess for my own part I see one great source of happiness snatched away." Closing the letter, Hamilton included the phrase, "I remain You Affectionate Friend" in the middle of a sentence. It has been observed that Hamilton did not make a spelling error when he wrote "You Affectionate Friend," but was moving from a polite formality to a direct expression of feeling, of love.[83] Hamilton included references to Angelica's husband throughout the letter, as would be expected in a letter of this type, but he and Angelica worked out a code in their correspondence that allowed them to convey different layers of meaning, those of intimacy and affection embedded within the conventional language of proper letters exchanged between a brother and sister-in-law.

Angelica and Hamilton exchanged two known letters in 1787. How often they may have corresponded after the Church's 1785 visit to America is unknown, but the two extant 1787 letters say much about their intimate feelings, shared understanding, and how they spoke in code. At the beginning of Angelica's October 2, 1787 letter to Hamilton she apologized for not responding sooner to his letter, indicating that there had been previous correspondence, now lost. She then said,

> Indeed, my dear, Sir if my path was strewed with as many roses, as you have filled your letter with compliments, I should not now lament my absence from America: but even Hope is weary of doing any thing for so assiduous a votary as myself. I have so often prayed at her shrine that I am now no longer heard. Church's head is full of Politicks, he is so desirous of making once in the British house

of Commons, and where I should be happy to see him if he possessed your Eloquence.[84]

Speaking in code, she wrote "my dear, Sir if my path . . . ," misplacing the comma between the words "dear" and "Sir," hoping—or assuming—that Hamilton would detect the mistake; she was, in fact, calling Hamilton "my dear." Angelica then went on to say that the "path of roses" he evoked made her lament her absence from "America." Decoded, it was he that she missed, he before whose shrine she had prayed, but whose votary had not yet heard her pleas. She missed him and wanted urgently to be with him. Indeed, he was her deity. By contrast, her husband could think only of politics. By referring to her husband not as "Mr. Church" or as "my husband" but by his last name she was, in this context, rejecting polite convention and belittling him, as what follows this form of reference indicates with full clarity: "Church's head is full of Politicks . . ." Angelica would be glad to have her husband in the "British house of Commons," where she would be rid of him. To heighten the contrast between her husband and Hamilton, and further to diminish her husband, Angelica said she would be "happy" to see her husband in Parliament if "he possessed your Eloquence," an obvious impossibility. Hamilton responded to Angelica's October 2, 1787 letter on December 6, 1787. He began by saying that he was writing just her, not her and her husband, who "has too much gallantry to be offended at this implication." The Churches moved in circles in both London and Paris within which sexual relations were fluid, in other words within which "gallantry" prevailed. He then told Angelica how much pleasure her letter gave him, a "feeble image" of which he wished to "convey." These "poetical" utterances were well and good; more to the point, he said, "I seldom write to a lady without fancying the relation of lover and mistress," by which he meant a certain lady in particular, the one he was addressing, Angelica. He was certain that she understood him, just as he understood her. "You ladies despise the pedantry of punctuation. There was a most critical comma in your last letter. It is my interest that it should have been designed; but I presume it was accidental. Unbridle this if you can. The proof that you do it rightly may be given by the omission or repetition of the same mistake in your next." Riddled with double entendres and flashing with wit, Hamilton's response to the misplaced comma in Angelica's letter says much about the understanding they had reached at this point in their relationship. The relationship was illicit by its very nature, as Hamilton did not hesitate to say in his closing sentences. "Betsey sends her love. I do not choose to say joins in mine. Tis old fashioned."[85]

Angelica arrived in New York in March 1789, without her husband and children, where she would spend the next eight months before returning to England in November. What happened between Hamilton and Angelica during this eight-month period is not entirely clear. Some historians have passed over this episode in silence, acknowledging that while Hamilton and Angelica were clearly drawn to one another it is difficult to imagine Hamilton betraying his trust to his wife,[86] or that in the absence of sufficient documentation there is no way to know if they had an affair.[87] But it has also been argued that there was an affair, and that by putting together bits and pieces of evidence the case can be made convincingly.[88] When Angelica left England her husband was much occupied with politics, aspiring to a position in Parliament, which he secured in the following year, 1790. Angelica had made it clear that she had no interest in her husband's political ambitions; additionally, she had compared him unfavorably to Hamilton in this context, the political. Socialite that she was, Angelica was not without serious interests, including interest in politics. She was her father's daughter; she was attracted to men of influence, intelligence, and power. That she drew Franklin into her orbit, and more importantly Thomas Jefferson, who invited her to stay with him at Monticello or travel with him to Niagara when they were both in Paris,[89] says much about Angelica Schuyler Church. She read her brother-in-law's political writings in London, and admired his mind and keen intelligence. In some measure that is what drew her to him. Angelica's arrival in New York in March 1789 was at a most propitious moment; Pierre L'Enfant was completing improvements on City Hall, undertaken at an expense of $65,000, which was to accommodate the House, Senate, a library, and a special room for displaying models of inventions. New York was humming with activity as preparations were made for Washington's inaugural on April 30, accompanied by festivities and celebrations. Washington asked Robert Morris to be Treasury Secretary, but he declined and both he and James Madison urged him to appoint his former aide Alexander Hamilton to the post, a decision whose importance to America's future no one could have foreseen. It was during the eight-month period when Angelica was in New York that Hamilton addressed problems of the greatest economic and political importance. Of these, the most immediate was the problem of the war debt, which Gouverneur Morris was also working on under very different circumstances in Paris and at the same time, as the agent of Robert Morris. The 20,000 word Report that Hamilton sent to Congress in January 1790, the product of staggering effort by Hamilton, called for Federal assumption of the states' war debt. The acceptance of Hamilton's debt plan had the unexpected effect of driving a wedge right through Washington's government, a political crisis of profound importance. And it was against the background of Hamilton's work on the debt issue that he and Angelica became lovers, or so it will be argued here.

When Angelica arrived in New York she stayed with her sister and brother-in-law, an arrangement that lasted for two months, but by mid-May she rented her own apartment in a nearby town house. Angelica arrived in New York with little money, and depended on financial assistance from Hamilton. He advanced Angelica the substantial sum of £500 on May 15 and Elizabeth contributed £100, taken from her own savings. Accustomed to fine things, Angelica was not to be neglected in New York; Hamilton set her up with a coach and matched horses and provided her with a coachman and stables for the horses. He also provided Angelica with a valet de chambre, which Angelica's husband was to pay for later, as Hamilton's accounts indicate. But in August Hamilton's bookkeeping system changed, making it difficult to follow the flow of money—to know how much was spent, or for what purposes. Angelica simply went shopping and presented Hamilton with the bills, which he took care of. It was at this time that Elizabeth left New York to be with her parents in Albany or Saratoga. Hamilton hired a new coach, one that allowed him to go here and there without being recognized, and he rented new rooms for Angelica, although his account books do not specify where. By this time he would appear to have been paying Angelica's expenses himself, or much of her expenses, which he was ill-able to afford and left his savings seriously depleted by the time of Angelica's return to England in November. Seen together regularly, gossip swirled around Hamilton and Angelica, as could have been expected. Where they spent evenings together is not known. Indeed, little is known about the details of Hamilton's life with Angelica in the summer and fall of 1789, his personal papers shedding little light on the matter. What is clear is that Philip Schuyler wrote Angelica, telling her that she must return to her husband. At the same time, John Barker Church wrote his wife that her children were ill, an added reason to book passage to England.

Elizabeth traveled to New York to see her sister off as she departed for England, but she was too ill, or distressed, to be on the dock when the ship set sail. Angelica wrote a letter to Hamilton after boarding ship that she expected Elizabeth to read, and was effusive in expressions of sisterly concern. "Do my dear Brother endeavor to sooth my poor Betsey, comfort her with the assurances that I will certainly return to take care of her soon." Having seen Angelica's ship leave port, Hamilton returned home and wrote her a letter which, as he explained, he would show to Betsey, who would add a note of her own. His letter is proper, laden with the conventional sentiments appropriate to an epistle written under these circumstances. Hamilton wrote this letter with both Angelica and his wife in mind. Filled with standard pieties and couched in the sentimental phrases of the time, the letter would have pleased Elizabeth, as it was intended to, and as Angelica would have understood. In the final paragraph Hamilton explained that he was about to give the letter to "Betsey to add whatever her little affectionate heart may dictate." The phrase "*little* affectionate heart" (my italics) could be seen as a term of endearment, but it also invited a different reading; Elizabeth's "little affectionate heart" was not like the heart of her sister; this was a coded message that Angelica could hardly have missed. Elizabeth's addition to Hamilton's letter to Angelica makes for sad reading, filled as it is with lamentations and grief. "I have seated myself to write to you (she had been lying down; just sitting up was an effort), but my heart is so sadned by your Absence that it can scarcely dictate; my Eyes filled with tears that I shall not be able to write you much." The letter ends with an incomplete sentence:

"I can no more"[.] After her initials, E.H., are the words *"heaven protect you"* [.]"[90] How can two sisters have been so different?

Elizabeth Hamilton was in Albany with her infant son and parents in the hot summer of 1791 when a 23-year-old woman of respectable New York family with a somewhat distant tie to the Livingstons appeared at the door of Hamilton's Philadelphia house. She told Hamilton that her husband "had for a long time treated her very cruelly" and abandoned her; she asked Hamilton, in the fullness of his "humanity," to render needed assistance. She gave him her address, he told her he would see what he could do, and he paid her a visit that night, the beginning of a disastrous affair. Having begun the affair, Hamilton urged Elizabeth to remain in Albany, and even when she returned to Philadelphia he continued to see Maria Reynolds, putting his political future at risk, along with all that he hoped to achieve as Washington's Treasury Secretary. And of course he ran the risk of bringing shame not only to himself, if he should be caught, but to his wife Elizabeth, a woman of unblemished reputation. So why did Hamilton enter into and continue the affair with Maria Reynolds? One explanation is that this was but another occasion in which Hamilton indulged libidinal impulses, but this might not be the entire story. Hamilton was always sympathetic to women in distress, abandoned or abused women, such as his own mother, whose cruel treatment he had seen as a boy. If he was susceptible to feminine allure, he was particularly vulnerable to the plight of abused women. And there had always been a self-destructive tendency in Hamilton, of which this episode was a striking example. Whatever the reason, Hamilton threw caution to the wind, as he had as a soldier, and risked everything when he entered into the affair with Maria Reynolds. Soon her husband, James Reynolds entered the picture, a scam artist who had probably orchestrated his wife's seduction to wring an office out of Hamilton, the Treasury Secretary, and when the office he wanted was not forthcoming he threatened Hamilton with blackmail. Hamilton paid blackmail, even though he was in debt and had to borrow part of the money; there were new demands, so great that Hamilton could not meet them; he said he would pay no more. The sordid episode continued through 1792, while Hamilton was shouldering a huge load as Treasury Secretary and working on some of his most ambitious projects, until matters came to a head in December. Reynolds, ever the conniver, landed in jail owing to his own machinations, but he suspected Hamilton was the culprit. He contacted several of Hamilton's political enemies, including James Monroe, accusing Hamilton of skimming money from the Treasury. When Monroe and two others saw Hamilton he admitted to the affair with Maria Reynolds, explained that he had been blackmailed by her husband, and persuaded them he had not abused his office. Embarrassed over these revelations, Monroe and his friends agreed that they would maintain silence over the Reynolds affair, but they kept incriminating documents, proof of Hamilton's affair. Someone, probably Monroe, leaked the documents to James Callender, a journalist seeking favor with Jefferson, and in 1796 Callender used them in an attack on Hamilton that included charges of corrupt speculation. To protect himself against those charges Hamilton published a long defense against Callender's charges, but in doing so he revealed in full detail his affair with Maria Reynolds. Up to this time Elizabeth had no knowledge of the affair, whose impact she now had to face. In making the decision to publish a full account of the affair, Hamilton had to make a choice between his public reputation and his private life, which he shared with his wife. That he placed greater importance on his public reputation, his honor, than his relationship with his wife is completely consistent with the mind and character of Alexander Hamilton. He had committed no public wrong; the charges of public corruption were totally false; to be defamed in this way by a creature with ties to Thomas Jefferson was unbearable; as a man of probity dedicated to the public weal who had carried out responsibilities of office with utmost integrity he could not let charges leveled against him stand. To clear his public record he had no choice but to expose his wife Elizabeth to the painful consequences that followed from his revelation. Out of this episode, the occasion of shame, anguish, and guilt, came a new and closer relationship between Alexander Hamilton and his wife Elizabeth.

Elizabeth had always been religious, attending church regularly and giving herself over to good and charitable causes. After the Maria Reynolds revelation Hamilton joined Elizabeth in her benevolent undertakings, and he returned to Christianity. He had attended church regularly as a student at King's College, but during the Revolution he became a rationalist who looked askance at organized religion as a source of superstition.[91] As Washington's aide-de-camp he wrote that "there never was any mischief but had a priest or a woman at the bottom"; as Treasury Secretary he wrote that "The world has been scourged with many fanatical sects in religion who, inflamed by mistaken zeal, have perpetuated under the idea of serving God the most atrocious crime." Hamilton was married in the Dutch church in Albany, but Elizabeth became an Episcopalian, and the Hamilton children were baptized at Trinity Church on Broadway Street in New York. She attended services there but her husband did not. In the aftermath of the Maria Reynolds episode Hamilton drew closer to his wife Elizabeth, personally and religiously. They took up charitable causes sponsored by Evangelical groups, they gave shelter to orphans, and they helped form an orphan society. Hamilton's son, John Church Hamilton, commented on his father's return to religious faith; his memories included those of his father praying daily, reading the Bible, and writing comments in the margins. An interior change took place within Alexander Hamilton in the last years of his life, owing in part to the squalid revelations of the Maria Reynolds affair, a source of shame and guilt. This forced Hamilton to reconsider his relationship with his wife. He had married her to advance his ambitions, not a worthy objective, as at some level he felt from the beginning. He had had an affair with his wife's sister. And he had had a sordid affair with a woman of no worth or character whatever—the pliable instrument of her scheming, base husband, a blackmailer. He had compromised his wife; he had shamed not only himself but her as well. Now it was time to make amends; this Hamilton would seem to have done in the last years of his life.

In March 1804 Hamilton made scathing comments on Aaron Burr while having dinner at the State Street home in Albany of Judge John Taylor, which Dr. Charles Cooper, who was there, described in a letter that he sent to a friend. In circumstances not clear even today, that letter was published, along with another letter by Philip Schuyler claiming that Hamilton could never have said the things about Burr that had been attributed to him. Someone sent the article containing Cooper's and Schuyler's letters to Aaron Burr, and it was that article that provoked the duel between Burr and Hamilton. Ironically, Philip Schuyler's letter written in defense of his son-in-law contributed to the duel that resulted in Hamilton's death. The episode is heavy with irony, and covered by layers of tragedy. In 1801 Hamilton's son Philip had been killed in a duel, fought over his father's reputation. Hamilton urged his son to fire in the air rather than aim at his rival. Philip Hamilton did what his father asked him to do, hoping to avoid bloodshed, but the other duelist did not follow his example; he fired a shot into Philip Hamilton's hip that ended up in his left arm. The death was slow and agonizing, the occasion of unbearable grief for Hamilton, Elizabeth, and other members of the family. Philip Schuyler asked his daughter and son-in-law to name their next son Philip, in honor of the brother he would never see. This they did; the next son was also named Philip. Another of the Hamilton children, Angelica, named after her aunt, became unhinged by the death of her brother, and never recovered her sanity. She lived to age 73, unable to escape from the inner prison to which she had been committed by the tragic death of her brother. When Aaron Burr challenged Hamilton to a duel, Hamilton did not take steps that could have avoided it, even after the recent dueling death of his son, on whom he doted, and in spite of his opposition at this point of his life to dueling. He decided to do precisely what he had asked his son to do, to fire his first shot into the air rather than at Burr. This is what he did, but Burr, an expert marksman, took deadly aim and hit Hamilton in the abdomen, a mortal blow. The same pistols, owned by Hamilton's brother-in-law, John Barker Church, were used in both duels. Hamilton and his son might have been killed by the same gun. Once again, family members had to witness the wretched death of one of its members; this time it was Alexander Hamilton who perished.

Hamilton received recognition in death that he had not received in his brilliant but troubled life in the funeral ceremony held in New York City on July 14, 1804. It seemed that all of New York appeared at the funeral in a city-wide outpouring of grief, marked by the firing of guns from the Battery, the ringing of church bells, and a parade comprised of a military band, militia units, civic, religious, and patriotic groups, various worthies who attended the ceremony, and Hamilton's children and relatives.[92] After the cortege wended its way through the streets of New York it ended up at Trinity Church, where the final obsequies were held. The funeral oration was given by Gouverneur Morris, whom Hamilton had known for almost 30 years. They sat together at the Constitutional Convention in 1787, and Hamilton asked Morris to participate in writing the Federalist Papers, but Morris declined, leaving the task to Hamilton, Madison, and Jay. Morris and Hamilton exchanged letters when Morris was in Paris, using code to avoid the scrutiny of authorities in France; Morris wrote Hamilton on March 21, 1792, thanking him for supporting his appointment as American Ambassador in France. Morris and Hamilton had been particularly close since Morris returned to America from Europe in 1798. When Morris visited his estate, Morrisania, in January 1799, the family house was in disrepair, and he decided to build a new one, at the cost of $60,000, a sizeable sum. As chance had it, Hamilton purchased property in northern Manhattan along the East River in 1798 and built a new home, the Grange, between 1800 and 1802, across the river and a short distance from Morris's estate in what is now the Bronx. How often Hamilton and Morris saw one another in the years between Morris's return to America at the end of 1798 and Hamilton's death in 1804 is not clear, but what is known is that when Hamilton lay on his deathbed his wife Elizabeth, overcome by grief, asked Morris, who had rushed to the house where his friend lay dying, to enter the room. According to David Ogden, who witnessed the deathbed scene, "The poor woman [Elizabeth] was almost distracted [and] begged uncle Gouverneur Morris might come into her room . . . She burst into tears, told him he was the best friend her husband had, begged him to join her in prayers for her own death, and then to be a father for her children."[93]

Morris had been elected to Congress in April 1800, and while in Washington DC, he and Hamilton exchanged letters, offering glimpses into the relationship between two leaders of the Federalist Party. Morris's election to Congress came when there was an impasse between Jefferson and Burr after a tie vote for president in the 1800 election. Hamilton, in New York, wrote Morris, in Washington DC on December 24, 1800 about the deadlock.

> Jefferson or Burr?—the former without all doubt. The latter in my judgment has no principle public or private—could be bound by no agreement—will listen to no monitor but his ambition . . . He is bankrupt beyond redemption . . . He is sanguine enough to hope every thing—daring enough to attempt everything—wicked to scruple nothing. From the elevation of such a man heaven preserve the Country![94]

Hamilton returned to the Jefferson-Burr problem two days later on December 26.

[If t]here be a [man] in the world I ought to hate it is Jefferson. With Burr I have always been personally well. But the public good must be paramount to every private consideration. My opinion may be freely used with such reserves as you shall think discreet.[95]

That Hamilton told Morris that he could share his opinions of Burr with others indicates that he was not averse to Burr knowing about his animus; seen in retrospect, he was setting the stage for the incident that resulted in his death at the hands of Aaron Burr. As for Morris, he was much less willing to take sides in the controversy over Jefferson and Burr. He felt that it was fitting and proper that Jefferson become president, as that was clearly the intention of the voting public; he stood back from the two rivals and considered the future of the presidency from a more detached position than Hamilton. Judging from Hamilton's letters to Morris he was unusually candid about himself, his life, and his role in the politics of the time. Hamilton wrote Morris on February 29, 1802, that

Mine is an odd destiny. Perhaps no man in the U[nited] States has sacrificed or done more for the present Constitution than myself—and contrary to all my anticipations of its fate. As you know from the very beginning I am still labouring to prop up the frail and worthless fabric. Yet I have the murmurs of its friends no less than the curses of its foes for my rewards. What can I do better than withdraw from the Scene? Every day proves to me more and more that this American world was not made for me.[96]

Reflecting upon the differences between himself and his friend, Hamilton wrote, "I have read your speech[es] with great pleasure. They are truly worthy of you. Your real friends had many sources of satisfaction on account of them . . . You, friend Morris, are by birth a native of this Country but by genius an exotic."[97]

In his funeral oration given from the portico of Trinity Church before a vast crowd Gouverneur Morris touched upon highlights in the life of Alexander Hamilton, whose "Heroic Spirit" had "flown to the mansions of bliss." He had been a student at Columbia, brought himself to the attention of the "penetrating eye of Washington," and shown "heroism" at Yorktown; he had attended the Constitutional Convention at Philadelphia, where he helped form the "constitution which is now the bond of our union, the shield of our defence and the source of our prosperity"; as Washington's Treasury Secretary he laid the financial foundations of the new nation; needing to care for his family, he resumed his profession, that of lawyer; even in that capacity he never lost interest in nor was he less devoted to the public interest, which he served tirelessly.[98] Morris set down his feelings about the funeral oration he was about to deliver in his diary on July 13, the day before the funeral ceremony. "The first Point of his

Biography is that he was a Stranger of illegitimate Birth. Some Mode must be contrived to pass over this handsomely. He was indiscreet, vain and opinionated. These things must be told or the Character will be incomplete—and yet they must be told in such Manner as not to destroy the Interest." Morris continued to reflect upon Alexander Hamilton as he again set down his thoughts in his diary on July 14, after delivering the oration. There was much over which he had had to draw a veil, particularly Hamilton's domestic life. Morris felt that Hamilton had "foolishly" made a public avowal of his infidelity, alluding to the Maria Reynolds affair. This he had not touched upon, but he had felt that he had to say something "to excite public Pity for his family which he has left in indigent Circumstances." When Elizabeth Hamilton asked Morris to enter the deathbed room, to pray for her own death, and to care for her children he dissolved in tears. He was sufficiently close to Hamilton to know about the deplorable state of his personal finances; it was he who organized a secret subscription fund to provide assistance for Elizabeth Hamilton. At the time of his death Alexander Hamilton left a debt of $50,000 to $60,000; Morris headed a group of some 100 subscribers who raised over $80,000 for the widow and children of Alexander Hamilton. A closely guarded secret, the fund was unknown until long after the death of Elizabeth Hamilton.

When Hamilton lay on his deathbed he told Elizabeth that in his duel with Aaron Burr he was unable, with the "scruples of a Christian," to aim his pistol at him. Continuing, he said, "you had rather I should be innocent than live guilty. Heaven can preserve me and [I humbly] hope will, but in the contrary event, I charge you to remember that you are a Christian."[99] Disconsolate over the death of her son in 1801, Elizabeth had to endure the loss of her sister Margarita, the wife of Stephen Van Rensselaer III, in the same year, and that of her mother two years later, in 1803. The tragic death of her husband in July 1804 had taken a large toll on her father, Philip Schuyler, who died four months later. The Schuyler family sold their Albany home, in 1806, and Elizabeth moved to Washington, DC, living on, remarkably, until 1854; she died there at age 97, the last of the Founding Mothers. She had moved to the nation's capital and was sitting in the backyard of her house one day in the 1820s when a maid presented her with a card, written by a former President who made a request to see her. James Monroe had come to see the widow of Alexander Hamilton. It was probably Monroe who turned over the incriminating documents concerning the Maria Reynolds affair to her husband's enemies; this is what Hamilton thought, and decades later it was what his widow thought. Looking at Monroe's card, according to her 15-year-old nephew, who was with her, "She read the name and stood holding [it], much perturbed. Her voice sank and she spoke very low, as she always did when she was angry. 'What has that man come to see me for?' " Her nephew said he had only come to pay his respects. "I will see him," she replied, and received him in her parlor. He had taken a seat, and rose when she entered the room; he bowed, and rather than ask him to take his seat again she stood opposite him. Elizabeth Hamilton understood well the rituals of refined society. Monroe bowed, and got to the point of his visit, explaining, in the words of Elizabeth's nephew, "that it was many years since they had met, that the lapse of time brought its softening influences, that they both were nearing the grave, when past differences could be forgiven and forgotten." "Mr. Monroe," Elizabeth replied, "if you have come to tell me that you repent, that you are sorry, very sorry, for the misrepresentations and the slanders and the stories you circulated against my dear husband, if you have come to say this, I understand it. But otherwise, no lapse of time, no nearness of the grave, makes any difference."[100]

Marie-Joseph-Paul-Yves-Roch-Gilbert du Motier, the Marquis de Lafayette (1757–1834), arrived in Albany on February 17, 1778, on a mission of greatest importance—or so he thought. Congress had placed him in command of an American army that was to invade Canada, a continuation of previous initiatives in 1775 and 1776.[101] The hopes this time were no better than before. The 1778 Canada expedition came out of efforts by Washington's rivals to bring about his removal as head of the Continental Army and the elevation of Horatio Gates to the position of Supreme Commander. The initial plan called for Thomas Conway, one of the intriguers against Washington, to lead the army that was to invade Canada, but as circumstances changed the plan took on another objective: It would detach Lafayette from his idol, George Washington. Without realizing it, Lafayette had become a pawn in a game whose rules he did not understand. High-minded, idealistic, brave, and devoted to the best and purest of causes—the American Revolution—Lafayette was so caught up in his sense of personal honor and so given to flights of knightly valor that he was all too susceptible to the intrigues and manipulations of the Conway Cabal.

Lafayette's father had been killed in the Seven Years War when he was two; his mother virtually abandoned him in the following year when she joined her family in Paris, leaving him in the care of his grandmother at the family estate in Auvergne. His mother summoned him to Paris when he was 11, bringing him into a sophisticated world utterly different from the rural simplicity of his country estate, of which he had been master, the object of much bowing and scraping. Now, in Paris, he was quite out of his element, and he was unhappy, miserable in fact. He did not have the social graces of others, and suffered from feelings of insecurity. The ornate, privileged world of Paris was hell to him. Then, in 1770, his mother died, and right after that his grandfather died. Suddenly Gilbert, as he was called, became one of the richest men in France, having inherited an income of 25,000 livres from one side of his family and 120,000 livres from the other side. He purchased a commission at age 13 and joined the royal hunt. Two years later a marriage was arranged that allied his family with the powerful Noailles clan, which had close and important ties with the court. Gilbert moved into the Hôtel de Noailles, hardly seeing the 13-year-old girl to whom he was engaged. He was 17 when they married in 1774. In the two years between the arranging of the marriage and the wedding ceremony Lafayette entered a riding school, where he became friendly with the Comte d' Artois, the dashing, rakish, younger brother of the Dauphin, soon to be Louis XVI. D'Artois mocked the clumsy, awkward Lafayette, reinforcing his insecurities. Gilbert's wife, Adrienne, was affectionate and the marriage went well, but that too, oddly, became a problem. In elite society, marriages did not assume fidelity of husband and wife; such marriages were unfashionable; a smart husband should have a mistress. Gilbert tried to have one but was rejected. Having a duel was pretty much obligatory; he challenged the Comte de Ségur to a duel, but the challenge was rejected. Lafayette's father-in-law, the Comte d'Ayen, found out about both episodes; he was willing to overlook Lafayette's failed effort at an affair, but he found the ridicule from the abortive duel odious. Yet, d'Ayen understood how miserable his son-in-law was and decided that he should have a position at court and arranged one; Lafayette was to be lord-in-waiting to the Dauphin's younger brother, the Comte de Provence. Gilbert's response to the appointment was to make an independent statement by deliberately offending Provence, and when the way was cleared for him to make amends he insulted him again. His father-in-law was furious with him over his outrageous behavior. Having gone to Metz to participate in military training, Lafayette met the Comte de Broglie. Broglie, himself frustrated, wanted to go to America to achieve goals that were impossible in France. Ideas of liberty were in the air, giving a patina of idealism to talk of serving noble causes, such as the American Revolution. To join that cause was to participate in a struggle against France's bitter enemy, England. Lafayette had particular enmity toward England; his father had perished on the battlefield at Minden in the Seven Years War, which cost France her possessions in Canada. Gilbert was put on inactive list in 1777, making him a failure at age 19. His course of action now became clear; he would join the glorious cause of the Americans in their struggle against England. To that end, he purchased a ship and supplies and went secretly to Bordeaux, and from there he set sail for America, a fugitive from monarchical France, without so much as telling his wife about his departure. In adventures right out of a novel he made his way to America, on whose shore he landed on June 13, 1777. He reached Philadelphia on July 27, along with other nobles who had sailed with him on his ship, *La Victoire.*

Washington did not care particularly for the French, whom he had fought in the French and Indian War, and he had little use for French aristocrats who came to America expecting to be officers in his army. When Lafayette arrived in Philadelphia he was one of 11 French aristocrats that Silas Deane had appointed officers in France before they went to America. When the officers presented their credentials to Congress in Philadelphia, Deane's appointments were not accepted, but an exception was made for Lafayette, who had purchased a ship and brought supplies for the Americans and explained that he would serve without pay. He was appointed honorary major general, but without an army to command. This only Washington could do. Lafayette had shown modesty and sincerity when meeting with members of Congress, making a favorable impression, unlike his older, more assertive, and demanding compatriots. When he met with Washington he again made a favorable impression, and he was overjoyed when Washington invited him to take up residence in his own house. Never having known his own father, Washington became a father figure, revered and venerated. For Washington's part, he seems to have liked the French youth, whose fine manners and civility made a favorable impression. Adroit at dropping important names, those of nobles in the highest offices in France—Maurepas, Vergennes, even the King—Lafayette presented himself as an intermediary between France and America. This made an impression. So too did Lafayette's bravery at the Battle of Brandywine, fought on September 11, shortly after he joined Washington's army as an honorary major general; he showed his mettle on the battlefield, in which he received a gunshot in the leg, an injury that he dismissed as inconsequential, a sign of character. Lafayette lived with Washington, sat at meetings of the war council, and felt that at long last he had found his place in the world. But he wanted a line command, which Washington was not prepared to give him. This made him susceptible to the machinations of Washington's enemies, those participating in the Conway Cabal.

As head of the Board of War, his reward for victory at Saratoga, Horatio Gates worked out a plan to invade Canada, which he sold to Congress. Washington thought the plan was mistaken, but not wanting to oppose a recommendation of the Board of War he said nothing. Aware of Lafayette's susceptibilities, Gates and Conway drew him into the Canada project, offering him command of the invading army. When Lafayette received instructions placing him in command of the army that was to invade Canada, he knew about Gates' and Conway's machinations against Washington, but he fell into their scheme anyway. They told him the plan was certain to succeed; the army he was to command would move up the Hudson-Champlain corridor and pass across Lake Champlain and down the Richelieu River to St. Johns. The army would then proceed to Montreal, whose capture Lafayette personally would carry out, bringing him honor and fame. Lafayette was given to understand that the French Canadians would rise up against their English masters, the Americans would offer to restore Canada to France, and Canada would enter the war on the side of their liberators. Lafayette took the bait, hook, line, and sinker, making him the instrument of Washington's enemies. That Lafayette was unable to see how he was manipulated says much about his political innocence, and how receptive he was to appeals to honor and his sense of importance. Lafayette's vision of brilliant success in Canada was a fantasy, completely at variance with the reality of actual circumstances in Canada, a flight of his romantic imagination, fueled by a wish to achieve fame.

Lafayette's correspondence before the Canada expedition reveals much about his thinking and state of mind. Writing Henry Laurens, president of Congress, on January 5, 1778, he recalled the campaigns of the previous year in which Gates had won a victory at Saratoga, whereas Washington had suffered defeat at Brandywine. Anyone, he wrote, could have defeated the British with the many advantages Gates had enjoyed, but with Washington battlefield conditions could hardly have been more different. Generals of old, great men such as Caesar, Condé, and Turenne would have suffered the same results as Washington. Over and over Lafayette harkened back to past times, times of great men and heroic exploits, an ongoing frame of reference that offered him models to emulate. He described his dedication to the ideals for which he and fellow Americans were fighting, what he called the "noble cause of liberty" in a January 26 letter to Henry Laurens.[102] Dedicated to the cause of liberty in America and waging war for a republican cause, Lafayette's mindset was that of a knight of old, keenly and proudly aware of a family pedigree that went back to the time of Hugh Capet and included an ancestor who had distinguished himself on the battlefield during the time of the Renaissance. In a January 6, 1778 letter to his wife Adrienne he described his "strange" destiny, confined to a winter camp in the "wilds of America."

> Honestly, dear heart, do you think that it would not require very strong reasons to induce me to make this sacrifice? Everything tells me to depart, but honor has told me to remain; and truly, when you know in detail the circumstances in which I find myself, the situation of the army, of my friend [Washington] who commands it . . . you will approve . . . My presence is more necessary to the American cause at this moment than you could imagine . . . [T]he English have said openly . . . [that] their hatred of me seems to grow stronger every day that I stay here . . . General Washington will be truly unhappy if I speak to him of leaving. His confidence in me is greater than my age allows me to admit . . . He finds in me a trustworthy friend to whom he can open his heart, and who always tells him the truth.[103]

The reality was that Lafayette was about to embark on a fool's errand that was concocted by Washington's enemies who exploited his vainglorious susceptibilities. When he received news of his appointment as commander of the Canadian expedition he wrote Henry Laurens, president of Congress, saying how honored he was, and how urgently he wished to justify the appointment. He would never think of "asking [for] any command, but I believe it is of my duty" to accept this one.[104] Having said that he would never request "any command," Lafayette requested the appointment of French officers to join him in the expedition to Canada, men older and with greater experience than he, whose savior he liked to think he had become. "I fancy that great many French officers, and even French soldiers scattered in the army will be given to me to establish the confidence of our fourteenth state" By "fourteenth state" he meant Canada, whose absorption into America was, in his mind, an accomplished fact.

As Lafayette made his way toward Albany he feared that Conway and William Duer, who had left a few days before he' did, would conquer Canada before he joined them. "They'll perhaps conquer Canada before my arrival, and I expect to meet them at the governor's house in Quebec."[105] Such worries were quite unnecessary, as Lafayette learned when he arrived in Albany on February 17, 1778 and set up his headquarters on North Pearl Street. He encountered complete disarray; nothing was as he had expected. He wrote the Albany Committee, Thomas Conway, and others right after his arrival, describing the problems and shortcomings with which he was faced. He wrote Henry Laurens on February 19, telling him of the "hell of blunders, madness, and deception I am involved in." He had been "deceived"; he found a "spirit of dissatisfaction everywhere"; he

> wished he had never set foot in America or thought of an American war. All the continent knows where I am, what I am sent for, I have wrote it through the whole [of] France and Europe . . . The world has theyr eyes fixed upon me . . . Men will have right to laugh at me, and I am almost ashamed to appear before some . . . No, Sir, this expedition will certainly reflect upon my reputation . . . I can not give up all ideas of penetrating into Canada, but I give up this of Going there this winter upon the ice. I will take further exertions. I Confess that I am exasperated to the utmost degree. . . .[106]

Writing Washington the same day, Lafayette again unburdened himself of his frustrations, again venting his sense of abuse and making the same charges of villainy against those who had deceived him. He had been "schamefully deceived by the board of war"; "this was certain to reflect on my reputation and I schall be laughed at." Yet he was not without hope: "[D]ear General, I know very well that you will do every thing to procure me the only thing I am ambitious of. Glory."[107] Lafayette continued to send letters to Congress, the Albany Committee, Gates, Conway, George Clinton, and Robert Morris. In a letter to Robert Morris, Lafayette explained that he needed money, and asked him to make some available. This letter is of particular interest, revealing as it does the extent of Lafayette's commitment to the American cause, which was intensely personal. He had purchased a ship and supplies before coming to America; now that he was a major general and actively involved in the American cause he would draw from his own accounts, personally financing operations in which he was involved. Men had to be paid in Albany and supplies needed to be purchased; Robert Morris arranged his finances so he could draw funds from his accounts in France. By the time the Albany episode was over Lafayette spent some $12,000 of his own money on the failed project, a substantial sum. As a leisured aristocrat who inherited vast wealth, Lafayette was in a position to use his money as he saw fit; this he did while he was in Albany during the abortive Canada expedition.

Within days of his arrival in Albany it was evident to Lafayette that the expedition to Canada had to be abandoned. Only half of the expected men were in Albany and there were no prospects of more coming. Supplies were hopelessly inadequate, with little chance of getting them in sufficient quantities. Having written Congress and Washington about problems that appeared intractable, Lafayette set about organizing things as best as he could, showing real ability as he did so. He inspected troops and worked with local authorities doing everything possible to procure provisions and supplies; he also tended to local defenses. There were constant demands for payment, both by soldiers and military suppliers, which he met in part by drawing from his private accounts. He talked to and worked with Philip Schuyler, and he talked to Benedict Arnold, who was still in Albany recovering from wounds incurred at Saratoga. Schuyler thought that if he had been in charge of the Canada expedition it would have succeeded. Arnold thought otherwise; for him the very idea of the Canada project was wrong and wrongheaded. Washington felt the same way. As Lafayette saw the Canada project coming apart before his very eyes he was drawn into other problems, first a rumored Tory attack on Albany that never materialized and then an expedition up the Mohawk to sort out Indian problems, which he did in cooperation with Philip Schuyler, long recognized as expert in dealing with Indians.

Lafayette joined Schuyler in an effort to pacify Indians, and to work out a treaty that would stabilize the area west of the Hudson, along the Mohawk corridor. He wrote Washington about the "distressing, ridiculous, foolish, and indeed nameless situation"[108] of the Indians; "Gal. Schuyller has told me that a parcel of French men would be of some use to the cause."[109] Lafayette wrote New York Governor George Clinton in Schenectady on March 3 while on his way to Johnstown where he would join Schuyler and other Indian commissioners who were already there. He reached Johnstown that night, having traveled by sleigh, a strange and bizarre episode in the life of a French aristocrat of bluest blood. While at Johnstown Lafayette met with half naked, brightly painted Indians who wore elaborate feathered headpieces, and whose ornaments included pierced ears and jeweled noses. Negotiations ran on for several days, but in time agreement was reached, after the smoking of peace pipes and distribution of gifts. Giving lavishly to Indians, Lafayette made a most favorable impression; they not only adopted him but gave him the name of Kayewla, after one of their fallen warriors. Back in Albany on March 11, Lafayette continued to work with Schuyler on local defenses and defenses along the Mohawk corridor, but it was clear to him that he had to move on. Still keenly aware of his reputation and eager to achieve fame and honor, he envisioned an attack on New York City, but he was given to understand that this was impossible. Congress had formally called off the Canada expedition and his plan for invading New York was a non-starter; there was nothing for him to do but return to Washington's headquarters at Valley Forge. He arrived there at the beginning of April. The Canada expedition had been a complete fiasco; its collapse spelled an end to the Conway Cabal. Lafayette had not gained the brilliant successes he sought, but he had acquitted himself capably, and on the balance showed himself resourceful and lavish in dispensing money from his own accounts, dedicated as he was to the virtuous cause of the American Revolution.

News of the French alliance with America arrived in late April 1778, weeks after Lafayette's return to Valley Forge. He saw himself as an important factor in the alliance between France and America, as in time he would be, but this was far from evident at the time. As was sometimes the case with Lafayette, there was a gap between his view of himself and the reality of his situation. He performed well at the Battle of Monmouth on June 28, 1778, but ran into difficulties at Newport in October. He was frustrated and wondered if it might not be best to return to France, where he could further the American cause by working the corridors of Versailles. Washington urged him to go home and to see his wife, who surely missed him deeply. The return to France was complicated by the facts of his 1777 departure, made without the King's approval; technically he was still under arrest, but after spending a week in the Hôtel de Noailles he was free to receive the acclaim rendered a hero who had taken up the American cause against Britain, now France's wartime enemy. Describing his return to France in his *Memoirs*, he admitted his error to the King, "which had such happy results . . . On my arrival I had enjoyed the honor of being consulted by all the ministers and, what was far better, being kissed by all the ladies. The kissing stopped the following day, but I retained the confidence of the ministry much longer and enjoyed both favor at Versailles and popularity in Paris."[110] For someone who needed acclaim as urgently as Lafayette did the adulation and praise in highest society, along with his newly-achieved stature at court, was deeply gratifying. The callow fugitive of 1777 was now an honored, respected 22-year-old major general who had fought alongside Washington in the war against Britain. The transformation was dramatic. With a surge of confidence, Lafayette threw himself into efforts to secure greater support for the American cause, and when he returned to America at the end of 1779 it was with Rochambeau, the general who was the architect of victory at Yorktown, in which Lafayette played an active part.

After Lafayette returned to America, Washington placed him in command of 2,000 men that he turned into a well-drilled unit. The Marquis de Chastellux, one of Rochambeau's staff officers, observed Lafayette's unit when he visited the American headquarters in New Jersey. "We found all his troops in order of battle . . . and himself at their head, expressing by his bearing and countenance that he was happier in receiving me here than at his estate in Auvergne. The confidence and attachment of the troops are to him priceless possessions, hard-won riches. . . ."[111] An acute observer whom we will meet again, Chastellux saw a confident Lafayette who would soon demonstrate real ability and leadership in the American War of Independence. As the British were committing additional forces to the 1781 campaign in the South, Washington sent two new units to counter them, one under General "Mad Anthony" Wayne, the other under Lafayette. The farther south the two American units went, the worse conditions became, leading to desertions of hungry, disaffected soldiers. To make an example, Wayne court-martialed six ringleaders and ordered their immediate execution, which their messmates carried out by shooting them at close range in front of their comrades, one of whom described the incident: "So near did they stand that the handkerchiefs covering the eyes of some of them were set on fire . . . The fence and even the heads of rye for some distance within the field were covered with the blood and brains."[112] This is not what Lafayette did. He told his men that they did not need to desert; they were free to go; he would approve leaves that would allow them to return to Morristown, but they would encounter a British army along the way. Or else they could remain with their comrades and as patriots fight an army of British soldiers. No one accepted the offer. Lafayette and his men followed Cornwallis' army farther south as the 1781 campaign was winding down. By following Cornwallis' vastly larger army closely, Lafayette made his adversary think his unit was much larger than it actually was, the very impression that he wanted to make. It was a calculated gamble that worked; it contributed to the dilemma in which Cornwallis found himself after setting up winter quarters at Yorktown. Having helped set the stage for the Battle of Yorktown, Lafayette added additional laurels by participating in the siege, and in the resulting victory, achieved by a combined French and American force of which he had become an important part.

Lafayette had grown from an insecure 19-year-old youth who wanted to prove himself worthy of his feudal ancestors into a soldier of worth and courage who won the respect of his soldiers and of the American and French military leadership, most importantly of George Washington. When he returned to Paris on January 19, 1782, he was the Hero of Two Worlds, feted and celebrated everywhere. He was in favor with Louis XVI, even with Marie Antoinette; when Adrienne saw him she fainted in his arms; poems were written in his honor, pamphlets circulated praising his achievements, and at the theater Mme Dorlay, a leading soprano, crowned a bust of Lafayette placed on the stage. Keen to achieve yet greater stature, he offered to participate in the peace talks with England, unable to recognize that someone who had fought against England was hardly suited to join peace negotiations. Lafayette's ambitions, his need for recognition, ran deep, deeper than he seems to have realized. It was not that he needed power, for this was not the case. Throughout an extremely long career in public life, Lafayette received many offers that would have given him high office, but again and again he turned them down. Achieving liberty and the participation of a sovereign people in political life were more important to Lafayette than exercising power himself; he dedicated himself to high-minded principles, placing the public good above his own personal interest. At least that was the ideal. His experience in America was the crucible within which this conception was formed. Lafayette took a five-month trip to America in 1784, visiting Washington and seeing all states in the Union; he received honors everywhere, was celebrated in dinners, and feted as America's great friend, a hero of the Revolution. The trip to America added to his luster in France; he rode the crest of his fame. Moreover, the cause to which he had dedicated himself, liberty, was all the fashion in Paris. Moving with the tide, he took up causes favored by the proponents of reform and progress. He became active in the cause to end slavery, to tolerate Protestantism, and to promote laissez-faire economic ideas; he wrote a study on the benefits of free trade. In all of this there was much high-mindedness, as when he suggested to Washington that they purchase a Virginia plantation together and emancipate its slaves. Washington did not take Lafayette up on his offer, so Lafayette purchased a plantation in French Guyana in order that he could carry out his plan there. When he went to America in 1777, Lafayette had no awareness of slavery as a problem, but after returning to France in 1781 this was no longer the case. Having embraced the cause of liberty in America he became aware of the terrible paradox of an American Revolution that had been fought in the name of liberty but did not extend that principle to blacks who continued to be bound to the institution of slavery. His purchase of a plantation in Guyana in 1786 that was to be worked by free-labor is evidence of how deeply Lafayette's thinking was transformed by his participation in the American Revolution.[113]

The France that Lafayette returned to in 1782 was experiencing serious internal difficulties, including those that resulted from her support of the American Revolution. The cost of the war resulted in a fiscal crisis in 1786; France was bankrupt; the budgetary situation was so severe that reform was essential, as Louis XVI's finance minister, Charles Alexandre de Calonne, understood full well. Calonne felt—correctly—that his plans for reform would encounter opposition in the parlements, a bastion of opposition to initiatives threatening the interests of the privileged classes, so he devised a strategy calculated to win needed support for his plan, summoning an Assembly of Notables.[114] Calonne's idea was to persuade the Assembly of Notables to support his reform plan, giving it a better chance of succeeding. The strategy did not succeed, and before the sessions ended the King dismissed Calonne, but in the course of the deliberations Lafayette, who was one of the 144 notables, came down resoundingly on the side of reform. Just before dismissal of the Assembly of Notables, Lafayette made a furious attack on abuses in the government, on profligate, favored court aristocrats, some of whom he named, and on the nobility as a separate class, whose end he called for. He also maintained that only the people could authorize new taxes, and he was the first to call for summoning the Estates General. When the King did summon the Estates General in May of 1789, Lafayette was an elected deputy of the Second Estate, and again he took a liberal position at every turn, calling for the Estates General to become a National Assembly—a step that, once approved, would turn France into a constitutional monarchy. And this is precisely what happened; again, Lafayette was marching in step with the advocates of progressive change, the cause of liberty and government subject to proper legal limits. These were principles to which Lafayette had dedicated himself in America; he now saw them coming into being in France. More than ever, Lafayette was the man of the hour.

In the heady days leading up to the summoning of the Estates General on May 4, 1789, and the subsequent transformation of the Estates General into a National Assembly on June 27, Lafayette carried on frequent conversations with Thomas Jefferson. Jefferson urged Lafayette to move with other liberal deputies of the first two estates and to join the third estate; Lafayette did not follow Jefferson's suggestion because he considered himself bound to the instructions of those who had elected him as deputy. Lafayette's mentor, George Washington, had always deferred to Congress; he steadfastly subordinated his authority to that of a duly constituted legal body. Washington felt that for power to be exercised properly it must be subject to legal limits. With Washington as a guide, Lafayette had learned respect for the law while participating in the American Revolution. Lafayette learned from both Washington and Jefferson; both were mentors whose examples and ideas gave him direction when the French Revolution was in its initial, moderate stage. It was from Thomas Jefferson that Lafayette acquired the theories, the ideology, of revolution, as set forth in the Declaration of Independence. When Lafayette wrote the Declaration of Rights of Man and Citizen in June and July 1789, he consulted with Jefferson, who helped him work his way through several drafts.[115] He presented his statement, ringing with lofty idealism, to the Assembly on July 11, and it was amended and accepted on August 26; even today it is the preamble of the French Constitution. It was on the very day that Lafayette presented the draft of his Declaration of Rights to the Assembly that the King dismissed his reforming minister, Jacques Necker, bringing in hard liners, conservatives whose charge was to impose order on a nation that the King, under intense pressure, had come to feel was spinning out of control. The King's cashiering of Necker set in motion a series of events that completely transformed the French Revolution, up to this point a political revolution carried out by elected deputies who transformed the Estates General into a National Assembly, thereby establishing the basis for constitutional monarchy, and by implication dissolving a society of legally separate orders into a modern, legally classless society with guaranteed rights. All that remained was writing the Constitution. Necker's dismissal changed everything. As soon as news of his dismissal reached Paris a huge crowd appeared at the Palais Royal, and it was there that Camille Desmoulins called the people to arms, thereby igniting a three-day insurrection that culminated in the storming of the Bastille and was followed by urban and rural insurrections across France.

Riots played an important role in the American Revolution, carried out by the people but typically directed by an elite leadership such as the Sons of Liberty. In France, popular disturbances, *émeutes* (to use the French term), had a very different morphology. The tensions and conflicts that fed into popular uprisings in France drew from anger that was a function of French history, the hatreds of a society divided into those who worked with their hands and those who did not, those with and those without privilege, the oppression and injustice of many centuries; and it drew from a popular culture in which scenarios of vengeance had been played out in times of previous crisis. Those scenarios were played out under different circumstances during the Paris insurrection of July 12–14, with consequences of profound importance. When the governor of the Bastille, Bernard Rene Jordan, Marquis de Launay, was taken to the Place de Grève on July 14 he was murdered and decapitated, as was Jacques de Flesselles, another hated official; both heads were placed on pikes and paraded through the streets of Paris, trophies of the people. The scenarios of violence were disturbing, as was the complete breakdown of royal authority in the capital. This called for an organized response. The result was establishment of the National Guard on

Figure 27. Jean-Louis Prieur, *The King at the Hôtel de Ville after the recalling of Necker*, July 17, 1789. Lafayette accompanied Louis XVI on this occasion.

July 15, the day after the storming of the Bastille and its unsettling aftermath. Lafayette rode from Versailles to Paris at the head of a delegation that was to assure those in the capital that the King had no intention of dissolving the Assembly, a message that he delivered after arriving at the Hôtel de Ville. Two royal official officials had been murdered and decapitated just outside the Hôtel de Ville on the previous day; maintaining order was now seen as essential, and choosing someone to undertake this responsibility had already been discussed. After delivering his speech in the Hôtel de Ville someone moved that Lafayette be appointed head of a National Guard and the assembled crowd chose him with one voice, but Lafayette declined the position; he maintained that his appointment needed the approval of the Assembly, and to be affirmed by popular election. He did agree to accept the position provisionally, and when Louis XVI rode in a carriage to the Hôtel de Ville on July 17 to acknowledge the popular revolution in Paris, he was accompanied by Lafayette. By this time the King had come to dislike Lafayette, but they exchanged polite civilities, and when Louis XVI accepted a red and blue ribbon, the colors of the city of Paris, Lafayette added white, the color of the Bourbons, expressing national unity in the tricolor, a revolutionary symbol. This gesture clarifies the position of Lafayette in the French Revolution perfectly; unity was his goal throughout, but it was a goal that he was unable to achieve; forces had been unleashed in Paris on July 12–14 that made Lafayette's goal of unity a chimera—a vision that was not to be realized. Nor would Lafayette's program of moderate, liberal reform be achieved; it too was a casualty of the popular revolution of July 1789, and its impact on the revolutionary dynamic in coming months, and beyond. Well-intentioned as Lafayette was, he was unable to give the Revolution the direction he sought; that he was unable to prevent descent from order to disorder was not his fault. No one could have directed the Revolution safely through the difficult waters that lay ahead. The course of the French Revolution was to be utterly different from Lafayette's model, the American Revolution.

The problems that Lafayette was to confront were revealed in all of their harshness eight days after the Fall of the Bastille when he tried to protect Foulon de Doué after he was forcibly returned to Paris. A mob inside the Hôtel de Ville, where he had been taken, wanted to lynch Foulon, but when Lafayette arrived he argued against such an outcome, and for respect of the law. By this time Lafayette had prevented some 17 lynchings; he would now try to do so again.

> You are trying to bring the man who stands before you to death without trial; it is an injustice which would dishonor you, tarnish me, and tarnish all the efforts I have made in favor of liberty—were I so weak as to permit it . . . But I am very far from trying to save the man if he is guilty; I desire no more than that he be taken to prison, to be tried by whatever tribunal the nation shall appoint.

Figure 28. Jean-Louis Prieur, *The Hanging of Foulon at the Place de Grève*, July 22, 1789. After lynching Foulon a crowd took the decapitated head and body up the rue St. Martin where another crowd was proceeding in the opposite direction, taking his son-in-law, Bertier de Sauvigny, to the Hôtel de Ville. Bertier was also a victim of popular justice on this fateful day. Lafayette was unable to prevent the lynching of either man; he tried to save both but was unable to. Lafayette wanted to observe the rule of law; furious crowds wanted to settle scores with their enemies.

> The stronger the presumption of his guilt, the more important it is that the forms be respected in his case, whether in order that his punishment be the more striking, or in order that he may be questioned and the names of his accomplices obtained from his mouth.[116]

Lafayette's appeal to an angry crowd inside the Hôtel de Ville was to no avail; the roar of protest was deafening as the people seized Foulon and dragged him outside to the Place de Grève, where he was hung from a lamppost and decapitated. As we have seen, the same fate awaited his son-in-law, Bertier de Sauvigny later in the same day. A similar unfolded in Troyes, east of Paris, when Claude Huez, the mayor, was dragged through the streets, still alive, with hay stuffed in his mouth. A crowd put out his eyes with a chisel and then killed him in the presence of his family. Lafayette tendered his resignation as head of the National Guard on July 23, the day after the murder of Foulon and Bertier de Sauvigny, but Bailly, the mayor of Paris, pleaded with him to retain a position that he argued no one could fill as well as he, as did the Assembly of Electors. Lafayette withdrew his resignation and remained head of the National Guard for an additional two years, until another crisis led to his resignation on July 19, 1791. On this occasion no one urged him to reconsider. What prompted Lafayette's resignation on this occasion was the July 17 Massacre at the Champ de Mars, when Bailly, the mayor of Paris, called upon the National Guard to maintain order in a time of extreme volatility following the abortive flight of the King and Queen to Varennes. Lafayette did as Bailly had requested and tried to maintain order, but the National Guard fired into a crowd at the Champ de Mars, discrediting both Bailly and Lafayette. Lafayette fled France in August 1792, but Bailly remained in Paris. When he was executed in October 1793, the guillotine was moved to the Champ de Mars, a reprisal for his role in the Champ de Mars massacre. The fates of Bailly and Lafayette, both leaders of the liberal revolution of 1789, say much about the political fragmentation within France as the Revolution veered in directions that no one could have foretold in the immediate aftermath of the Paris insurrection of July 14.

François-Jean de Beauvoir, Chevalier, and after 1784 Marquis de Chastellux (1734–1788), arrived in Albany on a snowy, wintry day on December 24, 1780, to see Phillip Schuyler, after making an arduous trip up the Hudson River. Chastellux is one of the most interesting of all visitors who came up the Hudson to see Philip Schuyler during the American Revolution. There is an historical marker in front of Schuyler Mansion, commemorating the visit of this French aristocrat, whose account of Schuyler and his mansion in his *Travels in Nortrh America* is of considerable documentary value. Chastellux was from a family of the French nobility whose castle was east of Paris, near the monastery of Vézelay, one of the jewels of French Romanesque architecture, in which he doubtless had little or no interest. A creature of the French Enlightenment, Chastellux was dedicated to reason, scientific objectivity, and perfection of life here on this earth. He was an apostle of progress, typical of the times. His best-known work was a treatise on happiness, *De la Félicité*, (1772), which Voltaire admired, and with whom he corresponded. Before writing this treatise he published an analysis of Frederick the Great's *Instructions militaire pour ses Généraux*; he also translated Shakespeare's *Romeo and Juliette* into French, giving it a happy ending, and he wrote various and sundry other works that made him a figure of some importance in Paris salons and within the world of eighteenth-century French letters. He was admitted to the Academy, a tribute to his reputation if not necessarily proof of great talent. An accomplished writer, he was a creature of the optimistic, liberal, civilized world of Paris salons in the second half of the eighteenth century. Fluent in English, he was well equipped to write a book that described his experiences in America during his three-year stay in the New World. He did this in his *Travels in North America*, written while serving as a major general under Rochambeau.

As a noble, Chastellux pursued a military career, typical of someone of his class. He entered the army at age 13 as a junior officer in the Auvergne Regiment, became a colonel at 21, participated in campaigns in Germany from 1756 to 1763 during the Seven Years War, and was made major general in 1780 before departing for America. By this time he had met Benjamin Franklin and Silas Deane; like other French intellectuals he was interested in the American Revolution, which he wanted to see at first hand. He knew Beaumarchais, whose idealized view of America he shared. He wrote in *De La Félicité* that

> . . . we may point out that all wars are not contrary to the welfare of mankind, just as all sicknesses are not harmful to the individual they attack. In both cases there may come a favorable crisis, which cures previous ills and produces a permanent state of robust health. What every philosopher must hope for is that America will continue to grow in population and in perfection; for reason, legislation, and the happiness that results from them, can never cover too much of this globe, where all is interrelated and all is linked as by a chain, now apparent, now hidden.[117]

Eager to see how things in America were connected in this best of possible worlds, he set out on the first of his travels when the 1780 campaign had, in effect, ended. As he put it, "For the first time I might now without risk absent myself from the army; but not wishing to show too much impatience . . . [I was able to set] out on a long tour upon the continent."[118] When he left Newport in November he was accompanied by two other officers, M. Lynch and M. de Montesquieu, each of whom had a servant; for his part, Chastellux had three servants. In the course of a trip that lasted from November 11, 1780 to January 9, 1781, Chastellux went through Connecticut, New York, New Jersey, and Pennsylvania as far as Philadelphia, and from there he traveled north until he reached the Hudson, along which he made his way to Albany, where he had made plans to see Philip Schuyler. Before reaching Albany, Chastellux met some important figures, both American and French. He met Colonel Jeremiah Wadsworth in Hartford on November 16, with whom he lodged. While in Hartford he looked up Governor Jonathon Trumbull, who made a fine impression: "his whole life has been devoted to public service, which he passionately loves . . . He has all the simplicity in his dress, all the importance, and even the pedantry becoming the great magistrate of a little republic."[119] Chastellux reached Washington's headquarters at Preakness, New Jersey on November 25, where he met Lafayette, Alexander Hamilton, and Henry Knox. He stayed with Washington, whose "goodness and benevolence" and "noble politeness" he found impressive; he was also impressed by the youthful Lafayette, whose private letters "have frequently produced more effect on some states than the strongest recommendations from Congress."[120] From Preakness, Chastellux continued on to Philadelphia, where he was caught up in the social whirl, meeting with the Shippens and other important families. He also met Gouverneur Morris at this time. Throughout his travels Chastellux was interested in and commented upon people who had fought at Saratoga, a battle whose significance was clearly on his mind. It was because he wanted to see the battlefield at Saratoga that Chastellux traveled to Albany to meet with Schuyler. Schuyler had been told that Chastellux was coming, and he was awaiting his arrival on December 24 when he appeared at the ferry on the opposite side of the river, directly opposite his Albany mansion.

Looking across the Hudson, Chastellux saw "A handsome house halfway up the bank . . . I had recommendations to [Schuyler] from all quarters, but particularly from General Washington and Mrs. Carter."[121] The Mrs. Carter to whom Chastellux referred was Angelica Schuyler Church, Schuyler's eldest daughter, whom he had met in Newport, and who had just attended the wedding of her sister Elizabeth to Alexander Hamilton. Two French officers had reached Schuyler's mansion the day before he did, the Vicomte de Noailles and the Comte de Damas. Chastellux thought he had seen Noailles looking at him through a telescope from a window in Schuyler's house, and guessed

> . . . that he was going to send somebody to conduct us on our landing to that excellent house, where we should find a dinner ready; I even pretended that a sleigh I had seen coming down towards the river was for us. Never was a conjecture more just. The first person we saw on the shore was the Chevalier de Mauduit, who was waiting for us with the General's sleigh, into which we quickly stepped, and found ourselves in an instant in a handsome drawing room, near a good fire, with Mr. Schuyler, his wife, and daughters. While we were warming ourselves, dinner was served, to which everyone did honors, as well as to the Madeira, which was excellent, and which made us completely forget the rigor of the season and the fatigue of the journey.[122]

Chastellux had made it known that he wanted to see the Saratoga battlefield and with Schuyler's assistance he made plans to depart the next day, December 25. As Schuyler was having one of his periodic attacks of the gout he was unable to accompany them, but Chastellux and his fellow travelers were to have the use of his home in Saratoga, and he sent his son ahead to make everything ready for their arrival. The travelers set out early in the morning as snow was beginning to fall, and by the time they reached the Hudson the snow was coming down heavily. Yet they wanted to continue on to Saratoga, just as Franklin and his fellow travelers had four years earlier, and under similar conditions. Chastellux and his companions rode along the Mohawk until they heard a dull roar, the sound of Cohoes Falls, which they found a stupendous sight to behold, with water "dashing over the cataract."[123] Continuing, they came to a ferry that was to take them across the Mohawk, but they were told the passage might not be possible. They tried, failed in the effort, and realized that they had no choice but to return to Albany.

Staying in an inn the night of the 25th, Chastellux was visited the next morning by Alexander Hamilton, who told him that Mrs. Schuyler was a "little indisposed," but that

> the General would be none the less pleased to receive us at his house during the evening. Accordingly he sent us his sleigh at nightfall. We found him in the drawing room with Mr. and Mrs. Hamilton. Conversation soon began between the General, the Vicomte de Noailles, and myself. We had already talked, two days earlier, of certain important facts concerning the northern campaign, about which we had asked for explanations. Mr. Schuyler appeared no less desirous of giving them. He is rather communicative and is well entitled to be so, his conversation is easy and agreeable; he knows full well what he is speaking of, and speaks well about what he knows. To give the best answer to our questions, he suggested letting us read his political and military correspondence with General Washington; we accepted the proposal with great pleasure, and leaving the rest of the company with Mr. and Mrs. Hamilton, we retired into another room.[124]

Going through the correspondence between Schuyler and Washington before the Battle of Saratoga and discussing events leading up to it, Chastellux came to know much about a battle in which he had keen interest. In the course of the conversation with Schuyler, Chastellux also learned of the abortive invasion of Canada, led by Lafayette, in 1778. It was evident to Chastellux that as he passed up the Hudson-Champlain corridor he was traversing ground of great military importance, on which battles had been fought whose outcomes were responsible for him being where he was, a French officer serving in a French army that was directly involved in the American Revolution.

Unable to cross the Mohawk at Cohoes on December 25, Chastellux and his aide-de-camp, Charles-Louis de Secondat, Baron de Montesquieu (grandson of the great philosophe), went to Schenectady by sleigh on December 27, where they were to spend the night before continuing north to Saratoga. Between Albany and Schenectady, Chastellux wrote, there was nothing but forest. Just before reaching Schenectady the travelers came to a squalid Indian village, occupied by some 350 natives, whom he speculated would become civilized some day. They received a letter from Schuyler the following day, December 28, saying that he was feeling better and that they should return to Albany in order that he could join them in the trip to Saratoga. Chastellux returned and "walked about Albany" on December 29, looking for weapons that had been used at Saratoga. He found "eight handsome mortars and twenty ammunition wagons, which formed part of Burgoyne's artillery."[125] He also visited a hospital where soldiers wounded at Saratoga had received treatment. The next day, December 30, the travelers set out for Saratoga in five sleighs, with Schuyler leading the way. They crossed the Mohawk and as they headed north Schuyler showed Chastellux some redoubts he had built while preparing defenses against Burgoyne's army. Continuing, they reached Gates' position at Bemis Heights, which they stopped to examine. They walked across the battlefield and surveyed the woods around Freeman's Farm while Schuyler discussed the battle in which he had not participated. He pointed out the place where Arnold had attacked the British: "I saw the spot," Chastellux wrote, "where Arnold, uniting the boldness of a 'jockey' with that of a soldier, leaped his horse over the entrenchment of the enemy." Chastellux continued his

> . . . reconnoitering until dark [after Schuyler left him]; sometimes walking in the snow, into which I sank to the knees, and sometimes proceeding still less successfully in a sleigh, my driver having taken the trouble to tip me over, very gently indeed, into a beautiful pile of snow. At length, after surveying Burgoyne's lines, I came down to the main road, passing through a field where he had established the hospital. We then traveled more easily, and I got to Saratoga at seven in the evening . . . [W]e found good rooms well warmed, an excellent supper, and gay and agreeable conversation; for General Schuyler, like many European husbands, is still more amiable when he is absent from his wife. He gave us instructions for our next day's reception to Fort Edward and to the great cataract of the Hudson River, eight miles above the fort and ten miles from Lake George.[126]

Chastellux went to Fort Edward the next day, saw the place where Jane McCrea had been murdered and scalped, and continued to Lake George, where he saw the results of scorched-earth warfare visited on bitterly contested land in a struggle that was of deep historical importance. Chastellux understood all of this full well; this was why he made the trip up the Hudson-Champlain corridor in the dead of winter. Schuyler took Chastellux and his traveling companions to the site of Burgoyne's surrender the next day, January 31. "We could not have had a better guide." Schuyler described Burgoyne's retreat, the burning of his house from "ill temper," and Burgoyne's stay at his Albany residence after his surrender. Chastellux's account of Burgoyne's stay in Albany is the fullest and best we have, replete with vivid detail, including that of a prank played by Schuyler's son.

> Mr. Schuyler's second son, then about seven years old, a spoiled little child, as are all American children . . . was running . . . all over the house, according to custom; he opened the door of the room, burst out laughing on seeing these Englishmen, collected there, and shutting the door behind him, said to them, "You are all my prisoners." This innocent remark was cruel to them, and rendered them more melancholy than they had been the evening before.[127]

Returning to Albany the next day, January 1, 1781, Chastellux heard New Year's Day celebrations. It was the beginning of a year that was to have a momentous outcome, one in which Chastellux played a role. He was with Rochambeau's army at Yorktown, participating in the climacteric battle of the American Revolution. This was after Chastellux visited the battlefield of Saratoga, the turning point of the Revolution; all was interconnected.

By the time Chastellux returned to France in 1783 he had visited Thomas Jefferson at Monticello, enjoying his distinguished host's fine hospitality, his fine wine, and his conversation, although he found Jefferson "grave and a little cold," at least at first. Jefferson warmed up, and it was if they were old friends by the time of Chastellux's departure. Upon returning to France Chastellux resumed his former way of life, liberal, tolerant, generous of spirit, his outlook having been broadened by his experiences in America. He was elected to the American Philosophical Society, the American Academy of Arts and Sciences, and received honorary degrees from William and Mary and the University of Pennsylvania. In 1784 he became the Marquis de Chastellux when his older brother died, the same year in which he helped Jefferson find a house when he arrived in Paris. He looked up Schuyler's daughter and son-in-law, the John Barker Churches, when they moved to Paris. But he was not in Paris when Gouverneur Morris, whom he had met in Philadelphia, arrived in February 1789; Chastellux died four months before Morris arrived in Paris, but he had written him a few months earlier about his marriage.

> A revolution has been wrought in my destiny, my dear Morris, diametrically opposite to that which has taken place in your country. When I saw you, I was free; I am no longer; or rather I have exchanged a painful and heavy chain for the most gentle hands . . . In this sad situation, obliged to be absent from Paris, to attend to my business as inspector, I resolved to visit the waters of Spa, in the interval between my reviews. My soul, my dear Morris,

was withered and overwhelmed. I saw nothing in the remainder of my career, to attach me to life, when that vast consciousness of strangers who assemble at Spa, presented to me one charming in my eyes as in those of all others; but especially fascinating by her mind, and most lovely character.[128]

Chastellux was 56 and the lovely woman he met at Spa, a member of the Duchesse d'Orléans' circle, was 28. They were married at the very moment at which political tremors, beginning in Paris, were about to pass across France. Chastellux did not live to see the changes wrought by those tremors, but an American visitor who looked up his wife after arriving in Paris was there, offering him a front-row view of the French Revolution. That visitor, of course, was Gouverneur Morris.

George Washington, accompanied by Governor George Clinton, General Henry Knox, and General Frederick B.A.H.F., Baron Von Steuben, arrived in Albany on July 27. 1782.[129] Twenty-eight years had passed since Washington lit the torch of war when he gave orders to his men to fire on a contingent of French soldiers some 40 miles from the Forks of the Ohio River. The fledgling officer who gave that order became the great hero of the American Revolution, an outcome that no one could have foreseen at the time of this incident. Washington began his ascent to fame with high hopes and great ambition but limited opportunities. His father, Augustine Washington, left his estate to George's older half-brother Lawrence, who had the benefit of an English education. Eleven at the time of his father's death, George had to make his own way in the world. Unable to go to college, he acquired the skills of a surveyor by the time he was 16, but powerfully built and a superb equestrian, he resolved to enter the rarefied world of the Virginia elite as a soldier. He was with Braddock in 1755 when his army was ambushed by a force of French and Indians; he commented afterward that he had "heard the bullets whistle and, believe me, there is something charming in the sound." He wanted nothing more than to receive a commission as an officer in a unit of British regulars, but this was not to be. Denied what he sought and subject to the slights of British superiors, Washington left the military while the French and Indian war was still in progress. Had he become an officer in a unit of British regulars he could conceivably have fought for Britain in the American War of Independence; as Commander in Chief of the Continental Army he became the very embodiment of the American Revolution and the most famous living American.

Awaiting Washington on a dock at the time of his arrival in Albany in July 1782 were Major General Philip Schuyler, Brigadier General Peter Gansevoort, Mayor Abraham Ten Broeck, and assorted local worthies and dignitaries. An address prepared by the "Mayor, Aldermen and Commonalty of the City of Albany" welcomed Washington and his distinguished traveling companions, a 13-gun salute sounded, and church bells began to ring, as they did for the next two hours. The guests walked to City Hall, located on what is now Hudson and Broadway, passing through a cheering crowd that lined both sides of the street. In a ceremony at City Hall, Mayor Ten Broeck gave Washington freedom of the city, symbolized by a document placed in a gold box. After the welcoming ceremony ended Washington and his illustrious companions rode up the hill in a carriage to The Pastures. Schuyler had invited Washington to visit him several times; now the renowned hero of the American War of Independence was enjoying his hospitality in his Albany mansion. General and Mrs. Schuyler organized a party for the evening, with officers in uniform attending, along with important Albanians, suitably dressed for the occasion. Musicians played and the guests danced, Washington and Mrs. Schuyler being the first to grace the dance floor, going through the formal steps of a minuet, according to accounts of the evening. Upon leaving the dance floor, men surrounded Washington and plied him with questions about the disposition of English armies still in America, the prospects for peace, when Congress would pay the army, and what land was like in the Ohio territory that lay to the west.

Washington did not come to Albany just to pay respects to an old friend, Philip Schuyler, with whom he had maintained regular correspondence since the beginning of the Revolution, even less for social reasons, although there can be little doubt that he did mix business with pleasure while in Albany. A combined French and American army had defeated and captured a complete British army at Yorktown seven months before Washington arrived in Albany, setting the stage for peace negotiations; but the war was by no means over and fighting continued in 1782, largely in the South. Warfare had been concentrated most heavily in the North and the Middle States in the first several years of the Revolution, but the British strategy changed, making the South the main theater of war. Yet, the North was never outside British military thinking. This, of course, included the Hudson-Champlain corridor. A British army in Canada might move down Lake Champlain again, or down the Mohawk from Fort Oswego. British forces in Canada were always a threat, and rumors began to circulate in the spring of 1781 of a plan to capture Philip Schuyler, perhaps at his estate in Saratoga, perhaps at his mansion in Albany. In early July, the Second New York Regiment was stationed in Albany, and on July 29, 1781, a gathering of men thought to be from Canada were seen lurking in a wooded area outside Albany. On August 7, a party of some 20 men raided Schuyler's Albany mansion while his family was there, breaking into the home in an attempt to capture Schuyler, on whose head a £200 reward had been placed. Schuyler had the presence of mind to shout out the window for men to rush to his rescue, quick thinking on his part since no men were there. The raiders stole silver and fled, having killed two of Schuyler's retainers and injuring a third. The raiding party had been organized at Saint Johns by St. Leger, in an effort to demoralize the revolutionary effort in New York. Simultaneously, 300 Indians and 90 Tories launched an attack from Niagara, striking as far east as Ulster County. In his report on the Albany episode St. Leger said:

> The Attack and defense of [Schuyler's] House was bloody and obstinate, on both sides, when the doors were forced the Servants fought till they were all wounded or disarm[e]d. The uproar of Mrs. Schuyler And the cries of the children obliged them to retire with two prisoners being the only persons that cou[l]d be mov[e]d on Account of their Wounds; two Men of the 34th were slightly wounded.[130]

Three months after the raid on Alexandre-Sébastien there was continuing fear of a British attack along the Hudson-Champlain corridor, a time of great strain for Schuyler. On October 9, John Stark asked him to come to Saratoga if his health permitted; he feared an enemy attack on Saratoga from Lake George, and on October 12, Stark told Schuyler that British invaders were moving south from Lake George and that Albany was threatened again. In Schuyler's absence, Stark built barracks around his house in Saratoga. This was late in 1781. While Yorktown changed everything, the military situation in New York was anything but clear; in early February 1782, Col. Marinus Willett tried to take Fort Oswego from the British but failed and problems with Indians continued. Schuyler and Washington worked together on supply issues in early 1782, and in June Schuyler was not yet certain that the British might not launch another attack down the Champlain-Hudson corridor. What the British might do was unclear; even if the prospects for peace were favorable, the British wanted to obtain the best terms possible, and might carry out military initiatives to that end. It was under these conditions that Washington visited Albany on June 27, 1782. Before departing for Albany on June 24 he posted a letter to Rochambeau spelling out his plans: "I am at this moment on the point of setting out for Albany, on a visit to my posts in the vicinity of that place. My stay will not exceed eight or ten days, and will be shortened if any dispatches should be received by you in the meantime." After spending the day in Albany on June 28, Washington rode on horseback to Saratoga on June 29 where, as reported by the Pennsylvania Gazette, "he inspected the theatre of the glorious campaign of 1777." He reviewed the New Hampshire regiment that was on duty, inspected the blockhouses, and saw officers who were eager to meet with the Commander in Chief. Having presided over the American victory at Yorktown, Washington now saw the battlefield of Saratoga that made it possible. After seeing Saratoga Washington rode to Schenectady where he met with a council of Oneidas and Tuscaroras, whose alliance with the American cause continued to be important. There were official ceremonies in Schenectady, as there had been in Albany a few days earlier. Washington rode to Albany in the evening, spent the night at The Pastures, and was aboard his sloop early the next morning, July 1, which took him back to headquarters in Newburgh.

Washington was in Newburgh with most of the Continental Army in March 1783, watching New York City, still occupied by the British. Hostilities had virtually ceased and negotiations were under way for a peace settlement, whose announcement all sides expected presently. Dissolution of the Continental Army in the near future was likely, and it was under these circumstances that officers, many in debt after years of military service and fearing that Congress would not meet previous promises on back pay and pensions, considered striking at Congress to secure what they believed had been promised them and was rightfully theirs. Washington's former aide-de-camp, Alexander Hamilton, now a member of Congress, wrote him a letter on February 13, alerting him to a conspiracy of officers who might march on Congress and impose its demands in a military coup. Washington responded to Hamilton's warning on March 4, thanking him for providing "foreknowledge" that he was "upon the brink of a precipice . . . [without being] aware" of his danger.[131]

In early March an unsigned declaration began to circulate through the army camp, the Newburgh Address, as it has come to be called, denouncing Washington for not giving sufficient support to his officers, whose fate, the instigators felt, was to live out "the miserable remnant" of their lives in the "vile mire of poverty" unless they acted. The declaration stated that if the officers' demands were not met they would disband; they were prepared to impose their demands on Congress. Having seen the declaration, Washington called a meeting of all officers, implying that he would not be there. After Horatio Gates called the meeting to order on March 15, a side door opened and Washington appeared, to the surprise of many and the chagrin of some. From Washington's point of view, the war for independence was, in effect, over; after eight years of heroic struggle and great sacrifices the Americans were at the cusp of victory. Throughout, Washington had steadfastly deferred to Congress, whose authority over the military he had insisted upon recognizing. For Washington this principle was to be one of the foundations of the American nation; sympathetic as he was to the plight of his officers, subordination of the military to Congress was a principle that he wanted, at all cost, to uphold.

Horatio Gates had not expected Washington to attend the meeting of officers on March 15, and was taken aback when he entered the room. The mood was tense and the outcome uncertain as Washington, not at ease when addressing audiences, began to read a speech that he had prepared. He did not mince words as he denounced the Newburgh Address, which he considered "insidious" and a "betrayal" of all that he and his men had fought for. It would "open the flood-gates of civil discord" and "deluge our rising empire in blood." These were not words that men on the verge of taking matters into their own hands wanted to hear, and sensing uncertainty, or restiveness, within the meeting place at Newburgh, the recently constructed Hall of Honor, Washington had the presence of mind to strike a different chord as he reached the end of his speech. In what appears to have been a spontaneous gesture, made on the spur of the moment, Washington took a letter from the inside of his coat pocket, which he began to read, but was able to do so only with difficulty, he said, as he stumbled over the first sentences. He reached into his pocket again, this time removing a pair of spectacles, which he had not worn publicly, and the sight of which was a surprise to his men. "Gentlemen," he said, "you will permit me to put on my spectacles, for I have not only grown gray but almost blind in the service of my country."[132] By the time Washington left his men after reading the meaningless letter, he had taken the wind out of the Newburgh Conspiracy. Eyes had welled up as Washington's improvised thespian exercise achieved its desired end. Officers on the verge of striking at Congress were made to remember that the general they had served under had been with them throughout the long struggle; he had shared their hardships; he was one of them.

Washington sailed up the Hudson to see Philip Schuyler a second time, in July 1783, having released his soldiers in the aftermath of the Newburgh Conspiracy. He again stayed with Schuyler, as he had before, and he rode north again, this time to see the beautiful and historically important Hudson-Champlain corridor without concern for a British military threat. He had made arrangements with Schuyler for Governor Clinton to accompany him on a tour of the battlefield that was the turning point of the Revolution, and this he did. Also, Washington wanted to travel up the Mohawk River Valley, which he had discussed with Schuyler, as knowledgeable about this part of New York as any living person and known for his interest in land speculation. Both Washington and Schuyler were aristocrats, landowners, and speculators in land, alert to opportunities for gain; this was perhaps the main reason for Washington's 1783 trip to Albany, which turned out very nicely for Washington. With advice from Schuyler he invested in land in Oneida County, from which he realized a fifty-percent profit when he sold it ten years later, in 1793.

One of the men who had traveled up the Hudson to Albany between 1776 and 1783 made the passage again in early October 1787. On this occasion, he was on a sloop with his wife Elizabeth, the daughter of Philip Schuyler, and they were on their way to Schuyler's mansion, where they had been married. Alexander Hamilton had been in Philadelphia as a member of the Constitutional Convention, which had disbanded on September 27, after completing a draft of the Constitution. Hamilton was not Philip Schuyler's only Hudson River visitor who sat with delegates of the Constitutional Convention in Philadelphia. So too did Benjamin Franklin, who had returned to America from France in 1785,

Gouverneur Morris, who spoke more often than any other delegate and held the pen that wrote the Constitution, and George Washington, who presided over the proceedings but spoke hardly at all.

A few days after Hamilton arrived in Albany, Philip Schuyler invited some friends to his mansion for an evening's entertainment, perhaps to show off his illustrious son-in-law, recently engaged in a matter of some importance in Philadelphia. Among those present at the dinner party was James Kent, who later described a discussion in which Schuyler held forth on the need for a national revenue system. Kent was surprised that "Mr. Hamilton appeared to be careless and desultory in his remarks," for this was a subject that interested him keenly. Reflecting on the conversation, Kent explained that "it occurred to me [only] afterwards that [Hamilton] was deeply meditating the plan of the immortal work of *The Federalist*." Elizabeth Hamilton, looking back at the early October visit to her father's Albany residence, said that "My beloved husband wrote the outline of his papers in *The Federalist* on board one of the North River sloops while on his way to Albany. . . ."[133] Hamilton was well aware of opposition to the Constitution; it was in the course of his trip to Albany in early October that the idea came to him to mount a defense of the Constitution. Comprised of 85 essays published as newspaper articles, *The Federalist* set forth arguments in favor of the Constitution and responded to the objections of its critics. Written under the name of "Publius," *The Federalist* has recently been described as "the best historical record, by far, of the uniquely American contribution to political thought and practice."[134] Hamilton asked three other men to join him in mounting a defense of the Constitution, John Jay, Gouverneur Morris, and James Madison. Morris declined, Jay wrote a few articles but dropped out after being injured in a street riot, and the authorship fell almost entirely to Hamilton and Madison. Hamilton could have chosen no better person to defend the Constitution than Madison, for he was its principal architect. It was he who wrote the Constitution for a nation that was to have the longest continuous democracy in the world. Perhaps it should be said that Madison *laid the foundation* for what was to become the longest continuous democracy in the world, for Madison was no democrat eager to place power in the hands of the people.

Among the delegates who assembled in Philadelphia, Alexander Hamilton was perhaps the most candid in expressing uneasiness about a "turbulent" people that "seldom judge or determine right." He wanted to arrest the democratization of America, not further it; for him the Constitution was to be a "shield against the 'imprudence' of democracy." Commenting on the Articles of Confederation, James McHenry of Maryland felt that "Our chief danger arises from the democratic parts of our constitutions." Elbridge Gerry of Massachusetts maintained that the "evils we experience flow from the excess of democracy," and that the delegates should find ways to restrain "the fury of democracy." For Madison, the answer to these nagging worries was what he later called the "republican remedy," mixed government that would prevent the "sinister views" of any single group from controlling central government. Like other delegates, Madison was deeply apprehensive over the people, whom he considered potentially disruptive. Those who held national office were to be of "a better class of leaders" drawn from "a better class" of society; in other words, Madison felt that America's leaders were to be of the elite.[135]

The delegates who met in Philadelphia in May 1787 gathered under the specter of Shays Rebellion, an uprising in western Massachusetts that began in the summer of 1786 and was a response to high taxes and the fear of court actions that threatened farmers with the loss of their farms. Some farmers had fallen into debt and been jailed. The leader of the uprising, Daniel Shays, a farm laborer with little education before the Revolution began, fought at Bunker Hill and Saratoga; like other farmer-soldiers he endured much in the long and trying War of Independence. Having returned to western Massachusetts in 1780, he was elected to local office and became a leader of resentful farmers who feared the money men in Boston and courts that they felt did their bidding. Having forced local courts to suspend sessions, Shays led a band of some 1,200 armed men who tried to seize the Federal arsenal at Springfield in January 1787. The insurgents were crushed by a superior force of 4,400 men, armed with cannon, led by General Benjamin Lincoln. When George Washington received news of Shays Rebellion he exclaimed, "Good God!"; like other men of property, he was afraid that the rebellion in western Massachusetts would spread to other states. "There are combustibles in every State, which a spark may set fire to." Washington feared that Britain might seize "every opportunity to foment the spirit of turbulence within the bowels of the United States." He—and others—wanted a national constitution that would give "energy and respectability to the Government."[136] The prospect of popular protest did not sit well with delegates in Philadelphia, none of whom were artisans or laborers; there were no leather apron men at the Constitutional Convention and there were no farmers. None of the framers of the Constitution worked with their hands; all were of the elite.

From the beginning of the Revolution elite leaders enlisted the support of ordinary Americans; while they fought side-by-side and struggled together in a common cause, the division between the elite and the people never disappeared. Revolutionary rhetoric proclaimed that "all men are born free" and it espoused the principles of liberty and equality, but this did not translate into the notion of social equality. John Adams said he wanted "a return to a 'Christian Sparta,' a virtuous egalitarian society," but he railed against the most forceful enunciation of democratic principles that appeared during the American Revolution, Thomas Paine's *Common Sense.*[137] Adams' fear of a "democratic tyranny" was shared by much of the Revolution's leadership; indeed, the fear was pervasive, and it was present at the end of the Revolution as well as at the beginning. It has even been argued that the Revolution *sharpened* the division between the elite and the people.[138] That division was of central importance to the eight-year struggle that unfolded in America between 1776 and 1783, which was at once a war of independence and a revolution. Those who came together in a common cause fought for independence from British imperial rule, but they also fought for ideas—for liberty, equality, and freedom. It was the latter struggle that was unresolved when Britain recognized America's independence in 1783. The Constitution was an attempt to resolve the deep contradictions within an America through which a division separating the elite from the people remained after America gained her independence. One could say that the system of mixed government that Madison constructed was the single most important stage of the American Revolution after the War of Independence. At the core of Madison's mental process as he worked his way through his design for the Constitution was fear of an unruly people and, at the same time, a search for political continuity and social stability. Among his guides was the Scottish philosopher, David Hume, who threw out the idea that republican government might be best suited for a large territory rather than a small one. Political theorists from Plato to Machiavelli had maintained that republics were feasible only in small political units, such as the Greek or Italian city-state; seizing on Hume's idea that republican government might work best in a large political unit, Madison combined that concept with the idea of mixed government, as advocated by the French philosophe Montesquieu. As conceptualized by Madison, and laid out in *The Federalist* No. 10, America would be a republic, and power would be dispersed through three branches of government. Built into the very form of government in the American republic was the idea that disagreement was not only necessary in the life of a political community but salutary. Power was to be checked by power.

To appreciate the order of Madison's achievement one need only consider the outcome of an assembly of men who came together in France to carry out needed change at almost exactly the same time that the Constitutional Convention met in Philadelphia. An Assembly of Notables gathered at the Salle des Menus Plaisirs at Versailles on February 22, 1787, summoned by the King's Finance Minister, Charles Alexandre de Calonne, who was faced with a fiscal crisis that can be traced back to the Battle of Saratoga. Calonne hoped not only to solve the problem of France's bankruptcy but to carry out extensive reform measures. The problem was that he was the man in the middle, with reactionaries on one side and liberals on the other. The most extreme of the liberals, as it turned out, was among Philip Schuyler's Albany visitors from 1776 to 1783. It was the Marquis de Lafayette who first called for a summoning of the Estates General, and when they were summoned he was among the deputies who assembled at Versailles in May 1789. He was one of the leaders of a French Revolution that was tied at the hip to the American Revolution. In contrast to the American Revolution, whose subsequent political history has been continuous, the French Revolution lasted a mere five years. It ended in the bloodbath of the Terror.

The division between the elite and the people went far deeper in France than in America, and it resulted in hatreds that were at the center of a revolution that began amidst rejoicing and euphoria in July 1789, but fell into fierce internal struggles that ended in tragedy in July 1794.

The seeds of the Terror were planted at the beginning of the Revolution, in the summer of 1789, when the people of Paris rose up in a three-day insurrection. In the weeks that followed the Paris Insurrection, deputies of the National Assembly discussed ideas for the Constitution, which they were to write. As the debates began one member of the Assembly, La Rochefoucauld, said that "Montesquieu will be opposed by Rousseau." This was indeed the case, and it was Rousseau's idea of a virtuous republic that prevailed, not Montesquieu's mixed government model, in which "power checks power." Montesquieu maintained that "Every man with power is led to abuse it. He presses on until he encounters some limit. Who would have thought it, *vertu* itself needs limits."[139] When members of the Assembly voted for a unicameral legislature in the summer of 1789, opting for Rousseau over Montesquieu, they set the Revolution on a path that led to Robespierre's Republic of Virtue, in which there was no room for dissent; between those for and against Robespierre's Republic of Virtue there was only the guillotine; when the Revolution imploded in July 1794 Robespierre was among those who went to the guillotine. If two eighteenth-century revolutions, the American and French Revolutions, were tied at the hip, they had very different outcomes.

Mme de La Tour du Pin's Two-Year Stay in Albany, 1794–96

A family of French aristocrats arrived in Albany in June 1794, having fled the Reign of Terror, which was at its peak at the time of their departure. The husband, Frédéric-Séraphin, Marquis de La Tour du Pin, had just become head of a distinguished family that had extensive landed holdings, largely in the south of France, after his father went to the guillotine in April 1794. Born in 1759, Frédéric Séraphin was 35 at the time of his arrival in Albany. His wife, Henriette-Lucy, the Marquise de La Tour du Pin, was 24 and the mother of two children, a four-year-old son and an infant daughter; her father had also gone to the guillotine before she and her family fled France and the Revolution. As soon as the de La Tours du Pin arrived in Albany they looked up Philip Schuyler, having been encouraged by him to come to Albany, with assurances that he would help them find someplace to live. Schuyler did help this family of aristocratic French émigrés find a place to live—they ended up on a farm a few miles north of Albany, on what is now Delatour Road—where they stayed until the Terror came to an end and they could return to France and reclaim their ancestral landed holdings. They returned to France in 1796, having lived in Albany for a period of two years. As it happens, we know a good deal about the stay of the de La Tours du Pin in Albany, and indeed about the larger story of this family. Mme de La Tour du Pin started writing her *Memoirs* in 1820, at age 50, and worked on them in years ahead, before her death in 1853, at age 83. Her *Memoirs* are among the best accounts we have of someone of privilege and high birth who was raised in the glittering, brilliant world of Ancien Régime France, lived through the French Revolution, and compiled a record of what she experienced in an age of social and political upheaval, narrated with skill and replete with a wealth of personal and historical detail.

Figure 29. The Palace of Versailles. I took this photograph when I first visited Versailles in April 1955 as a lad in the U.S. Army, stationed in Germany. It was being in Europe between 1954 and 1956 that led to my becoming an historian. Reading Mme de La Tour du Pin's *Memoirs* brought back a host of memories; I stayed on the rue du Bac in 1955, where Mme de La Tour du Pin lived before she was married.

Mme de La Tour du Pin—we will call her Lucy from now on—was from a family of officers in the French military; her father, Arthur Dillon, a general, commanded the Dillon Regiment, and her mother, Lucie de Rothe, was the daughter of a general. Lucy's family owned an estate 22 leagues outside Paris, Hautefontaine, which had rooms for 25 guests. The hunt was one of the favorite pastimes at Hautefontaine, with the sound of horns and staghounds heard often. The annual cost of maintaining staghounds came to 30,000 francs (the amount she gave in her *Memoirs*), an expense that her uncle shared with two other nobles. Looking back on her life of privilege before the Revolution, Lucy said,

> In those days, everyone with a decently dressed servant was waited on by him at table. No decanters or wine glasses were put on the table. At big dinners, there were silver buckets on a sideboard to hold the wine for various courses. There was also a stand of a dozen glasses and anyone wishing for a glass of one of the wines sent his servant to fetch it. This servant always stood behind his master's chair. I had a servant of my own who also dressed my hair. He wore my livery which, since our braidings exactly resembled those of the Bourbons, had to be in red . . . After dinner, which did not last more than an hour, we went to the drawing room . . . Afterwards, we often went visiting, carried in sedan chairs. . . ." (41–42)[1]

Carried by servants in sedan chairs, Lucy and others in her company were physically separated from people below them, and from the dirt of the street. As she put it, "this was the only possible means of transportation."

Lucy broke her leg while riding when she was ten, and to make her convalescence easier a puppet theater was brought into her room when she lay in bed. Both tragedies and comedies were given, with parts spoken in the wings. When comic operas were performed, those who could sing were assigned the vocal parts. The ladies amused themselves making clothes for marionettes used in the productions. Lucy was placed in the care of her first tutor at age seven, who helped develop her considerable intellectual curiosity. An English maid was assigned to her at age 11, much to her dislike, as she greatly preferred the care of a warm and sympathetic peasant woman, Marguérite, who had been her nurse but was now kept at a distance. With instruction from the English maid Lucy became fluent in English, most useful when she came to America. And she was widely read, with particular interest in English novels. She says that she avoided "immoral" French novels, of which there were many in the France within which she grew up.[2] Her family would seem to have enjoyed the *douceurs de vivre* in Ancien Régime France before the deluge of the Revolution. One of her grandfathers went through an inheritance of £10,000. As lady-in-waiting to Marie Antoinette her mother was at the center of the most exclusive of courtly circles. Lucy first went to court at age 11, after Marie Antoinette gave birth to the Dauphin, an occasion for much celebration. "I was taken to watch the ball given for her by the Gardes du Corps in the Grande Salle de Spectacles at Versailles. [Marie Antoinette] opened the ball with a young guardsman, wearing a blue dress strewn with sapphires and diamonds." (19) Lucy's mother died in the following year, 1782; during her illness Marie Antoinette sent a page to inquire after her health every day. When Lucy was formally introduced to the Queen after her marriage at age 17 she welled up with tears, so overcome was she by her presence. Lucy's wedding trousseau cost 45,000 francs; her husband's aunt, Mme d'Hénin, a fixture at court, gave her "a charming tea table and tea service [as a wedding gift]. The teapot, sugar bowl and other pieces were in silver gilt and the porcelain was of Sèvres. Her gift was the one which gave me the greatest pleasure. I believe it cost 6,000 francs" (65). Among her husband's wedding presents were "jewels, lengths of ribbon, flowers, feathers, gloves, blonde lace, lengths of cloth . . . many hats and elegant bonnets, as well as mantles of black or white muslin trimmed with blonde lace."

The guests at Lucy's wedding included "all the Ministers of the Government, the Archbishops of Paris and Toulouse, some bishops from Longuedoc who were in Paris . . . and many others whose names I do not remember" (66). After vows were exchanged, all of "the ladies embraced me, in order of kinship and age. Then a footman brought in a large basket of green and gold sword knots, favors, fans and cords for the Bishops' hats, to be distributed among the guests. Sword favors of the finest ribbon cost between twenty-five and thirty francs each. Military sword knots in gold and the tasseled cords for the Bishops' hats cost fifty francs, and the fans for the ladies cost between twenty-five and one hundred francs." Describing her wedding dinner, Lucy said it was served at four, but feeling "somewhat bored by that time" she and some friends decided to visit "the servants and the peasants. There was a table of one hundred places for the livery servants, whose variously colored coats and trimmings looked very picturesque, and another table for the peasants and workmen. They drank my health with a will. I was very much liked by them and they had the greatest confidence in me" (67). Lucy went to Paris the next day with her husband's aunt, Mme d'Hénin (although her face bore the marks of smallpox), with whom she was to establish close but not always congenial ties. A beauty and well-connected at court, Mme d'Hénin took it upon herself to prepare Lucy for the ultra-sophisticated and ritualized world that as a bride of 17 she was about to enter.

To prepare herself for formal presentation at court Lucy received lessons from a dancing master, M. Huart, who wore a wig, as if he were the Queen, showing her "just when to remove my glove and how to kiss the hem of the Queen's gown. He showed me the gesture she would make to prevent me. Nothing was forgotten or overlooked in these rehearsals, and my hair was only very simply pinned up. It was all very funny" (68). Describing her formal presentation at court after her wedding, Lucy said, "Thanks to M. Huart's good coaching, I made my three curtseys very well. I removed my glove and put it on again not too awkwardly. Then I went to receive the accolade from the King and his brothers," along with those of Princes of the Blood. As the center of attention, Lucy felt that she was "being stared at by the whole Court and being torn to shreds by every critical tongue" (69). The world of the French court was treacherous, with snares and traps everywhere, and from which no one was safe, particularly the Queen. In the last years of the Ancien Régime, Marie Antoinette was denounced in venomous publications that helped solidify public opinion against her, and against the institution of Monarchy. Much as Lucy regretted the "tragic" fate of Marie Antoinette during the Revolution, she did not pass over her need to be at the center of attention, and her propensity for sharp comments, sometimes directed at her. A Queen who had been "very kind and helpful to me" sometimes made "passing remarks which were almost cutting about my liking for bright colors and for the poppies and brown scabious which I often wore" (71).

Etiquette at the court of Versailles was tied historically to the refining process that was instrumental in shaping Western society from the time of the Renaissance to the time of the French Revolution. From the beginning, princely courts had been a seedbed of good manners, and from them came courtier's books that offered advice on proper behavior and correct etiquette. Originating in Italy, courtier's books found their way into princely courts throughout Europe, nowhere more importantly than in France, where the most admired of all courts in the Age of Absolutism was situated. Constructed by Louis XIV, the Palace of Versailles became a gilded cage within which the French nobility lived under the authority of the king, who adjudicated endless quarrels over etiquette, a means by which nobles of different rank tried to separate themselves from one another. Reduced to a leisured, parasitical group engaged in conflicts over rights of precedence at court, resentments built up within the court nobility that for some were all-consuming. To launch one's ship on these waters was treacherous, as Marie Antoinette discovered to her very great dismay, and as Lucy observed when she was at court in the years just before the French Revolution.

By the time of Lucy's presentation at court in 1787, Marie Antoinette was much altered from the 14-year-old girl who had married the Dauphin in 1770. Having traveled from Vienna to France for the wedding, her retinue met with another from the French court on an uninhabited island in the middle of the Rhine, where she was stripped naked and every possession was taken from her, including her jewelry and pug dog, as if to rid herself of her very identity as an Austrian, and to symbolize her becoming the Dauphine, the future Queen of France. The Austrian court was less formal than the French court, and with seven older siblings at the time of her birth (she was the 15th of Maria Theresa's 16 children; the others died in childbirth or during infancy) she always had plenty of company. At age 14 this changed abruptly when she married. Even before reaching Versailles she was nicknamed *L'Autrichienne*, stigmatizing her as a foreigner. Standing in a hastily-built pavilion on an island in the Rhine, the 14-year-old girl felt alone and vulnerable; confronted by the severe gaze of court ladies who looked at her dismissively, she threw herself into the arms of the Comtesse de Noailles, her *dame d'honneur*, to whom her mother, the Empress Marie Theresa, had said she should defer in all matters. To act spontaneously, as she did in this moment of emotional overload, was a complete breach of French court etiquette and for which she was quietly chastised. For Marie Antoinette, the Comtesse de Noailles became Mme Etiquette, the very embodiment of a formalized courtly regimen against which she rebelled, flaunting its rules as she surrounded herself with friends who shared her disdain for courtly procedures and distinctions, thereby generating deep hostility amongst nobles who resided at the Palace of Versailles. Adding to Marie Antoinette's burdens was a marriage that was unconsummated for seven trying years, and contributed to her reckless spending and rejection of proper restraints, a source of much concern to her mother who received regular reports of her behavior. By the time Marie Antoinette bore the children that were expected of her she was no longer the irreverent girl of earlier years, but she still had a sharp tongue, whose sting Lucy sometimes felt when in her presence.

Like others, Lucy found court etiquette trying, as indicated by her discussion of Sunday Mass, an ordeal for everyone:

It took great skill to walk [in a formal procession] without treading on the long train of the lady in front. Feet were never raised from the ground, and they glided over the gleaming parquet until the Salon of Hercules was safely crossed. Then, each lady threw her train over one of her panniers and, making sure she had been seen by her servant who would be waiting with a large, gold-fringed, red velvet bag, she rushed to one of the side galleries of the Chapel, trying to find a place as close as possible to the gallery occupied by the King and Queen and the Princesses, who had joined them either in the card-room or in the Chapel." (74)

After Mass, dinner was served, with members of the court arrayed around the King and Queen, according to rank. As usual, the "King ate heartily" (71). Describing Louis XVI on these occasions, Lucy said that he

> . . . was so short-sighted that he could not recognize anyone at a distance of more than three paces. He was about five foot six or seven inches tall, square-shouldered and with the worst possible bearing. He looked like some peasant shambling along behind the plough; there was nothing proud or regal about him. His sword was a continual embarrassment to him and he never knew what to do with his hat, yet in Court dress he looked really magnificent. He took no interest in his clothes, putting on without a glance whatever was handed to him. (71–72)

As was typical of females of her class, Lucy had not so much as seen her husband when the marriage contract was drawn up. She had been told that the man she chose to marry, the Comte de Gouvernet (before he became Marquis de La Tour du Pin at the time of his father's death), was "short and ugly," but that did not deter her. She felt his family lineage was most prominent among the various suitors who sought her hand in marriage, and within her scale of values, birth and pedigree were paramount. It turned out that Lucy did not take affront to her husband's physical appearance, and the marriage was close throughout, even with the unexpected and violent vicissitudes they experienced together when the Revolution brought an end to their privileged life. Their closeness was not typical of aristocratic marriages, which typically were arranged and based on family calculation rather than affection or close personal ties. Her mother married a second cousin, who was often away on military duty while she spent much of her time at court. Alluding to her mother's affairs, Lucy said her affection for her husband was "entirely sisterly," and that "she was not perhaps sufficiently distant in her relations with the men she liked, and whom the world considered in love with her" (14). When Lucy's mother died her father left her in the care of her grandmother, whom she hated, while he pursued a widow he met in Martinique, where he was in military service. They married, and her father gave her great uncle, the Archbishop of Narbonne, a proxy to marry her "as he saw fit." The wife of Lucy's father-in-law had carried on scandalously, more than the family was willing to accept, and she was sent to a convent to ruminate on her mistaken ways.

Scandal was pervasive in aristocratic society, and nowhere more so than at the court.[3] The single greatest scandal in pre-Revolutionary France was the Affair of the Necklace, a swindle perpetrated by intriguers who had entrée to the court and used Cardinal Prince Louis René Edouard de Rohan as dupe in the theft of a fabulously expensive necklace that made an innocent Marie Antoinette appear as the culprit. In the court of public opinion Marie-Antoinette was declared guilty, an episode that Napoleon later said started the French Revolution.[4] Lucy did not discuss the Affair of the Necklace, but she surely knew all about it: Among those who pursued her mother was Cardinal de Rohan's nephew, the Prince de Guéménée. So too did the Duc de Lauzun, the Duc de la Rochefoucauld-Liancourt, the Comte de Saint-Blancard, and the Comte de Fersen, a Swedish aristocrat who was close to Marie Antoinette and was widely thought to have been her lover. Her husband's aunt, Mme d'Hénin, was relieved when her husband established a liaison with the actress Sophie Arnould: "an unemployed man is so dull."[5] When it came to scandal within aristocratic society in pre-Revolutionary aristocratic society, Lucy had a front-row seat. Looking back on that world decades after it was blown away by the Revolution, Lucy said, "The profligate reign of Louis XV had corrupted the nobility and among the Court Nobles could be found instances of every form of vice. Gaming, debauchery, immorality, all were flaunted openly" (26).

As seen in Lucy's *Memoirs*, even bishops of the Church were drawn into a life of pleasure, display, and extravagance. After her mother's death she lived in Paris with her great uncle, the Archbishop of Narbonne, on the rue du Bac, in a home that she had inherited but which her great uncle and grandmother used, at her expense.[6] Lucy wrote that one would never know that she lived in the household of a high official of the Church. "I heard around me the freest conversations and the expression of the most ungodly principles. Brought up, as I was, in an Archbishop's house where every rule of religion was broken daily, I was fully aware that my lessons in dogma and doctrine were given no more importance than those in history and geography" (13–14). Her great uncle "went rarely or never to his diocese"; in effect, he was a " 'grand seigneur' in Paris and a courtier at Versailles." Her great uncle's archbishopric "was worth 250,000 francs, [but] he also held the Abbey of Saint-Etienne at Caen [built by William the Conqueror], which was worth 110,000 francs, and another smaller one which he later exchanged for that of Cigny, worth 90,000 francs" (16). Lucy said she received "no moral instruction" as a girl, and felt that traveling with her great uncle was like traveling with the most extravagant of aristocrats, with pomp and display openly and proudly flaunted. When she went to Montpelier with her great uncle,

> We traveled with eighteen horses, and an order would be sent through the administration to reach the posting stages several days ahead of us to ensure that fresh horses would be ready . . . The postchaise and the first courier would arrive an hour ahead of us to ensure that the table was ready, the fire lit and some good dishes prepared, or given at least a finishing touch by our own chef. He traveled with bottles of meat jelly and sauces prepared in advance, as well as everything else needful to make the bad inn palatable. (55)

Looking back decades later on the years before the Revolution, Lucy felt that in her "old age" she could see

> . . . symptoms of the upheaval which broke over us in 1789 . . . The rot started at the top and spread downwards. Virtue in men and good conduct in women became the object of ridicule and were considered provincial. I cannot quote chapter and verse in support of what I am saying. Many years have passed since the period I am trying to describe and they have transformed it for me into a purely historical generalization in which the individual has disappeared and I am left with only a broad impression. The older I grow, however, the more sure I become that the Revolution of 1789 was only the inevitable consequence and, I might almost say, the just punishment of the vices of the upper classes, vices carried to such excess that if people had not been stricken with a mortal blindness, they must have seen that they would inevitably be consumed by the very fire they themselves were lighting. (26–27)

Expanding on this theme, Lucy wrote that "It was the fashion to complain of everything. One was bored, weary of attendance at Court. The officers of the Garde du Corps, who were lodged in the Château when on duty, bemoaned having to wear uniforms all day . . . It was the height of style to complain of duties at Court, profiting from them none the less and sometimes, indeed often, abusing the privileges they carried. All the ties were being loosened, and it was, alas, the upper classes that led the way" (75).

Lucy held the King, the Queen, and leading officials at Versailles responsible for the disasters that struck France in 1789. She had attended the opening meeting of the Estates General, where speeches were made: "The speech of M. Necker seemed to me unbearably dull. It lasted more than two hours and . . . seemed never-ending" (106). No one knew what to do. Lucy felt that both the King and Queen were clueless. "The Queen knew only how to show displeasure, not how to act. She merely retreated. It must also be admitted that encroachments on the royal authority were so novel that neither the King nor the Queen realized that there was any real danger" (107), By seeing both the King and Queen as incapable of action in the 1789 crisis, Lucy failed to understand how differently they responded to it. If well-intentioned Louis XVI vacillated, hoping that accommodations could be reached by rival groups in the Estates General, Marie Antoinette joined the King's younger brothers and reactionary members of the court that pushed him to take a hard line rather than yield to calls for reform and liberal change. Marie Antoinette was among those who persuaded Louis to summon 30,000 troops to move toward the capital to maintain order. Rumors of troop movements passed rapidly through Paris and set the stage for the insurrection that broke out on July 12. Lucy understood that people in Paris were hungry, but she saw that problem as a conspiracy, not the result of a bad harvest, and more deeply as part of a structural crisis within France that was one of many factors in the making of the Revolution. She wrote that the King failed to realize that "foodstuffs were being purposely held up to create hunger in Paris and drive people to revolt . . . It is very easy now, fifty years later, after suffering all the consequences of this feebleness at Court, to say what should have been done! But at the time, when no one even knew what a revolution was, a course of action was less easy to decide" (107). For Lucy, the Revolution resulted from a decadent aristocracy that danced its way to the precipice of 1789, a "feeble court" headed by a weak King, a Finance Minister that failed to give decisive leadership when it was needed, and a liberal nobility that furthered the revolutionary cause until it was too late to pull back.

Nowhere was Lucy's aristocratic point of view more evident than in her verdict on the Assembly's legislation of August 4, 1789, which abolished feudal dues imposed on the peasantry for centuries. The peasantry was unburdened of ancient obligations, the oppression of centuries, but for Lucy the August 4 legislation "was a veritable orgy of iniquities," disastrous for her family.

> This decree ruined my father-in-law and our family fortunes never recovered from the effect of that night's session . . . We lost the toll crossing at Cubzac, on the Dordogne, which was worth 12,000 francs, and the income from Le Bouilh, Amberville, Tesson and Cénévrières, a fine property in the Quercy which my father-in-law was forced to sell the following year. And that was how we were ruined by one stroke of the pen. (116)

Initially, Lucy's family made accommodations to the Revolution and found a place within it, as did other nobles. Her father-in-law was appointed Minister of War, an important position, and given an apartment at Versailles. "As a Minister, my father-in-law received a salary of 300,000 francs, in addition to his pay as Lieutenant-General and Commander of a Province. But he had, in fact, to maintain considerable state and as well as the two weekly dinners for twenty-four people, there were also every week two lavish and elegant supper parties to which I invited twenty-five to thirty ladies of all ages" (117). As the Revolution swerved to the left, the position of Lucy's father-in-law changed. He resigned his position as Minister of War in November 1790, went to England in 1791, and upon returning to France during the Terror he was arrested and went to the guillotine. Her father also went to the guillotine during the Terror.

Among those Lucy held responsible for igniting the French Revolution was the Duc d'Orléans, a Prince of the Blood who hated the King and the court and manipulated the people in schemes designed to further his own political ends. Lucy was present at an incident in April 1789 that showed how Orléans turned popular discontent in Paris to his personal advantage. Having attended the races at Vincennes, Orléans returned to Paris in his carriage, which took him through the faubourg Saint-Antoine, a working-class district in the eastern part of the city. Passing through this district he came upon an angry crowd in front of the factory of a manufacturer of wallpaper, Réveillon, who had lowered wages amidst intense economic pressures in spring of 1789. Regarded as well-intentioned and dedicated to caring for his workers as best as he could, Réveillon's reduction of wages provoked a riot outside his factory. It was no accident that workers recognized Orléans as he passed through the faubourg Saint-Antoine on his way back to his residence, the Palais Royal, located in the center of Paris.[7] A protected aristocratic space when he inherited it, Orléans opened the Palais Royal to the public in 1780, turning it into a democratic space within which radical political ideas were pronounced and which attracted the people, workers from districts at the eastern end of Paris where they lived. When the Duc d'Orléans appeared before a crowd in front of Réveillon's factory they recognized him, their self-appointed friend. Commenting on the episode, which she witnessed, having also been to the races at Vincennes, and having also returned to Paris through the faubourg Saint-Antoine, Lucy said, "we found ourselves in the midst of the first riot, the one which virtually destroyed the worthy Réveillon's wallpaper factory . . . [As] we passed through the crowd of four or five hundred people which filled the street, the sight of the Orélans livery roused their enthusiasm. For a few minutes they held up the carriage shouting 'Long Live our Father! Long Live King d'Orléans!'" (103–4). When Lucy referred to the Réveillon Riot as the "first riot" she connected it to riots that were soon to erupt in Paris, in the month of July.[8] Those riots followed dramatic changes that had taken place at Versailles in May and June. By the time the Estates General met at Versailles in May 1789 Paris had been politicized; episodes such as the Réveillon Riots pointed toward the Paris Insurrection of July 12–14, which started at the Duc d'Orléans' Paris residence, the Palais Royal. Lucy says nothing about how the Paris insurrection began, or about the conditions among the people that made them ripe for an uprising that changed

France forever. Her perspective was from above; for her the Revolution was the result of a decadent aristocracy that had lost its way, a feeble court, unable to act decisively, and wayward nobles who contrived to manipulate the people by inciting popular protest. She does not describe the Paris insurrection of July 12–14 in any detail, concentrating instead on how she heard about the fall of the Bastille, the culminating event of the Paris insurrection.

Lucy's perspective of the French Revolution was distant, removed in time by events that had transpired many years before she wrote her *Memoirs*, and it was colored by the prism through which she viewed the events she described, that of her own experience. Her narrative achieves added clarity when it is seen alongside another narrative of the French Revolution, a pictorial narrative made by an illustrator who depicted the main events of the Revolution during its first three years. This illustrator, Jean-Louis Prieur, made drawings that were engraved and offered for sale, with accompanying descriptive texts. The *Tableaux historiques de la Révolution française*, for which Prieur did illustrations, is generally regarded as the best and most complete pictorial record we have of the French Revolution.[9] His perspective could hardly have been more different from that of Lucy; he was caught up in the popular revolution that erupted in Paris

Figure 30. Jean-Louis Prieur, *Paris guarded by the People on the Night of July 12–13, 1789*. This image portrays the people after their seizure of Paris at the beginning of the insurrection of July 12–14. From this point on the French Revolution was cast in a new mold.

on July 12–14, 1789, which he depicted in 18 tableaus; his images portrayed the violence that was at the core of the Paris insurrection. He was a Jacobin, active in his Section, and he was appointed to the Revolutionary Tribunal, the judicial body that sent enemies of the Revolution to the guillotine. There can be no doubt about where Prieur's political sympathies lay—with the people, and with the Revolution they made. All of this separates Prieur from Mme de La Tour du Pin, as their very different narratives of the French Revolution make abundantly clear. As it turned out, both Prieur and Lucy were both victims of the Revolution: Prieur went to the guillotine in May 1795, condemned to death as a Terrorist; Lucy's life was altered profoundly by a Revolution that brought her and her husband great misery and drove them from a France in which they were seen as enemies of the people.

Prieur's perspective of the French Revolution was from the street, Lucy's from the palace window. She was at Versailles on July 13, the day before the Storming of the Bastille. "Our feeling of security was so complete that at mid-day, and even later, on the 14th of July, neither my aunt [Mme d'Hénin] nor I had any suspicion that there had been the slightest disturbances in Paris" (109–10). Lucy heard about a "massacre" in Paris the next day, while riding in a carriage with "a maid and a maidservant" to one of her estates. She wanted to return "immediately" to Versailles, but her coachmen refused to take her, so she "had four post horses harnessed up . . . and set out for Versailles at a fast gallop. I reached there at about 11 o'clock. My aunt had a migraine and was in bed" (110). The next day her father-in-law told her

> . . . what had happened: the capture of the Bastille, the revolt of the Régiment des Gardes Françaises, the deaths of M. de Launay, M. de Flesselles and many other less well known people, the badly-timed and pointless charge on the Place Louis XV by a squadron of the Royal-Allemand commanded by the Prince de Lambesc. The following day, a deputation from the people forced M. de Lafayette to put himself at the head of the newly-formed Garde Nationale. A few days later came the news that M. Foulon and M. Bertier had also been murdered. (111)

Clearly, the events in Paris that Lucy described in a few sentences were dis comforting. Her aunt came down with a migraine when she received news of what had happened in Paris; writing many years later, Lucy passed quickly over the violence that was at the core of the Paris insurrection. By contrast, Prieur compiled a full record of the events of July 12–14, from the clash between German Guards in the Place Louis XV to the fall of the Bastille. He also showed the murder of two royal officials, Foulon and Bertier de Sauvigny, whom Lucy mentioned in passing in her brief description of the Paris insurrection. In his depictions of violence Prieur dramatized popular anger, seen in contorted faces

Figure 31. Jean-Louis Prieur, *The Death of de Flesselles*, depicts the shooting of a royal official in front of the Hôtel de Ville on July 14, 1789. This image captures the popular anger that erupted during the Paris insurrection. Lucy was quite unable to grasp the meaning of this event, as indicated by her comments in her *Memoirs*.

and in the body language of Parisians who settled ancient accounts with their oppressors.

A comparison of Prieur's and Lucy's French Revolution narratives shows that what he illustrated she often witnessed. She was at Versailles at the end of September 1789 when a regiment of Flanders infantry was summoned to the royal palace, where the Assembly continued to meet. A banquet was held for the newly-arrived Flanders regiment on October 1 in a "magnificent hall" that was "transformed into a ballroom . . . Towards the end of dinner, my sister-in-law and I went to watch the scene, which was magnificent . . . Suddenly it was announced that the King and Queen were to appear at the banquet: an imprudent step which produced a very bad effect" (124). Enthused by seeing the King and Queen,

> . . . certain ladies in the gallery . . . distributed white ribbons [sym-
> bolizing the House of Bourbon] . . . a most foolish thing to do,
> for the next day the disaffected papers, of which there were many,
> did not omit a description of the "orgy" at Versailles, which ended,
> they said, with a distribution of white cockades to all guests. I have
> since seen this absurd story printed in serious history books, yet
> in reality this thoughtless prank consisted of a bunch of ribbons

which Mme de Maillé, a heedless chit of nineteen, had taken from
her hat. (125)

Reports of this incident in Paris newspapers depicted a far more provocative
scene than the one described by Lucy. According to newspaper reports, soldiers in the Flanders regiment became unrestrained after many toasts, and in
their drunkenness they trampled on the Revolutionary tricolor; after they did
so white ribbons were circulated, expressing loyalty to the King and Queen
rather than to the Revolution. And this is how Prieur depicted the "Orgy of
the Guards in the Versailles Opéra," a scene of utter disarray. For Lucy, the
banquet at Versailles was devoid of any serious wrongdoing; for Prieur, who
followed inflammatory reports in the revolutionary press in his illustration of
the event, it was an "orgy."

Inflamed by the "orgy" at Versailles, the women of Paris marched to
Versailles on October 5, followed by the National Guard, demanding bread
that was too expensive for them to buy. In Lucy's lengthy description of this
episode she explains that she was riding in the gardens of Mme Elisabeth [sister
of the King] when she first received news of a huge crowd approaching Versailles. Soon she was confronted by an angry mob of women: "Some of them,

Figure 32. Jean-Louis Prieur, *Orgy of the Guards in the Versailles Opéra*, October 1, 1789.
Prieur's pictorial account of this event differs sharply from the written account in Mme
de La Tours du Pin's *Memoirs*.

Figure 33. Jean-Louis Prieur, *The Women of la Halle go from Paris to Versailles*, October 5, 1789. Lucy was at Versailles when an immense crowd arrived; she had a front-row seat to the historic event.

drunk, and very weary, took possession of the rostrums and benches inside the Chamber [where the Assembly held its meetings]. Night fell and a number of pistol shots could be heard: they came from the ranks of the Garde Nationale and were aimed at my husband, their commanding officer." Lucy's husband was an officer in the National Guard, and in her account he played an active role in efforts to prevent an eruption of unbridled violence at Versailles. Describing events of the next day, Lucy said,

> Dawn was just breaking. It was after six o'clock and the deepest silence still reigned over the courtyard. As he leaned against the window [her husband] thought he heard the sound of many feet, as if a large number of people were climbing the slope . . . to the forecourt. To his amazement, he saw a ragged crowd armed with axes and sabers, entering through a gate usually kept locked, whose key could only have been got through treachery. At the same moment, my husband heard a pistol shot. In the time it took him to rush down the stairs and have the door of the Ministry opened, the assassins killed M. de Vallori [his name was probably M. de Varicourt],

the guard on duty at the gateway . . . Part of the mob, not more than two hundred of them, rushed up the marble staircase, and the remainder threw themselves upon the sentry on duty . . . [who was] torn to pieces. (132–33)

As this was happening, Lucy and her sister-in-law were asleep in the apartment of her aunt, Mme d'Hénin.

> I was exceedingly tired and my sister-in-law had difficulty in waking me to tell me that she thought she could hear a noise outside. She asked me to go and listen at the window which looked out over the leads, for the noise seemed to be coming from that direction. I shook myself, for I had been very fast asleep, and then climbed on to the window . . . I could distinctly hear a number of voices shouting: "Kill them! Kill them! Kill the Garde de Corps!" I was terrified. Neither my sister-in-law nor I had undressed, so we rushed into my aunt's room . . . Her fear was as great as ours. We immediately sent for her servants, but before they had been roused, my good devoted Marguérite [her servant] came in, pale as death. She collapsed on the first chair within reach, crying, "Oh, Heaven, we shall all be murdered." (134)

Lafayette persuaded the King that there was nothing for him to do but go to Paris with the people. Much against their will and with great repugnance, the King and Queen made the long and harrowing trip to Paris, where they took up residence in the Tuileries palace in the center of the city. Before leaving Versailles, Louis XVI placed Lucy's father-in-law, who was Minister of War, in charge of the Palace of Versailles. Not only had Lucy been at Versailles when the women of Paris marched on the royal palace, both her husband and father-in-law were also there, and both played roles of some importance in the dramatic events of October 5–6.

Lucy saw the events of October 5–6 as violent and carried out by a murderous mob; what comes through in her account is her own fear and that of her sister-in-law, her aunt, and her servant; her perspective is that of a palace insider, someone against whom the wrath of the people was directed. Prieur's pictorial account of the events of October 5–6 is in three parts. His first tableau, "The Women of la Halle go from Paris to Versailles," shows the women of Paris, cheered by spectators and followed by rows of National Guards, making their way to Versailles. At the head of the procession is an empty cart that will carry bread for the hungry people when the crowd returns to Paris, a pictorial touch that lends legitimacy to the event. Prieur's second tableau, "The King promises to go to Paris with his Family," shows an artillery salvo in front of Versailles as files of National Guardsmen are lined up and the crowd makes

Figure 34. Jean-Louis Prieur, *The King and Royal Family led to Paris by the People*. A figure is seated on a lamppost in the far right-hand side of the image, looking down at the carriage with the King and Queen inside. By this time the lamp had become a symbol of popular justice. The message is that the King and Queen are now subject to the justice of the people.

ready for the journey to Paris. In his third and final illustration of the October 5–6 *journées*, "The King and Royal Family led to Paris by the People," Prieur shows the royal family in a carriage, surrounded by a crowd and followed by the National Guard as they enter Paris. A woman who stands next to the royal carriage raises her hand in a gesture of anger, directed at the King and Queen who are inside. At the head of the procession is a cart laden with sacks of wheat, appropriated for relief of the hungry people. Parisians are lined up on a wall, cheering, waving, and holding pikes aloft. At the far right-hand side of the scene a man sits on a lamppost and points at a lantern that hangs from it as he looks down on the King and Queen in their royal carriage. This is a warning to the King and Queen; living in Paris, as the people have mandated they must, they are subject to popular justice. At the beginning of the Revolution the people had hung their enemies from lampposts, and from that time on the lantern was a symbol of popular justice. "A la lanterne!" was the cry of the people, directed at their enemies, meaning, "String them up!" "Hang them!" In Prieur's tableau a man climbs a pole next to the lamppost, holding a branch in his arm, waving it triumphantly, as do others in the crowd below. The tree branch, like the lantern, became a patriotic symbol at the beginning of the Revolution, along with the bonnet rouge (a patriotic cap), and the pike (which expressed the people's militancy). Prieur's tableau bristles with all of these patriotic objects, symbols of revolutionary fervor. Fervor and anger come through in Prieur's tableau, "The King and Royal Family led to Paris by the People." Entering Paris, the King and the Queen are entering a different world, one far removed from the Palace of Versailles; they are entering the world of revolutionary Paris.

Relative calm descended on France after the *journées* of 5–6 October, the last of the 1789 uprisings. Two revolutions had taken place, one at Versailles, a constitutional revolution that brought the curtain down on the Ancien Régime and gave rise to a National Assembly, entrusted with creating a constitution for the new France; the other was a popular Revolution that began in Paris and spread to towns throughout France, and reached a climax in a massive peasant revolt, the Great Fear, which ended the feudal order. The two revolutions were interlocked, but they issued from different impulses and had goals that, if not conflicting, were far from being the same. Dramatic changes had taken place, accompanied by a widespread feeling of euphoria, but there was also uneasiness in some quarters, particularly among those who wanted stability, necessary for creating a constitutional government, based on the rule of law. Those who sought stability wanted ceremonially to announce the end of the Revolution; they wanted officially to proclaim its great achievements, and to declare it over. Out of that wish came the greatest of all festivals of the French Revolution, the Fête de la Fédération, held in Paris and in towns throughout France on July 14, 1790, commemorating the fall of the Bastille.[10]

The idea for patriotic festivals originated with National Guardsmen in the provinces who organized celebrations attended by young and old, men and women, rich and poor, and ministers and priests of rival faiths, brought together to commemorate the blessings of revolutionary unity. The idea of patriotic federative festivals took hold, and passed from the provinces to Paris; that the National Guard initiated these festivals was no accident. No group wanted stability more than the National Guard, and no person did so more than its leader, Lafayette. Preparations for the largest of the July 14 patriotic festivals, the one held in Paris, took weeks as stands were built around the Champ de Mars and as a patriotic altar was placed in its center. Some 400,000 observed the festival on the Champ de Mars on July 14, 1790, as endless files of National Guardsmen passed in review, and as patriotic oaths were sworn before the patriotic altar. A Mass and benediction was celebrated by Talleyrand, who rehearsed the text he followed the night before, revised for the occasion, hoping not to commit mistakes, as he was prone to do when celebrating Mass. Rain was falling as Talleyrand made ready for his part of the ceremony, putting out incense, soaking robes, and slowing units of National Guards who made their way into the Champ de Mars. Annoyed, Talleyrand muttered to his assistant, "Where are those buggers; when will they get here?"[11] After Mass was celebrated Lafayette dismounted and requested permission from the King to administer the patriotic oath to guardsmen. Having administered the oath to fellow guardsmen, Lafayette swore to "remain united with every Frenchman by indissoluble ties of fraternity." The King swore to uphold the constitution and the decrees of the National Assembly and the Queen held up the Dauphin amidst cheers of the people.

Among those who observed the Fête de la Fédération was Lucy, who saw it from a specially-built platform attached to the Ecole Militaire at the far end of the Champ de Mars. Lucy went to Paris on the night of July 13, so she could observe an event in which both her father-in-law and husband were involved. Aware of the role of the National Guard in the patriotic festival, Lucy wrote that the "Garde Nationale included all the more balanced elements of the population of Paris. It was considered a rampart against the spirit of revolution. All the shop-keepers, the great merchants, the bankers, the proprietors and members of the upper classes who had not yet left France were enrolled in it" (142). Lucy attended the patriotic festival with members of her family.

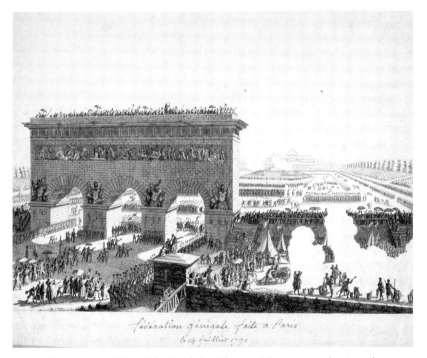

Figure 35. Jean-Louis Prieur, *The Fête de la Fédération*. The patriotic altar is in the center of the Champ de Mars and the Ecole Militaire is in the background. Lucy viewed the event from the Ecole Militaire, which can be seen in the distance in Prieur's tableau.

> Finally, on the evening of the 13th of July, I went with my sister-in-law . . . to stay in a small apartment in the Ecole Militaire overlooking the Champ de Mars, so that we would be on the spot the following morning. My father-in-law had an excellent meal sent over, with everything necessary to provide a large luncheon for the military who might come to see us during the ceremony . . . Monsieur le Dauphin was very glad to be able to share our luncheon.

Lucy's placement at the July 14 festival brought her into close contact with leading figures in the event, and it gave her a good view of oath-taking ceremonies at the patriotic altar in the center of the Champ de Mars. Commenting on two of the leading personages at the festival, La Fayette and Talleyrand, she passed favorable judgment on one and did not hesitate to criticize the other. La Fayette "was as fervent as any of us in his desire for the establishment of a wise freedom and the disappearance of abuses," but Talleyrand was much less sincere in his intentions.

> [The] King was so displeased, and rightly so, with [Talleyrand's] unpriestly behaviour that he refused to grant him a See . . . However, when . . . [his father] was dying, he asked as a last favour that his son should be raised to a bishopric and the King, who until then had withstood his petitions, could no longer stand firm in his refusal and [he] became Bishop of Autun. It was he who celebrated Mass at that Fédération of 1790 . . . I saw him himself, with my own eyes, at the steps of the altar, wearing an embroidered coat and a sword. (144)

If Lucy saw the Fête de la Fédération from the Ecole Militaire at one end of the Champ de Mars, Prieur viewed it from the opposite end in his illustration of the same event. Prieur's tableau underscores the event's grandness of scale and celebratory character, with salvos of cannon and people waving as files of guardsmen make their way toward the patriotic altar. Barely discernible in Prieur's illustration is the Ecole Militaire at the far end of the Champ de Mars, from which Lucy observed the same scene as that depicted by Prieur in his tableau, "Fête de la Fédération."

Efforts to bring closure to the Revolution through a festival commemorating unity had no real chance of success; divisions within the Revolution were too great, as events soon made clear. Among the most important of these events was the revolt of the Châteauvieux Regiment in Nancy at the end of August, six weeks after the July 14 festival. Military order was breaking down throughout France, and the Assembly took a firm line against rebellious units. Soldiers at the Nancy garrison requested better pay and better treatment; caught up in the spirit of revolutionary egalitarianism they chafed under a rigorous system of discipline, which they associated with the despotism of the Ancien Régime. Officers resented the claims of enlisted men, and tensions became acute; the punishment of an enlisted man led to confiscation of regimental funds by mutinous soldiers. Lafayette, who exerted considerable influence in the Assembly, was determined to make an example of the mutinous soldiers and the Assembly took his side, passing a decree that would "strike fear" into rebellious soldiers.[12] The Assembly sent an officer to Nancy to restore order, but he clashed with mutinous soldiers, wounding several with his sword, and fled after the incident. More concerned than ever, the Assembly sent Lafayette's cousin, François-Claude-Amour, Marquis de Bouillé, to sort matters out in Nancy. He managed to reach an agreement with two of the rebellious regiments, but not with Swiss troops of the Châteauvieux Regiment, and on August 31, 1790 a bloody battle erupted between Bouillé's men and the rebellious Swiss soldiers. The reprisals that followed were harsh, with 33 men broken on the wheel or hung and 41 committed to penal servitude. Many in France felt members of the Châteauvieux Regiment, which had been stationed in Paris at the time of the July 12–14 insurrection and had refused to fire on the people, had been right, and opinion began to shift in their favor and against an Assembly that had approved such harsh measures against soldiers seen as loyal to the Revolu-

Figure 36. Jean-Louis' Prieur's illustration of the Châteauvieux episode, *Affair at Nancy: Death of Désilles*, August 31, 1790. Lucy's husband was in the thick of the fighting.

tion. In time, the Châteauvieux Regiment would be rehabilitated, indicating a shift of public feeling within the Revolution. What this shift indicated was changing loyalty away from the original moderate leaders of the Revolution, such as Lafayette, and toward those farther to the left.

Lucy left for Switzerland with her aunt and a cousin in late July 1790 for a six-week visit at Sécheron, outside Geneva, "little thinking that I was to incur grievous anxiety" (145). This was a month before the revolt of the Châteauvieux Regiment, in which her husband would play a role. As she passed through towns and villages on the way to Switzerland she became aware of anger that was welling up within France, ancient hatreds to which the Revolution was giving release, directed at people of privilege and high birth, such as herself and her aristocratic companions. Two days out of Paris, "We crossed [a] town by a rather deserted road and except for a few shouted insults from passers-by, such as: 'There go some more on the way out, those dogs of aristocrats,' we managed to leave the town without incident. We had already met similar behavior in other places and had become accustomed to it" (145). After leaving town the next day they had to return because of complications over their passports, and when they passed through the "crowded market square" people began to greet them with insults, "then the storm increased as we advanced, and a voice suddenly shouted: 'It's the Queen!' We were stopped, the horses were unharnessed, the courier was dragged from his horse and there were shouts of 'A la lanterne!' " (146). Someone swore that Lucy, her aunt, and her cousin were the Queen and her two royal relatives, Mme Royale and Mme Elisabeth; unable to persuade their captors of their actual identity, the travelers were kept in detention for four days, until they were finally allowed to continue. They were first taken to the house of the local head of the National Guard, who at first did not know what to do; not wanting to be entangled in a matter that could be complicated, he took off, leaving a meal behind that he had just begun to eat. Sizing things up, Lucy and her companions "began to eat the abandoned dinner. An excellent stew, some meat paté and choice fruits soon satisfied our young appetites and we laughed heartily at our adventure and the cowardice of the chief of the national militia" (147). A cook was sent to Paris to get letters from Lucy's husband, her father-in-law, the Minister of War, and Lafayette, but while awaiting arrival of the letters there were altercations between local patriots and officers of the National Guard who sprang to the defense of the aristocratic travelers. The President of the National Assembly wrote a letter to the "President of the Commune [elected head of the town in which they were staying] . . . reprimanding him in strong terms for arresting us. M. de Lafayette sent a message to the commander of the National Guard who had so prudently remained invisible" (149).

When Lucy arrived in Sécheron there were letters from her husband, who as commander of a unit of National Guards had received orders to proceed to Nancy, "where the Régiment du Roi and the Régiment de Châteauvieux had barricaded themselves in . . ." (150). He was in Nancy when the fighting began. "M. de La Tour du Pin rode forward, but as he did so, the rebel soldiers fired and the gunners lit the fuse of [a] cannon, which was loaded with grape-shot . . . M. de La Tour du Pin's horse was killed and he himself had a terrible fall. Until his servant, who was there as a volunteer, managed to reach him in the field where his horse had carried him before collapsing, it was thought that he was dead" (152). Lucy's husband joined her in Switzerland after the crushing of the mutiny in Nancy, and together they returned to Paris six weeks later. By the time they reached Paris in October things were no longer the same. The Châteauvieux episode exposed rifts within the Revolution, and it contributed to a political shift within the Assembly that favored those on the left. One result of this shift was mounting uneasiness among many who had supported or at least accepted the Revolution but now found it difficult to do so. The disaffected were increasingly inclined to emigrate, as Lucy commented: "My father-in-law's distaste for his Ministry increased daily. Nearly all the regiments in the Army were in a state of revolt. Most of the officers, instead of meeting the efforts of the Revolutionaries with steady firmness, sent in their resignations and left France. To emigrate became a point of honour." Her father-in-law "was powerless before the intrigues of the Assembly and not finding in the King the firmness he had a right to expect, decided to resign from office" (155). This he did, on November 15, 1790.

Lucy's husband was appointed Minister Plenipotentiary in Holland in December 1790, but he did not take up the post until June 1791. In the 17 months the de La Tours du Pin spent in Holland, forces long at work within the Revolution brought about dramatic and convulsive changes. Conditions were so unstable in Paris that her husband's aunt, Mme d'Hénin, immigrated to England, as did her father-in-law. Mme d'Hénin often encouraged Lucy and her husband to join her in London, but immigrating would put their landed holdings at risk, so they remained in The Hague, waiting to see how things might turn out. During the last days of November 1792, Lucy wrote, "the Convention passed a decree against émigrés, ordering them to return within a given period—a very short one—under pain of confiscation of their property." Lucy and her husband decided they had no choice but to return to France. Her father-in-law also decided that he must return to France, and did. Leaving on December 1, 1792, Lucy heard the sound of cannon as she made her way to Antwerp, where she spent the night. She saw a glow emanating from the great Place in Antwerp after going to bed and went to the window to see what it was.

> I will never be able to forget the sight which met my eyes. In the midst of that vast Place had been lit a fire whose flames were leaping as high as the roof tops. Numbers of soldiers, drunk, reeling, unsteady, swayed about it, flinging in any furnishings they could

find: bedsteads, chests of drawers, sideboards, screens, clothes, baskets full of papers and then a mass of chairs, tables and armchairs with gilded wooden frames, all of which made the fire blaze higher minute by minute. Dreadful looking women, their hair loose and their dress in disorder, mingled with this gang of madmen, giving them wine . . . Wild laughter, foul oaths and obscene songs added to the general horror of this diabolic fling. For me, it was the embodiment of all that I had read about the capture of a town by assault, of the pillaging and terrible disorders which resulted. I stood at the window throughout the night, fascinated and terrified, unable to tear myself away despite my horror.

After leaving Antwerp the next day Lucy drove

> . . . through the entire French army which was camping there. These conquerors . . . had all the appearance of a horde of bandits. Most of them lacked a uniform . . . This medley, a vast human rainbow, stood out curiously against the snow which covered the ground . . . Forced to drive at almost a walking pace, the way seemed long. The roads, cut up by the artillery, were cluttered with wagons, ammunition carts and guns. We advanced slowly, amid the shouts and oaths of the drivers and the rough pleasantries of the soldiers." (171–72)

Returning to France, Lucy had "scarcely crossed the border when the Revolution was all about, dark and menacing, laden with danger" (174). The King's trial was in its final stage when Lucy arrived in Paris. Her father was working with others—including Gouverneur Morris—who were trying to help the King escape, but the plan failed.[13] She thought that even at the last moment efforts would be made to save his life, and she listened for the "rattle of musketry," the sound of guns fired by those who would not allow a "great crime" to happen without protest. "We stood there in shocked silence, hardly daring to say a word to one another . . . Alas! The deepest silence lay over the city like pall over the regicide city" (177). Lucy's father-in-law was arrested in March 1793 on false charges, and while he was released the incident was worrying; he decided that he should retire to his estate at Le Bouilh in the south of France, not far from Bordeaux. Lucy and her family also decided to leave Paris and departed on April 1, 1793, arriving at Le Bouilh in the middle of April, where they spent the next four months. Lucy was pregnant and her husband was worried about "the possibility of a house search or the stationing of a garrison in the Château at the time of my baby's birth" (181). The area around Bordeaux was given over to counter-Revolution, intrigue was ubiquitous, and life at Le Bouilh was increasingly precarious. Under these circumstances Lucy moved to a "small house . . . about a quarter league from Bordeaux in the village of Canoles." Her husband remained with her as she was about to deliver her baby, but their position became dangerous in the extreme when a Revolutionary army occupied Bordeaux in September, followed by two officials from Paris, Jean-Lambert Tallien and Claude Alexandre Ysabeau, who set about to impose Revolutionary justice. "The guillotine was set up permanently in the Place Dauphine [and so] . . . great was the terror" that when an order was published to hand over arms to the authorities every one did just that. "While all this was going on, I gave birth during the night to a daughter whom I named Séraphine, after her father, who stayed just long enough to give his blessing. At the moment of her birth, we learned of the arrest of many people in neighboring country houses" (184). A servant rushed to tell Lucy's doctor right after he delivered her baby that orders had been issued for his arrest. He spent the night hiding in the same closet as the baby. Three days later news arrived that orders had been drawn up for the arrest of Lucy's husband, orders that if carried out meant certain death. He fled, and after close scrapes found a locksmith who offered to hide him in an attic, "for a handsome consideration." Lucy wrote that

> Years later, I visited this dreadful hole. It was separated by only a thin plank from the shop where the boys worked and where the forge and bellows were installed. When the locksmith and his wife left their room, always taking the key with them, my husband had to lie quite still on his bed in order not to make the slightest noise. He was strongly urged not to have any light, in case it was seen from the workshop below. (190)

An acquaintance who was sympathetic toward Lucy found her a room in Bordeaux, where she lived in disguise, exchanging letters with her husband that were hidden in loaves of bread. Soon her position "in Bordeaux became daily more dangerous . . . I cannot see how I escaped death . . . I was in a state of most anxious uncertainty when Providence sent me a special protector" (195–96).

Lucy's protector appeared in the form of Thérésia Cabarrus, the mistress of Jean Lambert Tallien, who exercised extraordinary power in Bordeaux as a representative of the Convention, of which he was a member. Lucy had been introduced to Thérésia in Paris four years earlier; like everyone, she was struck by her beauty. Thérésia was the daughter of a French merchant, François Cabarrus, who went to Spain on business, fell in love with and married his employer's daughter, and became an important fixture at the court of Charles III. Along with other progressive, reforming ministers, Cabarrus was at the vanguard of efforts to modernize Spain. He founded the Bank of San Carlo and was among the liberal officials at the court of Charles III, whose portraits Goya painted. His Spanish wife took Thérésia to Paris for a convent school education. She was married at age 14 to a newly ennobled French aristocrat,

Jean-Jacques Devin, Marquis de Fontenay, an arrangement that conferred status on the adolescent bride and brought a substantial dowry to her husband, who kept a mistress openly, gambled, and earned his reputation as a rake. Thérésia took the first of several lovers at age 15. Her marriage, never anything but a matter of convenience, broke up over political differences; Fontenay was on the right politically, whereas Thérésia was on the left. She divorced her husband, took back her maiden name, and went to Bordeaux in May 1793 to live with a wealthy uncle, and while she was at the theater in October she was seen by Tallien, who had met her two years earlier. Tallien sought out the divorced beauty and became her lover.

When Lucy saw Thérésia in Bordeaux she wrote her a note requesting an interview, which she received. Thérésia was generous of spirit and sympathetic to the plight of those threatened by the Terror, particularly those of her own class and background; she took it upon herself to lend them her support, as she did when Lucy told her of her difficulties.

> I told her my position. She thought it even more perilous than I did myself and told me that I would have to flee and that she could see no other way of saving me. I replied that I could not leave without my husband and feared that if I abandoned my children's fortune, they would never see it again. She said to me: "See Tallien, he will tell you what to do. You will be safe as soon as he knows that you are my main interest here." (196)

Describing the woman whom "Providence" had placed in Bordeaux, Lucy said:

> No more beautiful creature had ever come from the hands of the Creator and, in addition, she was highly accomplished. Every feature was perfect in its regularity. Her hair, which was ebony-black, was like the finest silk and nothing could dim the radiance of her wonderfully fair skin. An enchanting smile showed a glimpse of perfect teeth. Her height recalled that of Diana the Huntress. Her slightest movement had a matchless grace. As for her voice, its melody and very slightly foreign accent gave it a charm which it is quite impossible to describe. (197)

When Thésésia arranged a meeting with Tallien, Lucy was completely direct as she explained her plight and that of her aristocratic husband, who was in hiding. Tallien said,

> 'All these enemies of the Revolution will have to go' . . . at the same time making a beheading gesture with his hand. Indignation surged up within me and, with it, my courage. I boldly raised my eyes to

the monster. Until then, I had not looked at him. I saw before me a man of twenty-five or twenty-six with a rather pretty face, which he tried to make severe [born in 1767, Tallien was 26, three years older than Lucy]. A mass of fair curls escaped on all sides from beneath a large military hat covered in shiny cloth and surmounted by a tricolour plume. He wore a long, tightly-fitting redingote of coarse blue cloth, over which were slung a cross belt and saber from one shoulder and a long silk tricolour scarf from the other.

Not to be intimidated, Lucy said, "I have not come here, citizen . . . to hear the death warrant of my relatives, and since you cannot grant my request, I will not importune you further . . . He smiled, as if to say, 'You are very bold to speak to me like this' " (198). Lucy left without further comment, fearing that her position was worse than ever, but when she met with Thérésia again she was told that she had made a good impression. Thérésia had accused Tallien of not treating her "kindly enough," and Tallien promised her that Lucy would not be arrested. Tallien was not one of the more severe agents of the Terror. Willing to dispatch those found guilty of treason, he was no butcher; keeping an eye on his own backside he moved cautiously. Suspected of taking bribes, he was sometimes under the scrutiny of others. Among those who suspected Tallien of irregularities was the other representative from Paris, Ysabeau, himself probably on the take, who Tallien feared might denounce him to protect his own skin. All of this placed Lucy in a most delicate and dangerous position. Her main prop was the hold of Tallien's mistress on him; what further compli-cated matters was Tallien's fear of being denounced, a consideration that at any moment could make him prove his dedication to the Revolution by striking down its enemies, hated aristocrats, a category to which Lucy and her husband belonged unequivocally.

As the winter of 1793–94 progressed, matters became more difficult for Lucy. The locksmith who had been hiding her husband—for a price—realized that if he were caught harboring an enemy of the Revolution he would go the guillotine, and ordered him to leave. Her husband went into hiding again, this time in a room in one of his family's châteaus, where he lived in constant fear, and barely escaped a search party. Summing up her own position, Lucy said,

> The terror in Bordeaux meantime reached its climax. [Thérésia] began to be anxious about her own safety and to fear that Ysabeau's denunciations would end in Tallien's recall. I shared her fears, for such a recall would have meant death for both of us . . . Every day there were executions of the people who had thought themselves safe . . . I could no longer sleep at night and every time I heard a sound, thought they had come to arrest me. I hardly dared to go out. My milk dried up and I was afraid of falling ill just at the

very moment when I needed my health more than ever before . . . It was then that, while paying a morning call on [a friend] who was still under house arrest [that] I happened to be standing by his table deep in thought when my eyes moved mechanically to the morning paper, which lay open. There, in the trading news, I read that: "The ship *Diana* of Boston, 150 tons, will leave in eight days' time . . ."

Unbeknownst to her, the American Ambassador in Paris, Gouverneur Morris, had succeeded in persuading the authorities to lift the embargo on American ships in Bordeaux. Lucy went straight to Thérésia and told her of her decision: She hoped to book passage on a ship that would take her, her husband, her son, and her daughter to America. Thérésia told Lucy tragedy was about to strike: Tallien had been reprimanded by the Committee of Public Safety in Paris, he had decided that he had no choice but to return to the capital to defend himself, and his departure was imminent. Thérésia "thought [Tallien's] recall would be the signal for even greater cruelty in Bordeaux and [she] did not want to stay on if Tallien left. We had not a minute to lose if we wished to be saved" (207). Acting quickly, Lucy took necessary steps to escape Bordeaux, France, and the Revolution. She first booked passage on the ship whose passage to America she had seen announced in the paper. She then needed to get a passport and, at real risk to himself, Tallien gave her a document that had the name Dillon (Lucy's family name) on it, but which needed an official signature. She sent for her husband, who managed, dressed as a peasant, to join Lucy, his son, and his daughter. The four of them went to the passport office for the required signature, fearing that they would be recognized. "When the passport was signed, we carried it off with a feeling of deep relief, though we were indeed still very far from safe . . . I went to see [Thérésia], thinking I would meet Tallien at her house . . . I found her in tears. Tallien had been recalled and had left two hours earlier. She herself was to leave the next day for Paris and did not hide from me the fear that Tallien's colleague, the fierce Ysabeau, would refuse a visa" (215), which they needed, the final document before they could depart for America. At this point, Tallien's secretary came to the rescue, presenting the obligatory visa to Ysabeau for signature, along with other documents that Ysabeau signed without so much as looking at them. That having been accomplished, Lucy, her husband, and daughter were free to board ship and sail to America. And they did.

Lucy did not describe and did know what happened to Thérésia and Tallien after they returned to Paris, where the Terror was in full swing. Robespierre's goal was nothing less than complete victory of the Revolution, which meant eradication of those who opposed it. A logic that had had been present within the Revolution from the beginning played itself out as Robespierre, searching for perfect unity in an indissoluble and virtuous Republic, sent original leaders of the Revolution to the guillotine.[14] These included men such as Camille Desmoulins, Robespierre's close friend, who had gone against him and was arrested and placed in prison. While awaiting execution, Desmoulins made friends with another prisoner, Arthur Dillon, Lucy's father. Dillon sympathized with the plight of Desmoulins' wife, Lucile, loved by all who knew her, and tried to smuggle a letter out of prison that he hoped would bring her needed help, but the letter was intercepted and used as proof of a conspiracy between Lucile and Lucy's father. Lucile was executed a week after her husband. From this point on there was mounting fear within the Convention that no one was safe; if men such as Robespierre's friend Desmoulins went to the guillotine, along with his wife, who was safe?

The Committee of Public Safety sent 19-year-old Marc-Antoine Jullien to Bordeaux to seek out those guilty of leniency or treason. At the time of Jullien's arrival, Thérésia was still giving assistance to those who were under scrutiny. He wrote Robespierre that "Bordeaux seems to have been until now a labyrinth of intrigues and waste. Revolutionary justice here is hungrier for money than blood. One woman has captivated the authorities of the entire town. The favorite is called Thérésia Cabarrus. It is she who forced the Committee of Surveillance to give free rein to her corruption."[15] Besides her "intrigues," she had been mistress of Tallien: "I denounce the free union between Tallien and this foreign woman. I accuse Tallien of softness and moderation." Having returned to Paris, Tallien was intriguing within the Convention, trying to save his skin. Thérésia was less fortunate; she also returned to Paris but was arrested at the order of Robespierre on May 30 and sent to one of the grimmest of revolutionary prisons, the Petite Force, where some of the bloodiest scenes of the September Massacres had taken place. She was strip-searched and given a straw pallet for a bed. For 25 days she was held in solitary confinement in a room in which there was no sunlight and during which she was given no changes of clothing. She wore the rough sleeveless dress they gave her throughout this period. Her feet and legs bore permanent marks of rats that bit her during her imprisonment. Robespierre had come to regard her with extreme enmity; when told of her circumstances he is reported to have commented, "Let her look in the mirror once a day."[16] Robespierre sent agents to see Thérésia, promising her freedom and a passport if she would give testimony of Tallien's wrongdoing. She replied that she would die first. Trying another tack, Robespierre sent her to lighter confinement at the Carmes on July 15, 11 days before his own fall and the end of the Terror. Devastated by Thérésia's imprisonment, Tallien took a room next to her prison, although he was unable to see her. He understood full well that he was in Robespierre's sights, and that if he were to save both Thérésia and himself extraordinary measures were necessary; the safest course of action was to take down Robespierre. Tallien played a key role in bringing about the fall of Robespierre on 9 Thermidor, July 27, 1794. Robespierre had gotten wind of a conspiracy against him when he spoke before the Convention, but when called upon to name the conspirators he refused; perhaps he did not know who they were. He was at a critical moment and knew it, and when the Convention met again the next day Tallien led the attack against Robespierre, preventing him from speaking, and calling for his arrest. Robespierre was incarcerated that night and went to the guillotine, with his followers, the following day.[17] Thérésia was released three days later, and it was at this time, after joining Tallien, that she conceived a child; she was four months pregnant when she finally married Tallien on December 26, 1794. Lucy had reached America by this time, and would hear news of Robespierre's execution when she was in Albany, New York; it was Philip Schuyler who told her the welcome news. But before seeing how this came about we must follow Lucy and her family as they make their way from France to America.

Lucy described the ship that carried the de La Tours du Pin to America, the *Diana*, as "a vessel of only 150 tons. Its solitary mast was very small, as in all American ships, and as there was no cargo except for our twenty-five cases (their baggage), the rolling was horrible" (220). The crew was originally four, but one of the men fell from the mast soon after they departed, reducing the crew to three. Lucy wrote, "My apprenticeship to the sea was of the very grimmest kind." Her infant daughter was lulled to sleep by the rolling of the ship during the day, but "for that very reason, she allowed me no peace when she felt me beside her at night and I could never sleep for more than half-an-hour at a time. I was so afraid of rolling over against her in my sleep and smothering her that I had a piece of cloth passed around the middle of my body and fastened to the wooden frame of the bed. I could neither turn nor change my position, but although at first it was torture I soon grew used to it" (221). Arduous as the passage was for Lucy, it was even worse for her husband. "For thirty days my husband did not leave his bed. He suffered terribly from seasickness and also from the bad food. The only nourishment he could take was tea made with water, and a few pieces of roasted biscuit soaked in sweet wine. As for me, when I look back across the years, I cannot conceive how I was able to withstand the weariness and the hunger" (220). Suffering from conditions such as these, Lucy had to make adjustments in her daily routine, and in how she thought about herself.

> My life on board, though hard, had one advantage: it put forcibly beyond my reach the small pleasures which we do not value when we have always had them. In fact, deprived of everything, without a minute of leisure, entirely occupied with caring for my children and my sick husband, not only had I not made what people call their "toilette" since going on board, but I had not even had time to remove my madras kerchief I wore on my head. Fashion still decreed quantities of powder and pomade. One day . . . I decided to dress

> my hair while my daughter was asleep. It was very long hair and I
> found it so tangled that, despairing of ever being able to restore it
> in order, I took the scissors and cut it quite short . . . My husband
> was very angry. I dropped the hair overboard and with it went all
> the frivolous ideas which my pretty fair curls encouraged. (224)

When Lucy arrived in Boston she was a different person, both inwardly and
outwardly, than the leisured, privileged aristocrat she had once been.

Yet, Lucy's identity remained aristocratic, within herself and insofar as the
rest of the world was concerned. While crossing the Atlantic she had helped
the cook in the galley prepare such food as there was, mostly hardened beans
that they had to soak before they could be made edible.

> The cook's name was Boyd. He was twenty-six and it was obvious
> that under his mask of grime and grease he was very handsome. He
> was the son of a farmer on the outskirts of Boston and much bet-
> ter educated than a Frenchman of the same class would have been.
> He understood at once that I was a lady, who wanted information
> about country ways and customs in his homeland. It was indeed
> thanks to him that I acquired a knowledge of the tasks that were
> to fall on me when I became a farmer's wife. (224)

A creature of the courtly world of Ancien Régime France, of châteaus on the
estates of her family, and of the finest districts of Paris (the rue du Bac, where
she lived as a girl, runs into the Louvre), Lucy entered a very different world
when she came to America, one that was essentially agrarian and whose back-
bone was farmers such as the cook on the *Diana* had been, whose education
struck Lucy as better than would have been the case with his counterparts in
France. And Lucy was right; ordinary people in America were better educated,
better fed, and physically larger than *le peuple*, those in France who worked
with their hands. Crossing the Atlantic in an American ship with a crew of
three, Lucy was on her way to a newly-formed nation, born of a very different
revolutionary experience than that of the France she had just left.

When the de La Tours du Pin arrived in Boston they were not just any
passengers seeking lodging; they were people of distinction, aristocratic émigrés,
a point that was not lost on others. Having landed in Boston, the captain of
the *Diana* "found a small lodging for us on the Market Square and he brought
offers of help from the owner of the ship. My husband resolved to call on him
the following day when we landed. The Captain told us he was a rich man
and greatly esteemed, and that we were very fortunate to be under his protection" (227). The ship owner, Mr. Geyer, "one of the richest men in Boston,"
was happy to put up the de La Tours du Pin in his own house, where they

were given fine accommodations and became the center of attention of "three generations of ladies," who doted on Lucy's children and wanted to hear all about their guests' adventures in France, as victims of the Revolution.

> The dangers through which we had passed in France evoked general sympathy and people were inclined to think our story had something of the miraculous about it. They insisted on believing that my hair had been cut short at the back as a preparation for execution. This belief still further intensified their interest in us and it was quite in vain that I explained that I had cut it for a very different reason. There seemed no means of persuading the good people of Boston that they were wrong. (230)

So taken by the de La Tours du Pin was their host, Mr. Geyer, that "he suggested we should live on a farm of his about eighteen miles from Boston" (230). They declined the offer, for they had decided to accept a different one; they had been encouraged to come to Albany, New York.

When Lucy was on board the *Diana* at Pauillac outside Bordeaux and about to begin the voyage to America, another ship pulled alongside hers, which was at anchor. Both ships were awaiting a favorable wind, which would allow their departure. The other ship was sailing to England, and Lucy wrote a "few hurried lines to Mme d'Hénin, who was living in London, asking her to write to us at Boston . . ." (228). Mme d'Hénin had fled to England and encouraged the de La Tours du Pin to join her there when she was in Holland, but they had declined the offer. Now Lucy was going to America, and hoping to remain in touch with her husband's aunt she asked her to write her in Boston. Mme d'Hénin did more than that; she wrote an American friend of hers, "a Mrs. Church [who] was a daughter of General Schuyler, who had so greatly distinguished himself during the War of Independence" (231). The Mrs. Church that Mme d'Hénin wrote to was the eldest daughter of Philip Schuyler, Angelica Schuyler Church, who had eloped with her British husband in 1777, much to the chagrin of her father. The Churches lived fashionably in London, and followed events in France closely, all the more so as they had spent some time in Paris before the Revolution. Like others of their class in England, and like Angelica's father, the Churches were opposed to the French Revolution after its early moderate stage, and gave assistance to those of high station who fled the Terror. "And so," Lucy wrote,

> Mrs. Church, seeing the deep and motherly interest taken in us by my aunt, who was a dear friend of hers, wrote to her parents and when we arrived in Boston, we received most pressing letters from General Schuyler, telling us to come without delay to Albany, assuring us we would find it easy to settle there. He assured us of

his full support in the matter. We therefore decided to accept his offer and shipped our belongings by sea to New York, and from there up the Hudson to Albany. We waited in Boston until we heard that they had arrived and then set out to follow them by the land route. We preferred to travel this way as the five hundred mile journey would give us an opportunity to see the country without involving us in any extra expense. (231)

Leaving in "the early days of June," she arrived in Albany after a two-week journey. "Despite my grief, I did find distraction in the beauty of the forests we crossed on our way to Lebanon, the last stage where we were to spend the night before arriving in Albany." Along the way the de La Tours du Pin "stopped for lunch in an inn set up not long before in the midst of this immense forest . . . The wooden house at which we stopped had reached the second stage of civilisation for it . . . was a house with glazed [glass] windows. But it is the incomparable beauty of the family who lived in it that particularly remains in my memory and which I still never forget" (235). To Lucy, it was as if the Americans had walked out of a Raphael painting. After lunch the venerable grandfather took off his cap and proposed a toast "to the health of our beloved President . . . the great Washington," an observance Americans made regularly. "Sometimes the health of 'The Marquis' was added. M. de La Fayette had left a much loved memory in the United States" (236). Staying in Lebanon before they reached Albany, the de La Tours du Pin heard a scream in the middle of the night, in French, coming from their traveling companion, M. de Chambeau.

In the morning we learned that towards midnight he had been awakened by a gentleman who was sliding, without so much as a "by your leave" into the empty half of his bed. Furious at this invasion, [Chambeau] promptly leaped out at the other side and spent the night in a chair listening to his companion's snores, for he had been in no way disturbed by M. de Chambeau's anger. This misadventure led to much teasing from everyone. When we arrived that evening in Albany, a small room was reserved for him alone, and that consoled him. (236)

Upon reaching Albany, the de La Tours du Pin made contact with Philip Schuyler, from whom they received "a welcome as flattering as it was kind. When General Schuyler saw me, he exclaimed: 'And now I shall have a sixth daughter.' He entered into all our plans, our wishes and our interests. He spoke French perfectly, as did all his family" (237). Ever the hospitable host, Schuyler escorted his aristocratic guests to a mansion north of Albany in Watervliet, the residence of his son-in-law, Stephen Van Rensselaer III and his daughter, Margarita.

On the very day of our arrival in Albany, as we were walking in the evening down a long and lovely street, we came across some enclosed grounds, planted with beautiful trees and flowers, and in it stood a pretty house, simple in style and with no outward pretensions to art or beauty. Extensive outbuildings could be seen stretching away behind it and these gave to the whole establishment the air and appearance of a splendid farm, wealthy and carefully looked after. A boy opened a gate to allow us to go down to the river bank and I asked him who owned this large house. "But," he said in amazement, "it's the Patroon's house." I told him I did not know who the Patroon was, and he lifted his arms to heaven exclaiming: "You don't know? You don't know who the Patroon is? Who can you be, then?" And he hurried off, horrified and slighty frightened at having spoken to people who had never heard of the Patroon. Two days later, we were received in this house with a kindness, an attentiveness and a friendliness which were never to change. Mrs Rensalaer (sic) was a woman of thirty who spoke French well, for she had learned it when visiting headquarters of the French and American armies with her father. She was blessed with a superior mind and a rare accuracy of judgment for both men and things . . . From the newspapers she had learned the state of the parties in France, the blunders which had caused the Revolution, the vices of the upper classes and the follies of the middle classes. With extraordinary insight, she had grasped the causes and effects of the disorders in our own country better than we had ourselves. (239)

Like Lucy, Margarita Van Rensselaer saw the French Revolution from above; from her elite perspective it was the errors of the "upper classes" and the "middle classes" that brought about the "disorders." The pressures from below that erupted with explosive force in the summer of 1789, and their underlying causes, are absent from the analyses of both aristocratic women.

The de La Tours du Pin did not want to settle in Albany, having decided that they preferred to buy a farm and live in the country. As he had assured them he would, Philip Schuyler found a place for them to stay until they were able to locate a farm they would purchase. The place Schuyler found for them was in Troy, the Van Buren farm, just across the Hudson from the Flatts, where Schuyler's brother lived.

The Van Buren's farm was an old Dutch house occupying a delightful position at the water's edge. It had no approach from landward, but was easily reached across the river. Opposite, on the road to Canada, stood a large inn where all the news, gazettes and sales notices were to be found. Two or three stage coaches stopped there every day. Van Buren owned two canoes and the river was always so calm that it could be crossed at any time. (241)

After Schuyler worked out arrangements for the de La Tours du Pin, Lucy wrote, "[we] went to stay with . . . Mr Van Buren to learn American ways, for we had made it a condition that we should live with the family and that they should not change the smallest detail of their ordinary routine. It was also agreed that Mrs Van Buren would let me help her in the house as a daughter would have done" (240). Accustomed to teams of servants who tended to her every wish, and to endless amenities due her as a person of noble birth in the privileged society of Ancien Régime France, Lucy was now staying on a farm in Troy, a fact with which, she understood, she had to come to terms. There is no reason to doubt Lucy's sincerity when she writes in her *Memoirs* that she wanted to accommodate herself to the domestic routine of an American farm, but at the same time this did not erase her aristocratic identity. She remained an aristocratic lady who was living in a very different world from her own, the one within which her identity had been formed. This was a fact that never went away.

Having heard of her father's death soon after arriving in America, Lucy went into mourning when she moved to the Van Buren farm. She had agreed to help Mrs. Van Buren in the house, as if she were her daughter, doing whatever work needed to be done. When she made a mourning dress in remembrance of her father it became evident to Mrs. Van Buren that she was an excellent seamstress: "seeing my skill with the needle [she] found it very convenient to have an unpaid sewing woman at her disposal. To engage one from Albany would have cost her a piastre a day, as well as food, including two lots of tea" (240). Lucy had not forgotten who she was; she was an aristocrat doing needlework for the wife of a farmer in upstate New York. There can be little doubt that Mrs. Van Buren was aware of the feelings that passed through Lucy's mind as she tried to fit into a life so different from that of her aristocratic past. After staying with the Van Burens for two months it was clear to Lucy that "they had had enough of us" (243). By this time Lucy's husband had found a farm that he decided to purchase, having been assured by Schuyler that it was worth the asking price. The farm was

two miles inland on the other side of the river, on the road from Troy to Schenectady. It was on a hill overlooking a wide stretch of country, and we thought it a very pleasant situation. The house was new and pretty, and in good condition. Only a part of the land was in cultivation. There were 150 acres under crops, a similar area of woodland and pasture, a small kitchen garden of a quarter of an acre filled with vegetables, and a fine orchard sewn with red clover and planted with ten-year-old cider trees, all in fruit. (242)

The owner did not want to move from the farm "until after the first snows," so having decided they should not stay with the Van Burens any longer, the de La Tours du Pin had temporarily to find another place. They found a "log house" in Troy that they were able to move into without delay, along with "a very reliable white girl," Betsey, who was to be married in two months, and who agreed to enter her service while her future husband was "building the log house where they were to live after their marriage" (243).

Lucy was fitting into a new way of life, as she understood she had to. "I resolved to equip myself to run my house as well as any good farmer's wife. I began by accustoming myself to never remaining in bed after sunrise. In summer, I was up and dressed by three o'clock in the morning" (241). She did work that had to be done.

> One day, towards the end of September, I was out in the yard, chopper in hand, busy cutting the bone of our dinner. As Betsey did not cook, I had been left in charge of everything concerned with food and, with the help of the *Cuisine Bourgeoise*, acquitted myself as best as I could. Suddenly from behind me, a deep voice remarked in French: "Never was a leg of mutton spitted with greater majesty." Turning quickly round, I saw M. de Talleyrand and M. de Beaumetz. They had arrived in Albany the previous day and had learned our whereabouts from General Schuyler. (244)

Talleyrand fled France after the Storming of the Tuileries in August 1792; he went to England and lived in London, until he was given five days to leave the country in January, 1794. While in London he made the acquaintance of the John Barker Churches—Philip Schuyler's son-in-law and his daughter, Angelica, the very couple that had been instrumental in the de La Tours du Pin's coming to Albany. Talleyrand was in financial need when he was told he had to leave England, and it was the Churches who subsidized his trip to America. Angelica wrote her sister Elizabeth, wife of Alexander Hamilton, recommending Talleyrand and a fellow émigré, the chevalier de Beaumetz. She told her sister that these two men were martyrs for "the cause of moderate liberty . . . To your care, dear Eliza, I commend these interesting strangers. They are a loan I make to you till I return to America, not to reclaim my friends entirely, but to share their society with you and dear Alexander the amiable." After Talleyrand arrived in Philadelphia, Alexander Hamilton tried to arrange a meeting between him and Washington, but sympathetic as Washington was to Talleyrand's position he decided he could not receive him officially, owing to the importance of maintaining neutrality toward France and Britain, now at war. Talleyrand and Beaumetz left Philadelphia and traveled through western New York to look for land for émigrés, hoping to reap whirlwind profits from sales; Talleyrand then decided to go to Albany, where he could meet Philip

Schuyler, whose daughters had served him so well, and while he was there he decided to seek out the de La Tours du Pin, whom he had been given to understand were living on a farm somewhere outside of Albany. He had known Lucy since she was a girl; seeing her would be like revisiting chapters from his own past. The day after he visited Schuyler in his Albany mansion he rode to the log house outside Troy where the de La Tours du Pin were staying, and it was there that he found Lucy turning a leg of mutton with "greater majesty" than he had ever seen.

Lucy invited Talleyrand and fellow émigré Beaumetz to join her and her husband for the leg of mutton, which they agreed to do the next day. But first, they were to have dinner with Philip Schuyler, and all rode from Troy to Albany. "We had a great deal to talk about on the way, and passed from one subject to another as people do when they meet after a long time. They had returned only the previous evening from their journey to Niagara and had therefore heard none of the latest news, which was worse than ever. Blood flowed everywhere in Paris. Mme Elisabeth [sister of Louis XVI] had perished. Each of us had relatives and friends among victims of the terror. Nor could we see an end to it." In fact, the Terror had come to an end.

> When we arrived at the good General's house, he was on the porch making signs from afar, shouting: "Come along, come along. There's fine news from France!" We hurried into the drawing-room and each seized a gazette. In them we found accounts of the revolt of 9 Thermidor, of the death of Robespierre and his supporters, the end of the murders and the executions of the members of the Revolutionary Tribunal. (244–45)

What Lucy did not know was that Jean Lambert Tallien, the lover of Thérésia Cabarrus, the woman who had given indispensable help to her in Bordeaux, had been instrumental in the overthrow of Robespierre, a most remarkable turn of events. Tallien, the suspect, turned the tables on Robespierre, helping end the Terror. To make all of this yet more remarkable, when Lucy received news of the fall of Robespierre it was when she arrived at Philip Schuyler's Albany mansion, accompanied by Talleyrand, whose path to Albany, like hers, had been cleared by Angelica Schuyler Church, Philip Schuyler's daughter. How strange the paths were between Paris, London, and Albany in the time of the French Revolution.

Talleyrand and Beaumetz had been traveling with Thomas Law, the younger brother of an English lord and the former governor of Patna, in India. Law had married "a very rich Brahmin widow," from whom he had inherited "a considerable fortune" at the time of her death. "He returned to England, but grew bored and decided to come to America and use part of the money he had brought from India to buy land. His intention was to discover whether this new nation merited the esteem he was ready to give it" (247). He had accompanied Talleyrand and Beaumetz on the trip to western New York before coming to Albany, where he was staying in an inn. When Talleyrand arrived at the mansion with the de La Tours du Pin he sought out Law and asked him to join everyone at Schuyler's mansion for dinner, which he did. Lucy considered Law among "the most eccentric of Englishmen"; for his part, Law was fascinated by Lucy and her husband—Lucy in particular, it would appear from her account of what transpired after they met at Schuyler's mansion. Law had booked passage for New York, but when he told Talleyrand that he would not make the trip as planned, Talleyrand asked why. The reason was that he had been deeply concerned over the plight of Lucy and her husband, whom he wanted to see again. He had understood that Talleyrand and Beaumetz would accompany the de La Tours du Pin to the log house in Troy the next day, where they were to have dinner together; he wanted to go with them. "I want to see that woman in her own home." Describing the visit, Lucy said, "In the evening, Mr Law came . . . to take tea with us. I already had a cow, and so was able to give them excellent cream. We went walking. Mr Law offered me his arm, and we talked for a long time" (247). There can be little doubt that Law, a widower in his forties and with two children, was smitten by Lucy. So too, some felt, was Talleyrand; rumors circulated about the reasons for Talleyrand's seeking Lucy out when he came to Albany, as she understood; she made it clear that the rumors were groundless (244). A profile of Lucy shows her as nice appearing, but the image tells us little about her as a person, either in the physical or psychological sense of the word. On one occasion in her *Memoirs* Lucy describes herself as tall, but she does not say how tall; what comes through in her *Memoirs* is a sense that others are drawn to her; one gathers that she had charm and *delicatesse*, qualities that were encouraged in females of her class, and which she would seem to have acquired.

Two days after Talleyrand, Beaumetz, and Law visited the de La Tours du Pin in the log house in Troy they all assembled together again, this time at Van Rensselaer Hall. They had all dined together several days previously at Philip Schuyler's mansion; now they came together in the mansion of the greatest landowner in New York. More aristocratic residences than these were not to be found in Albany. Present on this occasion were Stephen Van Rensselaer III and his wife, Schuyler's daughter Margarita, Schuyler himself and his wife Catherine, two French nobles of high pedigree, a former French bishop of noble birth, and an eccentric Englishman, son of a lord and a person of considerable wealth. Also present, although not mentioned, were servants. Outside the manor house were the manorial grounds, including a mill where tenant farmers were obliged to bring their grain for processing, and beyond the manorial grounds were families living on farms scattered across the Van Rensselaer patroonship under leasehold terms dictated by the Patroon, arrangements that for the most part were peculiar to the state of New York. Outside Van

Rensselaer Hall was one world; inside it was another. The aristocrats who came together inside Van Rensselaer Hall on this occasion shared much, different as they were in nationality and individual circumstances; what they shared was an aristocratic outlook, a sense that they *were* aristocrats, and that they should live as such. It was that awareness that bothered Thomas Law when he met the de La Tours du Pin, and saw the circumstances to which they had been reduced. Schuyler had been concerned over their plight; it was for that reason that he encouraged them to come to Albany, assuring them of his assistance; clearly the Van Rensselaers were similarly concerned, as their hospitality on this and other occasions indicated. And so it was with Thomas Law, who could not bear the thought that these once great French nobles were living under such meager circumstances in a log house in Troy. As Lucy explained: "After dinner, Mr Law took M. de Talleyrand by the arm and led him into the garden where they remained quite a long time

> . . . "My dear friend [Law said], I like these people . . . very much and it is my intention to lend them a thousand louis. They have just bought a farm. They need cattle, horses, negroes and so forth. So long as they live in this country, they will not repay my loan . . . in any case, I would not allow them to do so . . . I feel that to be useful to them will procure my own happiness and if they refuse . . . my nerves are very bad . . . I shall fall ill. They will truly render me a service in accepting my offer." Then he added: "That woman, so well bred! Who does her own cooking . . . who milks the cow . . . who does her own washing. I find it unbearable . . . the thought of it kills me . . . two nights now, I have not been able to sleep on account of it." (248)

When Talleyrand told the de La Tours du Pin of Law's offer they were "deeply touched," but they explained that they were at present able to manage by themselves. If in the future they should need assistance they would most certainly "have recourse to him." Knowing that the de La Tours du Pin would turn to him if they needed help seemed, Lucy said, to have "calmed Mr Law a little."

Talleyrand was also concerned over the prospects of his aristocratic friends, the de La Tours du Pin. Financially astute, he helped them rescue funds sent from Europe, "some twenty to twenty-five thousand francs . . . from Holland" that "had been consigned to the firm of [Robert] Morris in Philadelphia." Lucy explained that

> By a truly providential piece of luck [Talleyrand] learned one evening from an indiscreet conversation, that Mr Morris was to be declared bankrupt the following day. Not losing a minute, he went round to see the banker, forced an entrance when admittance was denied

him, and reached his office. He told Mr Morris that he knew of his position and obliged him to hand over certain Dutch bills of exchange which he held only in trust. Mr Morris allowed himself to be persuaded, for he greatly feared the dishonor into which he would have fallen if this breach of trust had become known—a course M. de Talleyrand would not have hesitated to take. He made only one condition, that M. de La Tour du Pin should sign a statement that the funds had been paid fully. M. de Talleyrand undertook that my husband would go to Philadelphia to settle the matter. He also advised me to accompany him. . . . (269)

So Lucy and her husband traveled down the Hudson in June 1795 to retrieve funds that were with Robert Morris in Philadelphia. They went first to New York City, where Lucy, who was ill, remained while her husband traveled to Philadelphia. "The three weeks that we spent in New York are among my happiest memories. My husband was away only four days, but had an opportunity to admire the fine city of Philadelphia and, what I envied still more, to see my hero, the great Washington. Even today, I still regret not having looked on the face of that great man of whom I had heard so much from his close friend, Mr Hamilton" (274).

The de La Tours du Pin were overwhelmed by the natural beauty of the Hudson as they sailed to New York, particularly the stretch of the river alongside the cliffs of West Point. "Although I have traveled in many lands and seen many grandeurs of nature, I have never seen anything to compare with that stretch of river at West Point" (272). They disembarked when they got to West Point and visited the scene of Benedict Arnold's treachery, of which Lucy gave a description in her *Memoirs.* She did not say, and perhaps did not know, that the person who had been responsible for her coming to Albany a year earlier, Philip Schuyler, had intervened on Arnold's behalf when Arnold was trying to persuade Washington to appoint him commander of West Point, the strategically important fortress that he planned to turn over to the British.[18] Schuyler, Arnold, and Washington had worked together through thick and thin before the Battle of Saratoga; knowing how highly Washington valued Schuyler's advice, Arnold persuaded Schuyler to use his influence with Washington to bring about his appointment as commander of West Point. The engineer who designed the fortifications at West Point in 1778 and oversaw their construction, Tadeusz Kosciuszko, had worked with Schuyler in 1777, throwing up obstacles between Skenesboro and Fort Edward that slowed Burgoyne's march to Albany. Kosciusko had also designed and overseen construction of the fortifications at Bemis Heights that contributed to the American victory at Saratoga. Judging from her *Memoirs,* Lucy knew nothing of these connections, nor, in all probability, did she know that Alexander Hamilton, whom she would soon see in New York, had been at West Point at the time of Arnold's treachery in the summer of 1780. Washington had traveled to Hartford with a retinue that included Hamilton and Lafayette to meet with Rochambeau, and on the way back to his headquarters he decided to inspect West Point, of which Arnold was in command. He sent Hamilton and another aide ahead to tell Arnold that he would be arriving presently, and that he should make ready for the forthcoming inspection. When Hamilton was having breakfast, Arnold received a note indicating that his treachery was certain to be discovered; excusing himself, he hurriedly gathered some belongings and rode away to join the British. Upon hearing of Arnold's betrayal, Washington said, "Whom can we trust now?" Little could Washington have imagined in this moment of despair that the stunning victory at Yorktown, the climacteric battle of the American Revolution, would take place in the following year, 1781, and that the French commander he had just met with in Hartford, Rochambeau, would be its architect. Moreover, two of the men who were with Washington at West Point, Alexander Hamilton and the Marquis de Lafayette, would be at Yorktown to share in the glory each sought fervently. What would Lucy have thought had she known of this as she walked about West Point in June 1795?

What would she have thought about what had happened to Rochambeau and Lafayette after Yorktown? Both were heroes of the American Revolution; both ran afoul of the French Revolution. Rochambeau was arrested and scheduled to go to the guillotine, but his jailors made a mistake and he escaped execution. Lafayette fled France and ended up in an Austrian prison. He had written the American Minister in The Hague, William Short, requesting money that would have allowed him to gain his freedom. Lucy was in The Hague at the time, she knew William Short, and she saw him the very day he received the letter from Lafayette requesting money to avoid imprisonment, but Short did not lend the money to Lafayette. "Mr. Short's refusal to intervene on behalf of a man who was a friend of Washington made me most indignant. Mr. Short was a very rich man and could have used his own money. He refused all the plans suggested and was later blamed by his own government" (168). Lafayette was initially placed in a Prussian prison in a dark, airless cell. Transferred to another cell in Prussia in January 1794, he was then sent to an Austrian prison at Olm tz under confinement so harsh that John Jay, American Ambassador in Vienna, complained, leading to relaxation of his imprisonment. Allowed to take daily walks, Lafayette attempted to escape, part of a finger was bitten off in the abortive attempt, and he was placed in solitary confinement. He fell sick, lost weight, and his hair began to fall out. As Lucy was walking about beautiful West Point, darkness descended on Lafayette in his grim prison cell in Austria. Lafayette's wife and two daughters joined him in imprisonment at Olm tz, sharing "all the rigors of his confinement," as Lucy wrote in her *Memoirs*. Lafayette's son, George Washington Lafayette, escaped to America and was taken in by Alexander Hamilton, who had not forgotten his comrade-in-arms, the gallant Marquis de Lafayette. Lafayette's son spent the summer of 1795 in the New York home of Alexander Hamilton; this was right after the visit to New York of the de La Tours du Pin.

For Lucy, the "three weeks we spent in New York [were] among my happiest memories." It was there that she met all the Hamilton family again.

> I had been in Albany when they arrived there in a wagon driven by Mr Hamilton himself. He had just retired from the Ministry of Finance [Treasury Secretary] to resume his legal practice, a profession more likely to enable him to leave some kind of fortune to his children. Mr Hamilton was then between thirty-six and forty years of age. Although he had never been in Europe, he spoke our language like a Frenchman and his distinguished mind and the clarity of his thought mingled very agreeably with the originality of M. de Talleyrand and the vivacity of M. de La Tour du Pin. (273)

Both Talleyrand and his English friend, Thomas Law, were in New York at the time of the de La Tours du Pin's visit, and all of them spent evenings together in conversations that Lucy remembered with particular fondness. And well she might. Among those with who conversed together in these evenings were two of the finest minds of the age, Talleyrand and Alexander Hamilton, along with Thomas Law, monsieur Emmery, an émigré who had been President of the Constitutent Assembly in January 1790, Lucy, and her husband, "and two or three other persons of note" (273), distinguished company by any standards. They "met after tea and sat on the verandah conversing under a beautiful starry sky and in a temperature of forty degrees. Whether it was Mr Hamilton telling of the beginnings of the War of Independence . . . Mr Law talking to us of his years in India, of the administration of Patna where he had been governor, of his elephants and his palanquins, or whether it was my husband raising some argument over the absurd theories of the Constitutent Assembly which M. de Talleyrand readily accepted, the talk never ran dry . . . (273).

Talleyrand held Alexander Hamilton in highest regard, so much so that looking back in later years at the men who bestrode the historical stage during the Revolutionary era he regarded Hamilton as one of the greatest. "I consider Napoleon, Fox, and Hamilton the greatest men of our epoch and, if I were forced to decide between the three, I would give without hesitation the first place to Hamilton. He divined Europe."[19] Between Hamilton and Talleyrand there were similarities of mind and attitude; both were urbane, polished and sophisticated, and both worked for stability in an age of upheaval. Talleyrand did fault Hamilton on one personal point: He felt that he did not respond sufficiently to the beauty of his wife Elizabeth. Also, he faulted Hamilton on his decision to step down from the office of Treasury Secretary in order that he could earn enough money as a lawyer to pay off debts and provide for his family. Lucy wrote that Talleyrand "found it strange that a man of [Hamilton's] quality, blessed with such outstanding gifts, should resign a ministry in order to return to the practice of law, and give as his reason that as a Minister he did not earn enough to bring up his eight children. Such an excuse seemed most odd to M. de Talleyrand, and in fact, rather stupid" (248). Walking by Hamilton's office in New York one evening, Talleyrand saw Hamilton working by candlelight. "I have seen a man who made the fortune of a nation laboring all night to support his family." This is not what he would have done. Talleyrand had benefited from office during the early, moderate stage of the French Revolution, lining his pockets as circumstances allowed, and he did the same after he returned to France in 1796 and became foreign minister, an office that in the span of two years allowed him to accumulate a fortune of thirteen to fourteen million francs. Lucy said of Talleyrand,

> . . . he was amiable . . . and his conversation had a grace and ease which has never been surpassed. He had known me since my childhood and always talked to me with an almost paternal kindliness which was delightful. One might, in one's inmost mind, regret having so many reasons for not holding him in respect, but memories of his wrong-doing were always dispelled by his conversation. Worthless himself, he had, oddly enough, a horror of wrongdoing in others. Listening to him, and not knowing him, one thought him a virtuous man. (246)

A French aristocrat who was traveling through the northern United States and Upper Canada paid the de La Tours du Pin a visit on their farm in the summer of 1795. Lucy referred to the visitor as the "Duc de Liancourt," but his full title was François Alexandre, duc de La Rochefoucauld-Liancourt. He added the distinguished name La Rochefoucauld to his title when his cousin, the Duc de La Rochefoucauld d'Enville, was stoned to death and disemboweled in the presence of his wife and mother at Gisors on September 14, 1792, in the aftermath of the September Massacres. As a progressive member of the nobility in the years before the Revolution, La Rochefoucauld-Liancourt established a model farm that included an arts and crafts school for the sons of soldiers. Elected to the Estates General, he supported the Monarchy while continuing to favor programs of social reform. It was he who told Louis XVI on July 15, 1789, that the disturbances in Paris were something more than a riot. "No majesty, it is a revolution." He became president of the Constituent Assembly on July 18, urged the King to seek refuge in Rouen, and when he declined the offer he assisted the king with the gift of a substantial sum of money. He fled France after the Storming of the Tuileries and sailed to America, where he traveled extensively. His *Journal de Voyage en Amérique* includes an account of his meeting with the de La Tours du Pin, and his distress over the straits to which the once-privileged aristocrats had been reduced—particularly Lucy, who was dressed in a woolen skirt and calico bodice when he saw her. "[I]t was only when he saw me appear in a pretty gown and a well made hat, though the milliner had had no hand in it . . . that he seemed to realize that we had not yet been reduced to beggary" (267). For her part, Lucy was struck by the frayed appearance of her aristocratic guest. "His clothes were covered in mud and dust, and torn in a number of places. He looked like some shipwrecked sailor who had just escaped from pirates. No one would have guessed that such an odd collection of garments clothed a First Gentleman of the Bedchamber!" La Rochefoucauld-Liancourt had received letters from Talleyrand recommending him to the Schuylers and Van Rensselaers, and he indicated to Lucy that he would like to meet the members of these prominent families. They rode into Albany the next day, but only after Lucy made La Rochefoucauld-Liancourt change his clothes. "I reproached him bitterly, especially for the patch on the knee of a pair of nankeen breeches, which must have come all the way from Europe, so worn were they from laundering." When they "made the call in the town" the next day the "transformation was not so complete" as she had hoped it would be. Lucy took La Rochefoucauld-Liancourt into Albany with the understanding that he would return to her farm for another visit, but he "visited the neighboring country instead . . . I never saw him again."

The de La Tours du Pin returned to France in 1796, the same year as Talleyrand, and lived through the upheavals of the Directory, the 15-year period of Napoleonic rule, and the return of the Bourbon monarchy during the Restoration. M. de La Tour du Pin held office again; he, Lucy, and their children fled France again; he even spent time in prison, where his wife joined him. In Lucy's story of her life, one that was marked by conflict, struggle, and violence, the two years she spent in Albany were a brief digression in a lifetime of extraordinary experiences in an extraordinary age. The two years she spent in Albany were a time of respite, a period she viewed nostalgically many years later when she wrote her *Memoirs*. Looking back, she recalled the 250-acre farm a few miles north of Albany that she and her husband had lived on with their two children. Settling into the regular rhythms of agrarian life on their farm, she and her husband experienced a way of life that was utterly different from that of leisured, privileged aristocrats who moved from one estate to another in Ancien Régime France. It was as if they had landed on another planet after leaving France. With the eye of an outsider, Lucy was intrigued by all that she saw; her *Memoirs* offer what is surely one of the finest accounts we have of life on a farm in the Albany region at the end of the eighteenth century.

Lucy explained that she wanted to fit into the country life she was entering, and to win approval of neighboring farmers: "I adopted the dress worn by the women on the neighboring farms—the blue and black striped woolen skirt, the little bodice of dark calico and a colored handkerchief, and I parted my hair in the fashionable way, piling it up and holding it in place with a comb" (266).

Figure 37. This was the site of the de La Tour farmhouse, which no longer stands.

As soon as we had the home to ourselves, we used some of our money to set it in order. It consisted of only a ground floor, raised five feet above the ground. The builders had begun by sinking a wall six feet down, leaving only two feet above ground level. This formed the cellar and the dairy. Above this, the remainder of the house was of wood . . . The gaps in the wooden frame were filled with sun-dried bricks so that the wall was compact and very warm. We had the inside walls covered with a layer of plaster into which some color had been mixed, and the whole effect was very pretty.

Philip Schuyler gave the de La Tours du Pin an "aged horse" that they used to make cider after they set up a cider press. They found that

> . . . putting aside enough [cider] for own use, we had eight or ten casks to sell. Our reputation for honest dealing was a guarantee that not a drop of water had been added to the cider, so that it fetched more than twice the customary price. It all sold immediately . . . The apple picking was followed by the harvesting of the maize. We had an abundance of it, for it is indigenous to the United States and

grows there better than any other plant. As the corn must not be left in the husk for more than two days, the neighbors collect to help, and they work without stopping until it is all done. This is called a "frolic." First the floor of the barn is swept with as much care as for a ball. Then, when darkness comes, candles are lit and the people assemble, about thirty of them, both black and white, and they set to work. All night long someone sings or tells stories and in the middle of the night everyone is given a bowl of boiling milk, previously turned with cider, to which have been added cloves, cinnamon, nutmeg, and other spices, and five or six pounds of brown sugar, if one is being very grand, or a similar quantity of molasses if one feels less grand. We prepared a kitchen boiler full of this mixture and our workers paid us the compliment of drinking it all, eating toast which accompanied it. These good people left us at five o'clock in the morning, going into the sharp cold, saying "Famous good people, those from the old country!" (278)

As an educated outsider, and a foreigner, Lucy took note of the ethnic and social types she encountered around her farm. Land agents made parcels available to "poor Irish, Scottish, or even French colonists" who arrived looking for land.

Let us follow one such group of colonists, people whom I knew, so that you can see how the system worked. The household consisted of the husband, the wife, a son of fifteen or seventeen, and two daughters. I saw them set off on foot, across the snow, the first three carrying shoulder packs. The husband was leading a poor horse harnessed to a small sledge on which he had packed two casks, one containing flour and the other salted pork, several axes, gardening and other tools, some bundles and the two small girls. (257)

With their meager possessions they would clear land, build a log house, and set themselves up as farmers, paying the Patroon "a small rent . . . either in wheat or money." Living amongst farmers of simple means, the de La Tours du Pin became accustomed to the rhythms of rural life. "When all the harvests had been gathered in and stored, we began the ploughing and all the other tasks which had to be finished before winter. The wood which we intended to sell was stacked under a shelter. The sledges were repaired and repainted." Helping run a 250-acre farm was not easy. "I never wasted a minute. Every day, winter and summer, I was up at dawn and my toilet took very little time." While the cows were being milked "I busied myself in the dairy, skimming the milk." Twice a week she helped in the making of butter, a task that was too demanding for her to do alone. But she did much of "the butter-making, and much other tiring work which still remained to be done, fell to me" (256).

As the winter of 1794 set in Lucy was buying some moccasins, when

> I saw [Indians] for the first time, the last survivors of the Mohawk nation whose territory had been bought or seized by the Americans after the war. At about the same time the Onondagas, who lived near Lake Champlain, had also sold their forests and dispersed, but now and again some of them were still to be seen. I was rather startled, I must admit, the first time I met a man and a woman, both stark naked, walking calmly along the road. But no one seemed to find it strange and I soon grew used to it. When I was living at the farm, I saw these people nearly every day during the summer time. (250)

At the beginning of winter an Indian asked Lucy if he could "cut branches from a kind of willow which has shoots five to six feet long and as thick as a finger, promising to weave baskets for me during the winter." She said he could cut the branches, but she did not expect him to keep his promise.

> I was wrong to doubt, for scarcely a week after the snow had disappeared, the Indian was there with his load of baskets. He gave me six, all fitting into one another. The first, round and very large, was so closely woven that it held water as well as any earthenware bowl. I wanted to pay for them, but he firmly refused and would only accept a jar of buttermilk, which the Indians like very much indeed. (259)

On another occasion Lucy was with a French officer, M. de Novion, who paid them a visit and wanted to see the country. Riding on horseback, she realized after a few miles that

> I had forgotten my whip. As M. de Novion had no knife with which to cut me a stick, he could not help. The undergrowth in the wood was fairly thick and at that moment, seeing one of my Indian friends sitting behind a bush, I called to him: "Squaw John." It is impossible to describe the surprise, almost the horror, of M. de Novion at the apparition which emerged from the bush and came toward us with his hand held out to me: a very tall man wearing only a strip of blue cloth passed between his legs and fixed to a cord about his waist. His astonishment increased when he saw how well we knew one another . . . As we walked our horses on, and before

I had time to explain how I knew such an odd person in such extraordinary garments, Squaw John leaped lightly from the top of a hillock which dominated the road and politely offered me a stick which he had stripped of its bark with his tomahawk. (261)

A cart passed the de La Tour du Pin farm often, laden with vegetables. The cart belonged to what Lucy called the "Quaker Shakers," today known simply as the Shakers. "The driver stopped at our house and I seized every opportunity of talking to him about their way of life, their customs and their beliefs. He invited us to visit their settlement, and one day we decided to go" (261). They went by wagon for several miles, passing through "thick forest," until they came to their settlement, "an offshoot from their main settlement at Lebanon." It was "bounded on one side by twenty thousand acres of forest belonging to the town and on the other by a river, the Mohawk." The Shaker community consisted of a "large number of fine wooden houses, a church, schools and the community house, the latter being built of brick." The Shaker (she called him a Quaker) that they knew took them on a tour of the community, starting with a vegetable garden where "Many men and women were busy tilling and weeding, for the sale of vegetables was the community's source

Figure 38. Road sign showing the location of Delatour Road where Delatour Road and Watervliet Shaker Road meet. As the sign indicates, a Roman Catholic religious institution is behind the site of the de La Tour farmhouse.

Figure 39. Delatour Road.

of income" (264). Lucy said nothing about the religious beliefs of the Shakers, or of the celibacy they practiced, but she described in some detail the separate schools for boys and girls, and the "perfect order and total silence" that was maintained. She was invited to see a building that was perhaps "150 to 200 feet long and about 50 feet wide . . . it was a very light room, bare of decorations, its smooth walls painted light blue. At each end was a small platform on which stood a wooden armchair." She was puzzled by lines of polished copper nails on the floor, wondering what use they might possibly have. At the peal of a bell a row of women entered the room from one side and a row of men entered from the other side, each row lining up behind the copper nails, careful "not to let even the tips of their toes pass beyond them. They remained motionless until [a] woman seated in [an] armchair gave a sort of groan or shout which was neither speech or chant. Then they all changed places. . . ." They carried out "several maneuvers" after an old woman muttered something in a language Lucy found unintelligible, and then everyone left the room in the same order in which they had arrived (264–65). Lucy had attended a Shaker ritual in Watervliet, the first of all Shaker settlements, founded by Ann Lee in 1774.

Among the more intriguing parts of Mme de La Tour du Pin's account of her life on a farm outside Albany is her discussion of slaves, hers and those of other farmers who lived nearby. She explained that a law allowed slaves to choose another master if they could find one willing to pay a stipulated sum; needing help on the farm, she and her husband learned of an intelligent and industrious slave who wanted to change masters, not because his master was unfair but because he wanted to escape the domination of his own father. "We went to consult General Schuyler and Mr Renslaer (sic), both of whom knew this negro by reputation. They congratulated us on his wishing to belong to us and made us promise to take him." The slave was grateful to the de La Tours du Pin for buying him, as were two other slaves, a husband and wife who had different owners and had been separated for 15 years. The de La Tours du Pin purchased the husband first, "an excellent man and a good worker," and then Lucy went to the farm of the "brutal and wicked man" who owned the wife. "Learning that I had bought her husband and wished to buy her also so that they might be reunited, the poor woman sank fainting on to a chair . . . I counted out the money [and told her] . . . that her husband would come to fetch her and her small daughter. This three-year old child had, by law, to go with her mother. And that is how we collected our negro staff" (254–55. Lucy felt that their "negroes" were "passionately devoted to us," and she came to care for them deeply. When the de La Tours du Pin returned to France they decided to grant their slaves freedom. Lucy explained that freeing their slaves was one of her most cherished deeds ever, one that she so wanted to savor that she asked her husband if she could be the one to tell their slaves they were to be freed.

> The poignancy of such a scene cannot be described. Never in my life have I known a happier moment. These people whom I had just freed, surrounded me and wept. They kissed my hands, my feet, my gown; and then, suddenly, their joy vanished and they said: "We would prefer to remain slaves all our lives and for you to stay here." The following day, my husband took them before the Justice of the Peace, for the ceremony of manumission, which had to take place in public. All the negroes of the town gathered to watch.

Looking back on that occasion, Lucy considered it "the finest day of my life" (282–83).

As an outsider, Lucy was alert not only to different ethnic and religious types she encountered on a farm outside Albany, but to the climate, the seasons, the forces of nature whose powers must have seemed formidable in a time that did not yet know modern amenities. A strong sense of Albany seasons and their harshness comes through in her *Memoirs*, as in her description of the onset and rigors of winter:

> We waited impatiently for the first snow to fall and for the moment when the river would freeze over for three or four months. The freeze-up happens suddenly, and if the ice is to be solid, it has to harden within twenty-four hours to a depth of two or three

feet. This was a local peculiarity, unaffected by latitude, and due solely to the enormous stretches of forest which covered that huge continent to the west and north of the settlements in the United States . . . Between the 25th of October and the 1st of November, the sky became covered by a mass of cloud so thick that the daylight faded. These clouds were driven violently before a horrible cold north-west wind and everyone began preparing to put under shelter everything that could not be left out and buried under the snow. Boats, canoes and ferries were hauled out of the water and those which were not decked in were turned keel upwards. It was a time of intense activity for everyone. Then the snow would begin to fall, so thickly that it was impossible to see a man at ten paces. Usually, the river would have frozen hard several days before. The first precaution was to mark out a wide path along one of the river banks with pine branches. Places where the bank was not steep and where it was safe to walk if the ice were similarly marked. It would have been dangerous to walk anywhere but between these markers for in many places the ice at the edge was not very solid. (249–50)

Living on a farm outside Albany at the end of the eighteenth century, Lucy experienced the numbing forces of winter, and she was in awe of the renewing powers of nature when spring arrived:

Speaking of spring, it is interesting to note the suddenness of its arrival in those regions . . . During the first days of March the north-westerly wind which had been blowing throughout the winter, dropped suddenly and was succeeded by a southerly one. The snow melted so fast that for two days the roads were raging torrents. As our house stood on a hillside, our white blanket disappeared very quickly. The winter snow had been two or three feet deep, protecting the grass and plants from the ice, and as a result, in less than a week after it had melted, the meadows were green and carpeted with flowers and the woods were filled with countless varieties of plants unknown in Europe. (258–59)

Yellow fever broke out in New York in June 1795, when Lucy and her husband were there to safeguard the funds they had placed with Robert Morris. As Lucy explained, "Fearing to be kept in New York by quarantine measures, I decided to leave immediately. We packed our trunk and went at daybreak to reserve places on a sloop which was ready to sail" (274). Both she and her husband had become severely ill in New York and were relieved to be back on their farm. "I returned to my country tasks with fresh ardor, for the change of air had cured my fever and I recovered with all my strength. I resumed my dairy work and the pretty patterns stamped on my butter told my customers that I was back." Then disaster struck.

> My small Stéphanie was taken from us by a short illness very common in that part of the continent: a sudden paralysis of the stomach and intestines without any accompanying fever or convulsions. She died within a few hours, and was conscious to the very end. The Albany doctor . . . told us immediately he saw her that there was no hope. He said the illness was very widespread in the country just then and that there was no known remedy for it. The Schuyler's small son, who had played with my daughter throughout the afternoon of the previous day, also died a few hours later from the same illness . . . His mother adored him, and called him my dear child's husband. (276)

Lucy had a "fairly severe attack" of measles at the "end of the winter of 1795–96," an illness that was "aggravated by the fact that I was in the first months of pregnancy" (281). She recovered quickly from the illness and "was no sooner better" than she received letters telling her that she and her husband could take possession of the family estate at Le Bouilh if they returned to France, but they had to do so within a year.

> The arrival of these letters at our peaceful farm had somewhat the effect of a firebrand, for in the hearts of all about me they suddenly set aflame thoughts of a return to our homeland, glimpses of a better life, hopes of achieving our ambitions, in short, they armed all those sentiments which animate the life of man. My own feelings were quite different. France had left me only memories of horror. It was there that I had lost my youth, crushed out of being by numberless, unforgettable terrors.

Those closest to her, those "all about me," were eager to return to France, but not she. But leave Albany and America they did, she, the members of her family, and other émigrés they had known during two years of flight from the French Revolution. In April 1796 the de La Tours du Pin sailed down the Hudson to New York, where they saw Talleyrand, who was also making ready to return to France. Because conditions in France seemed unpredictable the de La Tours du Pin went to Spain before returning home, gathering information as they proceeded.

Passing through Spain on her way back to France, Lucy had feelings of "horror and terror" that she was unable to overcome; she longed deeply for her farm outside Albany and the "peace we had enjoyed there." Having returned home she discovered that Le Bouilh had been stripped of everything; it was completely empty. She stayed in the "great house" while her husband was trying to sort things out on other family estates, and while he was away "gangs of brigands" were "spreading terror throughout the south of France," murder gangs that settled old political accounts from the Revolution. Violence had driven the Revolution into the Jacobin Terror; violence begat violence, and it continued during the Thermidorean reaction, in a new form. After the fall of Robespierre there was a White reaction, carried out by murder gangs such as those in the south of France who roamed the countryside around Le Bouilh, where Lucy was staying. "I often spent half the night sitting on my bed, listening to the barking watchdogs, thinking that any moment the brigands would break through the flimsy planks covering the ground-floor windows. I do not remember ever in my life having been more anxious! How I longed for my farm [in Albany], my good negroes and the peace of those months." Lucy wrote that "We lived at Le Bouilh right through the winter and for a part of the Spring. Towards July 1797, my husband realized it would be necessary to go to Paris to . . . finish putting his affairs in order. As if driven by presentiment, I asked to go with him" (302–03). Back in Paris, the de La Tours du Pin looked up relatives and old friends who had returned to France, including Mme d'Hénin, Mme de Staël, who had purchased Lucy's house on the rue du Bac, the Hôtel Dillon, where she had lived as a girl, Talleyrand, and Thérésia Cabarrrus, now Mme Tallien. The Paris to which Lucy returned was much altered from the city she had fled during the Terror. The Thermidorean reaction had been a time of rapid decompression and rejection of everything associated with the Terror, at least among the civilized elite, who reintroduced exquisite fashions and flaunted a life of easy-going frivolity and hedonism. Thérésia, now Mme Tallien, was one of the leading fixtures of this glittering, brilliant, some would say overly-refined society.

By the time of Lucy's return to Paris, Thrérésia had grown weary of Tallien and taken on a lover, Paul Barras, a leading political fixture who had tired of his mistress, Rose de Beauharnais, Thérésia's closest friend. One feels as if one needs a scorecard to keep track of liaisons in this indulgent and sexually free society, that of Paris in the late 1790s. Paul Barras had met a young Corsican artillery officer during the siege of Toulon in December 1793, and found him useful when a Royalist revolt threatened the Convention on October 5, 1795. This artillery officer, Napoleon Bonaparte, quashed the revolt with a "whiff of grapeshot," a most useful exercise insofar as Barras was concerned. Barras took his protégé to the home of his mistress's closest friend, Mme Tallien, whose beauty and allure captivated the inexperienced Napoleon. Napoleon made advances to Thérésia that elicited laughter; he then directed his attention to Barras' mistress, Rose de Beauharnais, at Barras' suggestion. Barras had set his sights on Thérésia, and was happy to dump his mistress on Napoleon, who preferred the name Josephine to that of Rose when he married her in the following year. When Lucy visited Thérésia in her fashionable Paris house, La Chaumière, Thérésia was pregnant, probably with Barras' child. Thérésia unburdened herself of her unhappiness when she discussed her circumstances with Lucy; she decided that she had never really loved Tallien, and that he had become jealous and unbearable. Tallien arrived while Lucy was visiting Thérésia, and she thanked him coolly for his former assistance. He said he would be pleased to render further assistance, should it be needed. And it was. Amidst the unstable politics of 1797 there was another Royalist revolt, that of 18 Fructidor; once again, Royalists were forced to go into exile. The de La Tours du Pin had just arrived in Paris to sort out their affairs; again they had to immigrate, this time to England. But getting passports proved difficult, and once again it was Tallien who stepped into the breach and secured the passports that allowed Lucy, her husband, and their children to flee Paris. Their time in England was one of utter misery for Lucy and her husband. They returned to France after Napoleon came to power in 1799, and M de La Tour du Pin held office again, under Napoleon. Lucy and her husband integrated into the governing elite under Napoleon, whom Lucy admired, and with whom she had several memorable meetings, most notably when her husband was deprived of his office. According to her account, a meeting she arranged with Napoleon was successful; while her husband did not recover the post he had lost, Napoleon, because of her intervention, arranged for him to receive another office. The de La Tours du Pin sided with the Bourbons at the time of the Restoration, and with the support of Louis XVIII's foreign minister Talleyrand (a post he had held under Napoleon), M. de La Tour du Pin was appointed ambassador at the Congress of Vienna. Lucy's *Memoirs* end in 1815, with her husband rushing to the south of France after Napoleon escaped from Elba and made his final, unsuccessful, bid for power.

The two years Mme de La Tour du Pin spent in Albany were a calm and peaceful interlude in a lifetime of political turmoil, ideological conflict, and social upheaval that began in 1789 and changed her world forever. Her life can be divided into three parts: the one that preceded her immigration, the two years she spent in America, and the many years she spent in Europe after her return in 1796. Twenty-six at the time she boarded ship in Albany for the return passage to Europe, she was a different person, a profoundly different person, than she had been seven years earlier, at the beginning of the French Revolution. When Lucy looked back at the moment in her life when she returned to Europe she viewed it from a distant perspective, that of 1843; she was in Lucca when she reached this point in her *Memoirs*, and she was 73. Reflecting upon the anxieties and apprehensions she had felt as she contemplated leaving Albany, she saw this as an important milestone, not only because she was about to return to Europe, but also because she realized that an internal change had taken place within her. As she recalled her state of mind when she was about to leave America she wrote that "only two sentiments" remained alive in her, love for her husband and for her children. They were eager to return to Europe but she was not. At that point in the narrative Mme de La Tour du Pin made a revealing comment: "[R]eligion, which from that time forward was my only guide in all my problems, prevented me from setting the slightest obstacles in the way of a departure which terrified me and filled me with dismay."

Religion was not a subject Lucy discussed often in her *Memoirs*. She did not refer to the religious practices or forms she observed; of that we know little. But as she recalled the momentous decision to leave America and return to Europe, the thought of which filled her with "unforgettable terrors," she said that "religion" removed the mental obstacles that filled her with "dismay." And when she said, "religion . . . *from this time forward* [my italics] was my only guide in all my problems" she recognized a personal change that had taken place within her. That change began with the dislocations and disruptions of the French Revolution that she had experienced. When she returned to France at the end of 1792 after spending 15 months in Holland, France was no longer the same, and she resolved that she would no longer be the same person. "Looking critically at my past life, I reproached myself for its futility." She would put her "carefree youth" behind her; she would devote herself to "carrying out her duty however painful or dangerous that may be. I felt by this means I would find my way back to the path which Providence had ordained me. In those troubled times, and without my being aware of it, God had enlightened me . . . From that day forward, my life was different, my moral outlook transformed" (174). In these comments Lucy explained the connection that she had come to see between her own life of "frivolity" and that of her class, the French aristocracy, a failure that she believed helped bring about the French Revolution. This was the Lucy who saw the aristocracy dancing toward the precipice of 1789, bringing about their own ruin. Lucy's new consciousness made her receptive to religious renewal, in effect a religious conversion. Looking back at the death of her infant daughter Stéphanie on her farm outside Albany in 1795, she wrote,

> Until then, though far from irreligious, I had not been much concerned with religion. During my childhood, no one had ever talked to me about it. During my early youth, I had been constantly surrounded by the worst possible examples. In the highest circles of Paris society I had seen the scandalous behavior repeated so often that it had become familiar and no longer distressed me. It was as if all concern with morality had been stifled in my heart. But the hour had come when I was to be formed to recognize the hand that had stricken me. I could not describe the change that had taken

place within me. It was as if a voice cried out to me to change my
whole nature . . . God granted me the grace of knowing Him and
serving Him; he gave me the courage to bow very humbly beneath
the blow I had received and to prepare myself to endure without
complaint those future griefs, which in his justice, he was to send
to try me. Since that day, the divine will has found me submissive
and resigned. (276–77)

Mme de La Tour du Pin was not the only aristocrat who saw Christianity in
a different light after experiencing the upheavals of the French Revolution.
Indeed, her return to Christianity was part of a larger structure of change in
the thought and feeling of those who lived through the pressures, burdens, and
disruptions of the Revolutionary age. Another such person was Lucy's contemporary, François-René, Viscount de Châteaubriand (1768–1848), an aristocrat
whose family estate was in Brittany, whom Lucy knew and did not like. Like
others of his class, Châteaubriand was initially receptive to the Revolution, but
the abortive flight of the King and Queen to Varennes in 1791 led him to
rethink his views, and in 1792 he joined a Royalist army at Koblenz. He was

Figure 40. The view from Delatour Road today is much as it must have been when
Lucy and her family lived there after they arrived in Albany, having fled the Reign of
Terror in France.

wounded at the siege of Thionville and went into exile in England in 1793, where he remained until 1800. It was during the years in exile, a period of misery and hardship, that Châteaubriand considered the causes of the French Revolution, of which several members of his family were victims; it was also during this period that he wrote the *Genius of Christianity* (1801), a seminal work in a movement of religious renewal that transformed the moral and political landscape of Western society. Châteaubriand had been skeptical of Christian doctrine before the Revolution; now he discovered the higher truths of a religion he had previously dismissed as irrelevant. The work in which he elucidated those higher truths, his *Genius of Christianity*, marked a turning point in Western life and thought; that it was written by a French aristocrat who fled the French Revolution suggests an obvious parallel between his experience and that of Mme de La Tour du Pin. Like Lucy, Châteaubriand underwent a religious conversion after witnessing the dislocations of the French Revolution; he too was an aristocrat whose sheltered and privileged life was torn asunder by a revolution that brought the curtain down forever on the *douceur de vivre* (the term is Talleyrand's) of Ancien Régime France. Châteaubriand made a public statement about Christianity in a widely-read and deeply influential book; writing many years later, Mme de La Tour du Pin described her return to Christianity in her *Memoirs*. She had lived in the glittering, carefree, pleasure-seeking world of France before 1789; it was when she lived on a farm outside Albany, New York, as she reflected on all that happened to her and to her family, that she understood the internal change that had taken place within her; religion became an anchor and safeguard for Lucy in a world whose convulsions she had experienced personally and directly.

4

Albany and the Erie Canal

The Erie Canal is one of the most important transportation projects in all of American history.[1] Three hundred sixty-three miles long, 40' wide, and 4' deep, it made inexpensive commercial transportation possible from the Hudson to the Great Lakes. That a project of such modest size unleashed forces that transformed the state of New York, made New York City the dominant commercial center in America, and fed into an historical dynamic that helped form a new economic global order seems most unlikely; but all of this is what followed completion of the Erie Canal in 1825. The Erie Canal was an immediate commercial success: The shipping cost for a ton of cargo from Buffalo to New York City plummeted from $90 to $125 per ton before 1825 to $4 per ton within ten years of the canal's completion. Revenues from tolls were even greater than expected; construction loans were paid off within seven years, and the first of several enlargements of the canal began in 1836. All along the 363-mile canal villages turned into towns, and towns became flourishing cities, throbbing with economic life. The population of Buffalo increased from 2,600 in 1825 to 15,600 in 1834 and to 42,000 in 1850. The population of Albany was 5,289 in 1800; it was 33,721 in 1840. The same demographic pattern unfolded all along the Erie Canal, in Rochester, Syracuse, Utica, Schenectady, and in smaller towns such as Canajoharie. Between 1820 and 1840 the population of New York State increased 77 percent. The rate of increase in this 20-year period was 167 percent in Albany, 330 percent in Utica, 769 percent in Buffalo, and 1,244 percent in Rochester. Albany, eastern terminus of the Erie Canal, was the ninth largest city in America in 1840. Rochester, Troy, and Utica were among America's 30 largest cities in this same period. Upstate New York was transformed by the Erie Canal; today 80 percent of the upstate population lies within 25 miles of the Erie Canal or canals that were linked to it, built soon after its construction.

The success of the Erie Canal was so great that it ignited a "canal fever" that swept across America; other states used the Erie Canal as a model, hoping to achieve gains such as those showered upon New York. The Erie Canal helped open up the vast region beyond the state of New York—the American Midwest—to agrarian and urban development. Rich mineral deposits that lay beyond the Erie Canal were made available by inexpensive water transport to markets in America and overseas, helping fuel the Industrial Revolution. Farmers in Ohio, Indiana, and Illinois had access to markets in the American East, a stimulus to increased production. American grain was less expensive owing to lower transportation costs made possible by the Erie Canal; this created tensions in overseas markets. The politically dominant landowning class in Britain passed legislation in 1815, the Corn Law, which imposed tariffs on grain, to protect their economic interest. Landowners were protected at the expense of workers in the Midlands, the center of the Industrial Revolution. Inexpensive grain would relieve pressure on workers, who were subject to low wages, were it to be available. And cheap grain was available, one of the sources being grain produced in America and shipped inexpensively through the Erie Canal to New York, America's most important port. Out of this complex of circumstances came repeal of the Corn Law in 1846, legislation that opened up markets for American grain in Britain; more broadly, this marked an important stage in opening world markets to free trade, or to trade less impeded by protective tariffs. The Erie Canal contributed to a new way of economic thinking, a paradigm shift, which resulted in a more dynamic global marketplace. Moreover, it contributed to a shift in the geographical center of global economic gravity, giving America a new place in the world community of nations.

Visionary as the men who planned and built the Erie Canal were, they could not have foreseen its enormous impact. By stimulating development of the area between Lake Erie and the Mississippi, the Erie Canal helped forge regional solidarity, binding states from New York to the Mississippi River more closely by common economic interests, thereby deepening the division between North and South. What further deepened that division was the role cities along the Erie Canal played in the Underground Railway, a role that was not lost upon the South. The Erie Canal contributed to tensions that ultimately culminated in the Civil War. The Erie Canal was more than a commercial corridor; it was a passageway that carried more than commodities laden on packet boats; a distinctive way of life developed along its length.[2] When construction of the Erie Canal began in 1817 local contractors hired men from nearby farms, villages, and towns to do the work, but increasingly immigrants made up the work force. Immigrants brought different habits and behaviors with them, contributing to a canal culture that was increasingly rough and tough. By 1830, 30,000 men, women, and children worked on the Erie Canal. By 1835 there were 1,500 grog shops along the canal. Prostitutes followed the grog shops. Children, leading horses and donkeys that pulled packet boats along the canal, worked long hours. For the most part they did not attend school. A culture of vulgarity grew up along the Erie Canal.

At the same time that a distinctive culture took shape along the Erie Canal there was a reaction against it, a call for moral and religious reform. The seeds of the Second Great Awakening had been planted before construction of the Erie Canal; they had their source in the political and ideological struggles of the Revolutionary age, and conflict over religion. By the time the curtain came down on the Revolutionary age Western society was more conservative, and more religious. This was true in Europe and in America. If the Second Great Awakening was part of a deeper and larger American impulse, nowhere was it felt more deeply than in upstate New York, along the corridor formed by the Erie Canal. Reformers strove to protect workers from a life of sin and degradation, sometimes couching their arguments in terms that took pragmatic facts into account. One reformer explained that "It is high time something efficient be done upon the lines of our canals, particularly the . . . [Erie Canal]; otherwise the vices of its population will soon become too firmly rooted to be eradicated, except by the destruction and perdition of one whole generation." Reformers warned that without moral improvement economic development would be undermined; "steady, honest, and respectable persons, of both sexes, will refuse to be employed on the canal. [Businessmen] will be reduced to the necessity of entrusting [their] business to the dregs of the community. . . ."[3] That Evangelical reformers were so attuned to business interests indicates the extent to which the Erie Canal furthered a business spirit, one of the central outcomes of the Erie Canal. If the Erie Canal came out of a vision of economic expansion, the growth that it unleashed created a new dynamic, within which business interests achieved new importance. Some of the men most instrumental in the planning and building of the Erie Canal were of the old elite; the transportation system they brought into being spawned an economic order into which they no longer fit easily. This is one of the many paradoxes of the Erie Canal story.

The story of the Erie Canal has, of course, been told many times, as has the story of the Battle of Saratoga. The Erie Canal story that will unfold in this chapter looks back to the Battle of Saratoga, and to the Albany visitors that traveled up the Hudson to see Philip Schuyler between 1776 and 1783. The same river systems that dictated military strategies during the American Revolution had vast economic potential, as men who participated in struggles along the Champlain-Hudson and Mohawk corridors understood. When independence was achieved some of these men lay down their arms and went forth with visions of economic growth, which they were convinced could be achieved within the wilderness of New York. The same river corridors that were of critical importance to wars fought in New York during the Revolution could be turned into avenues of commerce in time of peace. This is what some of his Albany visitors believed, and they were not mistaken. Some of the men that we have already met will appear again in this narrative, which is decidedly Albany centered. Having traced the development of the Erie Canal up to the time of its completion in 1825, we will look at the celebration of that achievement held in Albany. In looking at the 1825 Erie Canal celebration we will pay particular attention to two prominent Albanians, Stephen Van Rensselaer III and William James of Albany, both of whom participated in the event.

Among early American advocates of canals was Benjamin Franklin, the first of Philip Schuyler's visitors, who made his way up the Hudson in 1776 to help prepare an American invasion of Canada. In 1772, Franklin, still in Britain, had observed changes that were laying the foundations for a new economic order. A ten-mile canal had been built in 1759–61, the Bridgewater Canal, that linked Manchester and its bustling textile mills with coal mines, giving impetus to sharply increased production made possible by coal shipped inexpensively from nearby mines. Grasping the importance of canals to economic development, Franklin sang their praise in a letter to the mayor of Philadelphia, S. Rhodes:

> [In England] they look on the constant practicability of a Navigation allowing Boats to pass and repass at all Times and Seasons, without Hindrance, to be a point of the greatest Importance, and, therefore, they seldom or ever use a River where it can be avoided . . . Rivers are ungovernable things, especially in Hilly Countries. Canals are quiet and very manageable. Therefore they are often carried on here by the Sides of Rivers, only on Ground above the Reach of Floods, no other Use being made of the Rivers than to supply occasionally the waste water in the Canals.[4]

There is no record of Franklin having discussed canals with others in his company when he traveled up the Hudson on his way to Canada in 1776, staying with Philip Schuyler along the way. But we know that canals were discussed during the expedition, as an entry from the *Journal* of Franklin's traveling companion, Charles Carroll, makes explicit. Having reached Schuyler's estate at Saratoga on April 9, Carroll listened as his host held forth on his vision of a continuous commercial waterway between New York and Quebec.

> General Schuyler informed me that an uninterrupted water carriage between N. York and Quebec might be perfected at £50,000 sterling expense by means of locks and a small canal cut from a branch that runs into Wood Creek, and the head of a branch that runs

into the Hudson River. The distance is not more than 3 miles. The River Richelieu, or Sorel, is navigable for bateaux from the Lake Champlain into the St. Lawrence. The rapids below St. Johns are not so considerable as to obstruct the navigation of such vessels.[5]

In this conversation Schuyler thought of canals as linkages that brought larger bodies of water together by locks that formed a continuously navigable passage capable of facilitating the flow of commerce. Schuyler never departed from that vision, which differed from the type canal that Franklin held up as a model in his letter to the mayor of Philadelphia, in which canals were entirely man-made transportation corridors. Two types of canal were to be built in upstate New York in the expansive years of economic development that followed the end of the American Revolution. One was a waterway corridor comprised of existing bodies of water, rivers or lakes, joined by canal locks; the other was a completely man-made canal. Philip Schuyler introduced the first of these models in an unsuccessful effort to join the Hudson to the Great Lakes; it was his wartime visitor Gouverneur Morris, who first proposed the second model; it was he, years after his 1777 trip up the Hudson to see Schuyler, who originated the idea of the Erie Canal.

Ever the visionary, Morris saw the vast economic potential of New York's waterway system when he visited Philip Schuyler as Burgoyne's army was moving down the Champlain-Hudson corridor. A member of Schuyler's staff, Morgan Lewis, wrote that Morris held forth in evening conversations,

> . . . describing in the most glowing terms, the rapid march of the useful arts through our country, when once freed from a foreign yoke, the spirit with which agriculture and commerce, both internal and external, would advance; the facilities which would be afforded them by the numerous watercourses intersecting our country, and the ease with which they might be made to communicate; he announced in language highly poetic, and to which I cannot do justice, that at no very distant day; the waters of the great inland seas, would by the aid of man, break through their barriers and mingle with those of the Hudson.[6]

Gouverneur Morris and Schuyler shared this vision; both looked forward to time of peace, when the construction of canals would provide inexpensive transportation, essential to America's future economic development.

So too did another of Schuyler's wartime visitors, George Washington, who had received approval from the Virginia legislature before the Revolution to make the Potomac navigable, but Washington had to put his plans on hold as he led the struggle for American independence. Just before the end of the war Washington wrote the Marquis de Chastellux (another of Schuyuler's Albany visitors), describing the 1783 tour of the Hudson-Champlain and Mohawk corridors he had taken with Philip Schuyler.

> I have lately made a tour . . . through the Lakes George and Champlain as far as Crown Point; then returning to Schenectady, I proceeded up the Mohawk river to fort Schuyler, crossed over to Wood creek which empties into the Oneida lake, and affords the water communication with Ontario. I then traversed the country to the head of the eastern branch of the Susquehanna, and viewed the lake Otsego, and the portage between that lake and the Mohawk at Conajohario. Prompted by these actual observations, I could not help taking a more contemplative and extensive view of the vast inland navigation of these United States, and could not but be struck with the immense diffusion and importance of it; and with the goodness of that Providence which has dealt his favors to us with so profuse a hand. Would to God we may have wisdom enough to improve them. I shall not rest contented until I have explored the western country, and traversed those lines (or great part of them) which have given bounds to a new empire.[7]

For America's full economic development to take place after the Revolution it was necessary to build transportation corridors through mountains that extended along the Atlantic Coast from New York to the Carolinas, linking the eastern seaboard economically to the region that lay beyond the mountains. Roads were built through the mountains, two in Pennsylvania that passed through the Alleghenies and another that passed southward through Virginia, but they were wagon-roads that were not cost-efficient for transporting food or goods.[8] Transportation by water was far less costly than by land. Geography offered two passages through the long, coastal mountain barrier that held out the possibility of commercial transportation by water, those formed by the Potomac and Mohawk Rivers. As soon as independence was gained in 1783, Washington turned again to making the Potomac a transportation corridor that would facilitate commerce between the coastal region and lands west of the Allegheny Mountains, thereby binding "those people [to the west of us] by a chain which never can be broken." "The way is easy and dictated by our clearest interest. It is to open a wide door, and make a smooth way for the produce of that Country to pass to our Markets. . . ."[9] Washington was the driving force behind the Potomack Company, organized on May 17, 1785, with him as president. As plans for the project were moving forward Washington corresponded with fellow Virginian Thomas Jefferson, who shared his optimism. Both men felt a sense of urgency in opening up the Potomac for shipping; both were aware that New York was their rival in the development of a transportation corridor linking the coastal region to the frontier lands to the west. Jefferson wrote Washington, "Nature . . . has declared in favor of the Potomac, and through that channel offers to pour into our lap the whole commerce of the western world. But unfortunately [the route] by the Hudson is already open and known in practice; ours is still to be opened." Washington also felt that initiating the Potomac project as soon as possible was essential. "[Y]ou and I [are] satisfied that not a moment ought to be lost in recommending the business [of the Potomac], as I know the New Yorkers will lose no time to remove every obstacle in the way of the other communication."[10] Out of these efforts came the Potomack Company, which undertook dredging the Potomac and building lock canals to create the all-important transportation corridor between the coastal region and the rapidly developing interior. As it turned out, geographical obstacles were too great for the Potomack Company to overcome, and it declared bankruptcy in 1799.

An American from Plymouth, Massachusetts, Elkanah Watson, arrived in Albany in 1788, after visiting Washington at Mount Vernon in 1785. Taking notes at the time of his visit, Watson wrote,

> Both Virginia and Maryland have reciprocally incorporated a canal company, of which Washington had accepted the presidency. Preparations are now in full train to commence operations the ensuing spring; not only to open a free navigation of the Potowmac, but eventually to remove obstructions in such branches of the Ohio as point towards Lake Erie . . . To demonstrate the practicability of this, and the policy of preserving a commercial intercourse with those extended regions, especially should the Mississippi be opened, was his constant and favored theme.

In the three years after Watson saw Washington, he traveled through the Southern states, visiting possible sites for canals. He then went north and in 1788 traveled on horseback up the Mohawk to Fort Stanwix.

> It was on this occasion I first conceived the idea of the practicability of counteracting, at least by a fair competition the favorite plan Washington was then pursuing with zeal and ardour, to allure all the trade of the western regions, connected with the Ohio and the great lakes,—even the fur trade from Detroit and Alexandria. Doubtless many others may have conceived the same project many years prior, and probably subsequent to my first visit to Fort Stanwix, in 1788.[11]

In the following year, 1789, Watson moved from Rhode Island to Albany, hoping to push forward a project to develop a commercial waterway along the Mohawk corridor. He was not alone in that hope. In 1785 Christopher Colles,

Figure 41. Ezra Ames' portrait of Elkanah Watson, in the Albany Institute of History and Art. This work is a copy of John Singleton Copley's portrait of Watson, done in 1782. The Copley portrait is in the Art Museum of Princeton University. Watson presumably brought the Copley portrait with him when he came to Albany to develop a commercial waterway along the Mohawk River. It must have been a valuable learning experience for local artist Ezra Ames to copy a portrait by the highly accomplished Copley. Courtesy of the Union College Permanent Collection.

an Irish engineer who had immigrated to America in 1765, urged the New York State legislature to appropriate money to conduct a survey "of the principal obstructions upon the Mohawk river as far as Wood creek." The money was appropriated, the survey was made, and the results published and presented to the legislature. Colles then requested state funding in the amount of £13,000 to develop inland navigation between Cohoes Falls, Little Falls, and Fort Schuyler (Fort Stanwix). The legislature took no action on Colles' 1785 proposal, but the idea of developing a commercial waterway along the Mohawk corridor was in the air, as Elkanah Watson would have understood full well when he moved to Albany in 1789. Watson organized a tour of the Mohawk corridor in 1791, undertaken with Stephen N. Bayard and Jeremiah Van Rensselaer, during which he kept a *Journal* in which he described the opportunities that he expected would follow the construction of canals. Referring to saltworks near Lake Onondaga in his *Journal*, Watson wrote that "These works are in a rude, unfinished state,—but are capable of making about eight thousand bushels of salt per annum, which is nearly the quantity required for the present consumption of the country. . . ." The key to realizing this potential was transporting the commodity to markets, for which nature provided the answer. "Providence has happily placed this great source of comfort, and wealth" close to a body of water that, with a canal, would allow easy shipment to markets. "When the mighty canals shall be formed and locks erected, it will add vastly to the facility of an extended diffusion, and the increase of intrinsic worth."[12]

When Watson returned to Albany he drew up a report and arranged a meeting with Philip Schuyler, State Senator at the time. Also interested in developing a commercial waterway along the Mohawk, Schuyler had Watson send his report to the State legislature, and out of these efforts came the Northern Inland Navigation Company. As with the Potomack Company, the idea was not to build a continuous canal, but to make a river navigable, with locks to circumvent natural obstacles. Funding was provided by a grant from the state of New York and from the sale of stock shares to private investors, with Schuyler as a major investor. Originally, Schuyler subscribed to ten shares, but to jump-start the project he increased his purchase to 100 shares. From the beginning he and Watson were the two driving forces behind the company, which turned out to be a problem. They disagreed, and quarreled, over Schuyler's salary, and Watson grew weary of Schuyler's "tyrannical manner." Another problem was lack of engineers in the company, a shortcoming that Schuyler attempted to overcome by becoming chief engineer himself, for which he had no formal training. This left him vulnerable to criticism, and with inadequate funding, and technical problems beyond the company's capacity to address, it failed. Watson left Albany for Massachusetts, but not before local artist Ezra Ames painted his portrait, now in the Albany Institute of History and Art. Schuyler left the Western Inland Navigation Company to serve as U.S. Senator in 1803, marking an effective end by that company to improve navigation along parts of the Mohawk River. If those efforts fell short of the original plans, the company that Watson and Schuyler founded did improve navigation along parts of the Mohawk, and most importantly it initiated conversations that pointed toward a far more ambitious project, the Erie Canal.

Work on the Western Inland Navigation Company project began at Little Falls in April 1793 with 300 workers, but shortage of funds, a constant problem, forced a slowdown in September. Shares providing additional funds were issued in January 1794, and work resumed in May. By November five locks were completed that ran a length of 4,752 feet. Excavation for the canal was through solid and very hard rock, and was carried out with utmost difficulty. The problems were so great that in May 1795, a British engineer, William Weston, was hired for needed technical expertise. From this point on the Western Inland navigation project went from difficulty to difficulty, as a later report explained. One problem was "The want of able American engineers . . . General Schuyler was a man of great talents; but he was not a practical engineer. . . ." Another problem was that his successor, "Mr. Weston, a celebrated English engineer . . . was totally ignorant of the country and the people"; trained engineer that he was, Weston was unable to work effectively with others involved in the project. Moreover, the report continued, there was "great defect of funds . . . It was too great for any individual or company. . . ."[13] Work continued, but problems encountered in 1795 were never surmounted; the company that Schuyler was instrumental in founding failed just before he died.

As chance had it, Philip Schuyler's 1777 visitor, Gouverneur Morris, was in Scotland in 1795 inspecting the Caledonian Canal, the very year in which canal locks were built at Little Falls in upstate New York. Describing the visit in his *Diary*, Morris wrote,

> In my route I stopped twice to look at the canal . . . First I went to look at a succession of locks, which rise immediately after the canal has been carried over a river, and saw much [of] the execution in hewn stone, all in the best style. My second object was to see a number of vessels collected, and lading in the highest part of the canal, some brigs and sloops. On inquiry, I find that those, which draw only seven feet and a half of water, can go through. Also, that there are twenty locks, each of eight feet; so that the whole rise is one hundred and sixty feet. When I see this, my mind opens to a view of wealth for the interior of America, which hitherto I had rather conjectured than seen.[14]

Morris had envisioned a waterway transportation system in New York when he visited Schuyler in 1777; years later, in Scotland, he again conjured a vision of a waterway transportation system in New York. That vision took wing when he saw the Caledonian locks in Scotland; Schuyler, at this very time, was working on the construction of locks in upstate New York.

Morris traveled to Canada in 1800 on a trip that took him "up the Saint Lawrence and Lake Ontario to Niagara Falls to Lake Erie." He wrote a letter to John Parish a few weeks after completing the trip, in which he described seeing ships on Lake Erie as soon as

> the Lake broke on[to] our view. I saw riding at anchor nine vessels, the least of them above a hundred tons. Can you bring your imagination to realize the scene? Does it not seem like magic? Yet this magic is but the early effort of victorious industry. Hundreds of

large ships will, at no distant period, bound on the billows of these inland seas. At this point commences a navigation of more than a thousand miles. Shall I lead your astonishment up to the verge of incredulity? I will. Know then that one tenth of the expense, borne by Britain in the last campaign, would enable ships to sail from London through Hudson's River *into Lake Erie*.[15]

Morris' vision of a man-made waterway between Lake Erie and the Hudson River is the first such vision; up to this point ideas for a waterway that would connect the Hudson to the Great Lakes had Lake Ontario as the western terminus; it was Gouverneur Morris who first envisioned a direct waterway from the Hudson to Lake Erie. A few weeks after writing John Parish, Morris was at a dinner party in Washington, the newly founded national capital. The question arose of what the advantages might have been if the capital had been located in Newburgh, on the Hudson. Robert Morris, who was there, described the conversation.

> Gouverneur Morris, apparently drawn out by this question, went into the subject, and remarked upon the many and great advantages, which would have resulted from such a location. He extolled its beautiful site, its central position, its accessibleness to the sea, and the ease with which it could be protected from the approach of an invading enemy. "Yes," said he, "this would have been the place for the seat of government, and the members of Congress could have come from all parts by water." "Come by water, Mr Morris!" exclaimed the company, "but how?"—"Why, by tapping Lake Erie, and bringing its waters to the Hudson." "How could you bring them?"—"By an inclined plane."[16]

In this conversation, Gouverneur Morris set forth for the first time the idea, with modification, for what was to become the Erie Canal (it was not to be on an inclined plane, but it was, as Morris imagined it, independent of rivers). Further corroboration of Morris' claim to be the first to envision a canal that would go from the Hudson to Lake Erie is offered by Simeon De Witt, the New York State Surveyor. Writing to William Darby, De Witt said,

> The merit of first starting the idea of a *direct* communication between Lake Erie and Hudson River, unquestionably belongs to Gouverneur Morris. The first suggestion I had of it was from him. In 1803 I accidentally met him in Schenectady. We put up for the night at the same inn, and passed the evening together. Among the numerous topics of conversation, to which this prolific mind and discursive imagination gave birth, was that of improving the intercourse with

the interior of our State. He then mentioned the project of *tapping Lake Erie*, as he expressed himself, and leading its waters in an artificial river directly across the country to Hudson River.

Additionally, James Geddes, one of the principal surveyors of the Erie Canal, said it was his understanding that Morris was the first to conceive the project. One of the early canal commissioners, Stephen Van Rensselaer III, wrote, "I consider Mr Morris the father of our great canal, and every report and memorandum, of his should be preserved for posterity, who will render to him the honor he merited."[17]

In his extensive 1905 history of the Erie Canal, Noble E. Whitford saw the period 1798 to 1807 as one "of quiet before the people were ready to undertake the task which the conditions demand[ed]" for construction of the Erie Canal.[18] This was a period in which Gouverneur Morris and others thought about building a canal extending from the Hudson to the Great Lakes, and it was a period in which conditions nationally seemed propitious for construction of the canal. In his second inaugural address delivered in March 1805, Thomas Jefferson announced his intention of providing surplus federal revenue, when it was available, for the improvement of canals and roads to further America's economic expansion. In December 1806, he announced that surplus revenue was greater than anticipated, and suggested that applications could be made for federal support in the construction of transportation systems. By that time an upstate New York merchant, Jesse Hawley, had said in a discussion with one of his suppliers that an interior canal between the Hudson and Lake Erie could and should be built. If Morris was the first to envision construction of the Erie Canal, Hawley was "its first really hardheaded proponent."[19] Responding to Jefferson's call for canal proposals, Hawley put one together that outlined the advantages of "connecting the waters of *Lake Erie* and those of the *Mohawk* and *Hudson* rivers by means of a canal." He described the route of the proposed canal and in a series of subsequent essays he traced the course the canal would take and estimated the cost at 6 million dollars, which proved to be surprisingly accurate. Hawley wrote most of his essays in 1807 while in prison; he had been put there because of debts he was unable to repay. Also working on a plan to build a canal from the Hudson to Lake Erie was Joshua Forman, a member of the New York State Assembly from Onondaga. Responding to President Jefferson's call for canal proposals, Forman requested funding from the New York legislature on February 4, 1808, for a survey that could lead to construction of a state-wide canal. The survey was made and in late 1808 a report was issued and sent to Washington. Forman traveled to the capitol to meet personally with President Jefferson, to explain the "many advantages such a canal would bring to the nation as a whole." Jefferson's response was crushing:

Why sir, here is a canal of a few miles, projected by General Washington, which, if completed, would render this a fine commercial city, which has languished for many years because the small sum of 200,000 dollars necessary to complete it, cannot be obtained from the general government, or from, individuals—and you talk of making a canal of 250 miles through the wilderness—it is little short of madness to think of it at this day.[20]

Jefferson's flat rejection of the New York canal proposal in 1809 did not deter its proponents, who sent a resolution to the New York State Assembly recommending the formation of a canal commission. The measure passed unanimously. The New York State legislature was ready to push ahead with a canal project in spite of Jefferson's rebuff. Whitford wrote that: "The unanimity with which this resolution was passed indicates the change of public sentiment and the quicksand spirit for internal improvements which was abroad throughout the whole land. If this spirit were attributable to any one cause . . . it was [probably] due to a general awakening" to America's vast future potential.[21] Five members of the commission traveled across New York in 1810 to find the best route for a canal. The commissioners drew up a report and sent it to the New York State Senate on March 2, 1811. Having continued the canal initiative after Jefferson's rebuff, the New York State legislature still sought support from the federal government. Two members of the commission, Gouverneur Morris and De Witt Clinton, went to Washington in 1812, hoping to stir interest in Congress, but they sensed jealousy toward New York among its members and reached the conclusion that New York could not count on federal support for construction of a state-wide canal; for the canal to be built New York would have to go it alone. The commissioners concluded in their 1812 report that: "The maxims of policy . . . seem imperatively to demand that the canal be built by [New York State], and for her own account, as soon as circumstances will permit. . . ."[22] At the request of the commissioners a bill was introduced in the New York State Senate to take steps toward construction of a canal. The bill passed and became law on June 19, 1812. America had declared war on Britain on the previous day, thereby beginning the War of 1812, which lasted until 1815 and put the canal project on hold until the end of the war.

Men of high birth, natural leaders as they were still seen, were placed in positions of command at the beginning of the War of 1812. Among them was Stephen Van Rensselaer III, a member of the 1810 canal commission and one of the project's leading advocates and supporters. He was 48, a major general, and had no proper military training. Called to duty even through he opposed the war and had no field experience, he went up the Mohawk to Utica and then made his way to Oswego and Niagara, to undertake an American invasion of Canada. He wrote on August 19 that he lacked sufficient artillery and that his "troops [were] in a very indifferent state of discipline; finding myself in this truly unpleasant situation, I saw but one course of action to pursue which was to concentrate the troops scattered on this line [along the Niagara River], perfect their discipline as fast as possible, and order in such further detachments as might ensure success in my proposed operations. . . ."[23] Three days before this letter was written disaster struck on the shore of Lake Michigan, with General William Hull surrendering Fort Dearborn to the British without putting up a fight, news of which reached Van Rensselaer on August 26. His troops were dispirited by news of Hull's surrender; some of his men threatened to quit the field unless they were paid, and some wanted to retreat. Then, on September 29 reinforcements arrived and plans were made for battle. As events were pushing Van Rensselaer to take the offensive against British forces on the opposite side of the Niagara River, he sent a letter to Major General Dearborn in which he described his circumstances and revealed something of his state of mind.

> The United States declared the war. One army has surrendered in disgrace and another has but little more than escaped the reiteration of the blow. The national character is degraded, and the disgrace will remain; corroding the public feeling and spirit until another campaign, unless it be instantly wiped away by a brilliant close of this.

The prospects for victory were far from bright.

> Our best troops are raw, many of them dejected by the distress their families suffer by their absence, and many have not necessary clothing. We are in a cold country, the season is far advanced and unusually inclement; we are half the time deluged by rain. The blow must be struck soon or all the toil and expense of the campaign will go for nothing, and worse for nothing, for the whole affair will be tinged with dishonor.[24]

By the time the Battle of Queenston Heights took place on October 12–13 almost everything that could go wrong went wrong. The American forces greatly outnumbered the British on the opposite side of the Niagara River but they did not work together; boats that were to take them to the opposite side of the Niagara were not available in sufficient number; and oars were sent to the wrong place. The first group of men under the command of Van Rensselaer met sharp resistance from the British when they crossed the Niagara. To make matters worse, reinforcements that Van Rensselaer expected did not arrive. He crossed back to the American side and asked his men to board their boats, cross the Niagara, and join the battle, but they refused. The result was defeat, ignominious defeat, insofar as Van Rensselaer was concerned. Describing what had happened the next day, Van Rensselaer wrote, "to my utter astonishment I found that at the very moment when complete victory was in our hands the ardor of the unengaged troops had entirely subsided. I rode in all directions; urged the men by every consideration to pass over, but in vain." Mortified by his inability to stir his men to action, Van Rensselaer submitted his resignation on October 20. "After the evidence furnished me that the great body of militia could not in the most trying imaginable crisis be prevailed upon to cross the river, it was very evident that my future services would avail nothing. I have therefore retired from Lewiston . . . and have to request your permission that I may surrender my command." His request was accepted and on October 25 Van Rensselaer began to make his way back to his manor at Watervliet, north of Albany. Friends greeted him warmly as he traveled home, as indicated in a letter written after he reached his beloved manor house, Van Rensselaer Hall: "I cannot describe my feelings at the reception I met with in my journey home, if I had been a Victor, I could not have been more honored."[25]

At the beginning of the War of 1812 the average age of the eight generals in command of the regular army was 60; in 1814 the average age of new appointees was 35. America's military leadership had proven ineffective in the early stages of the war; commanding officers at the end brought what had been lacking to the war effort: resourcefulness and daring. Thomas Macdonough, a 31-year-old commander of an American fleet that did battle with a British fleet on Lake Champlain on September 14, 1814, epitomized the change in leadership during the War of 1812. Macdonough's skillful maneuver of his ship *Saratoga* (the ship's name was a reminder of an earlier battle that repulsed a British invasion of New York from Canada) helped bring about a victory at the Battle of Plattsburgh that Admiral Mahan has said "was to the War of 1812 what Saratoga was to the American Revolution."[26] Thomas Macdonough was the antithesis of Stephen Van Rensselaer III: the sixth of nine children, orphaned at age 12, he worked as a clerk until an older brother pulled some strings to secure a midshipman's warrant in the U.S. Navy in 1800, when he was 17.[27] He served in the Mediterranean during the Barbary War, and in 1812 was placed in command of a fleet on Lake Champlain that was to block a British force if it were to invade America from Quebec. With Napoleon's unconditional surrender and abdication on April 11, 1814, Britain was in a position to deliver a final blow to America in a war that been a sideshow since its beginning in 1812. General Sir George Prevost, governor-general of Canada and commander in chief of His Majesty's Forces in Canada, received orders on June 3, 1814; he was to lead "twelve of the most effective Regiments of the Army [that had served] under the Duke of Wellington together with three Companies of Artillery on the same service" down Lake Champlain in a British invasion of America.[28] Prevost's superbly trained and battle-hardened army moved south from Montreal, marching along Lake Champlain until they reached Plattsburgh on September 4. At that point the British army waited for a British fleet under Captain George Downie to do battle with the American fleet under Macdonough. The Battle of Plattsburgh, fought a few miles above Benedict Arnold's naval encounter at Valcour Bay in 1776, repulsed the British invasion of America from Canada. Like Arnold, Macdonough was resourceful and brave in battle, exhorting his men to fight on in spite of heavy pounding from British ships. Admiral Mahan wrote,: "the battle of [Plattsburgh], more nearly than any other incident of the War of 1812, merits the epithet 'decisive.' " In the evening after the September 11 battle Prevost's British force of 15,000 men that had fought against Napoleon in the Peninsular War and was arguably the finest ever to set foot on American soil started back to Canada, having destroyed its materiel and munitions before departing.

The 1814 British strategy called for another army to attack America from the mouth of the Mississippi. Britain continued to have ambitions in America; she was not yet prepared to concede control of the area west of the Mississippi to a nation whose future was still seen as uncertain. The first British fleet landed at Barataria south of New Orleans on September 3, 1814, and on November 26 a larger fleet under Vice Admiral Sir Alexander Cochrane set sail for New Orleans from Jamaica. Cochrane was to provide support to a British army under Lieutenant General Sir Edward Pakenham, brother-in-law of Wellington, who was to take on a ragtag American army made up of frontier miltiamen, Indians, and men of color from whom he expected little effective opposition. The American army was under the command of Andrew Jackson who, like a frontiersman from an earlier generation, Daniel Morgan, had little love of the British, and particularly British officers. In 1781, as a lad of 14, Jackson had refused to clean the boots of a British officer; when the officer struck him with his sword for insolence he protected himself as best as he could with his hand; the incident left him with lifelong scars. When Pakenham, whose troops were among the finest in British service, first saw the Americans with whom he was to do battle he felt that they moved about "in a most unmilitary fashion," and had "the appearance of snipe and rabbit hunters beating the bushes for game." Without uniforms, unlike the finely attired British redcoats, they were so many "dirty shirts," as he called them.[29] The Americans most certainly did not behave like proper soldiers. As soon as the British army set up camp Jackson sent his men in under cover of darkness to spread fear, smiting and killing as many as they could, a rude message that struck Pakenham as most uncivil. He sent a note to Jackson saying that such warfare was "ungentlemanly," as indeed it was. When the Battle of New Orleans was fought on January 8, 1815, it was a smashing American victory, with a mind-boggling disparity between American and British casualties. One outcome of the American victory at New Orleans, achieved after the Treaty of Ghent had been signed, was catapulting Andrew Jackson to a position of national prominence. He won a popular victory in the presidential election of 1824, but without the needed number of electoral votes the decision went to the House of Representatives, where the tie was finally broken by a Congressman from New York who been elected to a seat in the House vacated by the death of a relative, Solomon Van Rensselaer. It was Stephen Van Rensselaer III who cast the decisive ballot for John Quincy Adams, denying Andrew Jackson the presidency. Only as a result of the 1828 election would he become president.

As during the Revolution, the Hudson-Champlain and Mohawk corridors saw some of the bitterest fighting in the War of 1812. Once again New York's river corridors were the scene of conflict, along with Lake Ontario and Lake Erie; once again armies and supplies moved through the wilderness; once again the strategic importance of the New York waterways became evident. These lessons were not lost on proponents of the Erie Canal, who added military considerations to those already advanced when canal construction began in 1817. Not only was the Mohawk corridor that linked the Hudson to the Great Lakes important both militarily and commercially; so too was the Hudson-Champlain corridor. As a result, two canals were built at the same time, the Erie and Champlain canals, both of which had Albany as their terminus. Of these, the first to be completed was the Champlain Canal, whose opening celebration was held in Albany in 1823. Among those presiding over this celebration was Stephen Van Rensselaer III, who held the honorific office of Marshal. As one of the principal proponents and supporters of the Erie Canal, Stephen Van Rensselaer III was also present at the opening celebration of its completion in Albany in 1825. Indeed, as we shall see, Stephen Van Rensselaer III was the leading contributor to the elaborate (and costly) Albany celebration that marked completion of the Erie Canal.

Stephen Van Rensselaer III's letters written from Niagara at the beginning of the War of 1812 say much about him as a person. Honor, his own and that of America, was paramount. Dearborn's surrender was a "disgrace" that was a blot on the "national character," which he felt duty-bound to uphold. Further disgrace, he believed, would corrode "public feeling and spirit." A "blow against the enemy must be struck soon," lest the entire campaign end in failure and be "tinged with dishonor." Van Rensselaer's remarks bring his father-in-law Philip Schuyler to mind, an Albany aristocrat of an earlier generation. Like Schuyler, Stephen Van Rensselaer III was a man of progressive outlook, an advocate and apostle of progress. He was a Federalist who envisioned an expansive America, much as did his brother-in-law, Alexander Hamilton. Shortly after the Revolutionary War ended, he advertised 160-acre tracts of land in the southern part of the Van Rensselaer patroonship, free of rent for the first seven years, with payment thereafter of four fowl, 18 bushels of wheat, and a day's service, or some comparable payment. The village of Rensselaerville came out of this initiative, along with turnpikes built in the early decades of the nineteenth century that contributed to its vitality.[30] When Philip Schuyler organized the

Western Inland Navigation Company in the 1790s, Stephen Van Rensselaer III was among its supporters. And when the state of New York resumed its canal initiative in 1816, Stephen Van Rensselaer III was appointed to the commission that drew up plans for both the Erie and Champlain canals. There was opposition within the New York legislature, but with De Witt Clinton as a resourceful and single-minded advocate the opposition was overcome; amidst charges that "Clinton's Folly" was certain to end in failure, construction began in 1817. It took eight years to complete the two canals.

A celebration took place in Albany on June 11, 1825, in honor of the Marquis de Lafayette, who landed in New York in August 1824, to begin a triumphal tour of the United States. After arriving in New York, he sailed up the Hudson to Albany, where he was entertained by a newly-formed musical group, one of whose supporters was Stephen Van Rensselaer III.[31] Lafayette spent the winter in Washington and in March he began a tour that took him to all 24 states of the union. He arrived at Buffalo on June 6, 1825, and went by carriage to Lockport, the western terminus of the Erie Canal. He went along the canal by packet boat to meet De Witt Clinton at Utica on June 8, and after more celebrations he and Clinton proceeded by a special boat pulled not by mules but by a team of white horses that took them to Albany three days later, where they passed under a large stuffed eagle, whose wings were made to flap by some mechanical device. A ghost from the past, Lafayette was Philip Schuyler's only wartime Albany visitor who lived on to see completion of the Erie Canal. That he was again in Albany in 1825 is one of those historical incidents that can be seen to represent the end of an era, in this instance one that began with the American Revolution and came to closure in 1825. America was celebrating the fiftieth anniversary of the birth of the nation in 1825, and Lafayette was there to participate in events leading up to the national holiday, and in the patriotic event itself. Having arrived in Albany on June 11, Lafayette went to Boston, where he was present at the celebration of the fiftieth anniversary of Bunker Hill. From Boston he went through Maine, New Hampshire, and Vermont to Lake Champlain, and then passed down the Champlain Canal to Albany. Having come to Albany after passing along both the Erie and Champlain canals, Lafayette sailed to New York City where he participated in the Fourth of July celebration.

New York State staged grand festivities between October 26 and November 4, 1825, to celebrate the opening of the Erie Canal.[32] At the end of celebrations that began in Buffalo and ended in New York City, water from Lake Erie was emptied into the Atlantic Ocean, a "Wedding of the Waters" that symbolized completion of a man-made construction project of greatest significance to New York's future and that of America. After the opening festivities in Buffalo, marked by a parade and the firing of cannon, Governor De Witt Clinton boarded the specially appointed and decorated *Seneca Chief* that was to take him across the entire length of the Erie Canal. Followed by other dignitaries and a long line of boats carrying New York flora, fauna, birds, animals, and insects, the *Seneca Chief* arrived in Albany on November 2. The *Seneca Chief* and the other boats that passed through the eastern-most lock of the Erie Canal entered the recently completed Albany Basin, an artificial harbor built to accommodate the flow of commerce generated by the Erie and Champlain Canals. Albany Basin ran along the central part of the city, with an offshore pier 4,000 feet in length connected to the quay along the old riverfront by two bridges. Judging from contemporary accounts, vast crowds jammed Albany Basin and the riverside quay to cheer Governor Clinton and other personages who participated in the Erie Canal celebrations, including Secretary of State Henry Clay and Supreme Court Chief Justice John Marshall.[33]

Describing Clinton's arrival, the *Albany Daily Advertiser* wrote that cannon sounded and a "multitiude" welcomed the dignitaries with "shouts of gladness." "It was not a monarch which they hailed, but it was the majesty of genius supported by a free people that rode in triumph and commanded the admiration of men stout of heart and firm of purpose."[34] John Augustus Stone, "of the Albany Theatre," wrote an ode for the occasion that praised the "Fair stream [the Erie Canal]," "Richer than [the] Nile," "A people's wonder, boon and pride." The author of this ode saw the Erie Canal not only as the source of greatly expanded trade and commerce; it marked a new stage of history, carrying forward the work of an earlier generation that had thrown off the yoke of British tyranny and introduced an age of liberty. In this perspective, the Erie Canal would make a new way of life possible, one that was uniquely American:

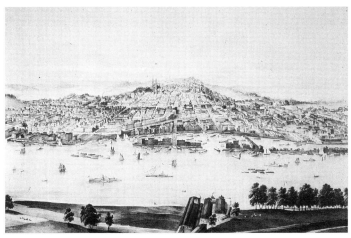

Figure 42. Albany Basin, as seen in an 1853 aerial view of Albany,

Oh! Dark was the age, overwhelming the gloom,
Whom bigotry forg'd for our fathers the chain,
When oppression exulted on Liberty's tomb,
And virtue wept over Britannia's domain! . . .
Hark! The shout is uprais'd, "the waters combine!"
From misty Niagara's bourne to the sea,
And Liberty looks, from her radiant shrine,
On her chosen dominion, and bids it "be free."[35]

In less poetic language the *Albany Daily Advertiser* wrote, "Wednesday last [November 2] was a proud day for the citizens of Albany; a great day to the citizens of New York, and an important day in the Union; for *then* we had occular demonstration that the great work of the age is completed, and our inland seas made accessible from the ocean."[36]

Observing carefully scripted arrangements for the Albany celebration, important leaders, civic groups, and a crowd that had assembled to witness the day's event moved from the bank of the Hudson up the hill to the New York State Capitol, where music was played, a prayer given, a dignitary gave a "neat and appropriate address," and another dignitary gave a much longer speech. A procession then wended its way down the hill to newly constructed Albany Basin, extending outward from the riverside quay. A temporary Gothic structure with 14-feet high pointed arches, replete with gilded Gothic turrets, had been built on the bridge that connected the quay to the offshore pier. Passing through the Gothic arches, those in the procession came to a tent that ran along the pier, under which there were two rows of tables, each 150 feet in length, lined with "plenty of the 'ruby bright' wines of the best vineyards of Europe," placed there for the 600 guests present at that part of the day's celebration.[37] Festivities continued into the night, including music, a theatrical performance, and horses and canal boats that passed through locks built on a stage. The Albany celebration commemorating completion of the Erie Canal was expensive, and it was necessary to solicit support from subscribers to pay for the event. The names on the list, a veritable who's who of prominent Albany families, included many old Dutch families: the Van Eyck, Staats, Van Vechten, Douw, De Witt, Bleecker, and Cuyler families.[38] It also included up-and-coming families of English, Scottish, and Irish ancestry: the Corning, Townsend, Hart, McKown, and Forsyth families. Also on the list was Philip Hooker, the architect who designed the most prominent buildings that participants in the celebration would have seen as they went from Albany Basin to the State Capitol, which he also designed, at the top of the hill.

At the head of the subscription list, with by far the largest contribution, is Stephen Van Rensselaer III, who donated $100. Second on the list is William James, who donated $50. That the next largest donation was $15 indicates the extent to which these two supporters of the November 2 Erie Canal celebration stood apart from all other donors. If these two men stood together as the most munificent contributors to the Erie Canal celebration in Albany, their backgrounds could hardly have been more different. The patent for Stephen Van Rensselaer III's estate of some 700,000 acres went back to the seventeenth century. William James was a first-generation Albanian who arrived in America in 1789 at age 18, a Scots-Irish immigrant who as a Protestant youth felt the breeze of liberty that wafted over Western society in the last several decades of the eighteenth century and came to America to make his fortune.[39] And this he did. By the time of his death William James was one of the wealthiest men in America; his wealth in New York is thought to have been second only to that of John Jacob Astor. He and Stephen Van Rensselaer III were almost exact contemporaries. Van Rensselaer was born in 1767 and died in 1839; William James was born in 1771 and died in 1832. The stories of both men are closely bound up with the Erie Canal, but in completely different ways. As we have seen, Stephen Van Rensselaer was one of the leading supporters of the Erie Canal; he sat on three canal commissions, those of 1808, 1810, and 1816, and he chaired the Canal Board from 1825 until the time of his death.

Figure 43. William James portrait. Courtesy of the Union College Permanent Collection.

He may be regarded as one of the Founding Fathers of the Erie Canal. It was quite otherwise with William James, an immigrant who came to America with little money, a Latin grammar, and according to family tradition a "desire to visit the field of one of the revolutionary battles."

It is not known if William James visited whatever battlefield he wanted to see when he came to America in 1789, but the chances are that he did; young William James accomplished just about anything he undertook. He seems to have come to Albany in 1793, and to have found employment in a local store. He owned his own store in 1795, and in 1797 he owned another store; by 1805 he owned five stores and a tobacco factory. His ascent of the ladder of success was so rapid that by 1804 (he was 33) he became one of the directors of newly founded New York State Bank on State Street, designed by Philip Hooker, Albany's most prominent architect. As a director of Albany's leading bank, William James helped make decisions on projects that enlarged opportunities for regional growth and profit, such as the Albany Turnpike, financed by State Bank. Three years later, in 1807, Robert Fulton's steamship, later named the *Clermont*, docked in Albany, an epoch-making event in the history of navigation, and one that greatly facilitated passenger traffic and the flow of commerce from Albany to New York City. Soon James was shipping commodities by steamship to his agent in New York City. Having become successful in commercial ventures in Albany, he turned over his businesses to others in 1818 and invested in real estate across New York State, including the 1824 purchase of 250 acres of land in what is now the center of Syracuse. This was the centerpiece of James' New York real estate holdings, which also included properties in New York City, Buffalo, Rochester, Utica, Schenectady, Troy, and Albany. All of these towns were on and benefited economically from the Erie Canal. William James built a house in Albany on North Pearl Street for himself and his family, now demolished but in its time very grand. It was a square stone house with a library and family rooms on the first floor, many bedrooms on the second floor, a covered piazza in the rear of the house, and a long walk that led to stables below where William James kept his carriage and several horses.

William James' speech for the Erie Canal celebration in Albany, given in the State Capitol, was the longest of the day. In his speech he viewed the stupendous achievement of the Erie Canal against the background of the American Revolution. The battles of Concord and Lexington, in his perspective, were the beginning of a 50-year period of remarkable growth; the battles that ignited the American Revolution unleashed a "republican spirit" that gave rise to a new society and a new nation, born of quest for liberty. "Who," William James asked, "can take a retrospective view of the beginning and progress of our government, not numbering more than half the years of some of our citizens, and not exult in every exhibition of its moral and physical power, and in every indication and prospect of future influence and greatness." The American nation was a new one, but its achievements were remarkable. "Our national history is short, but crowded with events of such a type and character as to confound the enemies and exhilarate the friends of rational liberty." Out of the new nation came progressive change, aided and abetted by men of science, "whose genius and talents have controlled and applied electricity and steam to useful purposes [and] are the benefactors of mankind." The new nation confronted many obstacles in its brief life, but men of vision, talent, dedication, and energy had forged ahead, the Erie Canal being among their most wonderful achievements; they had opened up and expanded America. "An excursion of the two lakes and canals cannot fail of administering mental feasts to the imagination of each class . . . Every section of the canal will present . . . sources of wonder and delight, exhibiting the power of mind over matter, and evidencing [this] country's greatness."[40] William James' lengthy speech must have taken over an hour to deliver.

Stephen Van Rensselaer III gave no speeches at the Erie Canal celebration in Albany on November 2, 1825, or at the earlier 1823 celebration that commemorated completion of the Champlain Canal. His cousin, Major General Solomon Van Rensselaer, was appointed Marshal for the 1823 celebration, but contemporary accounts do not discuss Stephen Van Rensselaer III in their accounts of the day's events. By contrast, William James was among the four speakers at the 1823 event, and of those who gave speeches at the 1825 celebration his was the longest. That Stephen Van Rensselaer III remained in the background in the November 2, 1825, Erie Canal celebration in Albany and that William James played a leading role is completely in character with the two men. One was a dignified aristocrat who avoided the limelight, the other, an immigrant who came to America to make his fortune. The drive, energy, and ambition James brought to everything he did was the embodiment of a thrusting capitalism that was transforming America. As an aristocrat with an ancient pedigree and vast landed holdings, Stephen Van Rensselaer III played an active role in the economic development of New York. None of the personages participating in the 1825 Albany celebration had been as actively involved in the Erie Canal project from beginning to end to the extent that he had. Yet, according to contemporary accounts, he was not an important participant in the November 2 festivities. De Witt Clinton received lavish praise; Stephen Van Rensselaer III deserved encomia but received none. And that is very well how he may have wished it.

Stephen Van Rensselaer's life story is one of continuous support of worthy and charitable causes. He was a congregant of the Dutch Reformed church in Albany, of which he served ten terms as deacon or elder. He was generous in giving donations to this and other churches, he furthered religious causes on his landed holding, and he granted land to churches. The years in which the Erie Canal was promoted and built was a time of religious revival in America, the Second Great Awakening, which passed through the Mohawk Valley in upstate

Figure 44. Stephen Van Rensselaer III portrait in the Albany Institute of History and Art, by Stuart Gilbert. That America's leading portraitist painted this work is a commentary on Van Rensselaer's stature. Courtesy of the Albany Institute of History and Art.

New York, the Burned-Over District, named after the fires of religious enthusiasm it ignited with transforming force. Religious societies played an important role in New York revivalist movements, most importantly the Bethel Union Society, of which Van Rensselaer was a supporter. The prevailing fear was that the Erie Canal would create temptations to those who worked on the canal, and this was indeed the case: There was, on average, a saloon every quarter mile along the full length of the Erie Canal. Other moral snares, in addition to saloons, also appeared along the canal, certainly in the eyes of reformers. Van Rensselaer gave generous support to Evangelical organizations; he was first president of the American Tract Society, and he was an original member of the American Bible Society. He was one of the founders of the American Home Missionary Society, and he was a leader in the Masonic Order. He donated lavishly to all of these organizations. He helped found the Society for the Promotion of Useful Arts and the Lyceum of Natural History, which merged and later became the Albany Institute of History and Art. He gave unstinting support to men of enterprise, the forces of scientific progress, and a host of causes that would further the development of farming and the practical arts. He supported local agricultural societies, both in Albany and Rensselaer counties. Of some interest in this connection is a very long speech he delivered at a meeting of the Albany County Agricultural Society in 1819, which began as follows:

> The first requisite of good husbandry, is undoubtedly a proper attention to manures; without their judicious application, the most fertile land becomes exhausted; when, on the other hand, they are indispensably necessary for those soils which are not properly prepared by the hand of nature for the purpose of soils, which are not considered as very advantageous for wheat, have the following succession: turnips, barley, clover, and rye or oats.[41]

What makes this speech interesting is the possibility that Van Rensselaer did not write it. An 1835 letter from Van Rensselaer to Amos Eaton suffers from weak syntax, and is, in fact, ungrammatical. "I received your letter the contents did not surprise me—we live in a World of Sin—we strive to injure our neighbour—to accumulate wealth this is the object of Worldly Man—you may rest in security—as long as I am able and blessed you shall not be oppressed—I will cause the necessary arrangements to me made for you (haste)[.]" Other letters by Van Rensselaer also suffer from grammatical and syntactic defects.[42]

Among Van Rensselaer's ghost writers was the same Amos Eaton, to whom he gave assurances of continuing support in the 1835 letter quoted above. Eaton was a 1795 graduate of Williams College who entered the New York bar in 1802, but became interested in the natural sciences, botany and geology in particular. He moved to Williamstown in 1817 and as an itinerant lecturer he gave talks on scientific topics, traveling through New England and the Hudson Valley. With interest in New York geography, Eaton proposed to Stephen Van Rensselaer in 1824 that he undertake a survey of the region through which the Erie Canal passed. Having completed the survey, Eaton recommended the founding of a scientific school, which Van Rensselaer agreed to support. The beginnings of the scientific school were modest in the extreme. Qualified teachers were to instruct the "sons and daughters of Farmers and Mechanics," who were to "apply themselves, in the *application of science to the common purposes of life*."[43] Classes were to be held in nearby farms and workshops; ten students enrolled in 1825, tuition was $100, and "corporal exercise" was obligatory. The school was to have the use of two farms on the Van Rensselaer manor. It was incorporated in 1826, and two years later, in 1828, Van Rensselaer announced his withdrawing of financial support from the school he helped found, although he responded to future appeals from Amos Eaton with periodic contributions.

While Van Rensselaer continued to offer support he wanted no publicity for himself. "I think it too ostentatious—I dislike being my own trumpeter. . . ."[44] In 1828 the State legislature passed an act to name the school Rensselaer Institute and in 1851 it became Rensselaer Polytechnic Institute. Van Rensselaer's contributions to the State University of New York, whose foundations he helped lay, were hardly less important; he became Chancellor in 1835. He was first president of the Albany Institute when it was formed in 1824, which merged with the Albany Historical and Art Society in 1900, thereby becoming today's Albany Institute of History & Art. Joining Van Rensselaer on the board of the Albany Institute in 1824 was a young science teacher at Albany Academy, Joseph Henry, about whom we shall hear more presently. What we should emphasize if we are to take the measure of Stephen Van Rensselaer III is the range and extent of his support of charitable, religious, practical, educational, and progressive causes. His support of the Erie Canal should be seen within this context. Dedicated to material progress and to moral improvement, Van Rensselaer lavished support on good causes, to an extent that he undercut his own economic position. Stephen Van Rensselaer III was lax in the collection of rents from tenants; rents were heavily in arrears in the last years of his life, so much so that he became concerned over the fiscal position of his eldest son and heir to the Van Rensselaer estate, Stephen Van Rensselaer IV. He called for strict collection of unpaid rents in his will, a measure that his son carried out when he inherited the family estate, thereby igniting the Anti-Rent Wars that broke out almost immediately and ended with the dismantling of the Van Rensselaer estate. By the time of the "Last Patroon's" death in 1839 the stage had been set for dissolution of the largest land holding in the State of New York.

Figure 45. The village of Rensselaerville today. Promoted by Stephen Van Rensselaer III to develop the southern end of the patroonship, it is now a refuge for elite families who bask in its scenic beauty and fine Federal-style architecture.

What we can gather about Stephen Van Rensselaer III from his correspondence is a strong sense of dignity and honor, evident in letters written during
the War of 1812. The mindset is that of an aristocrat who shared the values of
men such as his father-in-law, Philip Schuyler, and his brother-in-law, Alexander
Hamilton. He lacked the thrusting ambition of these relatives, but he was of
their age. He partook of the system of values of the Revolutionary elite, but
he lingered into a new age, whose leaders inhabited a different mental world,
men such as William James. No remaining in the wings for this newcomer,
not the William James who gave the longest of all speeches at the 1825 Erie
Canal celebration in Albany. Epitome of an expansive capitalist order, William
James had a grasp of history that set him apart from Stephen Van Rensselaer.
These men lived through the same history, but they experienced it differently.
One experienced it as a dedicated supporter of good and progressive causes, in
the tradition of aristocratic noblesse oblige; the other experienced the history
of the time as an immigrant who wanted to see an important battlefield of
the Revolution at the time of his arrival in America. For him the Revolution
unleashed forces of great transformation, made possible by independence from
Britain and by a republican government and society that was the proud and
worthy product of independence. What comes through in William James' speech
in the State Capitol in 1825 is a vivid sense of the stunning transformations
that had taken place between 1775 and 1825, a 50-year period of dramatic
growth in America, of which the Erie Canal was a clear example, emblematic
of a new moral and political order, as well as a transportation event of altogether new importance in New York and America. Having nothing to do with
construction of the Erie Canal, William James saw the vast opportunities it
held forth and seized them with a sure hand, gaining great wealth as a result.
This is in striking contrast to another Albanian, Stephen Van Rensselaer III,
whose family fortune had undergone major contractions by the time of his
death in 1839. From this point on, we will follow the paths of these prominent
Albanians, William James and Stephen Van Rensselaer III, after they observed
the Albany celebration of the opening of the Erie Canal. We will follow not
only the paths of these prominent Albanians; we will trace the history of their
families over several generations. Having done so, we will bring our story of
the Erie Canal to closure.

When William James reached the top of State Street hill to give the longest
speech of the day commemorating the opening of the Erie Canal he came to
two buildings, both designed by Philip Hooker. The State Capitol, where James
gave the speech, dates from 1809; adjacent to it and but a short distance away
was Albany Academy, which dates from 1814. While Hooker's New York State
Capitol no longer stands, Academy School is still intact, although a nearby

wooden stable has long since been demolished. An accident had taken place in the stable in the previous year, 1824, that was of no small importance to William James. His son, Henry, a 13-year-old student at Albany Academy, had participated in an experiment carried out by a 27-year-old teacher, Joseph Henry, that involved the use of a balloon. To float the balloon it was necessary to generate heat, which was done by lighting rags soaked in turpentine. When the balloon returned to the ground the rags were extinguished, but in the course of this experiment there were complications when the balloon reached the ground. A ball of rags was still burning, so boys kicked the ball, but in doing so one of them kicked it into the stable, creating the possibility of a fire. To prevent that from happening Henry James ran into the stable to extinguish the rags, but his clothing was soaked in turpentine and when he came into contact with the ball of rags his clothing caught fire, the result being serious burns over

Figure 46. Philip Hooker's 1809 NYS Capitol. This building was demolished when today's NYS Capitol was built.

Figure 47. Philip Hooker's 1814 Academy School. Hooker also did the 1829 Albany City Hall, which was destroyed by a fire in 1880. These buildings, along with Hooker's NYS Capitol, formed a triangle at the top of Capitol Hill, where Fort Frederick once stood.

much of his body. After many operations, surely painful in the extreme (no anesthetics), part of one leg was amputated. What might William James have thought if he looked toward the building close to Albany Academy where his son had suffered a grievous injury in the previous year as he stood before the New York State Capitol on the occasion of the Erie Canal celebration?

Dedicated to science and material progress, Joseph Henry, the teacher who carried out the experiment that exacted such a physical and emotional toll on William James' son Henry, was to carry out another experiment in Albany Academy that, six years later in 1830, was of such importance that he was invited to join the faculty at Princeton University. From there, Joseph Henry went to the Smithsonian Institution, of which he was the first Secretary. From a poor Scottish immigrant family that came to Albany, Joseph Henry left school at an early age and worked in a general store; he also worked as an apprentice watchmaker and silversmith, but he was consumed by interest in science, which he studied on his own. What he needed was support from someone to help him pursue his interests. Stephen Van Rensselaer III was that person. After completing a course at Albany Academy, and with a recommendation from the head of the school, Stephen Van Rensselaer hired Joseph Henry to tutor his children, which enabled him to become a full-time student at Albany Academy. Upon graduating, Joseph Henry became a teacher at Albany Academy; he began making experiments that in time made him one of the most important scientists in nineteenth-century America. His experiments in electromagnetics, carried out at Albany Academy, pointed toward and contributed to invention of the telegraph and the direct-current (DC) motor, and his experiments with balloons were a contribution to the science of aeronautics.

Young Henry James entered Union College in 1828 (he was 17), moving into the house of Eliphalet Nott, the college president. President Nott had undertaken a series of financial schemes to raise money for the college, but he ran into difficulties in 1823, and in 1825 the problems came to a head, at which time he turned to one of the college trustees, William James, for needed help. James loaned Union College $100,000, for which he took out a mortgage at 6.5 percent interest, meaning, in effect, that he owned Union College. No wonder that the seriously crippled Henry James moved into the house of Eliphalet Nott when he arrived at Union College in 1828. Getting from class to class was difficult, but with the sympathetic help of President Nott and other students Henry

Figure 48. Statue of Joseph Henry in front of Albany Academy, done in 1927 by John Flanagan. This photograph was taken by Tony Anadio, while standing on a ladder.

James managed, although his leg was so badly injured by the Albany Academy accident that he underwent another and far more serious surgery that resulted in amputation and application of a wooden leg. Throughout these medical episodes Henry James received continuing sympathy from his mother, as he recalled in his autobiography, written in 1880. He said little about his father's role during the period of painful operations and convalescence. William James was patriarchal, authoritarian, and moralistic, and he was distant toward the members of his family. He was consumed by his projects, early to go to work, late to come home for dinner and for the saying of prayers. Someone recalled that on one occasion William James told a woman who was approaching the front door of his house on Pearl Street that the lady of the house was not in; the woman, taken aback, announced that she *was* Mrs. James. Beneath the wall of exterior indifference to his family there was interior feeling within William James that did manifest itself on occasion, as when his son Henry's leg was amputated, which he witnessed. His wife Catherine said she had to restrain him as he witnessed a scene so painful that she feared he would shriek and throw himself upon the surgeon who was performing the operation. William James seems not to have communicated personal feelings to his son Henry in ways that had meaning to him. What is clear is that when Henry James went to Union College he rebelled massively against everything his father stood for. He spent money lavishly, first signing bills that his father was to pay, and when warned to mend his ways he indulged his whims even more extravagantly, surely knowing how his father would respond. Henry James left Union College during his senior year and went to Boston, where he found a position writing for a Unitarian newspaper, an affront to his staunchly Presbyterian father. Henry James returned to Union College and graduated in 1830, two years before his father's death in 1832, when he contracted typhus during an epidemic that passed from Asia to America, exacting a large toll in human life. William James of Albany was not yet 60 at the time of his death.

He had drawn up a very complicated will six months before his death, in which he tried, as it were, to dictate the lives of his progeny from the grave. He was survived by eight children and six grandchildren, a total of 14, for whom he made provisions in the will. He divided the estate into 12 equal parts, but did not give money directly to all of those he named in the will. Rather, he left it to the discretion of trustees to decide if those who were not yet 21 were worthy of receiving their parts of the inheritance when they reached maturity. What he feared was "the lamentable consequences which so frequently result to young persons brought up in affluence from coming into the possession of property. . . ."[45] Two of his sons did not receive portions of the will. They were given annuities that were to come out of interest derived from "rents and profits"; under no circumstances were their annuity incomes to come out of the 12 portions allotted to the other members of the family. The two sons excluded from the will were William James, the eldest son from his father's first marriage, and Henry James, the eldest son of the third marriage. William James (1797–1868) was to receive an annuity of $2,000 and Henry James (1811–82) was to receive an annuity of $1,200. Both had run afoul of their father, but for completely different reasons. Staunch Presbyterian that William James of Albany was, elder of First Presbyterian Church in Albany and a devout Christian who never neglected family prayers, he objected to his son's decision to become a Presbyterian minister. William James went to Princeton Theological School, was ordained at First Presbyterian Church in Albany in 1820, and became minister of Presbyterian churches in Rochester and Schenectady, precisely what one might expect a staunchly Presbyterian father to have wanted his son to do. But it was otherwise; William James of Albany opposed the path his son had taken and left him out of the will, except for the annuity that was dependent on "rents and profits" derived from his holdings. He dealt yet more harshly with his son Henry James, whose annuity was smaller than that of his older half-brother. This son had convinced his father that he was irresponsible in the extreme, an ingrate, a reprobate, and not to be trusted, particularly if he were to have a substantial sum of money at his disposal. As it happened, William James of Albany was not able to impose his will on his children from the grave, as he had intended. His sons William and Henry broke the will, pointing out in court that certain of its provisionary features were contrary to New York State law. While William and Henry James did not receive portions of the estate as their siblings did, they received considerably larger annuities than the will had provided for. Henry James received an annual annuity that has been estimated at between $10,000 and $12,500. Upon hearing that he had broken his father's will he is reported to have said, "Leisured for Life."

William James' fears when he drew up his will were not without basis; his progeny, on the whole, were unremarkable. Most died at early ages, never having accomplished anything of note in lives of leisured idleness. None followed in their father's footsteps; none followed the path of business, profit, and capitalist development. The trajectory of the James family after the death of William James of Albany is a long, slow decline into insignificance. That is except for one branch of the James family, that of the son who had disgraced himself in the eyes of his father. This son, Henry James, who left Albany for Princeton in 1835 to study theology, had a deep interest in religion, but he was a poor candidate for Princeton Theological School, which his older brother had attended earlier. Henry James' brother William fit into the Presbyterian scheme easily enough, but he did not; he stood apart from fellow students from the beginning, appearing at dinner table after grace was said and leaving before prayers. Henry had no interest and presumably little belief in the afterlife and he never completed the degree in theology. While at Princeton he again came into contact with Joseph Henry, who had gone from Albany Academy to Princeton; again the teacher and student were together, one of the many unexpected turns in the life of Henry James. Joseph Henry moved on to Washington as first

Secretary of the Smithsonian Institution and Henry James, his former pupil, dropped out of Princeton Theological School and moved to New York.

He met the woman he was to marry, Elizabeth Robertson Walsh, sister of a classmate, at her home at 19 Washington Square in New York at the very time he decided to drop out of seminary. He felt from the moment he met Elizabeth that she was the right person for him. As he told his friend, Ralph Waldo Emerson, later, "the flesh said, It is for me, and the spirit said, It is for me."[46] They were married three years later, in 1840. Altogether there were five children, four sons and a daughter. The story of Henry James' family has been seen as a "traumatic saga of dysfunction, competition, anxiety, aspirations often thwarted, confusion, repression, breakdown and sadness, of lifelong struggles to get away and an inexorable pull back to the powerful bond." At the center of that bond was "the eccentric and domineering personality of Henry James . . . unemployed, nomadic, scarred by the amputation of his leg in childhood," unable to exorcise his "inner demons."[47] The first two children of this marriage, William James (1842–1910) and Henry James (1843–1916), born within 15 months of one another, achieved greatness in their respective fields of endeavor, philosophy and literature; they are immortals in the realm of American thought and the life of creative imagination. As far removed as they were from their grandfather, William James of Albany, their achievements cannot be separated from him, or from his impact on their father, Henry James, the disinherited son. As a philosopher, William James was a pragmatist who saw the "cash value of ideas," and regarded money as the basis of power, and as a metaphysical force. In this way, it would seem that the legacy of William James of Albany, for whom money was the way to success and power, lived on, transmuted into philosophy. Isabel Archer in Henry James' *The Portrait of a Lady* visited an aunt in Albany, reminiscent of his Albany visits to see his Aunt Ellen at 4 Elk Street, a town house that still stands, and is opposite Albany Academy, where Henry James' father had suffered a tragic accident that left more than physical scars. What, one wonders, might Henry James have thought about his father and the terrible accident he suffered on the grounds that lay opposite the town house at 4 Elk Street on the occasion of Albany visits to see his aunt. Henry James' grandfather, William James, appears as a phantom figure in his story, "The Jolly Corner," a ghostly presence from the past.

Stephen Van Rensselaer III died in 1839, seven years after William James of Albany. When Van Rensselaer assumed the title of Patroon in 1785, at age 21, there were some 600 tenants on the Rensselaerwijck patroonship. This was in the immediate aftermath of the Revolution, when people from New England were pouring into Albany, many continuing on to territories to the west, but some settling along the Hudson River. Those who did so became tenants on the Van Rensselaer patroonship; by 1812 the number of tenants had grown from 600 to 3,000. A British traveler who passed through Albany in 1818 estimated the Van Rensselaer family fortune at 7 million dollars. According to a July 15,

Figure 49. The residence of Henry James' Aunt Ellen, at 4 Elk Street. She was married to the son of Martin Van Buren, and Henry James visited this townhouse as a boy. Franklin D. Roosevelt also lived here, between 1910 and 1912, when he was New York State senator. Photograph by Tony Anadio.

2007, article in the *New York Times*, Stephen Van Rensselaer III was the tenth wealthiest person in all of American history, with assets, corrected for inflation, of $62 billion. This changed. The economic contractions of 1819, severe not only in America but in Europe as well, resulted in reduced payment of rents by Rensselaerwijck tenants to their landlord; back rents continued to pile up over the years. Van Rensselaer never recovered from these difficulties, which were worsened by the depression of 1837, two years before his death. Throughout the difficult years, Van Rensselaer continued to contribute to good causes, civic, progressive, cultural, and religious; owing to his support of worthy causes and to lax collection of rents from tenants Stephen Van Rensselaer III had to borrow money; he left his heir, Stephen Van Rensselaer IV, with a sizeable debt, as he realized when he drew up his will. He owed creditors $400,000; his creditors had to be paid off. He gave instructions to his son to collect rents that were in arrears. Stephen Van Rensselaer IV's efforts to collect overdue rents came at a particularly bad time, in several ways. The depression of 1837 added to the difficulties of collecting rents; additionally, "feudal" rents were seen as anomalous and oppressive. The American economy was now carried forward by the forces of Jacksonian democracy, making arrangements between landlords and tenants that went back to the seventeenth century appear unbearable. Violent protests, the tin-horn rebellion, erupted as soon as Stephen Van Rensselaer IV tried to collect back rents; this he was never able to do effectively; by 1865 the Anti-Rent Wars were over; Rensselaerwijck, the ancient landed holding of the Van Rensselaer family was no more.[48]

Running parallel to the disappearance of the Van Rensselaer landholding was the disappearance of its physical center, Van Rensselaer manor, and of Van Rensselaer Hall, once one of the two finest mansions in Albany. Both Van Rensselaer Hall and the storied manorial grounds were depicted by Thomas Cole, the founder of the Hudson River school of landscape painting, in works that now hang in the Albany Institute of History and Art. According to the AIHA catalogue entry that discusses these paintings, "The Van Rensselaer gardens were celebrated as among the most beautiful and extensive in all of America, with elegant lawns, flower beds, ponds, and majestic trees."[49] Among those who visited the Van Rensselaer gardens in the early nineteenth century was Timothy Dwight, the president of Yale College, who passed through Albany between 1804 and the time of his death in 1817. He wrote,

> The mansion house in which [Stephen Van Rensselaer III] resides struck my eye as exhibiting an appearance remarkably comporting with the fact that for a long period it had been the residence of an ancient and distinguished family. The situation though not much elevated is fine, cheerful, and prospective. It is the front of a noble interval in the township of Watervliet, containing seven hundred acres. East of this interval flows the Hudson, and beyond it is seen a handsome activity rising from its margin, upon which stands the neat, sprightly village of Bath [today's Rensselaer, on the opposite side of the Hudson]. The house is large and venerable, and looks as if it was the residence of respectability and worth. The hospitality which reigns here has ever been honorable to successive proprietors.[50]

Little could Stephen Van Rensselaer have understood the impact the Erie Canal would have on Van Rensselaer Hall and the beautiful grounds on which it was situated when he passed alongside it in a canal boat with other

Figure 50. Thomas Cole's 1841 painting, *The Van Rensselaer Manor.* Tony Anadio, whose help in compiling the illustrations for this book (and taking some of the photographs) is writing his doctoral dissertation on Cole in the History department at the University at Albany. Courtesy of the Albany Institute of History and Art.

worthies who arrived in Albany to celebrate the opening of the Erie Canal on November 2, 1825. This project, to which he had given unstinting support, ran alongside his manorial grounds a mile or so before the Erie Canal reached its eastern terminus at Lock 53. In the years just before the opening of the Erie Canal, Stephen Van Rensselaer III undertook numerous improvements on his manorial grounds, frequently calling on Albany's leading architect, Philip Hooker, to carry out his various plans.[51] Hooker compiled three designs for a garden pavilion in 1811; he then carried out extensive additions to Van Rensselaer Hall in 1818–19, most importantly the construction of two one-story wings on both sides of the original 1765 house, which gave additional space for dining, a study, and a library, as well as the addition of new window sashes and a new porch. In 1820 Hooker designed a sundial stand for the gardens. Four years later, in 1824, Van Rensselaer commissioned Hooker to design two garden pavilions, one circular and the other octagonal. After the builders completed these projects, beautifying the gardens, Van Rensselaer paid Hooker to inspect the work, presumably to make certain that it conformed to his design and met with his approval. That Van Rensselaer selected Philip Hooker to carry out the improvements on his fabled manorial grounds says much about the care and attention he gave to the seat of his power; that he had Hooker inspect work for which he provided the designs says much about his concern that everything turned out right. Clearly, Stephen Van Rensselaer took keen pride in Van Rensselaer Hall, and in the manorial grounds.

The Erie Canal did not immediately compromise this refined space; rather, change took place by stages. Life on Van Rensselaer manor was still viable when Stephen Van Rensselaer IV moved into Van Rensselaer Hall after his father's death in 1839. He had Richard Upjohn (the architect of St. Peter's on State Street in Albany) undertake renovations between 1840 and 1843, but within another 15 years life in Van Rensselaer Hall was no longer as it had been. An 1857 map of Albany tells the story with full clarity. It shows not only slips alongside the eastern side of the Erie Canal, where workers stacked commodities that came in an always larger commercial flow, but also a railroad line that ran alongside the canal, facing toward the manorial grounds. Inhabitants of Van Rensselaer Hall looked down not only upon the Erie Canal and heard the noise of commercial activity, but were exposed to the sounds and smells of railway traffic that passed along the eastern end of the manorial grounds. By the 1870s the lumber industry in Albany reached its heyday, with some 50 lumber companies processing 700 million board feet annually. The Van Rensselaer strip with its 40 slips alongside the Erie Canal "was a veritable city of lumber piles, extending a mile and a quarter northward from . . . the Canal Basin."[52] Stephen Van Rensselaer IV continued to live in the old manor house until the time of his death in 1868, but his son William Bayard Van Rensselaer abandoned it in 1875. Huybertie Pruyn described visits there as a girl, before it was demolished. She thought it was a haunted house.

Figure 51. Cole's 1840 *Gardens of the Van Rensselaer Manor.* Courtesy of the Albany Institute of History and Art.

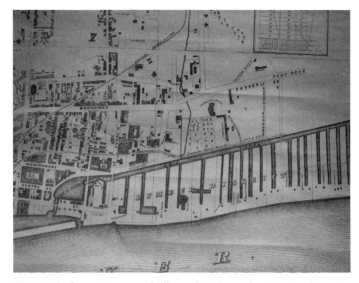

Figure 52. Detail of an 1857 map of Albany that shows the Erie Canal running along the eastern end of the Van Rensselaer Manor grounds. Slips where commodities were stacked line the entire stretch of the Erie Canal that runs alongside the Van Rensselaer manorial grounds. The map shows a railroad line that runs alongside the Erie Canal. The gardens ran all the way down to the railroad line and the Erie Canal; it is unclear to me if the gardens extended below the Erie Canal before 1825, as they might well have.

William Bayard Van Rensselaer decided to tear down one wing of the abandoned house in 1893 to make room for an extension of a railway line that was to run across the lower end of the manor, operated by New York Central Railroad. Marcus Reynolds, a cousin of William Bayard Van Rensselaer, who had visited the fabled house as a boy, thought it best to demolish the entire building, and to save as much of it as possible. Reynolds had been a Williams College undergraduate before going to Columbia University, where he studied architecture. Upon returning to Albany to set up an architectural practice, a unique opportunity presented itself when his cousin decided that something had to be done with the old manor house. There had been a fire in Reynolds' fraternity house at Williams College, Sigma Phi Lodge, and knowing that a new fraternity house would have to be built Reynolds persuaded William Bayard Van Rensselaer not to tear down one wing of the old manor house but to demolish the entire building, a project that Reynolds oversaw. The bricks crumbled when Van Rensselaer Hall was taken down, but the stone trim was saved; Reynolds identified and catalogued every stone that was to be incorporated into the new building, Sigma Phi Lodge, which he designed, and whose exterior was to be a replica of Van Rensselaer Hall. Reynolds scrupulously saved the interior decora-

Figure 53. 1893 photograph of Van Rensselaer Hall, presumably the last photograph of the storied building, taken in the year of its demolition. Courtesy of the Folsom Library, Rensselaer Polytechnic Institute.

Figure 54. The Sigma Phi fraternity House in Williamstown, designed by Marcus Reynolds. Reynolds' building in Williamstown did not include the two additions by Philip Hooker. The exterior was a near replica of Van Rensselaer Hall; the interior layout of rooms was by Reynolds. When Van Rensselaer Hall was demolished the brick crumbled, and was not usable for the new building. Only the stone trim and timber frame were usable and incorporated into Sigma Phi Lodge.

tion, most importantly the 1768 hand-painted wallpaper purchased by Philip Livingston in England and sent to his son-in-law, Stephen Van Rensselaer II, which Reynolds donated to the Metropolitan Museum in New York City. Now in the American Wing of the Metropolitan Museum, the wallpapers decorate the Van Rensselaer Room, which even today gives some sense of the elegance of what had been one of the finest houses in the Hudson River Valley.[53]

The disappearance of Van Rensselaer Hall was never complete; it was a strange disappearance that included efforts at preservation, some successful, some failed, some unclear even to this day. Williams College abandoned fraternities in 1963, and Sigma Phi Lodge was put to new use until 1973, when it was demolished to make way for an extension of the college library. The materials from Van Rensselaer Hall that Marcus Reynolds had saved were saved again, this time by Dr. Joseph Demis; they are now stored in Rensselaer Technology Park, having been donated to RPI in 1995–96 for the construction of a new president's house, to be built with materials from Van Rensselaer Hall in recognition of Stephen Van Rensselaer III, a founder of the Troy University. Other reports would have it that Marcus Reynolds incorporated parts of the decoration from Van Rensselaer Hall, including some of the interior woodwork, into the interior of the fine town house he designed at 385–389 State Street in Albany, commissioned by Reynolds' cousins, William Bayard Van Rensselaer

Figure 55. When I was told where I should go if I wanted to see piles of stones from Van Rensselaer Hall/Sigma Phi Lodge, Tony Anadio and I went, as directed, to an "old Dutch house" on the Rensselaer Technology Park on June 15, 2009. This is that farm house; it is the Defreest house, built at the same time as Van Rensselaer Hall, in the 1760s, on land that was leased from the Van Rensselaer family. This house is a little more than a stone's throw (pun intended) from the remains of Van Rensselaer Hall. Photo by Tony Anadio.

Figure 56. After Tony and I arrived at the Defreest house we walked, with the person I had talked to the previous day, Keith Van Amburgh (he couldn't have been more helpful), showing the way, through a field of wet bushes (it had rained the night before) to a fenced area. Inside it are the stones that were the object of our expedition, barely visible because they are covered with weeds. Every stone from the original building has been identified and marked. The idea originally was to use the stones from Van Rensselaer Hall/Sigma Phi Lodge in a new President's house at Rensselaer Polytechnic Institute, but that idea has been abandoned. The head of the Technology Park told Tony and me that he would like to use the stones to build areas around the Rensselaer Polytechnic Institute campus where students could sit, a nice idea indeed. If that happens, one wonders how many RPI students will know anything about the history of these stones, and their connection to the founder of the college that they attend. I must thank Dick Siegel, the holder of an endowed chair at RPI, and a good friend, for telling me about this pile of stones. Photo by Tony Anadio.

and Dr. Howard Van Rensselaer. Built in 1897, the timing for this transfer of materials would have been a perfect fit; the very person who ordered the demolition of Van Rensselaer Hall, William Bayard Van Rensselaer, commissioned a fine State Street town house into which he and his younger brother moved a few years later; the architect who oversaw the dismantling of the venerable manor house also designed the new town house. All parties were aware of the historical significance of the old building; all wanted to preserve it as best they could. So Van Rensselaer Hall lives on, in a sense, in the Van Rensselaer Room at the Metropolitan Museum, more obscurely in a pile of stones stacked inside a fenced-in space in a technology park on the eastern side of the Hudson, and (apparently) in interior decoration in one of the finest of Albany town houses, Marcus Reynolds' 385–389 State Street, done in the style of a Venetian palazzo.

Figure 57. Marcus Reynolds' fine townhouse, 385–389 State Street, 1897.

The economic success of the Erie Canal continued throughout most of the nineteenth century. It was enlarged twice, but it began to slip behind competition from the railroad, although not without a last-ditch effort to keep pace. Between 1905 and 1918 a new canal was built, the Barge Canal, whose eastern terminus is in Waterford, where the Mohawk passes into the Hudson. With construction of the Barge Canal the strip of the Erie Canal that ran along the Hudson from Cohoes to Albany was filled in. All traces of the eastern terminus of the Erie Canal are gone; all that remains is Erie Boulevard, a stretch of paved road perhaps a mile-and-a-half in length that begins a short distance above the Interstate 90 overpass and ends just beyond Colonie Street. That is where canal boats passed through Little Basin, paid their tolls, and came to the lock that let them into the Hudson, at the northern end of Albany Basin. This is where the *Seneca Chief* was lowered into the Hudson on November 2, 1825, when celebrations were held to commemorate completion of the Erie Canal; this is where cheering crowds gathered to celebrate completion of an engineering project they rightly considered a landmark event in the transportation and economic history of America. Going down Erie Boulevard today is a strange experience for those who know the history underneath the paving along which they pass. The canal is gone, the slips along it are gone, the lumber district it generated is gone, and Van Rensselaer manor is gone. So too is Van Rensselaer Hall, once one of the finest mansions in the mid-Hudson region.

An advertisement was placed in a Schenectady newspaper on December 16, 1825, calling for subscribers to invest in a proposed railway line between Albany and Schenectady. This was six weeks after the celebration of the opening of the Erie Canal in Albany. The connection between the opening of the Erie Canal and the newspaper advertisement was not accidental: In the 16-mile section of the Erie Canal between Schenectady and Lock 53 there were 19 locks, with canal boats backed up along the way. The idea for a railroad line between Albany and Schenectady was a response to this set of conditions. A railway line 16 miles in length would provide canal boat passengers with a faster passage from Albany to Schenectady. The result was New York's first railroad, the Mohawk and Hudson Company, chartered on April 17, 1826, and one of the first railroad companies in America. Stephen Van Rensselaer was its first president; the first locomotive was named the DeWitt Clinton, after the celebrated champion of the Erie Canal. A crowd gathered at what is now the triangle where Western and

Figure 58. Erie Boulevard today. I-90 passes over Erie Boulevard in this photograph.

Madison Avenues converge for the official opening of the Mohawk and Hudson rail line on September 24, 1831. No traces of the line remain, although there is an historical marker in front of the Pine Hills police station where people gathered to observe the first railway passengers in New York as they boarded the DeWitt Clinton steam locomotive train to travel to Schenectady.

Van Rensselaer manor, Van Rensselaer Hall, and the Erie Canal live on in the writings of William Kennedy. Kennedy wrote in *O Albany!* that "Colonie [Street] started along the river flats of the Basin, the sheltered harbor that began at the mouth of the Erie Canal and ran south to Hamilton Street. Colonie [Street] crossed Broadway and rose up the northernmost of the four steep ridges on which the city was built. . . ."[54] As a map of the eastern terminus of the Erie Canal indicates, Colonie Street ended right next to Lock 53 of the Erie Canal, precisely as Kennedy described it in the above passage. The Phelan family in Kennedy's novels had lived on Colonie Street; this was not accidental. Kennedy's father went to school at St. Joseph's Academy at Colonie and North Pearl Streets, attended by boys from a predominantly Irish and Catholic background, which of course is Kennedy's background. The Colonie Street that had close personal associations for Kennedy is no more, at least not as he knew it as a boy growing up in North Albany. Colonie Street now ends at North Pearl Street; public housing is located where Kennedy's father went to school. In Kennedy's novels,

Figure 59. Lock 53, the eastern terminus of the Erie Canal. Notice that piles of lumber are stacked next to the lock.

Figure 60. The toll house in Little Basin, where tolls were collected from canal boats just before they entered Lock 53.

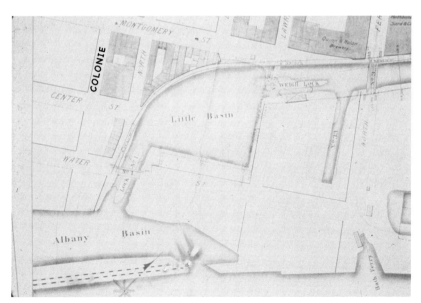

Figure 61. Map that shows Little Basin and Lock 53. Colonie Street is right next to Little Basin in this map.

the home where the Phelan family lived was on a Colonie Street that is largely gone. When Francis Phelan went on a rag-collecting junket in *Ironweed*, hoping to accumulate enough money to purchase a Thanksgiving turkey for the family he had abandoned in North Albany, he had to overcome interior obstacles as he walked down the street on which he had grown up, with scenes of his youth, and of his family, passing in review.

When Kennedy discussed the origins of Colonie Street in *Billy Phelan's Greatest Game* he connected those origins to the Van Rensselaer Patroonship:

> The street took its name from the Colonie itself, that vast medieval demesne colonized in 1630 by an Amsterdam pearl merchant named Kiliaen Van Rensselaer, who was also known as the First Patroon, the absentee landlord who bought from five tribes of Indians some seven hundred thousand acres of land, twenty-four miles long and forty-eight miles wide . . . Each power-wielding descendant of Van Rensselaer to assume the feudal mantle would maintain exploitative supremacy over thousands of farm renters on the enormous manor called, first, Rensselaerwyck, and later, The Colonie. Each Patroon

Figure 62. Colonie Street today, looking west from Erie Boulevard. The warehouse on the left can claim legitimately to be the ugliest building in Albany. Traffic is not continuous on Colonie Street below Pearl, thanks to the railroad viaduct that cuts through it at Broadway. The viaduct was built because so many people were killed at the railway crossing at Broadway and Colonie.

Figure 63. Colonie Street today. This is the only part of Colonie Street that is a residential street today. It runs from Henry Johnson Blvd. to Swan St.; much of the original Colonie Street is gone. Photo by Tony Anadio.

> would make his home in the Manor House, which rose handsomely out of a riverside meadow just north of the city on the bank of a stream that is still called Patroon Creek . . . [The Manor house] closed forever in 1875 [and] was later . . . dismantled brick by brick and reassembled in Williamstown as a fraternity house.

Continuing, Kennedy wrote that "Billy Phelan's great-grandfather, Johnny Phelan, a notably belligerent under-sheriff, was given safekeeping of the Manor House as his personal charge. . . ." Billy's friend and North Albany neighbor, Martin Daugherty, also had family ties that linked him to the old Manor House: "Martin Daugherty's grandmother, Hannah Sweeney, had been the pastry cook in the Patroon's kitchen and was famed for her soda bread and fruitcakes, which, everyone said, always danced off their platters and onto the finicky palates of the Patroon and his table companions. . . ."[55]

Francis Phelan, the protagonist of *Ironweed*, returned to Albany after abandoning his family years earlier. He is a street person, down on his luck, a former professional baseball player who is the victim of his addictions, aware of his tragic failings, and is finally at a time in his life at which he wants to

Figure 64. St. Johns, Green Street.

come to terms with his past. On a cold November night in 1938 he and his companion, Helen Archer, once a talented pianist but also fallen on hard times, visit a street mission on lower Madison Avenue, close to Green Street. He has decided that he will walk from South Albany to North Albany, a place of many memories, but before making the journey he has to do something with Helen. He walks with her down Green Street just past St. John's Roman Catholic Church (now boarded shut); he comes to an abandoned car off John Street (now filled in) with two street persons inside, making do for the long, cold night that lay before them. Francis deposited Helen in the car, explaining to her that this was the best she could do and that she would be alright, fearing that this was far from the case. And he was right; the street person in the front seat sexually assaulted Helen, who walked up Madison to cleanse herself ritually in church; she would have preferred going to the Cathedral of Immaculate Conception but was unable to make it that far and went to Saint Anthony's instead, on the corner of Madison and Grand. Meanwhile, Francis walked all the way up Broadway to North Albany, until he came to Main Street, where he turned east, toward the river. "He walked toward the flats, where the canal used to be, long gone and the ditch filled in. The lock was gone and the lockhouse too, and the towpath all grown over." He walked from Main Street to North Street, the last street that ran toward the river from Broadway, coming to an abandoned barn, Welt the Tin's Barn, "a shell, with a vast hole

Figure 65. The rear of St. John's. A sign on the building indicates—for those who are interested—that the abandoned church is "Available." This building is to South Albany what St. Joseph's is to Arbor Hill; once the anchor of a community, it is now a symbol of its breakdown. Efforts are under way to save St. Joseph's; one only wishes that the same were being done for St. John's.

Figure 65a. What was once John Street. The view is from the steps of St. John's; once continuous, John Street was filled in when they established the Historic Pastures District. It was in an alley off John Street that Francis left Helen in an abandoned car with Finny and another man.

in the far end of the roof where moonlight poured cold fire onto the ancient splintered floor." It was here that Francis Phelan encountered the ghosts of his past. "Bats flew in balletic arcs around the streetlamps outside, the last lamp on North Street, and the ghosts of mules and horses snorted and stomped for Francis." The ghosts of mules and horses that Francis encountered on North Street were those of animals that had moved packet boats along the foot path of the Erie Canal before it had been filled in. Standing there, Francis was within 75 feet of a deep personal tragedy, from which he had been running since the time of its occurrence. "Seventy-five feet from this spot, Gerald Phelan died on the 26th of April of April 1916."[56] On that day Francis had dropped his infant son, Gerald, while changing his diapers, killing him.

Francis decided, after years of abandonment, that he would again see his wife, who lived on North Pearl Street, where Kennedy himself had grown up. After seeing her he returned to his old haunts in South Albany, unable to overcome feelings of guilt. He and his friend Rudy, another drunk, drove up "Erie Boulevard, where the Erie Canal used to flow," in "Old Shoes' Car," until they came to a shantytown, "maybe seven years old, three years old, a month old, days old. It was an ashpit, a graveyard, and a fugitive city," where "people

Figure 66. Main Street below Broadway in north Albany—Francis Phelan's destination on that cold winter day in November 1938 when he confronted his past. The blue storage buildings in the photograph are at the bottom of Main Street; the Erie Canal was below these buildings; this was where "the canal used to be, long gone and the ditch filled in."

who had come . . . at journey's end to accept whatever disaster was going to happen next." And disaster was about to strike Francis, Rudy, and the other transients who were huddled together on a cold night within a "jungle" that "covered the equivalent of two or more square city blocks between the tracks and the river. . . ." Francis was "In the deepest part of himself that could draw an unutterable conclusion . . . My guilt is all that I have left. If I lose it, I have stood for nothing, done nothing, been nothing." At the precise moment Francis had these dark ruminations "men in caps entered the jungle with a fervid purpose." They were vigilantes, invading the shantytown with baseball bats and clubs, wielding them with dexterity to clear away the derelicts huddled together for the night. One of the vigilantes swung at Francis' friend Rudy with a baseball bat, felling him with what turned out to be a fatal blow to the head. Down-and-out street person that Francis was, the athleticism of old, the skill that had made him a professional baseball player, mysteriously resurfaced. An assailant went after him, but Francis

> sidestepped [the swing] as easily as he once went to his left for a fast grounder. Simultaneously he stepped forward, as into a wide pitch, and swung his own bat at the man who had struck Rudy. Francis connected with a stroke that would have sent any pitch over any center-field fence in any ball park anywhere, and he clearly heard and truly felt bones crack in the man's back. He watched with all but orgasmic pleasure as the breathless man twisted grotesquely and fell without a sound.[57]

Francis had killed the assailant; once again he fled Albany, bumming a ride on a Delaware and Hudson railway car that took him southward, a journey that took him alongside the Hudson as he reflected on his own tragic past, experienced in an Albany that had seen better times.

William Kennedy's novel *Ironweed* is a lament over the Albany in which he had grown up, an Albany whose history was closely bound up with the Erie Canal. The shantytown in the flats, between Erie Boulevard and the Hudson River, is a symbolic evocation of a world that had been transformed from busy North Albany to a desolate wasteland, a refuge for the outcasts of a very different age, America during the Great Depression. The shantytown and its derelict inhabitants were far removed from the Erie Canal that William James celebrated in the 1825 festivities, given at the time of its completion. In the 155 years between the opening of the Erie Canal and the publication of William Kennedy's Pulitzer-Prize winning novel *Ironweed*, the period between 1825 and 1980, the Erie Canal had been filled in, the lumber district it had spawned had all but disappeared, and little was left but an industrial wasteland. For William James the Erie Canal marked the beginning of a new era, one of vast hope and opportunity; for William Kennedy the Erie Canal had quite different

Figure 67a. A view of North Albany from Erie Boulevard. This photograph was taken directly below North Street. Kennedy's Sacred Heart church can be seen in the distance. This was Kennedy's church; he lived in three different houses on North Pearl Street, which is just behind Sacred Heart.

meaning. It was but a memory of a bygone age: The canal itself was gone; all that remained was a swath of desolation passing through a North Albany whose epitaph William Kennedy wrote in *Ironweed*.

In the years since William Kennedy wrote *Ironweed*, awareness of and interest in the Erie Canal has increased markedly, in Albany and throughout New York State. Most of it having been buried many decades ago, literally buried, the Erie Canal has re-emerged within the realm of historical understanding and imagination. Also, parts of the Erie Canal have been excavated in recent years, including a 2001 dig in Albany to uncover the precise site of the "wood-and-stone bulwark that lowered boats heading south to the level of the Hudson River and raised Buffalo-bound vessels for the trip along the high and mighty Erie."[58] Up to the time of this dig the precise location of Lock 53 was not known. Now we do know the location, owing to this exercise in historical recovery. In this

Figure 67b. 620 North Pearl Street. This is the house that Kennedy had in mind when Francis returned home to see the wife he had abandoned. It was Kennedy's own home.

way, as in others, the Erie Canal is coming back. As one of the pivotal events in the history of New York it could hardly have been otherwise; take away the Erie Canal and the history of New York is no longer the same. The Erie Canal was an engine of growth in New York State, and it was instrumental in making New York City the dominant city in America. That is the positive side of the Erie Canal story. The downside is the economic contraction of New York State that has been integral to its history since the shutting down of the Erie Canal as a corridor of commerce. Cities along the Erie Canal that were thriving centers of industry and teemed with urban vitality are now part of an extended "Rust Belt" that follows the course of the Erie Canal. Several generations of inhabitants in towns and cities along the Erie Canal have experienced the painful contractions that attended the closing of the Erie Canal. By the time the Erie Canal was filled in the communities through which it passed had grown old, it must have seemed. Old photographs show how tacky towns along the Erie Canal had become. The Erie Canal, for many who experienced its decline and after effects, was surely a bad memory. All of this is a stage in the history of the

Erie Canal, what one might call its death throes, its final rattle. But in recent decades a new stage has arrived in the ongoing story of the Erie Canal. From one end of New York State to the other, towns and cities have rediscovered the Erie Canal. This is true both of the original Erie Canal, "Clinton's Ditch," and the later Barge Canal. An Erie Canalway National Heritage Corridor has been established, with a central office in Waterford, the eastern terminus of the Barge Canal, completed in 1918. Visitors to Waterford today see the impressive concrete locks, vastly larger and technologically more advanced than the original locks of the Erie Canal, whose terminus was several miles to the south at the northern end of Albany Basin. There is nothing in Albany remotely like the Waterford locks. There are no locks at all in Albany. By the time the Barge Canal was completed, the heyday of canals was over. The Barge Canal, by far the most ambitious of New York's canals, is a final, paradoxical, commentary on the great age of canals; it is the product of thinking and planning that belonged to the past, not to a future in which other forms of transportation displaced canals. The eastern terminus of the Barge Canal is impressive, and it is not to be missed by those who have an interest in Albany and New York State history. But it does not belong to the heroic age of canals. It was the original 1825 canal that is of unique importance in this respect. The eastern terminus of the 1825 Erie Canal, Lock 53, was a focal point of sweeping economic change. It was here that two canal systems came together, one extending to Lake Erie to the West and the other to the Saint Lawrence to the north. Nothing of Lock 53 remains. Nor does anything remain of Albany Basin, built to accommodate the commercial traffic that flowed into it from the Erie and Champlain Canals. Albany Basin is no more; it too was filled in.

Let us, in imagination, walk down State Street with the dignitaries who celebrated the opening of the Erie Canal on November 2, 1825, after William James of Albany and other worthies delivered speeches in Philip Hooker's 1809 Capitol. These men, of an active generation, did not walk all the way down State Street to the area alongside the Hudson where Albany Basin had been built. They turned right on Pearl Street and walked to Lydius Street, now Madison Avenue; they then went down Lydius to Market Street, now Broadway; they then turned left on Market and made their way to Albany Basin, where the final Erie Canal festivities were held. How different today's Albany is from the Albany of 1825. The entire core of 1825 Albany is long gone, and Albany Basin, bedecked with Gothic towers for the day's celebration, is gone. Not only has it been filled in but the geographical space it occupied was shut off physically from the city of Albany by Interstate 787. How many drivers passing along I-787 today realize that east of where they are driving is where Albany Basin was constructed for the Erie Canal? Until the year 2001 the people of Albany were cut off from the Hudson River, the city's historic lifeline, and from the area that was once Albany Basin. This is no longer the

Figure 68. Barge Canal locks at Waterford.

case. Pedestrians can now cross a footbridge that takes them across I-787 and to the Corning Preserve, once Albany Basin, and to the Hudson River. This bridge begins at the end of Maiden Lane and ends at what was once the far end of Albany Basin pier. To walk across the Bridge today is to walk across what was once Albany Basin. Upon reaching the far end of the Bridge there are walkways that go down to the Corning Preserve bicycle path; if one takes the walkway on the left-hand side and walks north along the bicycle path one comes to an historic marker indicating the location of the eastern terminus of the Erie Canal. Along the way there are ponds with water from the Hudson River, a visible reminder of what was once Albany Basin, part of a bygone age. The Erie Canal historic marker on the bicycle path is next to a children's playground, across from an overhead maze of expressways and ramps, Interstate 787. To look in that direction, toward the maze of highways and ramps, is to look at what was once the eastern terminus of the Erie Canal, the end of an economic lifeline of incalculable historical importance.

As it happens, an actual segment of the original Erie Canal is close to Albany, the Mohawk Towpath Scenic Byway that runs through the Vischer Ferry Nature and Historic Preserve. This Byway allows today's visitors to walk along the towpath where horses and donkeys pulled packet boats along the Erie

Figure 69. The Albany Riverwalk Pedestrian Bridge seen from I-787. I-787 passes through what was Albany Basin until it was filled in after World War II; drivers who travel this section of I-787 pass through an important cross-section of history.

Canal. My wife, Anne, a friend, Candis Murray, who lives in Cohoes, and I walked along this towpath in the summer of 2005, Candis leading the way. It is a day that I shall not forget. No one else was there as we walked beside the moss-topped waters of the Erie Canal, which is remarkably well preserved. On

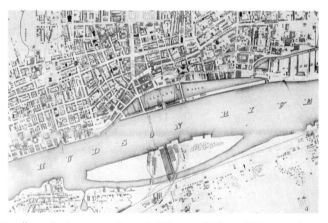

Figure 70. Albany Basin, as seen in an 1857 map of Albany. This map shows precisely where Albany Basin was situated; what was once Albany Basin is now the Corning Preserve.

Figure 71. Albany Basin, as seen in Len Tantillo's painting of Albany, c. 1860. This painting from 1985 launched Tantillo's highly successful career as an artist who has reconstructed the past visually after conducting exhaustive and meticulous research, essential to the historical accuracy that is always his objective. Albany has been extremely well served by William Kennedy and Len Tantillo.

one side of the footpath was the Erie Canal and on the other were backwaters of the Mohawk River, one of New York's historic river corridors. As a trip into the past I have seldom experienced anything like it; in my imagination I heard the sounds of the canal boys who led the horses and donkeys, and the

Figure 72. Pedestrians at the Hudson River end of the Riverwalk Pedestrian Bridge; they seem to be more interested in their dogs than the view of the Hudson.

Figure 73. Walkway to the bicycle path from the Riverwalk Pedestrian Bridge.

Figure 74. The bicycle path between the Riverwalk Pedestrian Bridge and the Erie Canal Historic marker. When I rode along this bicycle path for the first time in June 1998, I had no idea that I was passing over what had been Albany Basin, built to accommodate commercial traffic from the Erie Canal.

Figure 75. The Erie Canal historical Marker on the Corning Preserve bicycle path.

Figure 76. Historical marker for the Erie Canal on the Vischer Ferry Preserve.

Figure 77. A section of the Erie Canal on the Vischer Ferry Preserve, covered with moss.

Figure 78. The towpath alongside the Erie Canal on the Vischer Ferry Preserve.

Figure 79. Backwater from the Mohawk River, seen from the towpath on the Vischer Ferry Preserve.

snorts of the animals as well. What the canal boys and the animals did, taking packet boats along the Erie Canal, was of a different age, one that seems remote from us in all ways. And yet, primitive as this system of transportation was, it changed the world.

Conclusion

Albany, Past and Present

Observations and Images (with some musings thrown in)

At the beginning of the period covered by this study, 1775 to 1825, the two finest residences in Albany were Philip Schuyler's mansion, Schuyler Mansion, built in 1761, and Van Rensselaer Hall, built in 1765. By 1825 the Schuyler family had sold Schuyler Mansion, which became an orphan asylum in the second half of the nineteenth century, part of a larger transformation of South Albany from an elite neighborhood into one that has continued to see many changes down to the present. Today Schuyler Mansion is a state museum, restored as much as possible to its original condition, making it a fine place to visit, a building of great architectural and historical interest. For the visitor who understands the history with which this building is bound up, seeing it today is a strange exercise. Schuyler Mansion is in the middle of an urban ghetto with all of the characteristics that attend neighborhoods such as this. The street running along the north side of Schuyler Mansion, Catherine Street, was named after Catherine Van Rensselaer Schuyler, the wife of Philip Schuyler. Trucks are usually parked on a vacant lot at the corner of Clinton and Catherine, directly across from Schuyler Mansion. At the opposite end of Schuyler mansion there are abandoned row houses, with boarded up or broken windows. Two streets away from Schuyler Mansion is Alexander Street, named after Philip Schuyler's son-in-law, Alexander Hamilton. There was an article on Alexander Street in the *Times Union* in February 2007 that cited Alexander Street as an example of urban blight in the city of Albany. A photograph showed boarded-up buildings and pervasive decay. Much of South Albany is a wasteland, a sad and tragic commentary on the very different Albany of 1775 to 1825.

Matters are yet worse where Van Rensselaer Hall was once one of the two finest residences in Albany. Nothing remains of Van Rensselaer Manor, or of Van Rensselaer Hall; there is not even an historical marker. For an exercise in strangeness one can do no better than to visit the site of Van Rensselaer manor,

Figure 80. Abandoned houses next to Schuyler Mansion.

keeping in mind the visit to the same site by Mme de La Tour du Pin in 1794. The "well-tended park, planted with beautiful trees and flowers" that she saw right after she arrived in Albany is no more. Also gone is Van Rensselaer Hall, which was located not far from where the RTA Building (c. 1912) now stands, on Broadway just past Tivoli. Sitting atop the RTA Building is Nipper, a 25-foot, four-ton dog, the symbol of the RCA Company. Below Nipper, toward the Hudson, lies a jumble of warehouses, industrial buildings, and pavement where trucks are parked, giving the area the impression of an industrial wasteland, as do potholes that are filled with water after it has rained, as was the case when I first visited this site a few years ago. On that occasion I rode my bicycle to the far end of what had once been Van Rensselaer Manor, along which there is wild growth. Running through that growth there is a railroad track, the same one that is seen on an 1857 map of Albany, and next to the railroad track is Erie Boulevard, once the Erie Canal. Looking across Erie Boulevard to the left there is a former industrial building that in recent years has found a new use as a retail outlet, Huckleberry Finn. It is located where slips had been built

Figure 81. Broadway approaching what was once Van Rensselaer Manor, which began just beyond where Broadway turns to the left. Nipper, seen at the left of this photograph, is trying, without success, to hide behind a telephone pole. Where he is seated, atop the RTA Building, is a stone's throw from where Van Rensellaer Hall stood before its demolition in 1893.

to accommodate the commercial traffic generated by the Erie Canal. From Huckleberry Finn one can look across what was once Van Rensselaer Manor. Looking across that space one can see Nipper in the distance, looking down in puzzlement, it seems, at what had once been Van Rensselaer Manor, the center of the largest patroonship in the state of New York.

Figure 82. Nipper, up close.

Figure 83. Another view of Nipper, seen this time from a different perspective. I was standing in what had been the storied gardens of Van Rensselaer Manor when I took this photograph.

Oddly, there is a continuous link between the present and what in former times was the largest land holding in New York. There is a farm between Guilderland and Duanesburg, off Route 20, with a Federal-style farmhouse that has been in the same family since the original Van Rensselaer lease was drawn up in 1790, some 20 years after an immigrant farmer, Michael Lainhart, squatted on land that became the Lainhart farm.[1] The lease is framed and hangs on the living room wall, a reminder of a bygone age, a thread from the past. The

Figure 84. Potholes at what was once the eastern end of the Van Rensselaer manorial grounds.

Figure 85. Huck Finn is on the right-hand side of Erie Boulevard, in the distance.

document, an indenture, lays out the conditions of the lease in specific legal language, and is signed at the bottom, in elegant handwriting, "Stephen Van Rensellaer." There is another signature at the very bottom of the document, in a different hand but also in elegant script, that reads "Michael Lainhart." The signature is not that of Michael Lainhart; between the names "Michael" and "Lainhart" there is an "X," with a splotch of blood next to it; this was the mark of the immigrant farmer who settled on the 158½-acre farm that is still in the

Figure 86. View from Erie Boulevard at what was once Van Rensselaer manor. The railroad track can be seen in the middle of the weeds and wild bushes.

Lainhart family, located on Lainhart Road between the village of Altamont and Dunnsville, off what is now Route 20 but was once Western Turnpike.

When a celebration was held in Albany in April, 2002 to celebrate the 250th anniversary of the founding of Beverwijck, a member of the Van Rensselaer family, Edward "Ned" Maunsell Van Rensselaer, flew to Albany from California to participate in the event. A ninth-generation descendant of the main branch of the Van Rensselaer family, Ned Van Rensselaer traces his ancestry back to Kilian Van Rensselaer, and, of course, to Stephen Van Rensselaer III. As Paul Grondhal wrote in a *Times Union* article on April 7, 2002, "about all that survives from the first patroon in the possession of the last patroon are two massive, heavily carved chairs and a large stamp of the family seal." Ned Van Rensselaer explained that when his family moved to California "they sold off a lot of possessions and severed a lot of ties." With fierce determination, his aunt Caroline had tried to retain the family tradition, but he chafed under the pressure and with her death "all things Van Rensselaer passed with her." Ned now values his family heritage, but not enough to "drill his children in Dutch as his aunt once did." Ned's grandfather never worked a day in his life, but Ned does, as an investment banker in Southern California; he lives in Orange County, where I lived before coming to Albany in 1963.

While Van Rensselaer Hall no longer stands, that building lives on, as we have seen, in the Van Rensselaer rooms at the Metropolitan Museum in New York, and in Marcus Reynolds' 385–389 State Street town house, built in 1897 for his Van Rensselaer cousins in the style of a Venetian Palazzo, with fish scale and coral motifs on the superb terra cotta tiles on the exterior and (presumably) materials from Van Rensselaer Hall in the interior. Across the street from this town house is First Presbyterian Church, built a few years earlier, in 1883. In an assembly room next to the First Presbyterian sanctuary

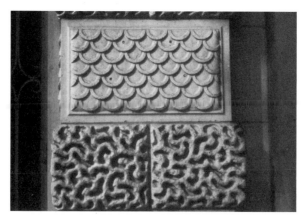

Figure 87. The terra cotta tiles on 385–389 State Street.

there is a life-size painting of Eliphalet Nott, President of Union College for 62 years. Nott delivered a sermon in 1804 after Alexander Hamilton's death in a duel with Aaron Burr. He was minister of First Presbyterian at the time of Hamilton's death, and his sermon, printed and widely circulated, brought him to the attention of the trustees of Union College, who selected him as president, a position that he held until the time of his death in 1866. Those trustees included Philip Schuyler and Stephen Van Rensselaer III. A short distance from the portrait of Eliphalet Nott in the assembly room of First Presbyterian is a stained glass window depicting Joseph Henry conducting an experiment at Albany Academy that made him one of the leading scientists in nineteenth-century America. Stephen Van Rensselaer III hired young Joseph Henry as a tutor for his children. Stephen Van Rensselaer III served ten terms as elder or deacon of First Church, the oldest church in Albany, which he joined in 1786. The church that he joined was still located at the bottom of State Street; it was demolished after Philip Hooker's church, one of the finest buildings in Albany, was built on North Pearl Street in 1798. No member of

Figure 88. First Presbyterian Church. This photograph was taken by Tony Anadio.

Figure 89. Portrait of Eliphalet Nott in the assembly room at First Presbyterian. This photograph was taken by Tony Anadio.

the congregation was more beneficent when this church was built than Stephen Van Rensselaer III. His donation took "the form of a major purchase of pews, apparently the largest such purchase."[2]

Within two years of Philip Schuyler's death in 1804 his children sold his Albany mansion, and from that time on the Schuyler family occupied a less prominent place in the city of Albany. Yet, a member of that family appeared on the local scene in the aftermath of World War II to play a role in the remaking of the city. General Cortlandt Van Rensselaer Schuyler, a four-star general in World War II who had been on General Eisenhower's staff, was appointed to a supervisory position when construction began on the Empire State Plaza in Albany in 1962. It has been said that General Schuyler was appointed to this position

Figure 90. Joseph Henry conducting his 1830 electrical experiment at Albany Academy. Joseph Henry was a member of First Presbyterian. The window is from the Tiffany Studio, and is signed. First Presbyterian has some of Tiffany's finest windows in the sanctuary. They have to be seen to be believed. Photo taken by Tony Anadio.

Figure 91. Hooker's 1798 First Church, seen in an old print. The classical portico, seen here, was removed in the middle of the nineteenth century so an organ could be installed. Later additions to Hooker's church, attached to its west end, would be installed in two major stages during the twentieth century. Except for Albany Academy, this is Hooker's only essentially intact Albany building. The latest addition, from 1989, has one of Tiffany's most glorious stained glass windows.

Figure 92. First Church today. Photo taken by Tony Anadio

because of his reputation for firm military command and efficiency, but it could not have hurt that was a member of the Schuyler family and was tied to the Van Resnsselaer family as well.[3] The problem was that General Schuyler had no construction experience; he had to turn to others to bring needed expertise to overseeing the construction project, which is said to have been the most costly complex of buildings in all of twentieth-century America. Construction of the vast project involved the displacement of some 3,000 families and the demolition of 90 acres of buildings in the center of Albany. Is it not a bit paradoxical that a descendant of the two most important families in eighteenth-century Albany was involved in a twentieth-century project that resulted in the destruction of much of the physical center of nineteenth-century Albany?

The lookout deck of the Corning Tower, the tallest building in the Empire State Plaza, offers a unique view of today's South Albany. From this perspective one can see the I-787 arterial that, along with urban renewal projects undertaken at the same time as construction of the Empire State Plaza, changed South Albany forever. The I-787 arterial passes over Madison Avenue below Green Street, now the last street above the Hudson River in the Historic Pastures District. Originally slated for demolition, this district is situated between Madison and Ferry and Green and South Pearl. It is comprised largely of row houses that date from about 1810 to the 1850s. To walk through this neighborhood today is to enter the past, but not without intrusions of the present, as I have observed while taking groups of students on walking tours of the Historic Pastures District. Starting at Madison and Pearl, we walk down Madison to Green, with the

Figure 93 (upper and lower). Albany before construction of the Empire State Plaza. These photographs offer different perspectives of the area razed for construction of the Empire State Plaza. New York State Archives, B1598. Aerial photographic prints and negatives of New York State sites, 1941–1957.

Figure 94. The Empire State Plaza.

buzz of traffic on the arterial just beyond Green Street ringing in our ears as we turn right. We pass by Herkimer and Gansevoort as we walk along Green Street, before coming to Ferry Street at the far end of this architecturally and historically important district. Upon reaching the corner of Green and Ferry the scene changes altogether: Rather than being surrounded by Federal- and Italianate-style row houses one encounters a large parking lot, and beyond it is the Department of Motor Vehicles building, which Albanians visit when applying for or renewing their driver's licenses. The contrast between the row houses on Ferry Street, with several Greek Revival entrances of surpassing beauty, and the DMV building across the street is most striking. While observing this scene at the corner of Ferry and Green with students a few years ago someone in the group said, "Look, there is Schuyler Mansion." We all looked up the hill, and sure enough, there it was, Philip Schuyler's 1761 mansion. Between us and Philip Schuyler's 1761 mansion lay the parking lot of the DMV building and a swath of urban blight, all part of today's South Albany.

How different the view of the Pastures was for the Marquis de Chastellux when he looked up the hill on the opposite side of the Hudson while visiting Philip Schuyler in 1780. Looking through a telescope, Chastellux saw someone in the window of The Pastures looking at him, also with a telescope. That person was the Vicomte de Noailles, a relative of Lafayette. Ever the hospitable host, Schuyler had made careful arrangements for Chastellux, his aristocratic French guest. Awaiting him with a sleigh at the Albany side of the ferry was the Chevalier de Mauduit, who whisked him up the hill. As Chastellux explained, "in an instant [we were] in a handsome drawing room, near a good fire . . . While we were warming ourselves, dinner was served, to which everyone did honors, as well as to the Madeira, which was excellent. . . ." At the time of Chastellux's arrival in Albany, in 1780 Schuyler's mansion stood virtually alone on the side of the hill, offering its inhabitants and their illustrious guests a commanding

Figure 95. View of South Albany from the lookout deck of the Corning Tower. I-787 cuts a swath right through South Albany. Urban renewal projects of the 1960s, along with the construction of this highway, sounded the death knell for South Albany as a vibrant neighborhood. The urban decay that passed through South Albany made its way to Schuyler Mansion; that decay has yet to be reversed.

Figure 96. Green Street, south of Madison. I-787 can be seen in the background, looming over the historic Pastures District.

Figure 97. A view of the Department of Motor Vehicles building, seen from Ferry Street.

Figure 98. Looking at Ferry Street from the Department of Motor Vehicles side of the street.

Figure 99. One of the Greek Revival houses on Ferry Street.

view of the beautiful Hudson River below. How different the scene Chastellux observed was from today's scene.

I led a group of students on a walking tour of the Pastures Historic District in the fall of 2007, as I had with other groups of students in previous years. We walked down Madison to Green, turned right on Green, and made our way to Ferry Street at the far end of The Pastures. We had walked up Ferry to the corner of Pearl, when I said to students in the group that we had to make a decision: we could end the tour, or we could see Schuyler Mansion. To my surprise, most students said they wanted to see Schuyler Mansion, so we began to walk down Pearl toward Schuyler Street, which ends up at Schuyler Mansion. As we were walking along Pearl someone shouted as he saw a tow truck drive by. It was his car being towed, which he had parked at McDonald's at Pearl and Madison, where we had begun our tour. I looked back and saw several students running toward McDonald's, where they too had parked their cars. Altogether, three students had their cars towed during this walking tour, a reminder of conditions in South Albany, some of whose ground rules they learned at their expense. I tried later to reimburse these students for their towing fees, but all refused.

Figure 100. McDonald's, at the corner of Madison and South Pearl, a scene of infamy for several of my students in 2007.

After the tow truck episode, I said we could still see Schuyler Mansion if anyone was interested, along with a model of the mansion and grounds in Schuyler's time that was on display in the Visitor's Center. Everyone said they wanted to continue, so we made out way to Schuyler Mansion. After ringing the doorbell of the Visitor's Center someone let us in, and we all looked at the model that showed us what Schuyler Mansion would have been like in Schuyler's time, when he received prominent guests, such as the Marquis de Chastellux. The sleigh that took Chastellux to Schuyler Mansion in 1780 traversed the same ground that students and I covered when we walked to Schuyler Mansion in the fall of 2007. How different the two trips were: how different today's South Albany is from the time of Philip Schuyler. One wonders what Philip Schuyler and his son-in-law Stephen Van Rensselaer III would think of today's Albany. Almost all of 1775 to 1825 Albany is gone. Yet, Schuyler Mansion stands, First Church stands, Albany Academy stands. All should be seen. All are links to an Albany that was at the center of events that changed New York, America, and the world between 1775 and 1825.

Figure 101. Model of The Pastures, which shows the gardens of Schuyler's 1761 mansion; it is in the Schuyler Mansion Visitor Center. Photo taken by Tony Anadio.

A new cemetery was established in Menands in 1841, Albany Rural Cemetery, a park-like setting that came out of a new way of thinking about nature, life and death.[4] It is here, in the beautiful surroundings of Albany Rural, that the remains of Philip Schuyler, Stephen Van Rensselaer III, and William James of Albany are to be found. In life these prominent Albanians lived along the most important street historically that ran through Albany along a north-south axis, Pearl Street; they now lie together in Albany Rural Cemetery. Philip Schuyler's tombstone at Albany Rural is next to a cenotaph built in his honor by the members of his family decades after his death. Not very far from the Schuyler monument at Albany Rural are the burial sites of Stephen Van Rensselaer III and William James of Albany—one an Albany aristocrat of ancient lineage, the other an immigrant who came to Albany to seek his fortune. As chance has it, Stephen Van Rensselaer III and William James of Albany were buried close to one another, where two paths converge. Different as they were in life, they lie almost next to one another in death; it is as if their spirits were within hailing distance of one another in death.

Figure 102. Philip Schuyler cenotaph at Albany Rural Cemetery. Photo taken by Tony Anadio.

Figure 103. Van Rensselaer and James monuments, Albany Rural Cemetery. It was Norman Rice who brought these sites to my attention while we were having lunch after attending Sunday service at the Presbyterian Church in Rensselaerville in the summer of 2008. Norman kindly offered to show me the Van Rensselaer, James, and Schuyler burial sites a few days later, with Anne Roberts and Tony Anadio also part of the group. The William James monument is in the foreground; the Stephen Van Rensselaer III monument is directly to the right of the tree that is next to the James monument. This photo is by Tony Anadio.

A recent article in the *New York Times* explains that New Yorkers think that the Erie Canal was filled in many years ago, as in fact the original canal was, or at least most of it; yet, the Barge Canal that replaced the Erie Canal is once again functioning.[5] The article describes brown water that flooded Lock 16 at Little Falls in the fall of 2008, lifting the barge *Margot* and its 2,000-ton cargo of steel "like a toy battleship in a bathtub." The Erie Canal carried 42 shipments in 2008, up from a total of 15 in 2007. Shippers are rediscovering the advantages of fuel-efficient water transportation; perhaps the Erie Canal, having gone into full eclipse as an avenue of commerce, has prospects for a new future, given the high cost of fuel in today's world. What might the spirits of Stephen Van Rensselaer III and William James of Albany, one a promoter of the Erie Canal and the other its leading beneficiary, think of this unexpected development if their spirits were to rise from their graves in Albany Rural Cemetery? "Well," they might say, "they buried us when our time ran out, and they buried the canal that meant so much to us when its time ran out. From dirt to dirt, that was the fate of the Erie Canal, whose opening we celebrated in Albany on November 2, 1825. We envisioned an expansive future for New York, and our vision became reality, but all too briefly. How dreary the spectacle of grim decline has been in towns and cities that sprang up along the Erie Canal. Might the Erie Canal, in which we invested so much, once again become an economic lifeline for New York State? It's a strange world: that a terrorist attack in New York City would lead to a war in the Middle East that made oil so expensive that transportation along the Erie Canal might again be viable seems too incredible to believe. It would seem that Clio, the Muse of History, is an ironist, with a perverse fascination for the bizarre and the paradoxical. Might Clio have some other tricks up her sleeve? Might the villages that became thriving towns along the Erie Canal recover some of their former luster? Our dream of a greater New York ended in a tattered rust belt, but the play isn't over until the last performer on the stage delivers her lines. Perhaps the play isn't over after all; perhaps the curtain is going up, and another act is about to begin. It sometimes seems that we mortals are but playthings of the gods; what do the gods—or the fates—have in store for Upstate New York, and for Albany, our city on the Hudson?"

Anne Roberts and I took a trip through upstate New York in June 2008. We found the villages, towns, and cities beautiful beyond belief; we concluded that New York is among America's best-kept secrets.[6] The early summer landscapes were magnificent, and the architectural treasures that awaited us with every turn of the road were an ongoing source of delight. Towns that had populations of 3,000 in the 1880s (and are sometimes the same size today) had opera houses that projected a sense of pride and worth in an age of expansion and economic vitality. These buildings, rich in ornament, still stand tall, statements from and about an earlier age. We drove through towns with Civil War monuments, rows of elaborately corniced buildings, churches in every conceivable style, and imposing Victorian mansions. Having gone west along the Southern Tier we drove north, where we picked up the Mohawk River corridor, which we followed on our way home, driving alongside today's Barge Canal. We stopped at Little Falls, and saw the locks that are once again conveying traffic along a commercial waterway that made New York the Empire State.

Anne and I took another trip in the summer of 2008, two months after the New York trip, to visit friends and relatives in Southern California. The contrast between what we saw on the two trips could not have been greater. We passed through beautiful towns and villages, saw breathtaking landscapes, and felt historical associations everywhere in the June trip through upstate New York. Driving from San Diego to Santa Barbara in August we passed along 14-lane superhighways, great swaths of concrete that carried endless flows of traffic. We drove by mega shopping centers with chain stores—Circuit City (which has gone belly-up since our 2008 trip), Home Depot, Walmart—all blending into a vast urban sprawl in which everything seemed the same and the people who inhabited this vast space seemed like so many atomized particles. I must say that all of this had a particular fascination, much as walking on the moon

Figure 104. The locks at Little Falls. I took this photograph while taking a trip through upstate New York with Anne Roberts in June of 2008.

Figure 105. The Erie Canal Visitor Center at Little Falls. This is where construction of the Erie Canal began in 1817.

surely would. I will take upstate New York any time; I will take Albany, with its rich and deep history, and its fine architecture: Albany, a city on the Hudson, along which a battle was fought in 1777 that changed the course of world history, Albany, the eastern terminus of a canal that helped lay the foundation of a global economy.

Appendix A

Thomas Jefferson and Angelica Schuyler Church in Paris

When Thomas Jefferson went to Paris in 1784 it was two years after the death of his beloved wife Martha, which left him disconsolate. He swore, at her request, never to marry again; he was not yet 40 at the time. Two years after he arrived in Paris he met Maria Cosway, a married woman who was bitterly unhappy with her philandering and much older husband, Richard Cosway, an artist who came to Paris to paint the children of the Duc d'Orléans. Beautiful, vivacious, and charming, Maria Cosway, herself an artist of note, swept Jefferson off his feet as soon as he met her; she stirred feelings that had lain dormant, or suppressed, since the death of his wife. It was to Maria Cosway that Jefferson wrote his famous "My Head and My Heart" letter, a dialogue in which he articulated the conflicted inner voices within himself

Maria's husband seems to have recognized her involvement with Jefferson and returned to London in 1787 with his wife in tow, perhaps for that reason. Among Maria Cosway's close friends was Angelica Schuyler Church, whom Jefferson first met in Paris in the winter of 1787. She too was beautiful, vivacious, and charming; she too stirred romantic feelings in Jefferson. Angelica was back in London in 1788 when Jefferson was beginning to make plans for his return to America, and he wrote her a letter in which he boldly invited her to meet him in New York.

> Think of it then, my friend, and let us begin a negotiation on the subject. You shall find in me all the spirit of accommodation with which Yoric began his with the fair Piedmontese. We have a thousand inducements to wish it on our part. On yours perhaps you may find one in depositions we shall carry with us to serve and amuse you on the dreary voyage . . . I shall flatter myself with the hope of seeing you in New York, or even at Albany if I am master enough of my time.

As William Howard Adams has written, by "alluding to Yoric and 'the fair Piedmontese,' [Jefferson] introduced a scene charged with sexual innuendo from Sterne's best-selling *Sentimental Journey*, which Angelica Church had no doubt read. The parson [Yoric] is forced to share a room with a lady from the Piedmont who has 'a glow of health in her cheeks.' "[1] Sterne's two characters spent the night together in an inn, separated only by a sheet, with Yoric suffering from proximity to his female companion, suggesting the complications that might attend Jefferson and Angelica if they were to travel together in America, perhaps to Monticello or Niagara, as Jefferson had suggested in an earlier letter. Angelica Schuyler Church did go to New York in 1789, the year of Jefferson's return, but not to be with him. At the time of Jefferson's arrival in New York Angelica had become close, very close, to her brother-in-law Alexander Hamilton, soon to become Jefferson's bitter political rival.

Appendix B

The Responses of Two Americans to the French Revolution

Gouverneur Morris and Thomas Jefferson

Gouverneur Morris and Thomas Jefferson responded very differently to the murder and decapitation of Foulon and Bertier de Sauvigny on July 22, 1789. Discussing the event in his *Diary*, Morris said: "[The] mutilated Form of an old Man of seventy five is shown to Bertier, his Son in Law, the Intendt. of Paris, and afterwards he also is put to Death, and cut to Pieces, the Populace carrying the mangled Fragments with a Savage Joy. Gracious God what a People." Writing to Maria Cosway in London on July 25, Thomas Jefferson made light of an event that horrified fellow American Gouverneur Morris: "[T]he cutting off of heads is become so much a la mode, that one is apt to feel of a morning whether their own is on their shoulders," but he assured his amiable correspondent that like all French fashions this one would pass, and that "the spirit of vengeance" would "soon be at rest," except for "a few of the obnoxious characters."[1]

Deeply conservative and apprehensive toward the people, Gouverneur Morris wanted stability in both the French and American Revolutions. He felt that legitimate government must rest on the consent of the people, but by this he meant people in the abstract; he did not mean that ordinary people, those who worked with their hands, should participate directly in government or that they should have the vote. He said in the Preamble of the Constitution—the words are his—"We the People of the United States, in order to form a more perfect Union . . . ," but in a 1774 letter to William Penn he referred to the people as "reptiles." Morris thought that aristocrats, natural leaders, men of education and intellect, should carry out the functions of government. Thomas Jefferson also felt that aristocrats were the natural leaders and best suited to exercise power, but unlike Morris he was not apprehensive toward the people.

Devoted republican that he was, Jefferson idealized a free citizenry and favored their protests against tyranny. He exchanged letters with Abigail Adams about Shays Rebellion in western Massachusetts in 1786, two years after he arrived in Paris. Jefferson expressed his support of a popular protest that his correspondent found deeply worrisome; he not only supported the rebellion but the principle of rebellion itself. "The spirit of resistance to government is so valuable on certain occasions, that I wish it always to be kept alive. It will often be exercised when wrong, but better so than not to be exercised at all. I like a little rebellion now and then. It is like a storm in the atmosphere." Jefferson wrote another correspondent later in the year about Shays Rebellion, not only defending it but the violence that attended it as well.

> [W]hat country can preserve it's [sic] liberties if their leaders are not warned from time to time that their people preserve the spirit of resistance? Let them take arms. The remedy is to set them straight as to facts, pardon and pacify them. What signify a few lives lost in a century or two. The tree of liberty must be refreshed from time to time with the blood of patriots and tyrants. It is it's natural manure.

Deeper waters had been stirred in France in July 1789 than Jefferson understood; the "spirit of vengeance" that he dismissed did not disappear from the Revolution, and when he heard of its continuation, and escalation, he disagreed sharply with those who denounced it. It was Jefferson's former mentor and secretary, William Short, who wrote him about the Storming of the Tuileries on August 10, 1792. "The mob and demagogues of Paris have carried their fury in this line, as far as it could go." In a postscript to his letter to Jefferson, Short described the subsequent horrors of the September Massacres, with "Arrestations without number of all description, and the people of Paris menacing the assembly to immolate these victims without delay. . . ."[2] Offended by Short's letter, Jefferson told him that he had not understood the importance of the cause for which French revolutionaries struggled. "The liberty of the whole earth was depending on the issue of this contest, and was ever such a prize won with no innocent blood? . . . Were there but an Adam and Eve left in every country, and left free, it would be better than it is now."[3] Still in Paris at the time of the September Massacres, Gouverneur Morris described the bloodletting in chilling detail in his *Diary*; for him the Revolution had been derailed. Emotionally and politically committed to the French Revolution, Thomas Jefferson, in America, continued to embrace it, along with the violence that accompanied it. This included the events of August and September 1792.

Appendix C

Talleyrand and the XYZ Affair

Mme de La Tour du Pin and her husband were having dinner with a friend, Mme de Valence, in Paris in July 1797, when "M. de Talleyrand was announced." He mentioned, with a "nonchalance that must be seen, for it cannot be described," that "New ministers have been appointed ... 'And who,' I asked, 'is at the Foreign Office?' 'Ah, at the Foreign Office? Well, I expect I am!' And taking his leave, he left." (*Memoirs*, 304) Having returning to Paris in 1796 after spending two years in America as an emigré, Talleyrand sought out his former mistress, Mme de Staël, now the lover of Benjamin Constant, an influential figure in Directory politics. In her account of Talleyrand's meeting with Mme de Staël, Lucy wrote that "Upon arriving at her house one day, and flinging on the table his purse, which held only a few louis, he said 'There is what remains of my fortune. I must have a Ministry by tomorrow or I shall blow my brains out. . . . [T]he appointment was not difficult to secure." (*Memoirs*, 305) When he received news of his appointment to the Foreign Ministry on July 18, 1797, an elated Talleyrand said, often repeating himself, "I'll hold the job." This was his golden opportunity, literally golden: "I have to make an immense fortune out of it, a really immense fortune."[1] Altogether, Talleyrand is thought to have amassed a fortune of between 13 and 14 million francs during his first two years as Foreign Minister. Yet, he was unable to cash in on one scheme that came his way several months after he took office. President John Adams sent three emissaries, Elbridge Gerry, Charles Coatesworth Pinckney, and John Marshall to France to enter into negotiations on a number of difficult issues. Upon arriving in Paris in the first week of October, the American emissaries presented their credentials and requested an audience with Talleyrand. Six days later Talleyrand's secretary met with them, raising questions designed to put the Americans on the defensive, as if to soften them up for some hard bargaining. But before negotiations could begin formally Talleyrand set forth a series of preconditions that he insisted be met, including "something for the pocket," a large bribe. The Americans refused to meet this condition, and returned home indignant over the outrageous demand by a French Foreign Minister that they could only regard as corrupt.

The failed mission placed President Adams in a difficult position, owing to deep political divisions in Congress. Proceeding cautiously, and not wanting to roil waters in Congress, or with France, Adams announced the failure of negotiations but without giving the reasons. Vice President Thomas Jefferson, once Adams' close friend but now his political rival, felt that the Americans were surely at fault for the failed negotiations, and along with Republicans in Congress he demanded release of the commissioners' report. Adams released the report, but with the names of the French negotiators who had insisted on a bribe replaced with the letters X, Y, and Z. If the report vindicated Adams, it furthered resentments between Federalists and Republicans. Congress was furious; the cry was "Millions for defense, but not one cent for tribute." The outcome of the XYZ Affair was abrogation of the Franco-American treaty and a quasi war in 1798–1800, waged between French and American ships in contested commercial waters. It was during this period that the corrupt and inept government of the Directory was swept aside in a military coup, that of 18 Brumaire (November 2, 1799), carried out by Napoleon Bonaparte. Predictably, Talleyrand had ingratiated favor with Napoleon, and taken part in the plans that brought him to power.

Appendix D

David's Depiction of Talleyrand
in *The Coronation of Napoleon and Joséphine*

When Napoleon first saw David's grand painting, *The Coronation of Napoleon and Joséphine*, on January 4, 1808 he praised the artist for the work that he had just completed: "It is good, Monsieur David, I am very pleased." Neither he nor others picked up subversive details that David insinuated into the painting. David would seem to have grown uneasy toward Napoleon, whose aggressive military policies had plunged France and all of Europe into destructive wars during the three-year period when he was working on the commissioned painting. David had proclaimed Napoleon his "hero" in 1797 when he first met him; while painting the *Coronation* he had second thoughts about the man who crowned himself emperor in December 1804 inside the Cathedral of Notre Dame.[1]

At the far right-hand side of the painting two altar boys do not look at Napoleon, who holds a crown above Joséphine; rather, they look at the hand of Eugène Beauharnais, Joséphine's son, which rests upon a sword. The altar boys are more interested in the sword than in the coronation ceremony that they and all others have been gathered to witness. Swords for David were symbols of patriotic virtue; having the altar boys look curiously at Eugène Beauharnais' sword was to comment ironically on a political regime from which patriotic virtue had been drained away. To reinforce this point, the ample figure of Talleyrand dominates the pictorial space within which this ironic commentary is to be seen.

That David placed Talleyrand in this part of the painting suggests how finely attuned he was to the inner workings of Napoleon's court. Talleyrand resigned his position as Foreign Minister under the Directory a few months before Napoleon's coup in December 1799 (which Talleyrand supported) and became Napoleon's Foreign Minister. If ever there was a political survivor it was Talleyrand; as the political winds changed direction so did he; he had served the Revolution and the Directory; he then served Napoleon; he would next serve the restored monarchy of Louis XVIII. Talleyrand was the most clear-headed and pragmatic of men, willing to serve one regime after another, able to make accommodations as circumstances required. He was a man of great intelligence and sophistication, whose cynicism served him well as governments rose and fell, one after the other. His aristocratic birth was an advantage to Napoleon, who wanted to build his regime on broadly-based social foundations; additionally, Napoleon genuinely admired Talleyrand for his learning, his cleverness, and his very great ability as a diplomat. And Talleyrand recognized Napoleon as a man of genius, whom he was willing to serve, even as he regretted a foreign policy whose dangers he recognized full well. As Talleyrand saw the dangers that lay ahead he entered into secret correspondence with Napoleon's enemies, positioning himself for whatever contingencies the future might hold in store. When Napoleon discovered this he summoned Talleyrand and unleashed pent up anger in a furious outburst; Talleyrand, he shouted, was so much "shit in a silk stocking." Talleyrand's response afterward was that it was a pity that such a great man had been brought up so badly.[2] This scene took place on January 28, 1809, over a year after Napoleon first saw David's completed *The Coronation of Napoleon and Joséphine*.

Had Napoleon looked carefully at the painting he would have seen how well David had taken Talleyrand's measure. Talleyrand had been thin in earlier years but he had taken on much weight; as a connoisseur of fine things he had enjoyed life's pleasures, including those of the table, which he had indulged to the full. David's Talleyrand is huge of girth, an ample presence who frames the far side of the painting. Looking toward Napoleon and the crown that he holds above Joséphine, Talleyrand views the scene with an expression that combines self-assurance with a trace of amusement. The fur-lined cape and feather-topped hat are nicely applied touches that reinforce the mock solemnity of David's perfectly rendered Talleyrand. Just behind Talleyrand are the altar boys who look at a hand that is placed on a sword.

Notes

Preface

1. Published by the Mount Ida Press in 1993.
2. Published by Penguin Books in 1983.

Introduction

1. Cantor, *The Civilization of the Middle Ages* (New York, 1993), 1–2.

2. In my reading on the American Revolution one book stands out as particularly helpful, Edward Countryman, *The American Revolution* (New York, 1985). It turns out that Professor Countryman is from Albany.

3. See Richard L. Bushman, *The Refinement of America: Persons, Houses, Cities* (New York, 1993).

4. See Norbert Elias, *The Civilizing Process: The History of Manners*, trans. Edmund Jephcott (New York, 1978), Maurice Magendie, *La Politesse mondaine et les théories de l'honnêteté en France. Au XVIIe siècle, de 1660 à 1660*, 2 vols. (Paris, 1925), and Warren Roberts, *Moarlity and Social Class*, 25–43.

5. Fernand Braudel, *The Mediterranean and the Mediterranean World in the Age of Philip II*, trans. Siân Reynolds, 2 vols. (New York, 1975), vol. 2, 704–65.

6. *Schuyler Mansion: a historic structure report, prepared by the Division for Historic Preservation, Bureau of Historic Sites* (1955), 14.

7. Ibid.

8. Ibid., 21.

Chapter 1

1. This was the verdict reached by R. W. Apple, Jr. in the Millenium edition of the *New York Times*. There is, of course, no way to prove that this battle or any other is most important, but the *New York Times* article does draw attention to the importance, surely vast, of the Battle of Saratoga.

2. Simon Schama, *Citizens: A Chronicle of the French Revolution* (New York, 1989), 60–71.

3. See J. H. Elliot, *Empires of the Atlantic Worlds: Britain and Spain in America, 1492–1830* (New Haven, 2008), and a fine discussion of this book by Linda Colley, NYRB (July 17, 2008), 43–46.

4. My two works that combine literature and history are *Morality and Social Class in French Literature and Painting* (Toronto, 1974), and *Jane Austen and the French Revolution* (London, 1979).

5. See Max M. Mintz, *The Generals of Saratoga* (New Haven and London, 1990). This study has been invaluable to me as I have tried to understand Burgoyne, Gates, and the Battle of Saratoga.

6. Richard J. Hargrove, Jr., *General John Burgoyne* (Newark, London, Toronto, 1993), 63.

7. Mintz, 44–45.

8. See J. H. Plumb, *England in the Eighteenth Century (1714–1815)* (Harmondsworth, 1950), 60–73.

9. Willard Sterne Randall, *Benedict Arnold: Patriot and Traitor* (1990), 26–27. This book has been extremely useful to me; I have drawn on it often, and in many ways.

10. Ibid., 29.

11. Don Higginbothom, *Daniel Morgan: Revolutionary Rifleman* (Chapel Hill, 1961), 49. This book has been a useful guide to me; I should like to express my debt to this study.

12. All 110 of the precepts are included in Caroline Tiger, *General Howe's Dog: George Washington, the Battle of Germantown, and the Dog Who Crossed Enemy Lines* (New York, 2005), appendix, 127–46. Historians have often commented on the importance of these precepts to the formation of Washington's social and ethical identity. See Joseph Ellis, *His Excellency: George Washington* (New York, 2004), 9, Gordon S. Wood, *Revolutionary Characters: What Made the Founding Fathers Different* (News York, 2006), 35–38, and Paul K. Longmore, *The Invention of George Washington* (Charlottesville and London, 1999), 7. For the importance of honor in the Southern plantocracy, see Bertram Wyatt-Brown, *Southern Honor: Ehics and Behavior in the Old South* (New York, 1982).

13. My discussion of manners comes from many sources and from my own thinking about and writing on this subject over many years. The seminal work on manners for me is Norbert Elias, *The Civilizing Process.* See footnote 3, Introduction.

14. Tiger, *General Howe's Dog*, 21.

15. Benson J. Lossing, *The Life and Times of Philip Schuyler*, 2 vols., (New York, 1860, 1879), vol. 1, 48–79.

16. *The Papers of George Washington: Revolutionary War Series*, ed. W. W. Abbot, 12 vols. (Charlottesville, 1983), vol. 1, 36–38.

17. Ibid., 47.

18. Ibid., 48.

19. Ibid., 331.

20. Ibid., 395.

21. Ibid., 181–83.

22. Ibid., 120.

23. Ibid., 188–89.

24. Ibid., 255–57.

25. Ibid., 255–59.

26. Bobrick, *Angel in the Whirlwind: The Triumph of the American Revolution* (New York, 1980), 245.

27. David Mc Cullough, *1776* (New York, London, Toronto, Sydney, 2005), 32–33.

28. PGW, vol. 1, 373.

29. PGW, vol. 2. 418.

30. Mintz, 82.

31. Sung Bok Kim, *Landlord and Tenant in Colonial New York: Manorial Society, 1664–1775* (Chapel Hill, 1978), 281–415. I should like top express particular indebtedness to Professor Kim, a colleague and good friend, whose office is next to mine, and who has helped me greatly in my work on this piece.

32. Lossing, *Life and Times*, vol. 2, 123.

33. Ibid., 121.

34. Bayard Tuckerman, *Life of General Philip Schuyler 1733–1804* (New York, 1905), 130. The copy of this study that I have used, taken from the library at the University at Albany where I teach, was donated by Philip L. Schuyler.

35. Gerlach, *Proud Patriot*, 182.

36. Tuckerman, *Life*, 153.

37. Ibid., 157–58.

38. Mintz, *Generals*, 126.

39. Richard M. Ketchum, *Saratoga: Turning Point of America's Revolutionary War* (New York, 1997), 55. I here express my indebtedness to Richard Ketchum, whose books on the American Revolution have been most helpful.

40. Mintz, *Generals*, 132.

41. Bobrick, *Angels*, 245. For mounting American distaste over British feelings of superiority during the French and Indian War see Fred Anderson, *The Crucible of War: The Seven Years' War and the Fate of Empire in British North America, 1754–1766* (New York, 2001), 410–14 and passim.

42. Ketchum, *Saratoga*, 68.

43. Ibid.

44. T. J. Stiles, ed., *The American Revolution: First Person Accounts by Men Who Shaped our Nation* (New York, 1999), 175.

45. Ibid., 177.

46. Robert Middlekauff, *The Glorious Cause: The American Revolution 1763–1789* (New York, Oxford, 1982), 314.

47. PGW, vol. 10, 363.

48. Ketchum, *Saratoga*, 247.

49. Lossing, *Life and Times*, vol. 2, 204.

50. Bobrick, *Angels*, 250.

51. Lossing, *Life and Times*, vol. 2, 227.

52. Ketchum, *Saratoga*, 330–31.

53. PGW, vol. 10, 234.

54. *Rebels and Redcoats: The American Revolution Through the Eyes of Those Who Fought and Lived It*, ed. George F. Scheer and Hugh F. Rankin (New York, 1957), 356.

55. PGW, vol. 10, 430.

56. Ibid., 410.

57. *Rebels*, 356.

58. PGW, vol. 10, 450.

59. Ibid., 91.

60. Ibid., 396.

61. PGW, vol. 10, 557.

62. *Rebels*, 257.

63. Ketchum, *Saratoga*, 363.

64. *Rebels*, 276–77.

65. Ketchum, *Saratoga*, 394.

66. Ibid, 399.

67. Mintz, *Generals*, 220.

68. Bobrick, *Angels*, 281.

69. Mintz, *Generals*, 225.

70. Ketchum, *Saratoga*, 429.

71. Ibid., 430.

72. Bobrick, *Angels*, 281.

73. *Baroness von Riedesel: Journal and Correspondence of a Tour of Duty 1776–1783*, trans. Marvin L. Brown (Chapel Hill, 1965), 55–65.

74. Ibid., 57–58.

75. Bobrick, *Angels*, 258.

76. Middlekauff, *Glorious*, 373.

77. Tuckerman, *Life*, 241.

78. Mary Gay Humphries, *Women of Colonial and Revolutionary America* (New York Heritage Series, no. 4, 1st ed., 1897), 162.

79. Gerlach, *Proud*, 325.

80. *Rebels*, 286–87.

81. Bobrick, *Angels*, 283.

82. For eighteenth-century warfare I have used J. R. Western, "Armies," in the *New Cambridge Modern History: The American and French Reolutions*, vol. 8, ed. A. Goodwin (Cambridge, 1965), 190–217; Alfred Vagts, *A History of Militarism: Civilian and Military* (New York, n.d.), 75–103; and Theodore Ropp, *War in the Modern World* (New York, 1962), 44–59. For America I have used Charles Royster, *A Revolutionary People at War: The Continental Army and American Character 1775–1783* (New York and London, 1979).

83. R. R. Palmer, *The Age of the Democratic Revolution: A Political History of Europe and America*, 2 vols. (Princeton, 1959, 1964).

84. John Wood, ed., *Beaumarchais: The Barber of Seville and the Marriage of Figaro* (London and New York, 1964), 19–20.

85. Elizabeth Kite, *Beaumarchais and the War of American Independence* (Boston, 1918); Samuel F. Bemis, *The Diplomacy of the American Revolution* (New York, 1935), 37; Orlando W. Stephenson, "The Supply of Gunpowder in 1776," *American Historical Review*, 30 (1925), 271–81; and Stanley J. Idzerda, *Lafayette in the Age of the American Revolution*, vol. 1, note 15, p. 14.

86. See Auerbach, *Mimesis: The Representation of Reality in Western Literature*, trans. Willard Trask (Princeton, 1968).

87. I draw here from my *Morality and Social Class*, 92–96. See also John Lough, *Paris Theatre Audiences in the Seventeenth and Eighteenth Centuries* (London, 1957).

88. Morgan changed as America changed; he was a Federalist and devoted follower of Washington when he became president, and he ran for and was elected to Congress. For an indication of how he changed, compare a letter Morgan wrote in 1771–72 with letters written in the 1790s. See note 11 above, Higginbothom, 13, 185–208. That a barely literate Morgan from the frontier days became a public-minded and verbally assured Virginian and member of Congress says much about Morgan and his experience during the Revolutionary and Federal era.

89. Stanley Weintraub, *Iron Tears, America's Battle for Freedom, Britain's Quagmire: 1775–1783* (New York, London, Toronto, Sydney, 2005), 164.

90. Ibid., 165.

91. Ibid., 235.

92. William Hague, *William Pitt the Younger* (London, New York, Toronto, Sydney), 161. See pp. 136–74 for the remarkable story of Pitt's coming to power at the end of 1783.

Chapter 2

1. Ketchum, *Saratoga*, 15.

2. John Ferling, *A Leap in the Dark: The Struggle to Create the American Republic* (New York and Oxford, 2003), 22.

3. *The Papers of Benjamin Franklin*, ed. Leonard W. Larabee et al., 38 vols. (New Haven), vol. 9, 774–75.

4. Ibid., 379–80.

5. *The Journal of Charles Carroll of Carrolton*, ed. Allan S. Everest (Fort Ticonderoga, 1976), 22.

6. Ketchum, *Saratoga*, 21–23.

7. Carroll, *Journal*, 23–25.

8. Ibid., 39.

9. Ibid., 49–50.

10. PBF, vol. 22, 425.

11. Ibid., 427–28.

12. Ibid., 429.

13. Carroll, *Journal*, 59–64.

14. Ibid., 57.

15. Ibid., 50.

16. PBF, vol. 22, 400.

17. Ibid., 432,

18. Ibid., 441.

19. Gordon S. Wood, *The Americanization of Benjamin Franklin* (New York, 2002), 72. I have also used Edmund Morgan, *Benjamin Franklin* (New Haven and London, 2002), and Stacy Schiff, *A Great Improvisation: Franklin, France, and the Birth of America* (New York, 2005).

20. Warren Roberts, *Morality and Social Class in Eighteenth-Century French Literature and Painting* (Toronto, 1974), 23.

21. Wood, *Americanization*, 400.

22. Thomas Fleming, *Liberty! The American Revolution* (New York, 1997), 231.

23. For a good account of this affair, see Bobrick, *Angel*, 297–307.

24. Fleming, *Liberty*, 314.

25. Jared Sparks, *The Life and Correspondence of Gouverneur Morris*, 3 vols. (Boston, 1832), vol. 1, 132.

26. Ibid., 134–35.

27. Ibid., 141.

28. William Howard Adams, *Gouverneur Morris: an Independent Life* (New Haven and London, 2003), 126. I hve also used Richard Brookheiser, *Gentleman Revolutionary: Gouverneur Morris, the Rake who wrote the Constitution* (New York, Toronto, London, Sydney, 2003); Melanie Randolph Miller, *Envoy to the Terror: Gouverneur Morris & the French Revolution* (Washington, DC, 2005); and Howard Swiggert, *The Extraordinary Mr. Morris* (New York, 1952.).

29. *A Diary of the French Revolution by Gouverneur Morris, Minister to the French Revolution, 1752–1816*, 2 vols., ed. Beatrix Cary Davenport (Boston, 1939), vol. 1, 5.

30. Ibid., 7.

31. Ibid., 45.

32. Ibid., 48.

33. Ibid., 49.

34. Ibid., 144.

35. Ibid., 144,

36. Ibid., 158.

37. Ibid., 158–59.

38. Maurice de la Fuye and Emile Barbeau, *The Apostle of Liberty: A Life of Lafayette,* trans. Edward Hyams (London, 1950), 96.

39. For popular riots in England and France, see George Rudé, *Paris and London in the Eighteenth Century: Studies in Popular Protest* (New York, 1973); *The Crowd in History: A Study of Popular Disturbances in France and England, 1731–1848* (New York, 1964); and *The Crowd in the French Revolution* (London, Oxford, and New York, 1959). For riots in America see Countryman, *American Revolution*, 67–97. See also, Roberts, *David and Prieur*, 19–52.

40. Roberts, *David and Prieur*, 19–20.

41. Morris, *Diary*, vol. 1, 44.

42. Ibid., 20.

43. See Dena Goodman, *The Republic of Letters: a Cultural History of the French Enlightenment* (Ithaca, 1994).

44. Adams, *Gouverneur*, 174.

45. Morris, *Diary*, vol. 1, 27.

46. Ibid., 19.

47. Adams, 185.

48. Morris, *Diary*, vol. 1, 21.

49. Ibid., 25.

50. Ibid., 31.

51. Ibid., 23.

52. Ibid., 17.

53. Ibid., 119.

54. Ibid., 157.

55. Ibid., 160.

56. Ibid., 164.

57. Ibid., 235.

58. Ibid., 238.

59. Ibid., 242.

60. Ibid., 242–45.

61. Ibid., vol. 2, 55.

62. Ibid., 244.

63. Ibid., 449.

64. Ibid., 483.

65. Ibid., 537–38.

66. Ibid., 598.

67. For Hamilton I have used Ron Chernow, *Alexander Hamilton* (New York, 2004); Richard Brookheiser, *Alexander Hamilton, American* (New York, 1999); Willard Sterne Randall *Alexander Hamilton, A Life* (New York, 2003); and James Thomas Flexner, *The Young Hamilton, A Biography* (New York, 1997).

68. Chernow, *Hamilton*, 84.

69. PAH, vol. 1, 353–55.

70. PAH, vol. 2, 36.

71. Ibid., 37.

72. Ibid., 270–71.

73. Ibid., 348.

74. Ibid., 543.

75. Chernow, 136–37.

76. PAH, vol. 2, 539–40

77. PAH, vol. 2, 563–64.

78. Chernow, 165.

79. Flexner, *Young Hamilton,* 329.

80. Ibid.

81. Randall, 314–15.

82. PAH, vol. 3, 619.

83. Randall, 315–16.

84. PAH, vol. 4, 279.

85. Ibid., 374–76.

86. Brookheiser, *Gentleman Revolutionary,* 47.

87. Chernow, *Alexander,* 282.

88. Randall, *Alexander,* 314–84.

89. Chernow, *Alexander*, 315–16.

90. PAH, vol. 5, 501–02.

91. For Hamilton's religious views, see Chernow, *Alexander,* 659–61.

92. PAH, vol. 26, 322–23.

93. Chernow, *Alexander,* 709.

94. PAH, vol. 25, 170.

95. Ibid., 274.

96. Ibid., 544.
97. Ibid., 545.
98. Ibid., vol. 26, 324–29.
99. Ibid.
100. Chernow, *Alexander,* 727–28.
101. For Lafayette I have used Louis Gottschalk, *Lafayette Comes to America* (Chicago, 1935), *Lafayette joins the American Army* (Chicago, 1937). *Lafayette between the American and the French Revolution (1783–1789)* (Chicago, 1950), and *Lafayette and the Close of the American Revolution* (Chicago, 1942), Lloyd Kramer, *Lafayette in Two Worlds: Public Culture and Personal Identities in an Age of Revolution* (Chapel Hill and London, 1996), Olivier Bernier, *Lafayette: Hero of Two Worlds* (New York, 1983), James R. Gaines, *For Liberty and Glory: Washington, Lafayette, and their Revolutions* (New York and London, 2008), and *Lafayette in the Age of the American Revolution: Selected Letters and Papers, 1776–1790,* 5 vols. (Ithaca, 1977–83).
102. Idzerda, *Lafayette,* vol. 1, 254.
103. Ibid., 223.
104. Ibid., 253.
105. Ibid., 87.
106. Ibid., 296–97.
107. Ibid., 329–31.
108. Ibid., 321.
109. Ibid., 325.
110. Ibid., vol. 2, 226.
111. Marquis de Chastellux, *Travels in North America in the Years 1780, 1781, and 1782,* ed. Howard C. Rice, Jr., 2 vols. (Chapel Hill, 1963), vol. 1, 102.
112. Gaines, *For Liberty,* 141.
113. See Melvin D. Kennedy, *Lafayette and Slavery* (Easton, PA, 1950).
114. Kenneth Botsford gave a paper at the Revolutionary Consortium conference in Huntsville, Alabama in February 2008, comparing Calonne's Assembly of Notables to the writing of the American Constitution, which took place in Philadelphia at the same time. His paper is part of an ongoing study of this timely subject.
115. William Howard Adams, *The Paris Years of Thomas Jefferson* (New Haven and London, 1997), 95–96. For Jefferson and the French Revolution see Conor Cruise O'Brien, *The Long Affair: Thomas Jefferson and the French Revolution* (Chicago and London, 1996).
116. Faye and Barbeau, 94–95. For a discussion of Lafayette's role in the French Revolution, particularly in its moderate stage from 1789 to 1791, see Roberts, *Jacques-Louis David and Jean-Louis Prieur,* 19–32. Susan Dunn discusses Lafayette and the American and French revolutions most usefully in *Sister Revolutions: French Lightning and American Light,* 3–8, 12–17, and 119–23.
117. Chastellux, *Travels,* vol. 1, 9.
118. Ibid., 65.
119. Ibid., 75.
120. Ibid., 108.
121. Ibid., 197.
122. Ibid., 198.

123. Ibid., 201.

124. Ibid., 202.

125. Ibid., 209.

126. Ibid., 213–14.

127. Ibid., 221.

128. Ibid., 19–20.

129. "Washington, Freeman of Albany," published without pages by the Albany Institute of History and Art (Albany, 1932).

130. Gerlach, *Proud*, 460.

131. Chernow, 178.

132. Ibid., 179.

133. Ibid., 246–47.

134. NYRB (March 26, 2009), 45.

135. Ferling, *Leap*, 290–92.

136. Ibid., 279–80.

137. Ibid., 62.

138. Gary B. Nash, *The Unknown American Revolution: The Unruly Birth of American Democracy* (New York, 2005), 387–402.

139. Roberts, *David and Prieur*, 197–98.

Chapter 3

1. Rather than footnote each quotation from Mme de La Tour du Pin's *Memoirs* I am placing the pages in parentheses; I will do this throughout the text. All quotations are from *Memoirs of Madame de La Tour du Pin*, translated by Felice Harcourt, with an introduction by Peter Gay (New York, 1971). The remarkable story of this French aristocrat who lived on a farm outside Albany after fleeing the Terror is the subject of a novel by Sheila Kohler, *Bluebird, or the Invention of Happiness, a Novel* (New York, 2007). Kohler places particular emphasis on the two years the de La Tours du Pin spent on a farm on what is now Delatour Road. As a novelist, Kohler tries to capture Lucy the person by entering her mental world—as it is revealed in her *Memoirs*—and creating dialogue that takes the reader imaginatively beyond the text of the *Memoirs*, doing what the historian cannot do. She does this most effectively. Caroline Moorehead has written an excellent full-length biography of Mme de La Tour du Pin, *Dancing to the Precipice: The Life of Lucie de La Tour du Pin, Eyewitness to an Age* (New York, 2009), which takes the story of her remarkable life down to the time of her death in 1853. Moorehead would appear not to have come to Albany. She says the de La Tour du Pin farmhouse was in Troy, and on one occasion she has Lucy walking across the Hudson River on logs. It was the Poestenkill Creek that she and her dog Black crossed, going from log-to-log. This was when Lucy and her family were staying in the Van Buren farmhouse south of Troy, across from the residence of Philip Schuyler's younger brother in Watervliet.

2. For a discussion of these novels see Roberts, *Morality*, 13–60.

3. Sarah Maza, *Private Lives and Public Affairs: The Causes Célèbres of Prerevolutionary France* (Berkeley, Los Angeles, London, 1993). See also Vincent Beach, "The

Count of Artois and the Coming of the French Revolution," *The Journal of Modern History*, XXX (December, 1958), 313–24, and *Charles X of France: His Life and Times* (Boulder, 1971), 1–50.

4. For a detailed account of the episode see Frances Mossiker, *The Queen's Necklace* (New York, 1961).

5. Antoinette Fraser, *Marie Antoinette, A Journey* (New York, 1971), 87. My discussion of Marie Antoinette draws from this biography; from Evelyn Lever, *Marie Antoinette, The Last Queen of France*, trans. Catherine Temerson (New York, 2000); and from Caroline Weber, *Queen of Fashion: What Marie Antoinette Wore to the French Revolution* (New York, 2006).

6. As chance has it, I stayed on the rue du Bac during my first three trips to Paris in 1955–56, when I was a lad in the U.S. Army. My wife and I stayed there in 1970, by which time the neighborhood in which the rue du Bac is situated had undergone marked change, some of its elite elegance having been restored.

7. For the Palais Royal and its role in the French Revolution see James H. Billington, *Fire in the Minds of Men: Origins of the Revolutionary Faith* (New York, 1980), 24 33. For commentary on political ferment in the Palais Royal in 1789 see Arthur Young, *Travels in France during the years 1787, 1788, and 1789* (New York, 1969), 104–05, 125–26, and 130.

8. I devote a chapter to the Paris insurrection in *Jacques-Louis David and Jean-Louis Prieur,* (Albany, 2000), 19–57.

9. See ibid., 59–91.

10. Mona Ozouf, *Festivals and the French Revolution* (Cambridge, MA, London), 33–60.

11. Simon Schama, *Citizens: A Chronicle of the French Revolution* (New York, 1989), 511.

12. I discuss the Chatêauvieux episode in *Jacques-Louis David and Jean-Louis Prieur*, 139–44.

13. Among those who participated in plots to save the King was Gouverneur Morris. See his *Diary*, 472–73.

14. I devote a chapter to Robespierre in *Jacques-Louis David and Jean-Louis Prieur*, 195–225.

15. Lucy Moore, *Liberty: The Lives and Times of Six Women in Revolutionry France* (London, 2006). 285.

16. Ibid., 290.

17. For the fall of Robespierre see *The Ninth of Thermidor: The Fall of Robespierre*, ed. Richard Bienvenu (New York, London, Toronto), 143–97.

18. See Randall, Benedict Arnold, pp. 501–03, which includes Schuyler's letter to Washington, written on Arnold's behalf.

19. Chernow, *Hamilton*, 466.

Chapter 4

1. For a recent book on the Erie Canal, which I have found most useful, see Peter Bernstein, *Wedding of the Waters: The Erie Canal and the Making of a Great Nation* (New York, London, 2005).

2. For the impact of the Erie Canal on New York life and culture see Carol Sheriff, *The Artificial River: The Erie Canal and the Paradox of Progress, 1817–1862* (1996).

3. Ibid., 150–51.

4. Whitford, *History of Canal System*, ch. 2, 14. I used the online text, www. history Rochester.edu/canal/bib/whitford/1906/Contents.html.

5. Carroll, *Journal*, 34–35.

6. Bernstein, *Wedding*, 82–83.

7. Whitford, *History*, ch. 2. 7.

8. Henry Adams, *The United States in 1800* (Ithaca, 1957), 1–2.

9. These quotes are from a Potomack Co. Web site; for a full-length study of the project see Joel Achenbach, *The Grand Idea: George Washington's Potomac and the Race to the West* (New York, London, Toronto, Sydney, 2002).

10. Bernstein, *Wedding*, 64.

11. Whitford, *History*, ch. 1, 10–11.

12. Ibid., 12.

13. Ibid., 21–22.

14. Sparks, *Life*, vol. 1, 498.

15. Ibid., 498–99.

16. Ibid., 500.

17. Ibid.

18. Whitford, *History*, vol. 1, Synopsis, 1–2.

19. Bernstein, *Wedding*, 102.

20. Ibid., 124–25.

21. Whitford, *History*, ch. 2, 11.

22. Ibid., 16.

23. Fink, *Stephen Van Rensselaer*, 87–88.

24. Ibid., 95.

25. Ibid., 103.

26. For Mahan's views on the War of 1812, see Harry C Coles, *The War of 1812*, (Chicago and London, 1966), 99–101; in addition to Coles I have used Walter R Borneman, *1812: The War of 1812* (New York, 2004).

27. For Macdonough and his role in the Battle of Plattsburgh, see David G. Fitz-Enz, *The Final Invasion: Plattsburgh, The War of 1812's Most Decisive Battle* (Cooper Square Press, 2001), 27–28 and passim.

28. Walter R. Borneman, *1812: The War that Forged a Nation* (New York, 2004), 200.

29. Ibid., 279.

30. For a history of Rensselaerville, see *People made it happen Here: History of the Town of Rensselaerville ca. 1788–1950* (Rensselaerville, 1977).

31. Ann-Marie Barker wrote an MA thesis on this musical group at the University of Albany in 2007, "Albany's Euterpean Club: Cultivators of Improvement in Musical Skill and Taste." As in so many local cultural initiatives, Stephen Van Rensselaer was among the patrons and supporters of the Euterpean Club. He met Lafayette on the occasion of his 1824 Albany visit.

32. For the statewide celebrations, see Bernstein, *Wedding*, 308–21.

33. For the Albany celebration, see Franklin B. Hough, "Albany Canal Celebration." *Hough Papers, 1840–85.* I have used the online text, www.nys.nysed.gov/msacra/

sc7009htm. I must thank Tony Anadio for placing these documents in my hands on a CD that he gave to me.

34. Hough, "Albany Celebration," 455.

35. Ibid., 457–58.

36. Ibid., 455.

37. Ibid., 468–69.

38. Ibid., 474.

39. My principal source for William James, and the James family, is R. W. B. Lewis, *The Jameses: A Family Narrative* (New York, 1991).

40. Hough, "Albany Celebration," 460–67.

41. William Bertrand Fink, *Stephen Van Rensselaer III, the last paroon* (Univ. of Michigan photocopy, 1950), 229–30.

42. Ibid., 215.

43. Ibid., 203.

44. Ibid., 212.

45. Lewis, *Jameses*, 27.

46. Ibid., 43.

47. The quote is from a July 6, 2008 NYT review by Hermione Lee of Paul Fisher's *House of Wit: An intimate Portrait of the James Family* (New York, 2008).

48. Charles W. McCurdy, *The Anti-Rent Wars in New York Law and Politics 1839–1865* (Chapel Hill and London, 2001), 10–15.

49. *Albany Institute of History & Art*, ed. Tammis K. Groft and Mary Alice Mackay (New York, 1998). 92.

50. Timothy Dwight, *Travels in New England and New York*, ed. Barbara Solomon, 4 vols. (Cambridge, Mass., 1969), vol. 2, 348.

51. Douglas G. Blucher and W. Richard Wheeler, *A Neat and Plain and Modern Stile: Philip Hooker and His Contemporaries 1765–1836* (Univ. of Massachusetts Press, 1993), catalogue entries 24, 44, 50, 53, 54, 74, and 88.

52. C. R. Roseberry, *Flashback: A Fresh Look at Albany's Past*, ed. Susanne Dumbleton (Albany, 1986), 88.

53. For a discussion of Reynolds' role in the dismantling of Van Rensselaer Hall, see Eugene Johnson, *Style follows Function: Architecture of Marcus T. Reynolds* (Albany, 1993), 12–15. See also Reynolds lamented the passing of Van Rensselaer Hall in "The Colonial Buildings of Rensselaerwyck," *Architectural Record* 4 (1894–95), 415–38.

54. William Kennedy, *O Albany!* (New York, 1983), 103.

55. Kennedy, *Billy Phelan's Greatest Game* (New York, 1983), 145.

56. *Ironweed*, 88–89.

57. *Ironweed*, 218.

58. NYT, November 25, 2002.

Conclusion

1. It was my good friends Vaughn and Hugh Nevins who told me about the Lainhart farm, and showed it to me on several occasions. A member of the Lainhart family, Vaughn introduced me to the current resident of the Lainhart farm, Sue Lainhart.

Vaughn Nevins also gave me a copy of her extensive family genealogy, which contains a wealth of information about the Lainhart family.

2. This quote is from a letter sent to me by the historian of First Church, James Folts, New York Archivist. Dr. Folts, a former student of mine many years ago, kindly went through the First Church archives to uncover this information.

3. Victoria Newhouse, *Wallace H. Harrison, Architect* (New York, 1989), 261.

4. See Barbara Rotundo, "Cemeteries for the Dead and Living," in Anne Roberts, *Experiencing Albany: Perspectives on a Grand City's Past* (Albany, 1986), 200–05.

5. NYT, November 3, 2008.

6. We stopped in Franklinville in western New York, where Anne Roberts' great grandfather was a country doctor; we visited the cemetery where he and his wife were buried. We also stopped at Stony Creek at the eastern end of Lake Ontario, where my family worked a farm from 1819 until the end of the Civil War, in which my great grandfather, Thomas served in the 110th infantry regiment. He was discharged in Albany in November 1865.

Appendix A

1. Adams, *The Paris Years*, 220–21.

Appendix B

1. *The Papers of Thomas Jefferson*, ed. Julian Boyd and Barbara Oberg (Princeton, 1950–2006), vol. 15, 305.

2. Conor Cruise O'Brien, *The Long Affair: Thomas Jefferson and the French Revolution* (New York, 1998), 140.

3. Ibid., 145.

Appendix C

1. Stanley Elkins and Eric McKitrick, *The Age of Federalism: The Early American Republic, 1788–1800* (New York and Oxford), 562.

Appendix D

1. I discuss this aspect of David's *Coronation* in *Jacques-Louis David, Revolutionary Artist: Art, Politics, and the French Revolution* (Chapel Hill, 1989), 150–64.

2. For a useful account of Napoleon's relations with Talleyrand see Alan Schom, *Napoleon Bonaparte* (New York, 1997), 240–50 and 488–94.

Index